Studies
in the
Perception of Language

Studies in the Perception of Language

Edited by

W. J. M. Levelt
Max-Planck-Gesellschaft
Projektgruppe für Psycholinguistik, Nijmegen,
and Nijmegen University

and

G. B. Flores d'Arcais
Leiden University
and Max-Planck-Gesellschaft
Projektgruppe für Psycholinguistik, Nijmegen

JOHN WILEY & SONS
Chichester · New York · Brisbane · Toronto

Library of Congress Cataloging in Publication Data:
Main entry under title:

Studies in the perception of language.

'Evolved from the Symposium on Language Perception
held at the XXIst International Congress of
Psychology in Paris.'
  Includes indexes.
  1. Psycholinguistics—Congresses I. Levelt,
Willem J. M. II. Flores d'Arcais, Giovanni B.
BF455.S755   401'.9   78-2548 .

ISBN 0 471 99633 5

Typeset by Preface Ltd., Salisbury, Wiltshire. Printed and
bound in Great Britain by Pitman Press Ltd., Bath.

Editorial Note

The preparation of this book was supported by the Max-Planck Projektgruppe für Psycholinguistik in Nijmegen, partly through a grant from the Stiftung Volkswagenwerk, Hannover, and by Nijmegan University.

Katherine Murphy gave us skilled and intelligent help with the editing of some of the papers: her work is here gratefully acknowledged. The editors are also grateful to William Marslen-Wilson for his helpful comments on the introduction.

Further assistance in the editorial work was provided by Charlotte Lauer, Ursula de Pagter, Edith Sjoerdsma, and Hilde Kleine Schaars at the Projektgruppe für Psycholinguistik.

The references and citations in this book follow the APA-norms, with the exception of Levelt's survey of the literature. Here references in the text are made by numbers, in the style of the Annual Review of Psychology. Complete citations of names and dates would have increased the length of the review considerably. The name index to the volume refers to pages in Levelt's chapters as if complete citations had been used.

List of Contributors

T. G. BEVER Columbia University, New York

J. P. L. BROKX Institute for Perception Research, Eindhoven

J. M. CARROLL IBM T. J. Watson Research Center, Yorktown Height

H. H. CLARK Stanford University

G. B. FLORES D'ARCAIS University of Leiden, and Max-Planck-Gesellschaft, Projektgruppe für Psycholinguistik, Nijmegen

W. J. M. LEVELT Max-Planck-Gesellschaft, Projektgruppe für Psycholinguistik, Nijmegen, and University of Nijmegen

W. D. MARSLEN-WILSON Max-Planck-Gesellschaft, Projektgruppe für Psycholinguistik, Nijmegen, and University of Chicago

S. G. NOOTEBOOM Institute for Perception Research, Eindhoven

J. PYNTE University of Aix-en-Provence

C. K. RIESBECK Yale University, New Haven

J. J. DE ROOIJ Institute for Perception Research, Eindhoven

R. C. SCHANK Yale University, New Haven

M. SEIDENBERG Columbia University, New York

M. K. TANENHAUS Columbia University, New York

L. K. TYLER Max-Planck-Gesellschaft, Projektgruppe für Psycholinguistik, Nijmegen

P. WILCOX   *MRC Applied Psychology Unit, Cambridge*

P. WRIGHT   *MRC Applied Psychology Unit, Cambridge*

Contents

Introduction

This book evolved from the Symposium on Language Perception which was held at the XXIst International Congress of Psychology in Paris, but there is only a partial overlap between what was presented at the symposium and the contents of the present volume. A chronicle of events and considerations can account for what has changed and what has remained, i.e. for what this book is about.

Though successfully held in Paris under the chairmanship of Professor Hörmann, Symposium 13 did have its unlucky moments. Its organizer (W.L.) had originally hoped to make it a truly international venture, in which researchers from both East and West should be involved. During the year of preparation it became frustratingly clear, however, that Eastern scientists would not react to letters, telegrams or telephone calls. The symposium therefore began tilting towards the West. The Western reaction was slightly different. The initial responses were positive, even enthusiastic, but a number of contributors had to withdraw at the last minute (all for good reasons of course), which was no less frustrating. In spite of this, so much intellectual power remained that a stimulating exchange of theoretical views and empirical findings could take place in Paris.

Two of the main features of this symposium are reflected in this book. Firstly, the symposium was one among several dealing with language. Among the other topics were semantic memory, language in apes, development of cognitive structures in children, language and cognition, perception in infancy, neuro- and psycholinguistics of aphasia, artificial intelligence. Because of this context, Symposium 13 dealt strictly with matters of language perception in normal adults, without stressing the AI-approach to language comprehension. The editors did not maintain the latter restriction in this book, but otherwise they kept to the original interpretation of the symposium theme. Secondly, the symposium contained a review paper followed by contributions which, as the invitation put it, 'should be something more than reports of partial works': they should relate facts and findings to more general theoretical issues. This pattern has been maintained in the present book: it starts out with a lengthy review paper, which is followed by articles mostly having a strong theoretical flavour.

At the same time, however, much has changed as compared to the symposium. The editors were very pleased that Riesbeck and Schank agreed to write a paper especially for the book, relating concrete work on artificial parsing of natural language to general theoretical issues of adult language comprehension. We were also able to add a paper by Marslen-Wilson, Tyler, and Seidenberg, which reflects a perspective on the study of language perception that otherwise would not have been directly represented in the book. These authors' work has focused in particular on what they call the 'on-line' aspects of sentence processing, and the paper contains an overview of their research into the word-by-word left-to-right structure of processing.

On the other hand, some new problems gave rise to various changes as well. Shortly after the symposium, the first editor accepted the challenging invitation to set up a Max Planck Projectgroup for psycholinguistics. This interfered badly with the completion of his own review paper, let alone the further editing of the book. At this point, the second editor came into the picture and kept things going where the first could not. One positive result of the consequent delay was that the review paper was able to include material published up to the end of 1976.

A further problem arose when Wanner, who had eloquently presented the Augmented Transition Network approach to sentence understanding at the symposium, also had to withdraw because of a change of professional position. We made great efforts to find a replacement, but in the end without success. We feel it to be a real omission that a fundamental paper on ATN-models is lacking from this book, the more so since developments in this direction are very much further along than the published literature would suggest. (It is for this reason that, as an exception, the review chapter of the book makes reference to several unpublished ATN studies.)

But this problem apart, the tortuous path of Symposium 13 led, in the end, to a satisfactory result: a collection of papers which, taken together, present a fair view of the major contemporary theoretical and empirical issues in the field of language perception.

Let us now consider the subject matters covered by this book and the ways in which the various papers relate to the main topic of language perception.

In the study of language, the term 'perception' has been used to cover a broad range of phenomena and processes. Students of speech perception have tried to discover the critical features of the acoustic signal which give rise to the identification of a speech unit, such as a phoneme or a syllable. On another level, psycholinguists have devoted much effort to the study of larger units such as clauses and sentences, and the processes by which these become interpreted as meaningful linguistic entities. In the broadest sense the study of language perception deals with the processes by which the intended meanings are attributed to spoken or written utterances; it covers the whole range from recognizing a phoneme to comprehending connected discourse.

This broad range of processes covered by the term 'language perception' implies several levels of perceptual decision-making, corresponding to several different levels of perceptual organization. The fact that these different levels can be considered separately does not, however, necessarily mean that perceptual processing at one level depends on the completion of the processing at some lower level. In fact, much of the available evidence points to a different conclusion: that language perception is a highly interactive process in which structure can be derived simultaneously at many different levels.

An important question in the study of the perception of language, related to the notion of different levels of perceptual organization which we have just outlined, is still: What happens during the initial stages of the comprehension process? Is the initial stage of a basically passive, receptive, nature, or is the listener right from the beginning actively using his knowledge of the language, the communicative situation, and of the task? It might, therefore, seem useful to make a distinction between those processes which take place during the input of the verbal material, and those which follow afterwards, since this distinction might help us to demarcate perception (the first phase) from comprehension, recall, inference, etc. However, this is not fully satisfactory. Since a linguistic stimulus is temporal by nature, the first analysis of one part of the speech event will very probably overlap with later stages in the analysis of earlier parts of the stimulus. It is sometimes possible, for instance, to give a verification response before the whole sentence has been uttered. Thus, probably, initial and later stages in the understanding of verbal material go on very much in a parallel fashion.

A distinction between 'perception' and later 'comprehension' stages of language processing is therefore a rather problematical one. Whether or not one would be able to define perception in this way is obviously very much dependent on one's theory of the structure of language processing. It is at this point that we find the essential differences between theories of language perception. There are, first of all, those global theories which do not single out an initial stage at all; they only tell us about variables which affect how language is understood. Secondly, there are those theories which make specific claims about the initial stages of comprehension. Here, the two major alternatives are theories where the initial stage is something like a general-purpose, task-independent parsing process, and those theories where no such independency is claimed. Many modern theories, and very diverse ones, are cases of the first alternative. These general issues underlie much of the empirical work on language perception of the last decade, and are extensively discussed in Levelt's survey of the literature which opens the book.

In the introduction to a book on language perception, which is intended to represent the trends in theory and research of the 1970s, it might be interesting to compare these trends with the approaches characteristic of the preceding phase of development of cognitive psycholinguistics. A major difference in theoretical approach between recent work in language perception, and the bulk of research in the late sixties, is the increasing interest for information 'flowing down' as opposed to information 'flowing up'. Models are much more 'top down' than they used to be. The active listener becomes endowed with semantic and pragmatic hypotheses which guide his search for structure. The expectations of the listener, his knowledge of the world, his awareness of mutual communicative agreements with the speaker, all have become central ingredients of models of language perception. This point of view has become very central in the theoretical approach of many recent psycholinguistic studies, sometimes even leading to a lack of sufficient concern for the way in which the stimulus information affects language perception.

We cannot, however, overlook the information flowing up. According to the circumstances, the listener is more or less dependent on stimulus information and on low-level perceptual processing. There may be no fixed pattern or direction of information processing in language perception. The listener adapts to the task and the circumstances, and his mode of processing may accordingly be tilted more to 'top-down' or to 'bottom-up' processing patterns.

This book reflects both kinds of approach. It contains, on the one hand, papers with a clear concern for the 'bottom-up' point of view—for example, in the question of how prosodic information affects sentence organization. Some other papers, on the other hand, are inspired by the 'top-down' approach, stressing for example semantically driven parsing, or the listener's awareness of the speaker's communicative intentions.

Both trends are traced in *Levelt*'s review of sentence perception which opens the book. Though the work on sentence perception is, clearly, only a subset of the extensive literature on the perception of language, it is a characteristic subset in that almost all general theoretical and empirical issues in the field of language perception arise in some form or another if one studies the perception of sentences. The paper is an extensive review of the psycholinguistic work in this area which has appeared within the last seven years. The length of the reference list and the variety of studies analysed can give an idea of the vitality of the field. The layout of the review and the approach taken in the analysis of the literature can be easily seen from the table of contents which precedes the chapter. The main theoretical approaches which run throughout the literature examined could be summarized as follows. The first is a linguistic approach: it aims at explaining how a linguistic representation or 'description' is derived from the speech input. The second is the conceptual approach: it is the derivation of a (task-specific) conceptual representation which is studied. The third approach, finally, can be labelled 'communicative'; here, the informational dependency between speaker and hearer is the topic of research: how is it that the hearer deciphers the intentions of the speaker in particular communicative settings? These approaches need not be mutually exclusive, but a substantial difference in tone between the three of them is clearly detectable.

After Levelt's review, the papers have been organized, rather traditionally, on the basis of an informal and intuitive notion of an increasing level of 'complexity' of the linguistic variable being investigated.

The paper by *Nooteboom, Brokx,* and *de Rooij* reviews several experiments and offers an integrated presentation of the ways in which suprasegmental features have been shown to affect perceptual segmentation. In spoken language, prosody is intimately related to the syntactic and semantic structure of the utterance. Prosodic information is used, together with the syntactic and semantic information, in the process of sentence segmentation. And it is probable that prosody is used as an important cue to guide the search for an appropriate structural organization of the incoming signal. But the contribution of this linguistic variable to the perception of language has until recently been largely ignored. In most psycholinguistic experiments prosody has at best been considered as a 'nuisance' variable to be controlled for. In many experimental papers we find statements such as 'the sentences were read with even intonation . . .'. Whether such an 'even intonation' represents a way of controlling this variable is rather questionable, for in some cases the choice of this 'even intonation' might indeed interfere with normal sentence processing.

But during the last few years the neglect of prosody has been compensated for by an increasing number of studies, as the reference list of Nooteboom *et al.*'s paper shows. And it is not difficult to predict still more interest in these areas in the future. The paper by Nooteboom, Brokx, and de Rooij represents some interim conclusions, and a point of departure for further research.

Pynte's paper offers a new contribution to the study of the processing of ambiguous sentences, an area in which the number of psycholinguistic studies is very large, much more than the apparent importance of ambiguity in linguistic communication would suggest. After all, in normal communicative situations with spoken language, no ambiguity arises, unless perhaps in very exceptional cases. But there are several valid reasons why psycholinguists have been so attracted to ambiguous sentences. Just as ambiguous figures in vision represent important paradigms for the study of visual perception, so ambiguous sentences might reveal something about the process of perceptual organization in language. For example, an indication of the moment at which, during input processing, the listener makes a perceptual decision of choosing one linguistic structure from among the two or more potentially available ones, is extremely important for the attempt to construct a plausible theory of sentence perception.

The questions asked by Pynte are not themselves new in the literature on ambiguous sentences. They are the questions of whether one or both possible interpretations are 'constructed' during processing, and whether disambiguation takes place during or at the end of the presentation of the sentence. Data on ambiguous sentence processing obtained with different methods, for example with the phoneme-monitor task, had shown that the point in the sentence at which ambiguity is resolved requires extra effort. Pynte's work represents an interesting elaboration on the same theme. An important feature of his work is the fact that the French sentences used are a very elegant material for a study on ambiguity, since disambiguation, and the choice of an interpretation, can take place at every single word of the sentence from the second one on. One of the contributions of this paper to a theory of sentence perception is the confirmation that some specific lexical knowledge has to be applied at various points in the sentence in order to make perceptual decisions about syntactic organization.

In their research work *Wright* and *Wilcox* adopt an experimental paradigm where the first phase of the task involves sentence perception. For the topic treated in this book, the first subtask reveals what strategies subjects may adopt in perceptually segmenting the instruction, and how the form of the instructions and the location of the presupposition in the sentence might affect perception. The approach taken in the paper represents a step towards a model of sentence comprehension quite different from those models which emerged from the numerous studies on sentence understanding based on sentence-picture verification tasks, whose generalizability is questioned by the authors of this study.

Beside the contribution to a general theory of sentence comprehension, the work reported is one of the first psycholinguistic studies on the comprehension of instructions. So far, sentence comprehension has mainly been studied with declarative statements in different forms. The use of a broader range of linguistic forms can not only enlarge our knowledge of psycholinguistic processes, but also represents a way of testing the models more critically. And if one tries also to look at psycholinguistic studies as a means to improve communication in daily life, it is clear that a better knowledge of how people understand instructions can be of enormous practical importance.

The work discussed in *Flores d'Arcais'* paper is much in line with the notion that the clause is an important unit in sentence perception, and that sentence segmentation takes place clause by clause: there is already some evidence for this hypothesis from the experimental work of the last few years. The main idea underlying the experiments discussed in this study is that a complex sentence made up of various clauses is processed at different levels, and that the clause represents an important level of such processing. The experiments reported are based on two assumptions. First, that a sentence is perceptually organized and stored in working memory clause by clause, and that at the end of the clause this memory is 'cleared' of clausal surface information. The second assumption is that the processing load tends to be higher towards the end of the clause, and that any additional tasks should therefore be more difficult to perform at that point.

The work reported confirms the notion that the clause is an important level of perceptual organization. But the paper also provides some evidence in favour of the hypothesis that the different types of clauses within connected discourse affect perceptual organization differentially and that some clauses might produce more load on the processor during perception than others. Also, an attempt has been made in the paper to specify some of the possible strategies hearers use when constructing clausal structures as they segment a sentence.

The work reported by *Carroll, Tanenhaus,* and *Bever* represents a further development along the same line, which has been pioneered by Bever and some of his associates, and which has been the subject of several important papers by these authors. One of the problems for a syntactic model of sentence segmentation concerns the use of surface information to form surface-structure constituents of various levels. But how can we construct such structural units within the constraints of the processing capacity of the perceiver (for example, within limits of working memory)? Carroll *et al.* propose that perceptual segmentation is based on perceptual cues which give signals to the hearer about the possible internal structure of the sentence. The work reported is an attempt to specify the types of cues which might be used, and to develop the notion of the functional unit as a basis for perceptual segmentation.

The paper by *Marslen-Wilson, Tyler,* and *Seidenberg* is also concerned with the role of clausal variables in sentence processing. They approach the issues from the point of view of an on-line interactive model of processing, and their paper has two main functions. On the one hand, they demonstrate that the serial clausal-processing hypothesis makes incorrect predictions about on-line processing phenomena at and around the mid-sentence clause boundary. On the other hand, they also attempt to account for the clausal structuring of the input in the context of their interactive processing theory. In this respect, their paper is consistent with the two preceding chapters, since it also emphasizes the role of non-syntactic interpretative variables in determining the organization of a sentence into clause-like processing sequences. The work reported shows that at least one 'interpretative informational variable'—the presence of a pronoun referring forward across the clause boundary—does affect the degree of clausal structuring of the material. This paper also provides something of a link between the psychological work and the artificial intelligence research described in the following chapter. Marslen-Wilson and coworkers share with Riesbeck and Schank an emphasis on the left-to-right structure of the word-by-word processing of the linguistic input.

The chapter by *Riesbeck* and *Schank* discusses the problem of human sentence processing in the light of the authors' recent work in artificial understanding of natural language. The purpose of this chapter, which is especially written for a psycholinguistic readership, is to explain the operating principles which should be adopted in order to make an artificial system which has the properties one would want to assign to the equivalent human understanding system. At the same time the paper discusses the thorny question of how AI models of human language understanding can have empirical predictive force. Although the theory distinguishes between a rather general-purpose parser

(ELI), and more task-dependent inferential activities—and this, as we have mentioned, is a characteristic of various modern theories of sentence under-standing—it also specifies the interdependencies between those two logical (not temporal) phases in the comprehension process. The authors' approach is very much conceptual in tone: the theory should explain how a conceptual represen-tation is derived.

Clark's chapter, finally, is a clear case of what we described as the communi-cative approach. How is it that the hearer derives the speaker's intentions in a given communicative context? Clark treats this as a problem-solving task, where several inferences have to be made in order to attain the required result. The way the hearer infers intentions is highly dependent on tacit agreements between speaker and listener. Clark tries to spell out such cooperative principles for the cases of understanding indirect requests, definite noun phrases, and shorthand expressions. A variety of empirical results is presented in support of these conjec-tures. This finishing chapter brings the student of language perception back to the question raised in the first chapter: what exactly should be explained? The process of understanding the literal meaning of what is said may be interesting to study, but—as Clark remarks—'speakers rarely mean what they say'.

W. J. M. LEVELT
G. B. FLORES D'ARCAIS

Nijmegen, 1977

Chapter 1

A Survey of Studies in Sentence Perception: 1970–1976*

Willem J. M. Levelt

1. AIMS

'The fundamental problem in psycholinguistics is simple to formulate: what happens when we understand sentences?' (Johnson-Laird, 143). 'The problem of when and how a sentence is understood is, in my view, the central problem of experimental psycholinguistics' (Gough, 109). 'How do we understand the relevant meaning of sentences used in ordinary contexts? This is a central problem in psychology and a primary preoccupation of the psycholinguist' (Tanenhaus *et al.* 244). These and many similar statements in the literature place the problem of sentence understanding at the very centre of psycholinguistics. The construction of a theory of sentence understanding is apparently expected to have spin-offs in various directions: the theory of language production, of language acquisition; it might even benefit cognitive psychology as a whole.

What, then, is the aim of a theory of sentence understanding? At this point authors are much less in agreement, or at least less explicit. In the early sixties the more or less implicit aim of constructing a theory of sentence understanding was to demonstrate the 'psychological reality' of linguistic notions, especially those developed in transformational linguistics. It is understandable in that light that such a theory was expected to stimulate developments in other areas of psycholinguistics as well. It is still an explicit purpose of many studies in language understanding to find out whether linguistic units are also relevant units in language processing. It has become abundantly clear, however, that proving 'psychological reality' of linguistic units and structures is too limited an aim for a theory of sentence understanding. Fodor *et al.* (80) convincingly show that reality studies have had only limited success. There is no doubt that such linguistic units and structures as words, constituents, and clauses show up in various experimental results; but generative rules, especially transformations, do not characterize processes of understanding. A major aim for a theory of

---

* The reader is referred to page 74 for a table of contents of this chapter.

sentence understanding is, therefore, not so much to validate linguistic structures as to explain how such structures are created by the language user. Fodor *et al.* call these structures *internal representations*, and they identify these with what linguists call *structural descriptions* (cf. 80, p. 21). According to this view, the purpose of a theory of sentence understanding is to explain how the hearer uses his knowledge of the language to encode sentences in terms of linguistic structural descriptions. Others describe the end product of understanding in non-linguistic terms. Schank (226), for instance, puts it this way: 'a parser should associate a linguistic input with what we will call a *conceptual structure*. A conceptual structure consists of concepts and the relationship between them'. The end-term, therefore, is a non-linguistic object. The aim of the theory is to explain how a linguistic object (a text, sentence, etc.) is mapped onto a non-linguistic object (a conceptual structure).

Many shades can be found between these two extremes (see, for instance, 102), and one very common claim is that deriving a structural description is a first step in deriving a conceptual structure. Varieties of this claim will be discussed and criticized in section 4. Here, it is only important to notice that the theoretical aims are much broader in the latter framework than in the former. One is more inclined to look into the role of context, especially of non-linguistic context within the conceptual framework. Also, the role of encyclopaedic knowledge in sentence comprehension is generally recognized and given attention: one is strongly inclined to hypothesize top-down and concept-driven parsing procedures. The former, more linguistic approach, being more limited in its aims, also tends to be more local. But in this way it has led to thorough analyses of syntactic and bottom-up procedures in sentence understanding.

Apart from this range of theoretical aims, authors vary in the degree to which they stress the importance of analysing the interaction between speaker and listener in the study of sentence comprehension. Hörmann (135) defines understanding as 'making sense at a point intended by the speaker'. How the listener manages to find out what the speaker's intentions are has increasingly become a more central aim for many researchers in recent years. Speech-act theory has captured the imagination of experimental psychologists. Clark (this volume) puts it this way: 'comprehension is conceived to be the process by which people arrive at the interpretation the speaker *intended* them to grasp for that utterance in that context'. And though the inference of such intentions is hard to study experimentally, Marslen-Wilson (186) explicitly defines it as an aim for the study of sentence perception: 'The normal listener . . . is a participant in a social event, trying to interpret the utterances he hears in terms of the communicative intentions of the speakers in question. Even if we cannot fully reproduce this situation under laboratory conditions, we can still try to capture, in our investigations of sentence perception, its essential goal-directed and dynamic properties'. .

So, in summary, the tasks which students of sentence perception have set themselves are at least threefold; let us call them *linguistic, conceptual,* and *communicative*. It is obvious that these aims are not mutually exclusive, and as a matter of fact it is hard to find studies that are pure cases of any of these three approaches, as will become clear in the course of this review.

What, then, is the aim of this review? Since the pioneering work of the sixties, the experimental study of sentence perception has had an explosive development in the seventies, which led to such an extensive literature that comprehensive reviews are available only for particular subfields and are mostly to be found in unpublished doctoral dissertations. It therefore seemed useful to collect a major part of the experimental literature from 1970 to 1976 and to analyse it with respect to method, results, and theory. In order not to be inundated by our material, it was necessary to place some severe restrictions on the review. Firstly, except for a few important manuscripts, only published material was taken into account. Secondly, the review ends at 31 December, 1976. Though many new findings about active research topics have been made since the end of 1976, it was not feasible to expect comprehensiveness of treatment for the first months of 1977; moreover, one has to stop somewhere. Thirdly, we have been strict on limiting ourselves to studies of sentence perception. Thus, on the one hand we have not reviewed studies of text comprehension, word recognition, word verification, or phoneme perception. On the other hand, studies of sentence memory, or sentence production have also been left out. Fourthly, we have left out the whole neurophysiological and aphasia literature. Fifthly, we have not incorporated the massive literature on reading. Sixthly, we have been forced to mention only in passing many studies—but such is the fate of all reviewers. We have been especially short on issues which are treated in other chapters of this volume. Finally, some omissions have occurred in spite of the effort to be comprehensive: the meshes of our net have apparently been too large here and there. But it may also be noted in this respect, that one had to be realistic and stop somewhere, apologizing to the fish that escaped.

The review is organized in the following way. Section 2 deals with experimental procedures in the study of sentence perception, because it became more and more clear to us that thorough analyses of experimental tasks and dependent measures are a necessary requirement for evaluating experimental results and theories. Section 3 deals with the independent variables, the linguistic and non-linguistic factors which have been manipulated to study their effects on sentence perception. It is especially here that variation in theoretical aims becomes apparent. Section 4, finally, is fully devoted to these theoretical issues.

2. TASKS AND DEPENDENT VARIABLES

Psycholinguists have been highly inventive in the development of experimental procedures (for a recent review see Olson and Clark, 205). The variety of experimental tasks which subjects have had to perform in studies of language perception is remarkable: click localization, dichotic switch localization, recall, completion, verification, paraphrasing, translation, judging comprehensibility or grammaticality, phoneme-monitoring, shadowing, etc. This productivity has its drawbacks, however. One cannot rid oneself of the impression that techniques are trademarks for research groups. This is especially clear in cases where different techniques are used to study basically the same theoretical issue. The issue of perceptual segmentation, for instance, has led one group (around Bever) to use click-localization tasks, another group (around Foss) to use phoneme-monitoring, a third group (around Wanner) to use a transient memory-load procedure, etc. Studies in which different methods are applied to the same material are very limited and tend to be rather inconclusive. As a consequence results obtained by different techniques have until now been less than cumulative. In this section procedures will be categorized into two major groups. The first group involves procedures where measurement takes place during reception of the stimulus, i.e. during the presentation to the subject of a clause, sentence, etc. These techniques will be called *simultaneous measurement*. One example is measuring pupil diameter while the subject listens to a sentence. The second group consists of procedures where measurement takes place after presentation of the stimulus. This will be denoted as *successive measurement*. An example is immediate recall of the stimulus. This distinction is important, since only in the first case can one be sure that results arise as a consequence of the input process, i.e. are strictly perceptual. In the latter case reconstruction activities, and therefore factors such as response bias, may codetermine the results. The results are perceptual only in the broad sense that they concern the way the subject reacts to a perceptual stimulus, and it is much harder, although not necessarily impossible, to determine in which phase of stimulus processing the experimental variable is effective.

It is quite simple to partition most techniques into these two classes, but a further qualification has to be made for a particular set of methods, those which can be called '*subsidiary task methods*'. Here, the subject has as a main task to interpret the verbal material, and as a subsidiary task to attend to something else in the mean time. Examples are click-localization and phoneme-monitoring experiments. Though the subsidiary stimulus is given during input of the test-stimulus, measurement can be either simultaneous or successive. Phoneme-monitoring is simultaneous since an immediate reaction to the subsidiary stimulus (the phoneme) is required. Click localization is successive, since the subject's response is given only after the full sentence has been presented. Subsidiary methods, therefore, fall within both main groups.

2.1 Simultaneous measurement

Three major ways of simultaneous measurement are in use: subsidiary task methods (which in simultaneous measurement are always monitoring methods), shadowing, and psychophysiological measurement.

2.1.1 Subsidiary task methods

During presentation of a word list, sentence, or text, the subject has to attend to the stimulus and at the same time to monitor for a particular test stimulus. (It is often only assumed that the subject attends to the sentence or text, without explicitly instructing him to do so.) This test stimulus can either be part of the verbal material, such as a particular syllable (191,222), word (1,249), or phoneme, or it may be an additional stimulus such as a light flash (272) or a click. The subject's task is always to react immediately to the test stimulus; reaction time is the dependent variable. Here we will give some attention to phoneme-monitoring and click-monitoring.

(i) Phoneme-monitoring. This technique was introduced by Foss and Lynch (92) in a study where subjects had to listen to a self-embedding or right-branching sentence which was followed by a comprehension test. Apart from understanding the sentence, subjects had the subsidiary task of pressing a reaction key as soon as they heard a word with / b / as the initial phoneme. The authors hypothesized the existence of a fixed-capacity decision mechanism (something like a working memory) where different decision-making processes have to share time. Difficulty of decision with respect to syntactic processing will therefore delay reaction to the test phoneme. Such difficulty was predicted for certain positions in self-embedded sentences. The authors found longer RTs for self-embedding than for right-branching sentences, provided the target phoneme appeared rather late in the sentence. Several phoneme-monitoring studies by Foss and his colleagues have followed this initial study (36, 37, 84, 87, 88, 91, 117, 118, 119, 120, see also 157). At this place we shall only discuss some issues related to the technique itself; the theoretical content of these studies will be treated in sections 3 and 4. A major issue is whether phoneme detection can be considered as an independent process, only competing for limited capacity. This was the original assumption, but after Savin and Bever's (222) finding that monitoring for a syllable is quicker than monitoring for its initial phoneme, Foss and Swinney (93) shifted to the assumption that the phoneme is identified after first analysing the word, i.e. word or syllable recognition is a condition for phoneme detection. Mortan and Long (201) show that this is not a necessary conclusion: phoneme detection can be relatively slow because of greater response inertia. But still, phoneme-monitoring reaction times are also sensitive to factors affecting recognition of the word to which the phoneme belongs. One such factor is transitional probability between the preceding word and the target

word. Morton and Long showed that this factor alone could induce a 70 msec variation in phoneme-detection time. This finding in itself necessitates caution in interpreting phoneme-monitoring results in all cases where this factor has not been controlled. It also sheds new light on experiments where the frequency of the preceding word affected monitoring reaction times (36, 87). If word recognition is a condition for phoneme detection, the target word's frequency itself should also be an important factor. The fact that several studies use different target words (with the same target phoneme) at different test positions in the sentence, makes this a major uncontrolled factor. There is not a single study known to this author which measured the effect of variations in target-word frequency.

A further, little understood, factor, which is probably a context variable that indirectly affects phoneme detection (through target-word identification) is the position of the target word in the sentence. Three studies (37, 87, 117) show relatively short RTs where the target word occurs relatively late in the sentence as opposed to early; two other studies (92, 120) show the inverse effect. Various factors can be involved here: transition probability, syntactic category of preceding word (see 37), increasing expectation, increasing processing load, response bias, intonational level, etc. (see especially 67), and rhythmic structure of the sentence (190, 233). Some of these factors are studied in a word-monitoring study by Marslen-Wilson and Tyler (187).

A final variable which has not been taken into account is the acoustical shape and environment of the phoneme. It is certain that in nearly all studies the target phoneme is not acoustically identical in different test positions. Moreover, its acoustical environment is also never controlled. Thus, variations in pitch, coarticulations, loudness, and so forth make it impossible to maintain that phoneme-monitoring studies provide the listener with physically constant test stimuli. The present dilemma for the phoneme-monitoring technique can be stated briefly as follows: either phoneme detection is an independent process competing for limited processing capacity, or phoneme detection is dependent on target-word identification and analysis. In the case of the former (and rather unlikely) alternative, it is essential to keep the physical stimulus and its immediate environment constant. This is hardly possible with phonemes as stimuli. In the second (more likely) case, one is essentially measuring word recognition. It is not only important, then, to control such nuisance variables as word frequency and transitional probability, but also to decide whether it would not make more sense to replace the indirect phoneme-monitoring by the more direct word-monitoring. The answer to that question will depend on the effectiveness with which one can control semantic and syntactic expectations in word-monitoring paradigms.

(ii) Click-monitoring. The subject presses or releases a key after detecting a click during presentation of a sentence. Abrams and Bever (3) introduced this

method with an argument similar to the one used by Foss and Lynch: detection of click and processing of the sentence are in competition for limited attentional capacity. If understanding is heavily loading the system, then detection will be relatively impaired. In retrospect we see that this initial study was merely exploratory; it was beset with experimental shortcomings (see 241), some of which also affected Holmes and Forster's study (130). (This latter paper seemed to show that RTs to clicks are relatively long in the midst of a clause.) The study by Streeter and Bever (241) controlled for relative frequency, transitional probability, acoustic shape, etc. A major finding was quicker RTs to clicks at the beginning of a clause than at the end, in correspondence with the attentional theory. An equivalent word-monitoring task tended to give the inverse effect: reactions to end-of-clause words were relatively quick.

The authors' interpretation is that the word, as an integrated part of the clause, is receiving attention contrary to the click. This conclusion makes it urgent to use the Streeter and Bever sentences in a phoneme-monitoring task. If phoneme detection is dependent on target-word identification and analysis (which as we have seen is rather likely), phoneme-monitoring should follow the word-monitoring results and not the click-monitoring results. Such a finding would be in good agreement with the close parallelism which Marslen-Wilson and Tyler (187) found between word-monitoring and rhyme-monitoring.

Bever and Hurtig (24) compared the Streeter and Bever (241) RT findings for supraliminal clicks, with detection for clicks at threshold. This is an essentially successive measurement situation, and response bias resulting from processing the whole sentence could affect the subject's yes/no decision which is given after the sentence. Though the results are compatible with those of Streeter and Bever, they should be interpreted with caution: inverted speech was used to control for acoustic masking by the sentence, a procedure based on the erroneous experimental assumption that forward-masking equals backward-masking. Click-monitoring is simultaneous measurement, as opposed to click localization (see section 2.2.1) and liminal click detection. Moreover, it is not beleaguered with most of the phoneme-monitoring problems. It is therefore surprising that click-monitoring has not been more widely used. Flores d'Arcais' (77) contribution to this volume gives further evidence of its usefulness.

2.1.2 Shadowing

Shadowing, i.e. the subject's repeating an acoustically presented sentence or text, insofar as possible in an on-line fashion, has been highly popular in former years. However, only a few studies since 1970 have made use of the technique. Rosenberg and Jarvella (216, 217) showed an effect of semantic integration of sentences on shadowing latency under noise conditions. Shadowing of word lists is used by Treisman, Squire, and Green (250) in order to test findings by Lewis (176), Garrett (101), and MacKay (182), regarding the semantic effects of words heard in the unattended ear on the interpretation of words heard in the attended ears. Treisman *et al.* (250) cast doubt on models postulating full lexical analysis of unattended words. Darwin (69) extends this work to sentences in order to study the effect of prosody. Marslen-Wilson (184, 185) used shadowing in order to demonstrate that so-called 'close-shadowers', who performed with a delay of about one syllable, were highly sensitive to syntactic and semantic aspects of the text. This demonstrates the immediacy of the syntactic and semantic processes during sentence processing. The origin of delays or errors in shadowing is not always self-evident. They can be due to a strictly perceptual failure or to complex difficulties in response selection.

2.1.3 Psychophysiological measurement

Psychophysiological studies of sentence processing are very much at an exploratory stage. Wright and Kahneman (273) studied pupil size as a measure of 'mental load' in tasks where the subject listened to a sentence, recalled it, or answered questions about it. Though results clearly indicated that effort was positively correlated with pupil size, no effects of phrase structure were found. It should be noted, however, that the experimental sentences, though complex, were essentially of a one-clause type. Two-clause sentences were used in a study by Abrams and Bever (3) in which the listener received slight electric shocks at critical points in the sentence. Galvanic skin responses were measured and turned out to be relatively strong for shocks occurring at the end of a clause. Unlike the pupil-size method, which does not interfere with the normal understanding process, the shock procedure is likely to divert the subject's attention from the syntactic material; it is probably the size of this orientation reaction which is reflected in GSR. This reviewer is unfamiliar with any follow-up study of these interesting beginnings.

2.2 Successive measurement

Studies on language perception using successive measurement outnumber, by a factor of about six, those using simultaneous measurement. It is impossible to review all the technical variations developed by inventive researchers. We will limit ourselves to the major types: subsidiary tasks, recall, recognition, paraphrasing, verification and question answering.

2.2.1 Subsidiary task methods

Apart from attending to the sentence, the subject has to attend to other simultaneously occurring events, but he is required to report on these only after the verbal stimulus has disappeared. The major method here is click localization; two other techniques are dichotic switch localization, and transient memory-load measurement.

(i) Click localization. Ladefoged and Broadbent (166) made subjects listen to a spoken message. The subjects had difficulty in locating the position of a short burst of noise (a 'click') which was presented during the message. The authors used the technique to determine perceptual units in the message. The subject's localization judgment would depend on what for him would have been a perceptual unit. In the psycholinguistic experimentation of the sixties, there was a real hunt for methods which could establish the 'psychological reality' of linguistic entities. The click procedure was discovered (79, 100) as an almost god-given measure to prove the perceptual reality of constituents, and/or clauses. Everybody's imagination was caught when it was observed that subjects were better at locating clicks presented in major constituent boundaries (79, 104) than at locating those presented just before or after such boundaries. Moreover, mislocations in the latter cases were more often than not in the direction of the boundaries. In short, boundaries 'attracted' clicks. At this point we will limit ourselves to a discussion of some of the technical questions which arose after the first euphoria subsided.

Let us recapitulate the original purpose of the click studies. They should show (a) the 'psychological reality' of certain linguistic units and (b) that this reality is strictly perceptual, i.e. that these units have their effect during input of the sentence.

With respect to (a), the main experimental problem was to disentangle the linguistic variable (i.e. the clause-boundary position) from other, often covarying, factors. The following covarying factors have been studied for their possible effects on click mislocation: serial position of the click in the sentence (21, 209), intonational pattern (210), and transitional probability (26). All these factors affected click localization, but for each of these factors it could be shown that the clause-boundary effect can occur if the factor is neutralized (see 21, and 25 for serial position; 104 for intonational pattern, and 26 and 104 for transitional probability). What has not been tried so far is to control for all these factors at the same time. One might still argue that even if one factor is neutralized, the click displacement is caused by one of the other factors, not by a 'pure' clause boundary effect. Thus, for instance, in a very careful study on response bias (23), which will be discussed later, the displacement effect could have been fully caused by intonation instead of by the clause boundary. The only way to control for all factors at the same time is to use the splicing method (as in 241). The study by Garrett *et al.* (104) comes the closest to this ideal.

Before treating the second issue of the perceptual origin of the effect, we should mention various additional factors which have been shown to affect click position. These factors, however, do not normally covary with clause-boundary position. Bertelson and Tisseyre (16) showed that prior knowledge of the sentence reduces preplacement of the click, and that separation of the click and sentence in acoustic space affected the degree of preplacement of the click (17). This effect apparently depends on reading direction, since in Hebrew it is inverse

(15). This spatial separation effect is not due to the response mode (written or oral report of click position, 18); it can explain the fact that negative displacement of the click is strongest if the speech is in the right ear and the click in the left ear (25, 26). Finally, click localization is more accurate (i.e. there is less of a clause-boundary effect) if the subject is free to ignore the contents of the sentence (see 21, 23, 229), especially if he is not required to recall, but receives a written version of the sentence on which to mark the click position (as in 16, 209, 210). This could not be verified in 131.

With respect to the second issue, regarding the perceptual origin of the click-displacement phenomenon, the click-localization technique shares the disadvantage of all successive measurement tasks: the effect arises somewhere between the initiation of the sentence and the subject's response, and it is hard to find out exactly where. Since the localization response usually occurs several seconds after presentation of the sentence, there is good reason to consider whether the mechanism of response selection is partly or wholly responsible for the click shifts. We will in the following pages go into some detail in order to demonstrate that even with sophisticated experimentation it is extremely troublesome to argue for the (strictly) perceptual origin of a phenomenon on the basis of a successive measurement technique, be it click localization or anything else. The obvious way to check for response selection factors is to compare real click localization with 'click localization' when no click is presented. Ladefoged (165) was the first to try this out in an exploratory way; it was followed by an equally exploratory study by Reber and Anderson (210).

The first experiment systematically measuring the distribution of guessing bias was Reber's (209). It revealed a rather dramatic guessing effect: subjects clearly preferred to locate the non-existent click in or around the major syntactic break. This is the case in spite of the fact that subjects are not requested to recall the sentence, so that one would expect such results *a fortiori* if the subject were also set to actually recall the sentence. When this was tested by Bever *et al.* (23), the results were negative: they found only a small effect of clause break for the 'subliminal' click condition. The graph of their results shows that there is a bias to locate the non-existent click either a half-syllable before the break or in the break. But the attraction of breaks is significantly stronger in the real-click situation, although there is also in this case a bias towards preposing the click. It is certainly correct to conclude from these results that the clause-boundary effect is stronger for real clicks that for non-existent clicks, and therefore that since guessing cannot fully explain the click-displacement effect, something more strictly perceptual is also involved. It cannot be concluded, however, that this perceptual factor is the clause boundary *per se*. In this experiment, clause break was contaminated with intonation, and it therefore could have been a perceptual effect of intonation alone (which has been shown to be an important variable; see 210). The fact that Bever *et al.* (23) found a lesser effect for guessing than Reber did (209) needs explanation. The recall set in Bever's study as opposed to

Reber's is difficult to interpret as a possible cause since Reber found strong guessing-bias effects in a situation where no recall was required. It is not clear why this bias should disappear if the subject is forced to attend to the contents of the sentence. There are additional differences between Reber's and Bever's experiments which should be explored in more detail. The first possible cause of this difference is that Reber used 'normal intonation', whereas Bever *et al.* used 'monotone intonation'. In view of the strong effect of intonation on click localization (210), this experimental difference is worth a further check. The second possible cause is to be sought in the number of response alternatives. Reber's subjects could localize the non-existent click at any position in the sentence, i.e. at any of 25 possible locations (within and between syllables). Bever *et al.* gave their subjects a 'window'; that is, a limited region on the typed-out sentence within which the click should be located. This region contained nine possible positions. If one now looks at the clausal break and the two immediately adjacent positions, one will see that they make up 12% of the possible positions in Reber's case, and 33% in Bever's. Reber found 33.8% (subliminal) click localizations in this region and Bever 52%—in both cases substantially more than could be expected on a non-bias basis. The fact that Bever's curves are less 'peaked' than Reber's can therefore be partly due to the window technique: the subjects have to 'pile up' their responses in a limited region. A final difference between the two experiments may have worked the other way. Reber used a control group for his 'subliminal' click condition, whereas Bever *et al.* used click and non-click conditions mixed within subjects. In their experiment the response window for the subject was always centred around the real click position; the subject might therefore conclude that this was always the case, and apply this knowledge in the non-click condition; i.e. he might position the click in the middle of the window on the answer sheet. This would have favoured the break $\pm$ 1 positions.

In summary, it has been shown that a great many factors can influence click localization, some of them presumably affecting early stages of the decision-making process (especially intonation). The experiments showing an early origin of the clause-break factor contaminate this factor with other factors; on the other hand, clause break also seems to have an (early or late) effect of its own if it is uncontaminated.

(ii) Dichotic switch localization.   This method was introduced by Wingfield and Klein (267). The subject listens to the sentence dichotically. The sentence starts out in one ear, and at some point switches to the other ear. It is the subject's task to localize the switching point after he has heard the sentence. The method is very much akin to the click-localization technique, and in fact it gives very similar results. Wingfield (266) and Wingfield and Klein (267) used the tape-splicing method of Garrett *et al.* (104), which is an effective control for prosody

and transitional probability. An example is given in the following sentence pair
(1) and (2):

(1) Besides *commercial uses of colour movies*, they are simply enjoyable;
(2) Among the *commercial uses of colour, movies* are most typical,

where the middle part of the sentence can be spliced into the other sentence.

Results showed that switch localization was more accurate if the switch
coincided with the clause boundary. However, this was the case only if prosody
'agreed' with the clause structure (i.e. in unspliced sentences). If clause structure
conflicted with the prosodic pattern (i.e. in the spliced versions), there was no
significant clause-boundary effect, only a significant effect of prosody.
Wingfield also found, in agreement with the click studies (21, 23, 229), that
localization is more accurate if the subject is not required to recall the sentence.
In conclusion, there is also here at most a very slight effect of clause boundary,
but a strong effect if it coincides with prosodic pause. Darwin (69) used
sentences similar to Wingfield and Klein's (i.e. normal and cross-spliced
sentences) in a dichotic switch situation where the subject did not have to
indicate the switch position but simply to write down the sentence. Darwin
analysed errors as a function of switch location in the sentence. Cross-spliced
sentences led to substantially more syntactic errors, but not to more lexical
errors. Errors near the intonational boundary had highest rates if an
intonational boundary preceded (rather than followed) a major syntactic
boundary. We will return to this finding in section 3.1.

Can one control for response bias in the switch-localization technique? Flores
d'Arcais (see his paper in this volume) has managed to do so by presenting both
parts of the sentence to both ears while manipulating the loudness balance
between the ears: a switch is then perceived as a small 'shift in the head' of the
message. In this manner fake shifts can be interspersed (by not affecting the
balance at all) in order to measure response bias effects.

(iii) Transient memory-load.   Savin and Perchonock (223) measured the
mental load of incoming syntactical material by additionally giving the subject
(either just before or just after the sentence) a short word list to remember. The
number of recalled words was supposed to be an indication of the spare STM
capacity during the processing of the sentence. Foss and Cairns (90) used this
technique to show that recall of complex sentences was worse than recall of
simple sentences if the subject's first task was to remember the word list. Wanner
and Shiner (261; see also 259, 260, 262) extended this method in the following
way: a sentence is presented visually word by word. The sequence is interrupted
at some (test) position for presentation of a short list of words to be
remembered; after this the sentential sequence continues. The subject's task is
(i) to comprehend the sentence and (ii) to remember the list of words. Wanner

and Shiner (261) showed the validity of the technique on a visually presented arithmetic task. Wanner *et al.* (259, 260, 262) used it in psycholinguistic experiments, especially to test predictions from an Augmented Transition Network (ATN) model (see section 4.3.2) of sentence parsing. In these experiments the authors use a combined comprehension plus recall score as their load measure, a concession which expresses the feeling that the situation is not really one of a main plus an additional task but one of two main tasks. The combined measure, however, is quite sensitive. A major disadvantage for study of sentence perception is the unnatural character of the presentation: a slow word-by-word presentation combined with a major interruption. It is likely that the perceptual process itself is also slowed down, and is quite different from the process which occurs in normal listening.

2.2.2 Recall

Recall is an obvious procedure to be used in the study of memory. Psycholinguistic studies of memory of sentences are very numerous (see 172), and various recall methods have been used for this purpose. Here we will limit ourselves to studies where the researcher's interest was basically in sentence perception but where some form of recall was used in the experiments. Many of these studies have been designed to show that a certain variable affects the subject's processing of verbal material, without much concern for the particular stage between stimulus presentation and recall at which the variable accomplished this. These are often loosely referred to as studies in comprehension. Examples are Bransford and Johnson (32) and Frederikson (96), who used free recall to study the effect of context on the understanding of text. Both studies claim that the effect of context is located somewhere in the encoding process, not in the recall phase. Only the first study systematically varies context before or after the prose passage. Results show that context placed before is much more effective, which certainly makes it likely that context is helpful during reading in these cases. Kintsch *et al.* (158) varied the number of word concepts in a text and found an effect on recall; the variable also affected reading time, indicating that it might operate during encoding. In other studies more specific perceptual claims are made, and they invariably lead to more difficulties in interpretation. A typical example is Levelt's (169) experiment where subjects were presented with sentences embedded in white noise; after each sentence they had to write down what they had heard. The data were analysed in terms of conditional probabilities that word j would be reproduced when given that earlier word i had been reproduced, for all words i and j in the sentence. In this way it was possible to show that the data structure was strongly hierarchical, and it was concluded that 'hierarchical left-to-right chunking will often be an adequate model for sentence processing'. It is not at all certain, however, that the hierarchical structure reflects the way in which the sentence is chunked during presentation. Loosen (179) repeated this experiment with one change. He presented the sentences with their word order scrambled, but asked the subjects to reproduce these word lists in the form of a sentence (if possible). The data were very similar to Levelt's, even though the subjects could not have chunked the words in the way hypothesized in that study. The hierarchical structure must have resulted during a complicated storage or retrieval process. (Kempen, 155, could show that it is in fact a retrieval effect.) Of course this does not prove that the original conclusion was wrong, but it certainly shows that it was insufficiently motivated. Dooling (72) used a similar technique to Levelt's in a study where subjects were set for a particular rhythmic and/or surface structure. Only change of rhythm had a (major) effect on subject's sentence reproduction, and it appeared quite likely that rhythmic expectations enhance perceptual efficiency. Still, it is not impossible that the subject's response selection is facilitated by a given rhythmic structure. If a perceived element is not quickly read out of STM it may be lost, and reading out may be hampered by a change in the response rhythm. An experiment of Forster (84), using immediate sentence reproduction in combination with a rapid visual presentation technique, did control for the possibility of losing a perceived element from STM. (The technique of rapid serial visual presentation, RSVP, involves a quick word-by-word presentation of the sentence in such a way that successive words are centred at the same visual localization.) Here, subjects were requested to monitor for a word beginning with a particular pair of letters. Subjects performed better at monitoring than at recall. This indicates that in the recall of rapidly presented sentences, perceived elements may get lost during retrieval from STM. A recall technique alone is insufficient for deciding on the stage where the effect arises. Carpenter (43) combines the technique with a verification reaction-time procedure.

Immediate recall is also used in the experiments by Jarvella *et al.* (140, 141, 142), but here the purpose is rather different. Jarvella gave a spoken (142) or written (141) text to his subjects; it was interrupted at some point and the subjects' task was to recall immediately as much of the text as they could. A major finding was that verbatim recall was at a high level for the last clause and/or sentence only. In this way Jarvella could distinguish between stages of comprehension: the earlier material had already been interpreted and only the last clause or sentence was still available in verbatim, uninterpreted form. Here also, control was necessary to exclude retrieval as the sole explanation for the findings. It could be that the subject started out by reproducing the last clause and only thereafter went back to earlier material. This time-lag might explain the results, but Jarvella controlled for such a possibility in an experiment in which subjects were presented with prompt words and were requested to recall from that point on. The results corroborated the earlier ones: a prompt word was most effective if it had been selected from the final clause. Jarvella's experiments have been extended by Marslen-Wilson and Tyler (188), to whom we will return (section 4.1.2). For a similar method, see 211.

2.2.3 Recognition

Retrieval processes which are always at work in recall tasks are less important in recognition tasks. A good example is Caplan's (38) study where a word-recognition test followed the presentation of a sentence. The subjects' task was to judge whether the word had occurred in the sentence, and reaction time was measured. The results confirm very well Jarvella's recall findings (141, 142): the last clause has a substantially higher verbatim availability. See also Kornfeld (161) for replication and extension of these findings.

Larger units, such as complete sentences, have also been used in recognition tests. The classic study here is by Sachs (212), who gave her subjects a story in which a critical active or passive sentence had been embedded. The story was followed by a recognition test for either the same sentence of its transformed version. If the sentence was the last sentence in the story, recognition was close to perfect; but if the critical sentence had occurred earlier in the story, recognition went down to about 60%. This shows, again in agreement with Jarvella's findings, that the verbatim version of a sentence is quickly lost. Anderson and Bower (5, 7) have used and extended Sachs' technique with essentially similar findings. A signal-detection analysis of Sachs-type data can be found in 235. Although reconstructive retrieval processes are probably eliminated in recognition experiments, they share the disadvantage of all successive measurement techniques that it is impossible to differentiate input explanations from storage explanations. How was the sentence registered in memory, and how well was it kept there? It is likely that in all the above experiments recognition failure resulted from forgetting, not from failure to detect in the first place. But only independent detection tests, such as Forster's (84), can be decisive in this respect.

Finally, caution is needed with the often implicit assumption that recognition equals recall minus reconstruction. Carey and Lockhart (41) show for word lists that subjects employ different encoding operations, dependent on whether they expect a recognition task or a recall task (see 251 for a similar result). Nothing is known about whether the same task dependency is operative in sentence or text comprehension.

2.2.4 Paraphrasing

Though paraphrasing tasks are often used for the sole purpose of forcing the subject to interpret the sentence, there are some studies where paraphrasing, especially paraphrasing reaction time and accuracy, is used to determine the perceptual complexity of a sentence. Examples are the studies by Fodor et al. (80, 83), where among other variables self-embedding and verb complexity were shown to affect paraphrasing accuracy and reaction time. Just as with the recall studies, it is ambiguous at which stage between stimulus and response the variable is effective. Hakes (117) writes 'Paraphrasing seems to require that the S

Table 1.1 Paraphrase and phoneme-monitoring results in relative pronoun deletion, self-embedding, and complement-that deletion

| Authors | Independent variable | Ph.mon.RT | Paraphrase | | | Sent. compl. |
			Acc.	RT	Acc/RT	
Fodor and Garrett (1967)	Rel. pronoun deletion	0	0	0	+	0
Fodor, Garrett and Bever (1968)	Verb structure	0	+	−	0	0
Foss and Lynch (1969)	Right branching vs self-embedd.	0	+	0	0	+
	Rel. pronoun deletion	0	−	0	0	−
Freedle and Craun (1970)	Degree of self-emb	0	+	0	0	0
Hakes and Cairns (1970)	Rel. pronoun deletion	+	+	−	0	0
Hakes (1971)	Verb structure					
	Expt 1	−	+	0	0	0
	Expt 2	−	−	0	0	0
Hakes (1972)	That-deletion in complement:					
	Expt 1, Easy sentences	+	−	0	0	0
	Expt 2, Diff. sentences	+	+	0	0	0
Hakes and Foss (1970)	Relative pronoun deletion	+	−	0	0	0

0 dependent variable not tested.
+ dependent variable tested and significantly affected.
− dependent variable tested and not significantly affected.

at least: (1) comprehend the presented sentence; and (2) by modifying the sentence's lexical content and/or structure, construct another sentence that is roughly synonymous. Thus, while a paraphrasing error might reflect a comprehension failure, it might also reflect a failure occurring during the construction of the paraphrase'. Hakes *et al.* in a series of papers (117, 118, 119, 120) tested some of the original Fodor *et al.* variables comparatively in paraphrasing and phoneme-monitoring tasks. The results of these and some similar studies are summarized in Table 1.1. These results are at best confusing. Relative pronoun deletion has been studied in three experiments. Fodor and Garrett (82) measured both paraphrasing accuracy (Acc) and paraphrase delay (RT). They expressed their data in Acc/RT. If one reads their text carefully it appears that in at least one experiment delay itself is significantly affected by the variables. Foss and Lynch (92) used two other dependent measures, phoneme-monitoring and sentence completion. Neither showed an effect of relative pronoun deletion. Hakes and Cairns (119), finally, found significant effects on phoneme-monitoring RT and paraphrasing accuracy, but not on paraphrase delay. Thus, each dependent variable showed an effect in just one study. Verb structure was manipulated in two studies. Fodor *et al.* (83) found an effect on paraphrasing accuracy, but not on paraphrase delay. Hakes (117) found an effect on paraphrasing accuracy in one experiment, but not in the other, and no effects on phoneme monitoring. Degree of self-embedding was manipulated in two studies, using different dependent variables: phoneme-monitoring and sentence completion in Foss and Lynch (92) and paraphrasing accuracy in Freedle and Craun (97). All showed significant effects. These and the other results on Table 1.1 show that paraphrase delay, paraphrase accuracy, and phoneme-monitoring behave quite independently and differently for different variables. Thus, there is no basis for the strong generalizations that can be found in some of these papers.

2.2.5 Verification

In a typical verification experiment, the subject is presented with a sentence and is asked to verify its truth with respect to some other source of information (a picture, another sentence, or pre-existing knowledge of the world). There are two dependent variables, reaction time and error rate. Mostly (but not always; see 137), reaction time is the critical variable. It is used to discover or test processing stages mediating between stimulus and response. The basic assumption is Donders' (71) notion that a response is the result of a linear sequence of operations, with each operation taking a certain amount of time, with these times being additive. Donders' so-called subtraction method consisted of adding or removing an operation in the sequence and registering the resulting increase or decrease in RT. The difference would amount to the characteristic time for that operation. A much-used application of the subtraction method in sentence verification is the following. It is supposed that coping with a negative involves an independent operation. In order to measure its effect, negative sentences are compared with affirmative sentences and differences in RT are determined. More important than determining characteristic operation times is demonstrating that a certain operational stage is really independent. It has to be shown that the stage contributes to the RT independently of what happened in earlier or later stages.

In a very fundamental paper, Sternberg (238) extends Donders' method in order to show the additivity and independence of processing stages; this is called the *additive factor method*. This method does not require the elimination of a processing stage but only the manipulation of the processing durations of each of the hypothesized stages. If two stages are supposed to be independent and successive, then it should be possible to find an experimental variable which specifically affects the duration of one stage but not the other, and inversely. Experimentally this should show up in the absence of an interaction between the factors in an analysis of variance (on the raw RT data). This confirms additivity but not necessarily independence. For independence it is, moreover, required that the higher cumulants of the RT distribution (i.e. variance, skewness, etc.) are also additively affected by the factors. Donders' method is a limiting case of Sternberg's in the sense that eliminating a stage is equal to reducing its processing duration to zero. Verification RT measurement, while successive in character, does not share all the disadvantages of other successive measurement techniques, but only by making additional assumptions. More specifically, one has to make assumptions about the successiveness, nature, and order of stages. If, for instance, a perceptual stage is hypothesized, then one can define an experimental variable which, by the nature of the stage, will affect its processing time. By manipulating the variable one can find out whether the stage is really independent and what its temporal characteristics are. Thus although neither Donders' nor Sternberg's method can decide on the *order* of stages, it is possible to hypothesize such an order on independent grounds and then to verify the model by choosing appropriate experimental variables in a factorial design. To take just one example, Banks, Clark, and Lucy (13) presented subjects with such questions as 'Which balloon is higher/lower?' and 'Which yoyo is higher/lower?' followed by a picture of two balloons tied up at different heights or of two yoyos hanging down at different heights. The subject had to press the left or right reaction key in correspondence with the highest/lowest balloon or yoyo. The model is a two-stage model: a perceptual followed by a linguistic stage. At the perceptual stage the picture is registered. Various factors may specifically influence the duration of this stage. The authors selected as their experimental factor discriminability, i.e. difference in height of balloons (or yoyos). They used three levels for this factor. The linguistic stage is supposed to compare the perceptual output with the linguistic representation of the question sentence. A factor which might specifically affect the duration of this is the congruity between perceptual and linguistic code. If a balloon is perceptually coded in terms of 'high', and a yoyo in terms of 'low' (the authors' hypothesis), the congruent question ('Which balloon is higher', 'Which yoyo is lower?') should be easier than the incongruent question ('Which balloon is lower?', 'Which yoyo is higher?'). It turns out that the two factors have additive effects on mean RT; there is no statistical interaction, testifying to the successiveness of the perceptual and the linguistic stage. The authors do not test the additivity of the higher moments of the RT-distribution; strictly speaking, therefore, the independence of the stages has not been shown. There is. however, not a single sentence verification study where the additivity of higher cumulants is analysed—a very general technical omission in these experiments. Otherwise, this study is an exemplary application of Sternberg's method. If the two test factors do show statistical interaction, then one must reject the possibility that there are successive independent stages. The interpretation of the way in which the two processes interrelate, then, depends on whether the joint effects of the two experimental factors is super- or subadditive. Sternberg points out that superadditivity may indicate limited capacity sharing of two parallel processes, whereas subadditivity may indicate parallel processing where RT is determined by the slowest of the two operations. Krueger (162) did an experiment where subjects matched a short phrase (such as 'is north', 'isn't east') with the position of a small circle with respect to the typed phrase (above, below, left, or right). He tested whether negation coding ('isn't' versus 'is') occurs at a different stage from feature matching (e.g. comparison of 'north' and position above). He found an interaction, and the interaction was superadditive. His conclusion was that the two processes occur in parallel but have to share a limited-capacity central processor.

These examples suffice to show some of the purely technical possibilities and difficulties attached to the verification method. The major issue in this review article should, of course, be the theoretical 'stuffing' of the different stages. We will return to this point in section 3.5. Here we will conclude by distinguishing three types of verification tasks. The main set of verification studies is concerned with sentence/picture comparisons. Coming back to our trademark metaphor, we see that this is certainly the trademark of Clark and his colleagues (see 13, 44, 45, 49, 50, 54, 56, 57, 58, 60, 148, 149). But it has also been widely used by others as well (65, 75, 98, 108, 160, 162, 204, 215, 247, 248, 256, 257) especially for the study of ambiguity (40, 89, 205). Table 1.2 (see section 3.5) summarizes most of these studies. (Word-verification studies are not mentioned.)

The second variety of verification studies has the subject test the truth or falsity of a sentence presented in isolation on the basis of his common knowledge of the world (e.g. 'Lions are more ferocious than sheep'—true or false?). Most studies in this category are basically interested in the organization of semantic memory and employ test sentences having the form of quantified statements ('All canaries are birds') (see 63, 106, 107, 134, 192, 213, 214). Other studies concern comparatives (43, 75) or variation of imagery value (147). Another set of studies is concerned with the relationship between clauses of a sentence; e.g. verifying the truth (151) or oddness (231) of 'if . . . then' statements. These latter studies are similar to the third variety of verification studies.

This last, and smallest, group of studies involves some sort of sentence/sentence verification. A test sentence has to be verified on the basis of some earlier presented sentence. Here one can either vary the delay between the sentences (5, 42) or present the two sentences simultaneously, as in Stillings' (240) experiment. Since we have categorized the Banks *et al.* study (13) in the picture-verification group, even though it is essentially a question-answering task, we should also mention here some question-answering RT experiments using sentences as test material. These are mostly inference experiments (e.g. 'A is better than B, B is better than C. Who is best?'; see 146, and also 52, 139), and are concerned with an imagery versus congruence explanation of the latency data. For a review of this Clark/Huttenlocher discussion, see Johnson-Laird (144). Amnon *et al.* (4) studied latencies for answering questions about self-embedded constructions and compared their results with probe-latency data. Garrod and Trabasso (105) studied latencies for answering questions about earlier presented text, very much as Anderson (5) has done.

2.2.6 *Question answering*

Question answering (QA) is the trademark of researchers in semantic memory. With respect to sentence comprehension we have already mentioned the QA latency studies in the framework of the preceding section. QA accuracy has been used in just a few studies. Among them are Blaubergs and Brain (27), who investigated self-embedding constructions as opposed to right-branching ones. Wright (271) measured QA accuracy as a function of syntactic correspondence between question and answer. Finally, three studies (Smith and McMahon, 234, Bever, 19, and Locatelli, 178) deal with the comprehension of sentences expressing two-event temporal orders. The paradigm is to ask the subject, 'Which event occurred first?' Neither Smith and McMahon nor Locatelli found an effect of order of mention on QA reaction time. Bever relates this finding to data on 2–4 year-olds where order of mention does matter.

2.2.7 *Miscellanea*

Various other tasks have been given to subjects in order to study sentence comprehension. In *comprehension latency tasks*, subjects are requested to push a button as soon as they grasp the meaning of the sentence. Examples are 59, 126, 159 and 207. Sometimes a subject is merely asked to make a *comprehensibility judgment* (123, 133, 196, 228, 254, 255). *Grammaticality, acceptability,* or *meaningfulness* judgments were collected in various studies (55, 127, 197, 199). In *choice tasks* the subject is requested to choose between two meanings (175) or two implications (160) of a sentence. In some experiments subjects had to *judge compatibility* of sentences (35, 74, 111, 112), and various other more idiosyncratic techniques have also been used to study sentence comprehension.

2.2.8 Some conclusions

In the preceding sections some of the major experimental procedures used in studies of sentence comprehension have been reviewed. Among others, the following observations can be made:

(i) The research group is often a better predictor of a research method than is the theoretical problem.

(ii) Comparisons between methods, if made at all, are mostly inconclusive since apart from changing the dependent variable, one nearly always changes the independent variable as well.

(iii) If the research objective is merely to show the 'psychological reality' or 'validity' of some linguistic notion, then most of the procedures we have mentioned can be appropriate.

(iv) If moreover, one wants to determine the stage at which a certain variable is effective, it is preferable to use either a simultaneous measurement procedure or a (successive) reaction-time method. The former is especially adequate if one is interested in the strictly perceptual stage, i.e. the processes operative during input of the sentence. The latter in principle allows for a Sternberg-type additive-factor method, but one has to make assumptions about nature, successiveness, and order of stages.

(v) Contrary to the original interpretation of phoneme-monitoring results in terms of the sharing of a limited capacity, detection and analysis of the target word seems to be a condition for phoneme detection. It is therefore necessary to control for all variables which might affect detection of the target word—which is rarely done.

(vi) Psychophysiological measurement during sentence perception is still an underutilized procedure.

(vii) Click localization can be affected by a great variety of factors, some of which clearly affect the very early stages of processing. It appears to be very troublesome, however, to vary just one of these factors, while keeping all others constant.

(viii) A major problem for recall tasks is to control for reconstructive activities which take place between the stimulus presentation and the response.

3. LINGUISTIC AND EXPERIMENTAL VARIABLES

The experimental measurement procedures discussed in the former section have all been developed to study linguistic and other factors which could be expected to affect language perception. In many cases these independent variables had been derived from more encompassing theories, in other cases they seem to appear out of the blue, so to say, derived from interesting observations, well-known phenomena, and so forth. Whatever their origin, we will summarize the most important experimental variables that have figured in studies of sentence perception. In section 4, we will go deeper into the more general theoretical considerations which have been in the background of some of these studies.

3.1 Prosody and rhythm

Though the importance of suprasegmental features in the perception of sentences has never been seriously denied, variables such as pause structure, intonation contours, and speech rate have often been treated as nuisance variables which had to be controlled in order to study the effect of more important factors such as syntactic complexity and constituent structure. The result is that relatively little is known about the role of suprasegmental features in sentence perception, and especially little about how these features interact with other factors in the perceptual process.

Martin and his associates (189, 190, 233, 242) have done some basic work on the role of rhythm in sentence perception. They varied the structure of sentences by splicing tapes, inserting pauses or stretches of white noise at different places in naturally spoken sentences, or removing short stretches of speech. Their main measurement procedure has been phoneme-monitoring. They found a strong increase in reaction time when the rhythmic structure of the sentence was mutilated, even if the mutilation took place long before the target phoneme. Martin (190) concludes that 'the main outlines of syntactical structure often are communicated relatively early in an utterance', and 'suprasegmental cues enable the listener to expect or anticipate rough outlines of speech not yet heard'. Dooling (72) confirmed this latter claim by showing that if a subject was set to recognize sentences (in noise) with a certain rhythmic pattern, he would tend to fail if a sentence with a different rhythmic pattern was suddenly presented.

Dooling counterbalanced syntactic changes that might also be involved and found that only the rhythmic changes were effective. In view of the above-mentioned 'nuisance' status of suprasegmental features, it is no surprise to find various studies in which such features are 'traded against' syntactic structure, as in Dooling's article. As we have already noticed in section 2, some effort has gone into showing that suprasegmental features, and especially intonation, do affect phoneme-monitoring results (e.g. 67, 233), click localization (210), dichotic switch localization (266, 267), and bias in ambiguous sentences and phrases (173, 274). A similar effort was put into showing that these features were not the sole ones and that syntactic variables alone would also be effective (80, 104, 241).

A more integrative approach would be to study exactly how the listener uses prosodic information to make early quesses about the clausal structure of the sentence. Here we should mention the pioneer work on intonation contours by Cohen and his associates at the Institute for Perception Research (61, 62, 124, 125, 154). They found that in order to render a syllable or word more prominent the speaker could use either a rise or a fall in intonation, or both. In the latter case, such a rise/fall has little predictive value. However, if only a rise is used, then at some place before the end of the sentence the intonation should go back to normal. The speaker has two options here: he could either go back to normal at another prominent word, using the fall as a marker there, or—and this is the critical issue—maintain his high intonation until the end of the clause and then begin the next clause at the normal level. This latter way of speaking does not lend prominence to the first word of the new clause. Thus, if a high intonation is maintained by the speaker after a rise, the listener can predict that either a second prominent word or a clause break will follow. The experiments show that listeners do have such expectations, and that they mostly expect clause breaks. Also the experiments by Darwin (69) mentioned earlier (sections 2.1.2 and 2.2.1) show that intonational cues are used to listen selectively and to delimit higher-order syntactic units. The question remains whether speakers normally provide sufficient prosodic information to enable the listener to use it predictively. Levelt *et al.* (175) found that disambiguating prosodic information is nearly absent if the ambiguous sentence is spoken in a disambiguating context. Here, clearly, the listener is supposed to be able to derive the correct reading of the sentence by using other sources of information.

Finally, variations in rate of presentation have also been studied, but almost exclusively in connection with visually presented sentences. High presentation rates have been used to study the effects of linguistic complexity under borderline conditions (84, 86, 129, 132, 163). Schwartz *et al.* (228) found that under high-rate conditions subjects failed to understand sentences but were still able to judge reliably the comprehensibility of the verbal material. This is in correspondence with Mistler-Lachman's results on levels of processing (197, 198, 199) which will be discussed in section 4.1.2. Miron and Brown (196) studied the effects on intelligibility of speeding up acoustic material. It was found that speech-pause times especially could be reduced without much effect on intelligibility.

3.2 Syntactic complexity

Studies of syntactic complexity originated from the aim to test the 'psychological reality' of linguistic notions. As was discussed in section 1, this aim was twofold: to demonstrate the psychological validity of linguistic units and structures, and to show a one-to-one relationship between linguistic (transformational) rules and perceptual processes. The former goal was achieved more successfully than the latter. Characteristic of studies of the latter sort were efforts to vary the transformational complexity of sentences and to show that comprehensibility would covary. Although Fodor and Garrett (82) unmasked and disproved the 'Derivational Theory of Complexity' (DTC) underlying these studies, active/passive and affirmative/negative variables have continued to be used in studies of sentence perception, although usually not for the purpose of proving DTC.

3.2.1 Voice

Although there is a general tendency for passive sentences to be harder to comprehend than active sentences—in correspondence with DTC (see e.g. 177)—a closer look at the situations of use has shown that passives may lose this additional difficulty if they structurally match other aspects of the task situation. Olson and Filby (204) found that verifying a passive sentence with respect to a picture is easier if the picture evokes a 'passive' encoding—for example, if the largest or the focal object is the recipient of the action. A similar finding was reported by Flores d'Arcais (76) in an experiment where appropriateness of the descriptive sentence was judged by the subject. Wright (271) showed that answering questions about nouns in a sentence is relatively easy if the question corresponds in voice to the sentence. Green (112) found that voice correspondence between two sentences facilitated judgments of sameness and difference in meaning. Garrod and Trabasso (105) gave subjects short paragraphs of four sentences followed by a question about one of them. Apart from generally longer latencies for passive than for active questions, they found an interaction between voice of question and voice of sentence: if the two correspond, latencies are shorter, at least for the first and the last short sentence in the paragraph. A similar correspondence effect is reported by Anderson and Bower (7), especially for the last sentence in a relatively long text. These experiments were all inspired by the original study of Sachs (221), who showed that active test sentences at the end of a text are not recognized as passive (and vice versa), but that such confusions are the rule if the test sentence appeared earlier in the text.

The basic question, given these ubiquitous correspondence effects, concerns the availability of the surface and the underlying form of the sentence to the subject. On the one hand the correspondence effects can only be explained if the subject is able to work from a surface representation, while on the other hand there is evidence (see, for example, Clark, 54, Fodor *et al.*, 80) that subjects can operate on the basis of underlying structure. One solution is to assume that subjects have the surface form, and therefore the voice of the sentence, available for a rather short period, but that they will lose it as soon as the sentence has been interpreted.

This assumption is compatible with the theory that the sentence clause is available verbatim in STM but that only its interpretation is transferred to

LTM. For the voice experiments this theory is contradicted by the following evidence: (i) Wright's (271) finding that the correspondence effect still occurs if the subject is forced to count backwards between test sentence and question—this activity presumably erasing STM content; (ii) Garrod and Trabasso's (105) finding that not only the last sentence in their list of four, but also the first (which should have been overwritten in STM) shows the correspondence effect; and (iii) the finding of Sachs (221) and of Anderson and Bower (7) that some correspondence effect remains even if the test and the recognition or question sentence are far apart.

The other solution is that both surface and underlying form are available to the subject for a relatively long period, as already suggested in Garrod and Trabasso's article. Further evidence is given by Anderson (5). This solution is compatible not only with the idea that the surface form is available both in STM and LTM (and Baddeley, 9, 10, gives convincing evidence that the recency effect can very well occur for information in LTM), but also with the more radical view that memory is not multi-store (see Craik and Lockhart, 66) but that perceptual (surface) and propositional (underlying) information have different rates of decay. This issue will be further discussed in section 4.1.2. That traces of such surface information can remain available in memory may be due to the communicative function of active versus passive sentences.

A final set of studies is concerned with the function of passives in discourse. Anisfeld and Klenbort (8, 160) showed that subjects preferred implications from passive sentences in which the logical subject is also the focal information point (comment). Passives are more markedly topic-creating in this respect than are actives. Grieve and Wales (115) and Hupet and Le Bouedec (138) show that voice can be confounded with definiteness of subject and object noun-phrase, especially in full passives, and that definiteness had a topicalizing effect of its own. Hupet and Le Bouedec show that these variables are not independent in normal communicative usage: subjects clearly prefer the grammatical subject to be definite in both passive and active sentences, indicating that the passive voice is used if the logical object is presupposed, and that the logical subject carries the assertional information. Further evidence for this presupposition-creating function of passives can be found in Hornby's (137) study. Presumably, listeners assume this functional interaction between surface form and presupposition when they interpret passive forms.

3.2.2 Negation

'What is so difficult about negation?' is the title of one paper (Wales and Grieve, 253). One answer is that negative sentences are transformationally more complex than affirmative ones and are therefore harder to understand. This answer, however, is a variant of DTC and clearly not satisfying. Wales and

Grieve conjecture that a possibly important factor is 'confusability', i.e. the degree to which the negative statement's interpretation resembles the affirmative's interpretation (e.g. 'seven plus nine is not fifteen' should be harder than 'seven plus nine is not seventy seven'). Though this factor seems to work, Greene and Wason (113) show convincingly that confusability does not interact with negation. The two factors are additive. One could say that they involve independent stages (in Sternberg's sense) in the comprehension process. The stage-approach to negation has been popular in many of the verification studies (see section 2). In particular, many of the studies by Clark and his associates (45, 57, 58, 149) use negation as one of the independent variables (see Table 1.2); and the classical finding is that true affirmative (TA) sentences are the easiest and true negatives (TN) are the hardest to verify. Somewhere in between are false affirmative (FA) and false negative (FN), usually in this order. The initial processing models developed for the explanation of these findings (see in particular Clark, 54, and Trabasso *et al.*, 248) have in common an independent stage where the negative is recoded as a positive proposition. For instance, if the ball in the picture is either red or green, then the sentence 'The ball is not red' gets internally represented as 'GREEN (BALL)'. But at the same time, Clark (54) calls this model 'cheating', since normally there will be more than two alternatives, thereby excluding the possibility of this easy transformation. The two-alternative case does occur naturally, however, in the case of marked versus unmarked adjectives. Negating an adjective may lead to recoding (see, e.g., 150), and the use of a marked adjective badly complicates the understanding of double-negative sentences (232). Not only marked adjectives but also connectives such as *or* with a single alternative (*and*) behave as if they are psycholinguistic negatives (see 237). Clark (54), as well as Trabasso (247), handles the multiple-alternative case by assuming that the negative is encoded as a positive proposition embedded in a negative (e.g., Neg (RED BALL)). Since the picture is assumed to be positively coded, the Neg-element must lead to a change in the truth value when comparing sentence and picture codes. This requires additional time. This model can therefore handle the longer latencies for negative sentences, since an (additional) change of truth value is required if the picture coding is assumed to be positive. Tanenhaus *et al.* (244) object to this solution, especially to Carpenter and Just's (45) version of it, and we will return to the issue in section 3.5.

It should be noted that all these laboratory studies concern the cases TA, FA, FN, and TN, and that in such experiments negatives are usually harder to process than affirmatives. One might wonder whether these cases reflect the normal communicative uses of negation. Why, indeed, use negatives if they are harder to understand? Johnson-Laird (145) gave a first experimental example where negatives are in fact easier: One of the test sentences 'John is not rich' or 'John is poor' could follow the statement 'Either John is intelligent or he is rich'. The subjects found the negative test sentence easier to use when inferring that

John is intelligent. Johnson-Laird made the point that negation has a natural function. Wason and Johnson-Laird (263) present a thorough review of experimental studies of negation—to which the reader is referred for further details—and they analyse what this natural function might be. They firstly cite Russell (220): 'When I say truly "this is not blue", there is on the subjective side, consideration of "this is blue", followed by rejection, while on the objective side there is some colour, "different from blue" to suggest that the natural function of a negative is to deny a certain preconception'. This hypothesis was first tested and confirmed in two inventive studies by Greene (111, 112), who found, basically, that if a subject had to judge the agreement of meaning for a pair of sentences, one affirmative and the other negative, the task was easier if the sentences disagreed than if they agreed. The natural function of negation is to signal a change with respect to an existing belief or expectation. Wason and Johnson-Laird point out that contrary to most laboratory situations, in normal life listeners do not have to 'transform' negatives into affirmatives, since the affirmative is already there as a preconception—otherwise the negative would not have been used. Or to state it in the terms of the original laboratory experiments: negatives are normally used only as false negatives. The listener can be sure that the negative sentence is used to falsify an existing expectancy or belief. True negatives are unnatural laboratory constructions and they are harder because of their unnaturalness. This philosophy fits nicely in Clark and Haviland's (59) 'given/new' theory. One could say that the negative should only be used if the corresponding affirmative is given. Levelt and Noordman (174, 202) add to this a so-called principle of minimal change: the given affirmative is not fully rejected; it is instead maximally maintained: only a single component (argument or predicate for sentences, semantic component for lexical items) is affected by negation. This is at least so for 'normal' communicative settings. Language does provide means, however, for more radical negation, namely by negating sentences containing positive polarity items (e.g. 'John indeed didn't answer the letter'). The borderline grammaticality of such constructions will lead to an 'echo' interpretation, that is, it will negate a verbatim repetition of what the former speaker said. In such a case the whole positive preconception may be dropped (cf. Baker, 12). This, however, has never been studied experimentally. A thorough and comprehensive review of negation studies can be further found in Clark (54).

3.2.3 Relatives and complements

Section 2.2.4 described various studies which used paraphrasing and phoneme-monitoring tasks. Many of these studies used variations in relative clause and complement structure as dependent variables, and we refer to Table 1.1 for a summary of the major results. It was mentioned there that deleting the relative pronoun gave varying and in some cases conflicting results; it led to longer phoneme-moniyoring RTs in 119 and 120, but not in 92; it decreased paraphrasing accuracy in 82, 119, had no effect in 120, and increased accuracy in 92; and it had no effect on paraphrasing reaction time (119). The major rationale for these studies of relative-pronoun deletion was the so-called deep-structure clue theory: the listener makes direct inferences from the surface properties of the sentence as to its underlying structural relations. The relative pronoun could, for instance, function in a decoding strategy (see section 4.1.1) that might run as follows: For the sequence NP-Rel-NP$_2$, interpret the constituents NP$_1$ and NP$_2$ as object and subject of the same verb. Deleting the Rel might interfere with the strategy. The strategy is not error-proof, as Foss and Lynch (92) have shown, and the empirical evidence for this instance of the deep-structure clue theory is dubious.

Another reason for experimenting with relative constructions is the old question of why centre-embedded sentences are so difficult to understand. (The issue of self-embedding in psycholinguistics stems from Chomsky's proof that English is not a regular language; see Levelt, 172, volume 2.) Nearly all studies show centre-embedded constructions to be harder to understand than corresponding right-branching constructions, as long as the degree of embedding is two, or in some cases more than two (see Blaubergs and Brain, 27, with a recall task, Foss and Lynch, 92, with a phoneme-monitoring task, Freedle and Craun, 97, and Hakes and Foss, 120, with paraphrasing accuracy, Hamilton and Deese, 123, with comprehensibility rating, and various other studies). Note, however, that Hakes and Foss (120) did not find the predicted self-embedding effect in a phoneme-monitoring task and that Hakes *et al.* (121) criticized earlier studies because they had confounded self-embedding versus right-branching with object versus subject relatives. In a phoneme-monitoring experiment, and without this confounding, the author could not find a difference between self-embedding and right-branching constructions. However, some effect of self-embedding did occur for a paraphrase task. Blaubergs and Brain (27) were able to show that some learning did take place in the handling of self-embedding constructions, when subjects had been trained by performing tasks involving lesser degrees of embedding (but not inversely). Baird and Koslick (11) showed that verb-object relations were better recalled if the relative clause was of the subject-focus type ('The boy who kicked the ball chased the girl') than if it was of the object-focus type ('The boy whom the girl chased ran home'). Moreover, subject-verb relations were equally well recalled in nested and non-nested constructions, thus casting doubt on an interruption theory of self-embedding complexity.

Finally, we should mention three experiments with complements. Forster (84) showed that, with the exception of a few complement constructions, two-clause sentences were generally more complex than one-clause sentences (method: rapid serial visual presentation). Holmes and Forster (132) were able to extend this finding to include *that*- and *for to*-complements. They conclude that sentence complexity is not related simply to the number of clauses. Hakes (118) found an effect of *that*-deletion in *that*-complement constructions, namely that in phoneme-monitoring RTs were longer in the deleted constructions. The effect of deletion on paraphrasing accuracy, however, was dubious.

3.2.4 Verb structure

The deep-structure clue theory also assigned a major role to the main verb of the sentence. Verbs have characteristic underlying structures in which they can occur, so that direct structural inference should be possible on the basis of the verb-token in the sentence. Such inference should be relatively difficult to make if the verb has several underlying structures into which it would fit. Fodor *et al.* (83) tested this prediction for 'complex' verbs such as *know*, which can take either a *that*-complement or an object-NP, as compared with 'simple' transitive verbs such as *meet*, which do not allow for a *that*-complement. The results were partly positive: paraphrasing accuracy and anagram solution accuracy were higher for simple verbs than for complex verbs. However, this variable affected neither paraphrasing RT nor anagram solution RT. Hakes (117) confirmed the paraphrasing accuracy result, but failed to find an effect on phoneme-monitoring. Holmes and Forster (132) used their rapid visual presentation method and showed that sentences with simple verbs were recalled better than sentences with complex verbs. These different results can be explained if the effect of verb complexity is merely reconstructive; that is, the creation of a complex verb sentence (in the paraphrasing recall and anagram tasks) may be harder, but this does not necessarily imply additional perceptual complexity. Levelt *et al.* (174) showed that sentences containing either simple or complex verbs of motion (like *move* vs *rise*) could be verified more quickly for complex verbs than for simple verbs, in perceptual situations where both sentences were true. In such situations, for example where one observes a quickly rising dot, the complex verb is more appropriate, in accordance with Grice's (114) maxim of quantity. A very different approach to verb structure is exemplified by Stillings (240). The subject was typically presented with a sentence such as 'Mary just loaned a book to John', and then had to verify the further sentence 'John didn't have the book'. The verification model predicting the reaction time is based on a system of meaning rules, which are written as programs for converting one sentence into the other. Stillings compared *borrow* and *loan* in various verification tasks and was able to substantiate his model.

3.3. Ambiguity

The effects of ambiguity on the comprehension of sentences have been studied intensively since the papers of MacKay and Bever appeared (180, 183). Initially a fruitful distinction was made between lexical, surface, and deep-structure ambiguities. The first type involves ambiguous lexical items, as with 'the soldier put the gasoline into the tank'; the second involves word-grouping ambiguities as in: 'the three masted British ships were sailing south', and the last involves underlying relations without surface-grouping effects: 'Italians like opera as much as Germans'. Only the first and last variety are genuine homophones. Surface ambiguities are at best homographs; they should be, and in fact are, perceptually non-homophonic with explicit pronounciation (175). Experimental results with lexical ambiguities have sometimes been rather different from those with underlying ambiguities. Since there are theoretical reasons why they should be different (see 22, 91), and since almost all studies are on lexical ambiguity, we will begin with a review of lexical ambiguity and conclude this section with a few remarks on deep-structure ambiguities.

3.3.1 Lexical ambiguity

The main issues in the study of lexical ambiguity have been the following: (i) Does lexical ambiguity complicate the processing of a sentence? (ii) Are both meanings of the lexical item computed during sentence perception, or only one? (iii) How does context affect ambiguity resolution? (iv) When is ambiguity resolved: immediately or with a short or long delay? These questions are not independent; moreover, each of them needs further qualification. Let us consider them in turn.

(i) *Does lexical ambiguity complicate sentence processing?* The following studies have compared sentence processing with and without lexical ambiguity: 22, 35, 37, 64, 88, 89, 91, 101, 128, 180, 183, 197, 206, 230. These studies involved a large variety of tasks, and in almost all cases an effect of ambiguity was found. In particular, one finds longer reaction times in the ambiguous case if the subject has to judge compatibility between the test sentence and a second sentence (35) or a probe word (230), or even if one has to judge the colour of the visually presented probe word (64). Longer RTs are also found for phoneme-monitoring if the test phoneme shortly follows the ambiguous word (37, 88, 91). Verifying the truth of a sentence (205), deciding on the ambiguity of the last word of a sentence (128), and verifying the sentence vis-à-vis a picture (89), all lead to longer reaction times in the ambiguous case. Furthermore, clicks are less accurately localized (101) in lexically ambiguous sentences. On the basis of a depth of processing argument (see section 4.1.2), Mistler-Lachman (197) predicted and found no effect of lexical ambiguity on RT in a meaningfulness judgment task.

The only tasks for which the results are conflicting are completion tasks. If the subject is asked to add an appropriate continuation sentence to the test sentence one finds either no effect of lexical ambiguity on RTs (22), or an effect with unspecified statistical significance (197), which, moreover, seems to appear if the test sentence is preceded by a disambiguating context sentence. Also, if the subject has to complete an ambiguous sentence fragment, then the effect of lexical ambiguity is unclear when the fragment is an incomplete clause. MacKay (180) found 0.5 sec longer completion times (measured by stopwatch) for lexically ambiguous fragments; the effect is of unspecified significance. Olson and MacKay (206) found a significant effect on completion RT, but Bever *et al.* (22) and Cairns and Kamerman (37) did not. These differences, however, may be more apparent than real: in the latter two studies, (insignificant) differences in RT of 240 and 200 msec were found respectively, whereas Olson and MacKay found a (significant) RT-effect of 200 msec, which is of the same order of magnitude. It should be added, moreover, that the statistics used in all of these studies are subject to Clark's (53) critique. At any rate, production tasks are not very sensitive to lexical ambiguity. All other tasks, however, showed the predicted effects of ambiguity, so that it makes sense to pose the next question:

(ii) Are both meanings of the lexical item computed during sentence perception, or only one? The additional effort of computing both meanings may explain several of the foregoing results. However, the question (which is asked in several of the reviewed papers) is highly confusing if it is not further qualified. What does it mean to 'compute' both meanings of a lexical item? It is certainly insufficient to state that 'both readings are in some sense available' to the listener (164), or that 'both meanings are activated in memory' (64). One might use Morton's (200) logogen-model to distinguish two senses of 'available'. If a homophone activates both logogens in LTM, they both become more available since both have an increased probability of reaching activation-threshold. If, moreover, both logogens do reach threshold they both fire (simultaneously, or in quick succession), thereby delivering the responses to working memory. This is a second and stronger sense of availability: the subject is conscious of both meanings. Foss and Jenkins (91) explicitly proposed this latter strong sense of availability. In the literature strong availability is often determined by asking the subject whether he noticed the ambiguity. If one trusts this test, as Foss and Jenkins apparently do, and if in the majority of cases the subjects turn out not to have noticed the ambiguity (a very general finding), it is in my view contradictory to maintain the strong version of double availability. In my opinion the test is not fully satisfying, and we are therefore left with three possibilities.

(a) During a lexically ambiguous sentence the homophone initially activates one logogen only. At a certain moment it fires, and that particular meaning is in working memory for structural integration.

(b) The homophone activates both logogens until one fires: one meaning becomes conscious, the other logogen gradually turns back to rest state. We call this the *weak theory of double availability*.

(c) The homophone activates both logogens up to threshold level: both meanings become conscious. This is the *strong theory of double availability*.

Alternative (a) should be dismissed. It contradicts substantial experimental evidence (see Morton, 200), and it is unclear how the homophone would 'know' which logogen to activate. However, there are naive versions of the so-called *one-meaning* or *unitary perception* theories that come close to (a). Both (a) and (b) are one-meaning theories in the sense that only one meaning of the word becomes available to working memory. Originally, many authors did not consider the possibility of activating a meaning without making it conscious. In Lashley's (167) *garden-path* paper, but also in Foss (88), Carey *et al.* (40), Cairns (35), and Hogaboam and Perfetti (128), we find the theory that only the most likely meaning of an ambiguous word becomes conscious and that as long as the most likely meaning is also the correct meaning (given the context and the task) there is no difference whatsoever from the unambiguous case. Problems only arise if the secondary meaning is intended. The subject should then retrace the blind alley and find the other meaning, this leading to longer reaction times. There is evidence, however, that even though only one meaning becomes conscious, the secondary meaning gets activated during comprehension; this is exactly the difference between models (a) and (b). The evidence mainly derives from the dichotic studies of Lackner and Garrett (164) and the extensive replication thereof by MacKay (183). Basically, these authors found that one can bias the interpretation of a lexically ambiguous sentence, presented to one ear, by simultaneously presenting a word to the other ear, which is related to one or the other reading of the ambiguous word. The stimulus conditions are such that the subjects are unable to reproduce the biasing word. If only the dominant meaning were retrieved in the way of model (a), it would be impossible to bias one way or the other (see 164). It seems necessary to allow for the possibility that both logogens become activated, as in model (b). In that case the biasing word might add to the activation of the corresponding logogen, increasing the chance that it will fire first. The other bit of evidence against model (a) is Olson and MacKay's (206) result that the completion of an ambiguous sentence fragment takes longer than the completion of a non-ambiguous control sentence. If the subject completes according to the first meaning which comes to mind, there will be no retracing, and model (a) would not predict the RT difference. Would model (b)?

To answer this question, one has to look into the relevant results in more detail. The authors find an effect of lexical ambiguity on completion RT only for those cases where the two possible interpretations are about equally likely (bias range of 40–60%). They propose the so-called *perceptual suppression theory*: the two sets of features (*logogens* in Morton's terminology) are supposed to interact: in order to activate one logogen to reach threshold level, the other one has to be de-activated. It is not hard to suppress the recessive logogen activity in the case of a 90/10 bias; the reaction time will not be noticeably different from the unambiguous case. Suppression, however, is difficult in a 50/50 bias situation since both logogens have a high level of activation. It should be remarked that in Morton's model logogens are independent; and one should ask whether that simple principle should be abandoned in the light of these data. Not yet, I believe. In the same way as it is agreed that it takes relatively much effort to suppress a likely meaning (as in the 50/50 case), one could state that it takes relatively much effort to activate the other logogen up to threshold. This might be very easy for the dominant meaning in the 90/10 case—one does not need a suppression model here. Olson and MacKay give two further arguments for their suppression theory, but these concern the case where one meaning is already conscious. Suppression here means erasure from working memory. This has nothing to do with interaction between logogens. And finally, all other existing evidence for logogen interaction with homographs points to facilitation instead of inhibition, i.e. in order to activate one logogen, the activation of a related one may be helpful. This is the homograph effect reported by Rubenstein and his associates (218, 219), and Schvaneveldt and Meyer (227). (Whether this effect is due to logogen-interaction, however, is doubtful, in view of the long reaction times in these experiments.) So far model (b), the weak theory of double availability without subthreshold suppression, seems to suffice. What about model (c), the strong theory of double availability? It seems to me that it is in general not necessary to suppose that both interpretations are simultaneously present in working memory. Except for the relatively infrequent cases where subjects notice the ambiguity, there are no compelling data in the literature suggesting that the strong model (c) should be adopted. There is substantial confusion here about the requirements of the weak and the strong theory, especially with respect to the role of context. Let us, therefore, turn to the next question.

(iii) How does context affect ambiguity resolution? We have already mentioned the findings by Lackner and Garrett (164) and MacKay (182) in which biasing information in one ear affects the interpretation of the material presented to the other ear. Normally, disambiguating context either precedes or follows the ambiguous item; some authors have studied the role of such context in the comprehension of ambiguous sentences. Foss and Jenkins (91) distinguish two ways in which prior context can influence the interpretation of an ambiguous word in a sentence. In the so-called Prior Decision Model, the prior context activates (to use Morton's terms) all related logogens: the logogen corresponding to the contextually appropriate reading of the ambiguous word thus gets an activation advantage before the word itself has appeared. This is the weak model (b) above. According to the Choice Point Decision Model both interpretations of the ambiguous word are activated and transferred to working memory: context asserts its effect only later, i.e. it helps to select from among items already present in working memory. This is clearly the strong model (c), which predicts an effect on working memory-load regardless of whether disambiguating context has been presented. With a phoneme-monitoring task, Foss and Jenkins found strong evidence for the latter model: biasing prior

context does not affect monitoring RTs, whereas ambiguity itself quite clearly does so. This supports the strong model. Quite similar results were obtained by Conrad (64), who also found that biasing prior context had little or no effect on her colour-naming task: after the (to be remembered) sentence had been presented, the subject was visually presented with the ambiguous target word (a category name, which was either appropriate or inappropriate to the correct interpretation of the ambiguous word) or a control word. The subject had to name the colour of the printed word. RTs were longer for ambiguous words and their category names than for control words. But again, the effect of biasing context was negligible. Conrad concludes that apparently an independent stage of lexical search exists. But though this finding fully agrees with the results of Foss and Jenkins, Conrad favours 'a theory in which contextual information increases the strength of one or more of the activated meanings of a word to the point that it reaches threshold and becomes conscious'. This, however, is the weak model (b)!—so essentially the same results are interpreted as confirming the strong theory in one case and the weak theory in another. Putting this confusion aside, there are at least four reasons for not adopting the strong theory: Firstly, Foss and Jenkins found that most subjects had been unaware of the ambiguity, and that both the aware and the unaware subjects gave essentially the same results with respect to the critical variables. This is unlikely to have happened if the two interpretations had been in working memory, i.e. conscious (see above). Secondly, Foss and Jenkins correctly state that an effect of context might be critically time-bound, i.e. a disambiguating context appearing either too early or too late might not be effective at the moment of entrance of the ambiguous word. This may also be the case for Conrad's results, who is measuring a fairly long time after the lexical search process (the visually presented test word follows the acoustically presented sentence), and is therefore using a successive measurement technique (see section 2.2) that does not allow direct inferences as to the precise moment of the lexical search. Thus, further measurement might show a context effect, such as found by Morton and Long (201) in a phoneme-monitoring task with non-ambiguous material. Thirdly, there are the general problems with the phoneme-monitoring technique, discussed in section 2.2.1. Finally, as Hogaboam and Perfetti (128) state, one should consider these experimental results from the point of view of the primary and secondary meanings of the ambiguous word. Even if a word has a 50/50 bias, an individual subject will (given the weak theory) allow one (his primary) interpretation to occupy working memory. Measurable effects may occur in just those cases where this (primary) interpretation conflicts with the context which requires the secondary meaning. Summing over subjects will then show an overall effect of ambiguity but no context effect, as found by Foss and Jenkins and by Conrad. Although this fully fits the weak theory (b), it should be noted that the effect of context is supposed to take place in working memory, and not directly through activation of logogens. Hogaboam and Perfetti's experiment is itself, however, somewhat inconclusive, since asking the subject whether the last word of a sentence was ambiguous is highly unnatural, just as in Olson and Mackay's (206) study, where he subject is asked to find a second meaning after one has already been given. Such conscious search is not typical for sentences containing ambiguous items.

(iv) When is lexical ambiguity resolved? If the weak theory of double availability (b) is correct, the effect of lexical ambiguity should come to an end as soon as the one meaning is transferred to working memory. Only in cases where later context requires the alternative meaning will reprocessing become necessary; this is the well-known *garden-path* effect. In all other cases, however, one would expect the effect of lexical ambiguity to be very shortlived. Note that in the alternative strong theory (c), where both interpretations are available in working memory, longer lasting effects could be expected since rejection of one of the two meanings will depend either on later disambiguating information or on the arrival of the end of the clause (as Bever *et al.* (22) propose). The available evidence is limited but in agreement with the weak theory; there is not the slightest evidence for long-lasting effects of lexical ambiguity (apart from garden-path effects). In order to test the duration of the ambiguity effect one can only use simultaneous measurements (see section 2.1). The Bever *et al.* (22) sentence-completion task (on visually presented materials) is a successive measurement; moreover, in spite of their theory, lexical ambiguity had no effect on completion latencies. The only simultaneous measurement experiments are those of Foss *et al.* (88, 91) and of Cairns and Kamerman (37), who used the phoneme-monitoring technique (with all its disadvantages; see section 2.1.1). Foss (88) found a significant 40 msec effect of ambiguity on monitoring latency. However, this was a mixture of lexical and underlying ambiguities. How large the non-significant differences between the two types was is not stated in the paper. Also, the target phoneme was given at different delays after the ambiguous element, but this was not a systematic variable. Foss and Jenkins (91) found a significant effect of lexical ambiguity of 38 msec. The target delay never exceeded two words in this experiment, and it was mostly shorter. The only experiment where target delay was systematically varied was conducted by Cairns and Kamerman (37). At zero delay, where the target phoneme immediately followed the ambiguous lexical item, a significant 20 msec delay was found, but at a two-word delay the ambiguity effect disappeared. The authors conclude that lexical decisions are taken immediately before, and not after, transfer to working memory. In summary, although lexical ambiguity can clearly complicate sentence comprehension, there is little evidence that working memory is involved in this additional load (except for garden-path phenomena or any other task where later recomputation is required for the subject). Rather, a weak theory of double availability can explain all available data: the ambiguous element—as well as earlier context—can activate both logogens, but

normally only one reaches threshold, so that one interpretation becomes available to working memory; this happens very rapidly after the appearance of the lexical item. This interpretation is in good agreement with the general notion that semantic and syntactic processing is very much 'on-line' activity, (see section 4.1.1, and especially the work of Marslen-Wilson).

3.3.2 Deep-structure ambiguities

Deep or underlying-structure ambiguities have been the subject of various experimental studies (see 22, 28, 39, 49, 88, 89, 164, 180, 181, 182, 183, 197, 262). Here we will limit ourselves to a few remarks about the question of whether in comprehension tasks underlying ambiguities behave differently from lexical ambiguities. Evidence shows that in most experiments this is not so. Apart from cases where subjects are led up a garden path, i.e. spontaneously produce one interpretation when another interpretation is required (see for instance 89), or cases where subjects are asked to find the other meaning (as in 183), underlying ambiguities are not more difficult to handle than lexical ambiguities (see 88, 164, 197).

There is, however, some evidence that underlying ambiguities can be distinguished from lexical ambiguities in critical tasks. Bever *et al.* (22) found that sentence completion may be relatively quick if an underlying ambiguous clause (in contrast to a non-ambiguous clause) is presented to the subject. This is not the case for lexical ambiguities. If the presented clause is incomplete, however, deep ambiguity tends to slow down completion. Again, this is not so in the case of lexical ambiguities. This different behaviour is explained by Bever *et al.* by assuming that the hearer 'is carrying out two distinct perceptual operations during presentation of a sentence fragment with an underlying structure ambiguity'. If completion is required before the end of the clause, the subject must choose between two incomplete and independent interpretations. In lexical ambiguity there is less independence, which supposedly makes the choice easier and less forced. If completion is required at the end of a clause, the fact that there are two independent interpretations available increases the chance of finding (at least) one completion. Apart from a need for confirmation of these results (the effects are around borderline significance and no Min F'-test (see Clark, 53) has been used), there is a need for clarification of 'carrying out two distinct perceptual operations'. This would require parallel processing in working memory, and one would like to see a more explicit model of the operations involved. The best available model here is Wanner's (259, 262). Based on an ATN analysis of relative-clause parsing (see section 4.3.2), Wanner and Shiner (262) predict a preference for a direct object interpretation of ambiguous sentences of the sort 'The patient that the nurse brought the doctor, hated rainy days'. In an experiment with control of semantic bias, strong evidence was obtained for this prediction. At the heart of the Wanner model is a mechanism where syntactic function assignment is postponed until the relevant information arrives. Therefore, contrary to the Bever *et al.* notion, Wanner and Shiner suppose that neither are both interpretations computed nor a single one: rather none is computed; the decision is postponed, and since postponement requires the storage of information, it is a load-increasing process.

3.4. Constituent and clause structure

In this section we will limit ourselves to presenting some of the major opinions about perceptual units of segmentation to be found in the literature. Since many of the studies on segmentation employed the click-localization technique, we should keep in mind the methodological difficulties proceeding from this technique (see section 2.2.1). Also, the recall techniques (see section 2.2.2) that seem to support the psychological reality of clause structure do not necessarily show that this reality is perceptual. Relatively little simultaneous measurement has been used for segmentation units (see, however, 3, 24, 77, 186). In the search for the psychological reality of linguistically defined segments, major constituents were among the first candidates of investigation. Fodor and Bever (79) claimed perceptual reality of major constituents on the basis of click-location results. Bever, Lackner, and Kirk (25) modified this view in the sense that only those constituent boundaries which related to deep-structure sentoid boundaries were able to attract clicks. Opposition to this position came from Chapin *et al.* (48) and Toppino (246), who tried to show that surface boundaries not relating to sentoids could attract clicks. Fodor *et al.* (80) challenged Chapin *et al.*'s critique on the basis of an analysis of the linguistic material which they had used for their experiment. After a review of the major literature on clause structure, Fodor *et al.* (80) conclude that 'surface constituent boundaries which correspond to junctures between sentoids define the potential points of perceptual segmentation of sentences; whether any such point is in fact taken as the boundary of a perceptual unit may depend on a variety of other structural features' (p. 339)—a rather cautious statement. An important addition to the search for reality of linguistic segments was an effort to determine the functional role of such segments in the perceptual event. Fodor *et al.* (80) propose the theory that 'As the sentence is received, it is assigned to a short-term store where the fragments that constitute each of its sentoids are collected together. Material is dismissed from this storage as soon as it can be asigned to a completed sentoid. It is because each sentoid is dismissed from this store en bloc that the clause functions as a unit of speech perception) (p. 342–343). Thus, at the end of the clause the materials are assembled and assigned relations according to the sentoid structure. There have been reactions against both the sentoid interpretation of segmentation units and the clause-by-clause processing theory. In spite of the fact that Fodor *et al.*'s most recent statement about segmentation units was quite modest, Tanenhaus and Carroll (243) attacked the position that the segmentation unit could be *structurally* defined; in its place they propose the notion of 'functional clause', which expresses, among other things, so-called 'functional completeness': A clause can be a candidate for a segmentation unit only if it expresses a complete set of grammatical relations (as, for example, in '*After Mary finished the cake*, she took an apple', and not in '*After finishing*, Mary took an apple'). It was mainly Marslen-Wilson (184, 185, 186, 187, 188) who attacked what he called the 'staggered serial model', i.e., the notion that syntactic analysis would only take place after a whole syntactic unit, such as a phrase or clause, had been gathered. His shadowing and word-monitoring experiments clearly show that syntactic analysis takes place right from the beginning of the clause, inter-actively with phonetic and semantic analysis. A more formal model of such on-line processing has been proposed by Wanner *et al.* (259, 260).

What is lacking at the present moment is a restatement of the relationship between segmentation units and working memory. If clausal 'reality' is not in fact caused by end-of-clause interpretation plus release from working memory, are we then bound to dismiss clausal reality after all, or should we seek its cause among other memorial functions? The contributions of Marslen-Wilson *et al.* and Carroll *et al.* to the present volume shed a wholly new light on this issue.

3.5. Pictoral context

Many studies in sentence perception have used pictoral variables in order to study how sentence comprehension interacts with non-linguistic perceptual context. Almost all of these studies were of the verification type (see section 2.2.5). Table 1.2 gives a summary of the linguistic and pictoral variables used in these sentence-verification studies, as well as of the major results obtained.

What are the major principles which govern most of these results? All theoretical accounts (45, 54, 56, 58) are based on the assumption that the sentence is internally represented in abstract propositional format. The same is assumed about the internal representation of the picture. Verification proceeds through a serial process of comparison between these two internal representations, with the order of comparison being determined by the propositional hierarchy. Reaction times are determined by the number of operations to be performed in the serial comparison. The number of operations critically depends on the number of mismatches between the two propositional representations: this is known as the *congruence principle* (Clark, 54).

In general, the serial nature of sentence/picture verification processes finds substantial support in the literature; see, however, our earlier remarks in section 2.2.5. Though the congruence principle seems to find similarly strong support, it should be noted that this support depends on (a) the representation one chooses for sentence and picture and (b) the order of comparison one assumes. With

Table 1.2 Sentence-picture verification experiments

Authors		Linguistic variables	Pictoral variables	Order	Main results
Banks, Clark and Lucy (1975)	1	Which balloon/yo-yo is higher/lower? Which string is longer/shorter?	A or B and varying string difference	S → P	Balloon/yo-yo × A/B interaction (congruency) No congruency × length difference effect
	2	Same	A or B constant string-length (1 cm)	S → P	Congruency effect. No congruency × height diff. effect
Cary, Mehler and Bever (1970)	1	Set-list of four Adjectival (A) (they are incoming signals) or Progressive (P) (they are unearthing diamonds) sentences, followed by ambiguous test sentence (they are lecturing doctors) Ear of entry	Pictures for which both interpretations are true (TT) only one (TF or FT) or both false (FF)	P → S	For ambiguous sentences A/P × ear of entry interaction for reaction times. Interpretation bias according to set. No true/false effect
	2	Same	Same	P → S	No interpretation bias
Carpenter and Just (1972)		Type of quantifier: minority/majority, few/ many (of the dots are red/black)	A 2 black, 14 red dots B 2 red, 14 black dots	S → P	Interaction between quantifier and locus of fixation (i.e. red or black subset)
Carpenter and Just (1974)	1	Negation and colour name: It is (n't) true that the dots are (n't) red/green	16 dots of 1 colour: red, green or black	Simultaneous	No negation × colour congruence interaction. RT increases with number of constituent comparisons
	2	Same	Same	S → P	Same

Table 1.2 (continued)

Authors		Linguistic variables	Pictoral variables	Order	Main results
Clark, Carpenter and Just (1973)	1	Which is taller/shorter Which is deeper/shallower		Simulta-neous S → P	RT (tall/short) < RT (deep/shallow). RT (tall, deep) < RT (short, shallow). No interaction simultaneous/S → P with any variable
	2	Same	A ... B ...	S → P	RT (tall/short) < RT (deep/shallow). Interaction A/B x (tall, short)/(deep, shallow)
	3	Same	Five boxes 'looked into' from different angles	S → P	Interaction box-type x (tall, short)/(deep, shallow)
	4	Dimensionality of comparative: which is taller/shorter/bigger/smaller? which is wider/narrower/bigger/smaller?	Two rectangles, one being a square differing only in width. Two rectangles, one being a square, differing only in height	S → P	Two-dimensional terms quicker, one-dimensional terms slower for square
	5	Same	Same, but no square rectangles	S → P	One-dimensional terms quicker, two-dimensional terms slower for the more rectangular figure
Clark and Chase (1972)	1	Star (plus) is (n't) above (below) plus (star)	Two pictures: star above or below plus	Simulta-neous	RT (above) < RT (below) Aff < Neg True < False. No interactions
	2	Same	Same	S → P P → S	Same, plus interaction pos/neg x true/false S → P quicker than P → S

Reference	No.	Task / variable	Stimulus	Direction	Result
Clark and Chase (1974)	3	Same	Same, instructions to attend bottom/top of figure, or whole figure	P → S	RT (whole) < RT (bottom/top). No interactions
	1	Dependent linguistic variable (spontaneous descriptions)	Relative prominence of objects, i.e. star above (below) line (prominent) or circle (non-prominent)	P → S	Preference for above. Above-bias for non-prominent picture independent of orientation; for the prominent picture dependent on orientation
	2	Star (line) is (n't) above (below) line (star), or star (circle) is (n't) above (below) circle (star)	Same	S → P	No above/below x star/position interaction
Clark and Lucy (1975)		Ten different types of request to either or not ('polarity') colour circle blue or pink	Blue or pink circle	S → P	Truth x polarity interaction
Cormish (1971)		The circle is not all blue (red, green, yellow)	Circle with different differently large sectors of red (etc.)	S → P	Non-monotonic sector size effect on verification RT
Flores d'Arcais (1974)	1	Comparatives with 'marked' vs 'unmarked' adjectives (tall vs short, etc.). Orally presented	Pictures with two persons, animals, etc. differing on the antonym's dimension	S → P	Longer RT for marked than for unmarked. True quicker than false
	2	Comparatives with marked vs unmarked adjectives. Orally presented	Two long test lines among small ones, or two short test lines among long ones. Test lines differed in size. Similarly for	S → P	Longer RT for marked than for unmarked. True quicker than false. No effect of size of test lines (etc.)

Table 1.2 (continued)

Authors	Linguistic variables	Pictoral variables	Order	Main results
		positions of weighing balance, more or less filled glasses, smaller or larger blocks		
3	Same as 2	Same as 2	P → S	Same as 2
4	Marked or unmarked cue-adjective presented before picture. Sentences with larger vs smaller, or less large vs less small	Large and small circle	P → S	Same as 1, plus cue-adjective × sentence adjective interaction
Foss, Bever and Silver (1968)	Ambiguous or non-ambiguous sentences	Pictures for which sentence is either true or false	S → P	Longer RTs for ambiguous sentence only if picture presents unexpected meaning
Glucksberg, Trabasso and Wald (1973)	$\left.\begin{array}{l}\text{Car}\\ \text{truck}\\ \text{bus}\\ \text{train}\end{array}\right\} \left.\begin{array}{l}\text{hit}\\ \text{passed}\\ \text{pulled}\end{array}\right\} \left.\begin{array}{l}\text{fence}\\ \text{pole}\\ \text{tree}\end{array}\right.$ In either active or passive (A/P) form. Thus, some reversible, some irreversible (R/I)	Corresponding pictures	P → S, S → P	For true sentences: A/P × R/I interaction for S → P only. For false sentences: A/P interaction with locus of mismatch
Hornby (1974)	1 Cleft/pseudo-cleft sentences	Picture true, or picture false with respect to resp. focus or proposition	S → P	More errors for false/presupposed than for false/focused

Study	Exp	Sentence manipulation	Task	Direction	Results
	2	Standard/cleft/pseudo-cleft sentences (S/C/P) Sentence voice (A/P)	Same	S → P	More errors for false/presupposed. A/P-effect (for errors) S/C/P-effect
Just and Carpenter (1971)	1	Three types of negatives: syn-not (not, none, no) syn (few, scarcely, hardly) sem (a minority, a small proposition etc.)	4 x 4 array of dots. All 16 same colour or two with different colour	Simultaneous (sentence left)	RT (Neg) > RT (Aff) Aff/Neg x True/false interaction for syn-not and syn. Type of neg x Aff/Neg x True/False interaction
	2	Same	Same	P → S	Aff/Neg x T/F interaction only for syn-not
	3	Two types of negatives: syn and sem	Same, but instruction to code colour of larger or smaller subset	P → S	For 'code larger subset' same interactions as in expt. 1; for syn and sem. For 'code smaller subset' inverse interaction
Krueger (1972)	1–4	Is (n't) north east south west	Circle above, below, left of, right of sentence	Simultaneous	Interaction Neg/Aff x location of circle
Olson and Filby (1972)	1	The {car/truck} hit the {truck/car} Active/Passive	Picture for which sentence true or false. Two directions of movement, two instructions: attend subject/object of action	P → S	RT (Act) < RT (Pass) Instruction x A/P interaction
	2	Same	Same, but other instructions: attend car/truck	P → S	RT (Act) < RT (Pass) RT (True) < RT (False) Instruction x position (car/truck) interaction

Table 1.2 (continued)

Authors	Linguistic variables	Pictoral variables	Order	Main results
	3 Same	Presentation of one vehicle, followed by presentation of the other higher or lower on the slope (focus)	P → S	RT (Act) < RT (Pass) RT (True) < RT (False) Focus × Act/Pass interaction
Roncato and Sonino (1976)	'A {inside / outside} B', where A, B are different figure names. Visual presentation	Embedded or juxtaposed figures (circles, squares, triangles), which corresponded or did not correspond to figure names in sentence	S → P P → S	S → P faster than P → S Faster RT if smallest object is mentioned first. Faster RT if figure does not correspond to name. True faster than false
Wannemacher (1974)	1 Active/Passive (A/P) Reversible/Irreversible (R/I)	Pictures such that they create mismatch for subject, verb, or object of sentence or combinations thereof ('treatments')	P → S	Different RTs for 'treatments' (object mismatch slowest). A/P-effect, R/I-effect Interactions: A/P × R/I A/P × treatment A/P × R/I × treatment
	2 Same	Same	Simultaneous	Same
Wannemacher (1974)	1 As in Wannemacher (1974)	As in Wannemacher (1974)	S → P	Interaction R/I × treatments
	2 Same	Same, but only the three one-component mismatch types	S → P	Same i.e. serial self-terminating comparison: logical subject → verb → logical object

respect to the representation of sentence and of picture, different authors give different solutions. These are partly notational variants, but for another part important empirical issues are involved. The question is whether the same sentence (resp. picture) can be represented in different formats, dependent on task and practice, and on the prior presentation of the picture (resp. sentence). It is indeed the case that these factors can affect the way in which the subject codes the information. Examples of task and practice effects have already been mentioned in section 3.2.2, especially Trabasso *et al.*'s (248) finding that subjects apparently represent the sentence 'The ball is not red' by 'GREEN (BALL)'. But this occurs only if there is no more than one (colour) alternative, and after the subject has had some practice. This is called the *recoding strategy* (45, see also 150); it is assumed to have taken place if the true negative (TN) is judged faster than the false negative (FN). One wonders whether recoding is not a mere laboratory artifact. Interdependence between sentence and picture representations has been shown to exist by Clark, Carpenter, and Just (56); it has especially been demonstrated that the representation of the picture can be affected by prior presentation of the sentence.

Recoding and interdependence give the theorist quite a lot of leeway in modelling his data. One would like to have independent evidence that a particular situation leads the subject to recode (i.e. independent of the finding that TN < FN); and similarly for interdependence. But otherwise, there is nothing against invoking such principles. Tanenhaus *et al.* (244) in a sharp critique of Carpenter and Just's (45) paper, to which we will return shortly, criticize the arbitrariness in the use of a once-chosen format of representation. They refer especially to inconsistencies in the use of an affirmative embedding predicate (AFF) in the internal representations, inconsistencies which do indeed affect predicted reaction times. More agreement, however, seems to exist with respect to the order of comparison one must assume. The principle seems to be 'inside out': the embedded propositions are verified before the embedding propositions.

Let us, finally, return to the Tanenhaus *et al.*'s (244) critique of verification studies, which was mostly addressed to Carpenter and Just (who reacted to it in 46). Apart from technicalities relating to the question of whether the choice of internal representations is ad hoc, the exchange of views is primarily demonstrative of a clash in aims. The Tanenhaus *et al.* paper demonstrates what we have called the linguistic aim in section 1: to explain how the hearer uses his knowledge of the language to encode sentences in terms of linguistic structural descriptions. It is argued that the verification approach does not tell us how the verification representations are derived but only how the comparison is done. The latter is said to be of marginal interest for a theory of sentence understanding. Carpenter and Just, on the other hand, place themselves much more in the communicative framework: how does the listener use linguistic and non-linguistic information in order to answer questions? For this, it is highly important for the listener to find out the referents of what is said, and this process is studied in the verification literature. So far, the discussion has little theoretical import: if one is mainly interested in studying the derivation of internal representations, one should not join the verification club. If, however, one's aim is to find out how linguistic information is used vis-à-vis perceptual or encyclopaedic knowledge, then verification studies can be quite useful. An important theoretical issue does arise, however, if one wants to realize both aims at the same time. Tanenhaus *et al.* assume that the verification representation which is used in the verification process, and which is task-dependent, is in its turn derived from a prior, and much more general-purpose representation. This is, of course, the structural description mentioned earlier. Here is an interesting empirical assumption: deriving a structural description is a first step in deriving anything else (a conceptual structure, a verification representation). This issue will be taken up again in section 4.1.1.

3.6. Non-pictoral context: Given and new information

In section 2.2.5 various studies were listed in which a sentence had to be understood (verified), given another sentence or certain encyclopaedic knowledge. In most respects these studies were concerned with the same theoretical issues as the sentence/picture verification studies (i.e. congruence, markedness, etc.) Here we will limit ourselves to mentioning some studies of a different theoretical flavour, namely those deriving from Clark's notion of the given/new contract. Clark and Haviland (59) starting from Grice's (114) notion of a 'cooperative principle' in conversation, propose the existence of 'cooperative' information-exchanging strategies used by speaker and listener. At any moment the speaker presupposes certain items of information to be available to the hearer. These are the 'givens' to which the speaker can then add new information. The speaker will use special linguistic devices to express what he supposes to be given, and what he intends to be new. The listener, in his turn, will match this strategy by using what is linguistically marked as 'given' in order to locate the appropriate information in memory. He can then proceed to add the information linguistically marked as 'new' to the existing data structure. Clark and coworkers did various studies to show that violations of this given/new contract lead to complications in the comprehension process (59, 126, 236). A typical paradigm is to switch the linguistic marking of given and new, as in the following examples:

Context: Michelle ignored Sam, who was waiting at the bar. Turning her back, she began talking to a group of strangers. Sam was wild with jealousy.'

Sentence (a): 'The dancer *who disregarded Sam*, motioned to Jack.'

Sentence (b): 'The dancer who motioned to Jack, *disregarded Sam*.' If the context is followed by sentence (a), everything is according to the contract. The relative clause expresses (as it should) information already given in the context.

In (b), however, the relative clause (linguistically marking information as given) in fact expresses new information. Clark found longer reading and comprehension times required for (b) than for (a). In (b) the listener is forced to switch the roles of given and new in order to integrate the sentence with the earlier context.

Though the given/new notion has a long tradition in linguistics, these are the first studies where its role in sentence processing is studied. It appears from two other studies (Hornby, 137; Just and Clark, 151) that given (presupposed) information is harder to verify than new; this is in accord with the general theory. (See especially Clark's contribution to this volume.)

3.7. Some conclusions

In the preceding review of linguistic and other independent variables used in sentence-comprehension studies, some of the major observations were:

(i) There is a gradual shift from considering prosody as a nuisance variable to a genuine interest in the comprehension of spoken (as opposed to written) language.

(ii) The effects of linguistic complexity on processing are not uniform. Not only are some complexity variables, such as verb structure, only marginally effective, but in many cases (voice, negation) the effect depends on the communicative setting in which the sentence is used.

(iii) Lexical ambiguity almost always increases the processing load of a sentence. However, in all but garden-path and similar cases, working memory seems not to be involved in this.

(iv) It is still undetermined which perceptual mechanisms cause clause-like entities to function as processing units.

(v) The controversy about the usefulness of verification studies for a theory of sentence understanding signals a clash of aims in the psycholinguistic literature.

4. THEORETICAL CONSIDERATIONS

In section 1 it was pointed out that there is little disagreement about the central importance of a theory of sentence understanding. There is also little controversy about the general aim of a theory of sentence comprehension, which should be able to explain the processes involved in understanding sentences used in ordinary contexts. But from this point on every single step is controversial. There is a double tension to be noted in the literature. Firstly, there is a disagreement concerning the definition of understanding. Fodor *et al.* (80), Tanenhaus *et al.* (244), and others reserve the term for what I will call *immediate linguistic awareness* (ILA): the almost instantaneous awareness of the underlying propositional structure of the sentence. Others (Schank, 226, Bransford, 30, 34) use the term to denote the process mediating between syntactic input and the completion of a linguistic or non-linguistic task (memory task, paraphrase task, verification task, etc.). This difference is not a matter of the mere restriction of empirical domain. That would be the case if the latter type of processes would necessarily contain the former type as proper subpart. This is, rather, an empirical issue. The question is whether in all sentence comprehension there is an initial stage during which the underlying linguistic structure of the sentence is derived. We will call this the *immediate linguistic awareness* (ILA) *hypothesis*. Closely connected to this issue is the question of whether this initial stage, if appearing at all, corresponds to the existence of a separate memory mechanism, a short-term store, or whether one has to assume a continuum of depth of processing. This is the subject of section 4.1.

The second tension concerns the measure in which the theory should be formalized and the type of formalization to be chosen. There is the full range, from completely unformalized theories such as the one proposed by Bransford and his associates (e.g. 31, 34) to completely formalized ones such as Wanner's ATN models (259, 260, 261). Usually the formalized theories either concern a very limited aspect of comprehension or, if more generally applicable, are still very limited in the range of phenomena for which they have been worked out and empirically tested. They are discussed in section 4.3. That section is preceded by some remarks on the role of context in comprehension (section 4.2).

4.1. Immediate understanding and depth of processing

4.1.1 Immediate awareness and task dependency

All experimental studies on sentence perception involve some explicitly stated or implicit task for the subject. This is not entirely artificial: in ordinary language perception also the hearer listens for something. Dependent on the situation, this can be almost anything: whether the voice is male or female, whether there is an implicit request, whether the sentence answers an earlier question, etc. If there is any truth to the claim that laboratory studies of sentence perception are *ipso facto* unnatural and thus meaningless, it cannot be ascertained simply because of the fact that specific tasks are set in the laboratory. Subjects participating in laboratory experiments never tell us that this is not the real world. The only argument for the claim could be that the task dependency of linguistic processing is not sufficiently studied in itself and that too general conclusions are drawn from too limited task environments. Various studies have show that sentence processing is critically dependent on the task requirements (4, 41, 95, 96, 110, 197, 199, 252), and one could conjecture that sentence understanding is idiosyncratic to the task and that generalizations from laboratory studies are not allowed. Although some authors come close to this position, there is a very general tendency in the literature to gravitate towards another solution. We called this the 'immediate liguistic awareness (ILA) hypothesis', and a general formulation of it could be as follows: *The initial part of any sentence comprehension consists of deriving a complete underlying representation of the sentence.* The ILA hypothesis involves two strong empirical claims. First, the initial stage is identical for any comprehension task, and thus task-independent. Second, the output of the initial stage is a complete underlying representation. Since the derived representation should be general purpose (i.e. suitable for any task), it should be an almost complete linguistic analysis of the sentence, containing all semantically relevant information. Authors who adhere to the ILA hypothesis differ substantially in the characterization of this initial internal representation, as will appear from the following enumeration:

The immediate perception hypothesis has its roots in what in the 1960s was called the *coding hypothesis*: a sentence was supposed to be coded in memory in the form of its deep structure (see Johnson-Laird, 143; Levelt, 168; and Fodor *et al.*, 80 for detailed statements and analyses of the coding hypothesis). The hypothesis was proved to be false (see especially Bransford *et al.*, 30, and Fodor *et al.*, 80), but the idea that the underlying structure of the sentence becomes available at some time during sentence processing is still rather generally endorsed. Clark (51) stresses the importance of 'the base strings': 'they constitute the essential part of the interpretation of the sentence and should therefore play an important part whenever the interpretation is needed at a later time'. Clark (54) proposes a 'deep-structure hypothesis' to characterize the internal representation of the sentence. Even if the subject's task is such that he should ignore the literal interpretation of the sentence—as is the case in coping with conveyed requests—Clark and Lucy (60) have shown that this literal interpretation is nevertheless derived first, thus testifying to the empirical validity of the task-independency of the immediate linguistic awareness. A similar claim is made by Cutler (68).

Garrod and Trabasso (105) also express the deep-structure hypothesis: 'the prior sentence is held long enough for a deep-structure representation to be derived and stored in long-term memory'. They add the claim that surface information may be stored in LTM as well, which is further supported by a study by Anderson (5). Fodor *et al.* (80) argue extensively that the internal representation of a perceived sentence coincides with the linguistic structural description. If empirical data show that the structural description proposed by transformational theory is not available to the subject, Fodor *et al.* (81) would prefer that the linguists change their theory rather than have the psychologists forfeit this principle of identifying internal representation and linguistic description. It should be noted, however, that Fodor (78) argues for a much shallower immediate processing: 'The representation of a sentence that must be recovered in understanding it is relatively *un*abstractly related to the surface form of the sentence' (p. 154). Another example of the ILA hypothesis can be found in Tanenhaus *et al.* (244). As discussed in section 3.5, these authors severely criticized Carpenter and Just's (45) processing models derived from sentence/picture verification studies mainly because the sentence encodings (i.e. internal representations) which are proposed are different for every study, rather arbitrary in nature, and extremely task-dependent. In section 3.5 we mentioned that the theoretically important part of the criticism is that a model of sentence understanding should adhere to the ILA-hypothesis. The authors propose a two-stage model: 'First, they (the subjects) understand the sentence, developing a representation for it. Then they extract a *verification representation* from the comprehension representation. The form of the verification representation depends on the particular verification task'. The first stage is what we called 'immediate linguistic awareness', and it is task-independent. The exact nature of the comprehension representation, however, remains unspecified in this paper; it is even left open whether it can be linguistically defined. Forster and Olbrei (85) take the risk of making themselves extremely vulnerable at this point: 'when syntactic analysis is required by the task conditions, it is executed without regard for the meaning of the sentence. This conclusion tends to suggest that there must be a psychologically real level of description which is purely syntactic, and quite independent of the semantic representation'. The statement does not imply the two-stage model, but Forster and Olbrei's experiments (see also Gamlin, 99) would make a strong case for Tanenhaus *et al.*'s comprehension representation to be syntactic. Miller (193), inspired by the work of Davies and Isard (70), proposes a stage of immediate awareness, by disconnecting 'the understanding of a sentence from any actions it might entail'. One can refuse to *obey* a command, but not to *understand* a command. In computer terms the first stage ('understanding') consists of compiling the program, with natural language functioning as a higher-level programming language. The output, then, is a set of lower-level sub-routines which may or may not be executed, dependent on the task-environment. If this output is linquistically characterized by means of grammatical rules, then these rules are abstractions from the computer (resp. language understander); they are not components of it.

Thus, although all these authors assume the existence of a task-independent initial phase, the character of the initial internal representation differs widely: a syntactic deep structure (semantically uninterpreted), a propositional hierarchy, a much shallower surface-related representation, and a set of (semantic, conceptual?) subroutines have all been used as representations.

The different variants of the ILA hypothesis are empirically interesting only if they are explicit about the structure of this internal representation. The existence of a task-independent representation can only be demonstrated if one is fairly precise about the nature of that representation. I am not familiar with any empirical evidence (either in favour or against) which is of this strong nature. The advantage of these theories is, however, that they are stronger than alternative theories in which understanding is completely task-dependent. Stronger theories are more stimulating, even if they are quite probably false.

Another major obligation of these theories is to describe the processes by which this initial internal representation is derived. In this respect the situation is plainly poor. Clark (54) does not propose a parser for this deep-structure hypothesis; he is clearly more interested in later task-dependent aspects of comprehension. Fodor *et al.* (80) propose and empirically test some so-called strategies. One of them is the *canonical sentoid strategy*: whenever the hearer encounters the surface sequence NP-V(-NP), he or she assumes that these items are, respectively, subject, verb and object of a deep sentoid. Although there is empirical evidence for the correctness of some of these strategies, or parsing principles (see also Kimball, 156), there is a major lack of clarity about how these strategies interconnect, whether they are hierarchically organized, what happens if two strategies lead to opposite results, at which point in the sentence a strategy is called for—in short what sort of control structure is involved in sentence perception.

One way to explore these questions more systematically is to cast strategies in the form of augmented transition-network (ATN) models; we will return to this in section 4.3.2.

As far as derivational processes have been proposed, one is left with the impression that the hearer accumulates surface information during presentation of the clause, and that by the very end of the clause there is a flurry of internal processing, leading more or less immediately to determination of the underlying structure. As we have seen in section 2, such theories are mostly based on successive measurement, which supplies little information about the precise structure of the knowledge which is accumulated during the input of the sentence.

There are, moreover, theoretical and empirical arguments against this view of processing. If one looks into Riesbeck's (212) parser, which is intended to be psychologically realistic, it is clear that processing at *all* levels (phonological, syntactic, semantic, conceptual) takes place right from the beginning. Parsing is not hierarchical in the sense that syntactic operations precede semantic and conceptual operations; it is heterarchical: a process at one level is able to call a process at any other level without a hierarchical transfer of control (see Haggard, 116; Winograd, 268).

One of the most challenging of empirical issues is to demonstrate the psychological reality of such distributed control. Apart from the ATN-work (see section 4.2), the shadowing experiments by Marslen-Wilson (184, 185, 186, 187) should be mentioned here. Phonological, syntactic and semantic effects on shadowing performance could be demonstrated to be taking place already at the very beginning of the sentence, even if shadowing delay were not more than one syllable. A similar simultaneous availability of phonological and semantic information could be shown by measuring monitoring latencies: reaction times for rhyme-monitoring were the same as RTs for (semantic) category-monitoring. Also, Mistler-Lachman's experimental results (see section 4.1.2) suggest that a full syntactic analysis, if performed at all, may follow semantic analysis. If sentence processing is of this heterarchical nature, there is reason to doubt an immediate derivation of deep structure (as in Clark, 54; Garrod and Trabasso, 105; Fodor *et al.* 80, Tanenhaus *et al.*, 244). If conceptual parsing is taking place from the first word on, it seems to be rather awkward, as Marslen-Wilson (186) remarks, 'that the initial target of the processing system is a deep-structure representation of the input'. This doubt is also expressed by Bransford and McCarrell (34): 'It seems reasonable to assume that the surface structurally similar sentences *The house squeaked* and *The window squeaked* are understood differently *not* because one first discovers a deep structure and then interprets the meaning of the lexical items, but because one's knowledge of the entities and events in the sentence forces different semantic interpretations to be made'. Other statements of this so-called constructive view of sentence comprehension can be found in 14, 30, 94, and 136. However, there is certainly not enough empirical evidence now to reject all versions of the ILA hypothesis, especially those which are more semantic in nature. Much more precise experimentation is necessary to refute the existence of a task-independent first processing stage and of a general-purpose internal representation.

4.1.2 Stores versus levels of processing

An attractive though not essential processing model for variants of the ILA hypothesis is a multi-store model, consisting of at least a short-term and a long-term store (STS, LTS). The STS would contain a verbatim representation of the sentence or clause, which is maintained until the parsing operations involved in deriving a deep structure have taken place. The resulting deep representation is put into LTS, to be available for further processing. This is essentially the model proposed by Jarvella (141) and Fodor *et al.* (80). Garrod and Trabasso (105) and Anderson (5) have argued that surface information may as well be sent to LTS; they maintain, however, that STS will not contain deep information. Since decay of the memory trace is quicker in STS than in LTS, variants of this successive-stores model can explain the longer persistence of propositional over verbatim information.

An alternative view has been expressed by Craik and Lockhart (66). These authors reject the multi-store model but try to explain the longer persistence of semantic information from the deeper level of processing necessary for deriving this information. The store model is initially replaced by a stage model. If extracting meaning presupposes the recognition of words, an early stage of processing would involve word recognition, whereas meaning extraction would take place at a later stage. These stages cannot be identified by pointing to successive stores with their own preferred internal code and their own decay time. The character of these stages is only stimulus- and task-dependent. Later in the same paper the authors qualify the stage terminology; they do not mean that logically prior analyses necessarily take place at earlier stages, and they refer to Savin and Bever (222) who showed that the syllable is usually more quickly recognized than is its initial phoneme. 'Spread' of encoding would be a better term than 'depth' of encoding, and the stages in fact form a continuum of increasing spread. This notion of spread of encoding agrees with the earlier mentioned idea of heterarchy: there is no hierarchical ordering of processing, neither in terms of stores, nor in terms of logical order.

Experimentally, depth of processing has been manipulated in two ways: by task and by stimulus. Most studies manipulate by task. The best examples are found in the studies by Mistler-Lachman (197, 198, 199). In 197 she presented sentences to subjects with or without ambiguity. Two of her tasks were: judgment of meaningfulness and constructing a good continuation of the sentence. She measured reaction times in the two situations. Presumably judgment of meaningfulness does not require ambiguity resolution: processing can be relatively shallow. Deeper processing is required for the other task, and presumably ambiguity should be resolved. RTs on sentence continuation indeed turned out to be longer for ambiguous sentences, whereas ambiguity did not affect the time required for making a meaningfulness judgment. In 198 Mistler-Lachman showed that the thus demonstrated shallower processing in meaningfulness judgments leads to a quicker decay of the memory trace, as predicted by Craik and Lockhart. Gamlin (99) also used tasks as a variable: question-answering probe latency with similar results.

One can also affect the level of processing by manipulation of the stimulus material. Marslen-Wilson and Tyler (188) repeated Jarvella's experiments (see section 2.2.2) but varied the quality of the text: it could either be normal text, so-called 'syntactic prose', text which is semantically uninterpretable but syntactically correct, and random word-order text. The Jarvella-effect, i.e. less accurate recall of the penultimate clause, was substantially more marked for syntactic prose than for normal prose. Syntactic prose prevents deep (semantic) processing, and since recall is a function of depth (Craik and Lockhart), the theory correctly predicts this substantial forgetting of syntactic prose. It is not obvious how a two-store model would make the same prediction. Although task-dependency is naturally handled in the depth of processing model, the existence of an initial task-independent phase in sentence comprehension is not contradictory to this view: the dependability of multi-store models remains an empirical issue. For a critical discussion of the sort of information that might discriminate between single-and multi-store models, see Wickelgren (264).

4.2. Comprehension in context

Language understanding is largely a matter of finding out the speaker's intentions. This review was originally to have included a section on the various means and processes by which the listener can determine intentions on the basis of literal meaning of what is said plus the context in which it is said. I would have discussed empirical work on given and new information, conversational postulates, anaphoric and definite reference, and major attention would have given to the work of Clark and coworkers. In view of Clark's own very full treatment of these issues in this book, my own review would be superfluous; it is therefore omitted. It is only for referential completeness that the bibliography contains numbers 14, 28, 31, 32, 33, 59, 60, 73, 94, 126, 135, 137, and 151, which are relevant to the issues under concern.

4.3. Formal theories of sentence understanding

4.3.1 Transformational models

Transformational models of sentence perception emerged during the sixties as a psychological answer to the newly developed transformational linguistics. Extensive reviews of these models and their empirical tenability can be found in the literature; the reader is especially referred to Levelt (170), and to Fodor *et al.* (80). Both reviews show that initially transformational grammar was adopted as an isomorphistic model; this isomorphism had two related but separable characteristics: the first is the *derivational theory of complexity* (DTC), the second is the so-called *coding hypothesis*. DTC means that the processing of a sentence simulates the transformational derivation of the sentence on a micro-scale: each rule in the grammar has a one-to-one relationship with a particular psychological operation. This can still be done in very different ways, such as inversing transformations (Petrick, 208) or analysis-by-synthesis (Halle and Stevens 122).

If rule-for-rule isomorphism exists, one would also expect input-output isomorphism, i.e. at some early stage in comprehension the hearer is supposed to have available a surface-structure-like representation of the sentence, whereas after applying the transformation-related rules, this has been replaced by a deep-structure-like representation. This latter view is called the coding hypothesis (for different senses of the coding hypothesis, see Levelt, 170). Of course the latter can be valid, without DTC being valid, and that is the position taken by Fodor *et al.* (80). Carroll and Bever (47) put it this way: '(1) There is a variety of evidence for the psychological reality of linguistically defined surface and deep-structure representations of sentences. (2) There is no consistent evidence for the perceptual reality of transformations as perceptual processes'. This conclusion is not drawn in Levelt's (170) review, where both DTC and deep-structure output theories are characterized as empirically untenable. The point is sharply made by Wanner (258) in his review of the Fodor *et al.* book: 'Why should we believe that deep-structure phrase markers are determined during compre-hension, when the characteristics of deep structure are partially selected just in order to simplify the operation of the transformational rules, which themselves lack psychological reality? So far as I can see, there is no compelling reason to adhere to such a belief. One can search in vain through the deep-structure experiments which FBG review without finding any which test the psychological reality of the transformationally motivated aspect of deep structure.'

Miller and Johnson-Laird (194) make a similar point by stating that 'Fodor, Bever, and Garrett assume, however, that the decoding processes compute the same structural description that a grammar does (p. 369), as if parsing were an end in itself, rather than an abstraction from (or trace of) the computations required to translate a sentence into an executable routine'. We will return to this point at the end of the next section.

4.3.2 Perceptual strategies and Augmented Transition Networks

Given the theoretical framework of Fodor *et al.*, the important psychological problem is to define and test psychological operations which can derive underlying structures from surface forms. These operations need not be linguistically justifiable (see 20), and they are not necessarily foolproof. One example is the canonical sentoid strategy, mentioned above in section 4.4.1. There is no doubt that this approach has partly freed psycholinguists from their linguistic captivity: one could resume the search for interesting perceptual operating principles without being hampered by existing linguistic rule systems. This openness has led to a variety of highly interesting empirical observations, for which the reader is referred to the Fodor *et al.* book.

At the same time, however, this approach has created a theoretical vacuum. As already noted in section 4.1.1, he control structure of the strategies approach remains unspecified; there is no theoretical basis for distinguishing possible from impossible strategies or for limiting the number of strategies to an 'optimal', or canonical set. This vacuum is not easily filled so long as the aim of parsing is defined in deep-structural terms: formal objects which have no relevance for understanding will have to be created by the parsing process, whereas linguistic constraints are ignored in defining the perceptual operations. Augmented Transition Networks (ATNs) may provide the formal means of leaving the vicious circle. Some important arguments are:

(i) Transformational grammars can always be translated in the ATN-formalism, since ATNs have Turing machine power. By doing so, properties of TG-generated structures which are only there for the sake of TG-*formalism* can disappear in an ATN representation. There is no further need to generate them by the parsing process.

(ii) The ATN is a *linguistic* theory; but as I have written elsewhere (170), 'It is no longer the psychological theory which is adapted to the grammar, but rather the grammar which is written for the representation of psychological processing operations. If such a network at the same time provides all input sentences with their correct grammatical parsing, this new isomorphism is of a more acceptable kind than the naive isomorphism discussed (above)'. Therefore, the ATN does behave properly according to linguistic constraints.

(iii) The output of an ATN need not be a deep structure (even stripped from its incidental formal characteristics). Underlying grammatical relations will be operative at various stages of the parsing process, without necessarily being represented in the end-product of the parsing process.

(iv) ATN networks allow for semantic and pragmatic conditions on transitions and for building operations which create semantic and pragmatic output (see especially Miller and Johnson-Laird, 194).

Though syntactic and non-syntactic aspects of ATNs are clearly separable, ATNs give a natural means for expressing distributed syntactic—semantic control. Specific operating characteristics of ATNs which make them especially 'human' (such as left-to-right processing) have been enumerated by Wanner and Maratsos (260).

Rather then enumerate these advantages, we shall present an example of an ATN network, taken from Wanner *et al.* (259), and designed as a demonstration example.

In the ATN of Figure 1.1 circles denote states, and arrows transitions. The initial state is S_0 (S for 'sentence') and the upper network is the sentence network. A set of conditions and a set of actions is assigned to each transition. Conditions are given over the arrows in Figure 1.1, actions are listed separately. If the ATN is in a given state, a transition from there to a next state can be made if the particular condition is fulfilled. For instance, the transition from S_0 to S_1 requires that an NP has been detected (i.e. one has to 'seek' an NP in order to make a transition). To go from S_1 to S_2 requires the input of an item (word) of category V, i.e. a verb, and so on. In the case of SEEK conditions, control has to be shifted to the appropriate network. In order to satisfy the SEEK NP condition from S_0 to S_1, the state S_0 is pushed down and control shifts to the NP network, specifically to NP_0. If this network is successfully passed, i.e. reaches the NP_4-end state, control is popped to S_0 and the transition to S_1 can be made. An ATN may consist of several networks, between which control can shift back and forth. If there is more than one possible transition from a given state, as in NP_1, it is customary to arrange them clockwise in such a way that the first arc after 12 is tried first, and so forth. The final state is reached when (a) the ATN is in the end state of the sentence network, and (b) there are no states left in the push-down store.

Actions can be of several kinds. If one wants to use an ATN as a syntactic parser which gives phrase structures as output, actions have to assign category symbols (such as NP) and/or grammatical functions (such as subject), and to assemble types of structures. In other words, a phrase (e.g. an NP), when built and categorized, is stored in a functional register (a subject-register, an object-

sentence network:

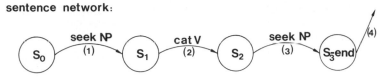

noun phrase network:

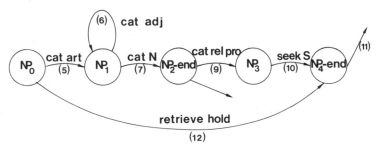

Arc	Action
1	ASSIGN SUBJECT to current phrase
2	ASSIGN ACTION to current word
3	ASSIGN OBJECT to current phrase
4	ASSEMBLE CLAUSE
	SEND current clause
5	ASSIGN DET to current word
6	ASSIGN MOD to current word
7	ASSIGN HEAD to current word
8	ASSEMBLE NOUN PHRASE
	SEND current phrase
9	HOLD
10	CHECK HOLD
	ASSIGN MOD to current clause
11	ASSEMBLE NOUN PHRASE
	SEND current phrase
12	(no action)

Figure 1.1. A simple ATN grammar for sentences with relative clauses (from Wanner, Kaplan, and Shiner)

register, etc.). But actions can equally well be of certain semantic types. Miller and Johnson-Laird (194) call such actions *executions*. These may be very task-specific activities which the listener chooses to perform. One example is that at a certain transition the referent of the particular word or phrase, specified in the condition, is looked up in long-term memory. (Such examples are not given in Figure 1.1.)

Wanner *et al.* (259) demonstrate the working of the example ATN by parsing the sentence 'The old man that the boy loved caught the fish'. Roughly, the parsing proceeds as follows. From S_0, control shifts to NP_0 in order to find an NP. 'The old man' leads via transitions 5, 6, and 7 to state NP_2-end. In order to make transition 9, one needs a relative pronoun, which is in fact present ('that'). The action taken here is important. The categorized information (i.e. DET, MÒD, HEAD; see actions 5, 6, 7) are put in a special register, the so-called HOLD register; that is, no grammatical function (subject, object) is assigned. This is postponed to a later stage. There is a good reason for doing this, since the grammatical function of the first NP in a relative-clause sentence depends on later information. In order to make the last transition within the NP network, control has to be transferred to the sentence network (i.e. at the moment S_0 and NP_3 are on the push-down store). For the first transition control has to go again to the NP network, which parses 'the boy' as an NP. From S_1, the verb 'loved' leads to S_2, after which the NP network takes over again. Since transition 5 cannot be made, transition 12 can be made by retrieving the information from the HOLD register (The$_{DET}$ old$_{MOD}$ man$_{HEAD}$). Transition 11 leads to assembling this as an NP; and at popping back to S_2, this NP is assigned to OBJECT-function. In this way, the ATN takes care that 'the old man' becomes the object of 'loved'. The further steps are obvious: After assembling the relative clause (4), control returns to S_0, transition 1 can be made, and the verb 'caught', followed by the NP 'the fish', leads to S_3-end, plus an empty push-down store.

Returning now to the ATN-literature, it should be remarked that the notion stems from Thorne *et al.*'s (245) parsing system for English, and was further developed by Bobrow and Fraser (29) and Woods (270). It found its first psychological application in Kaplan (152), who showed how some of Bever's 'perceptual strategies' could be cast in the ATN formalism. Further psychological applications were made by Kaplan (153), Stevens and Rumelhart (239) on a reading task, by Wanner *et al.* on relative clause comprehension (259, 260), and by Wanner and Shiner on structural ambiguities (262). Wanner and Maratsos (260) give evidence for the memory-loading effect of using the HOLD register (see above). The elegant theoretical analysis deserves further empirical verification by means of acoustical simultaneous measurement techniques.

But the theoretical concepts also need further psychological interpretation. It is normal for an ATN to have various stores and registers: a push-down store for keeping track of control shifts, registers for assigning functions to built subtrees, and a HOLD register for keeping uninterpreted structures. How do these stores relate to working memory, short- and long-term storage, levels of processing, and similar concepts described in the memory literature? In this connection, Anderson's (6) critique of the ATN approach should be especially mentioned. Anderson clearly recognizes the various attractions of ATNs but doubts whether they will ever become psychological models. Because of their Turing machine power, they have no intrinsic limitation. Human cognitive limitations, therefore, should be explicitly imposed on the models. The question is whether there are natural ways to do so, or whether one is forced into an arbitrary set of limiting assumptions. Anderson shows, for instance, that HOLD cannot be the only reason for the increased processing load of centre-embedded sentences. The recursive shifts of control (SEEK operations) should be a cause as well, but then right-branching structures should also be difficult, since they involve the same SEEK operations. Moreover, there is no natural limitation on the size of a network, nor therefore on the size of the structure to be assembled after reaching the end-state. Would a large assembled structure use up so much memory capacity that it would interfere with the assembling of further structures? In addition, ATNs are of little help for syntactically scrambled or incomplete sentences which may still be interpretable. And in actuality, human listeners often skilfully interpret such utterances. Clearly, therefore, ATNs cannot be the answer to all problems; and in fact Anderson replaces it by his so-called ACT model, which retains some of the ATNs advantages but is less powerful and claimed to be psychologically more realistic.

What is important is to recognize that we have a class of models here which is at the 'right' level of theorizing. They are more local and experimentally more testable than are AI-models of language understanding (see the following section), but at the same time they are more structured than mere lists of perceptual strategies.

If we now reconsider the 'ILA hypothesis' (section 4.1.1), we see that ATN models may be able to give a refined version of it. Miller and Johnson-Laird (194) use ATNs to 'translate' the sentence into routines, as in a compiler. These (semantic) routines may or may not be executed, depending on the task and the motivation of the hearer; but the compiling process itself is automatic, and in general outside voluntary control. 'Immediate awareness' here means compiling, it is not task-specific, and it is the first phase of understanding. However, it is the first phase only in a logical sense; this does not mean that one has to wait until the end of the clause or sentence in order to execute the routines. Routines appear at successive stages of the ATN parsing process, and execution can be done as soon as the routine appears. Thus, syntactic and interpretative activity may go on in parallel, in correspondence with Marslen-Wilson's empirical findings (184, 186, 188), whereas at the same time a distinction is maintained between automatic-general and voluntary task-specific operations in language understanding.

One thing, however, is not taken care of so long as one maintains the logical priority of 'translation'. There is some evidence that the results of executing routines can feed back to the translation process. Marslen-Wilson and Tyler's (187) finding that word-, rhyme-, and category-monitoring are slower for syntactic (i.e. meaningless) prose than for normal prose points in this direction. From these and other results Marslen-Wilson concludes that syntactic and semantic analysis proceed in parallel and interactively. In order to describe such an inverse (top-down) flow of information more formally, one has to consider what is called *goal-oriented parsing* in artificial intelligence.

4.3.3 *The artificial intelligence approach*

Riesbeck and Schank's contribution to the present volume contains a thorough statement of the principles and structure of goal-oriented, natural language parsing. This makes it somewhat superfluous to review these issues here. We will limit ourselves to a few general remarks. The parallel-interactive features of sentence comprehension are a natural consequence of AI-parsing principles, at least those of Schank (224, 225, 226) and Wilks (265): 'The common linguistic model with a syntactic analysis phase followed by a semantic interpretation is a good example of what we are against. The modules in the understanding process affect each other in both directions' (Riesbeck and Schank, this volume). If the ultimate goal of parsing is to extract meaning, i.e. to derive a conceptual representation, semantic considerations should have priority over syntactic ones. The latter become important if the interpretation is highly unexpected. 'I think that syntax exists so that we can say improbable things' (Garrett, 103). Parsing in these systems goes from left to right, without much backing up. It is essentially expectation-based, where expectation is due to knowledge of the world as well as to prior (con)text. It is encouraging that such systems can be built.

One should keep in mind, however, that even the most promising systems still have serious limitations. Like ATNs, they all have Turing machine power, and the question which has to be answered is what sort of restrictive principles have to be imposed in order to make these programs human-like. Also, in spite of their power, all present systems show time characteristics which make them unrealistically slow if their knowledge of the world, or data base, is expanded to a more realistic size. Efforts to partition the data base into 'frames' (195) or 'scripts' (2) are very much in a beginning phase, whereas the whole notion is badly undefined. Levelt (171) discusses how existing systems are unable to account for language acquisition. Anderson (6) makes a similar point and enumerates several other weaknesses of computer language systems. Nevertheless, there can be no doubt that AI (and AI-related research) has become increasingly influential in the study of language understanding. Some major sources in this literature are by Winograd (268, 269), Anderson and Bower (7), Anderson (6), Norman and Rumelhart (203), Schank (226), and Miller and Johnson-Laird (194). The recent convergence of insights from AI and experimental psycholinguistics gives one the hope that essential AI principles (as opposed to accidental properties of parsing programs—and authors are often not very clear about this distinction) will lend themselves to empirical tests in the near future.

4.4. Conclusions

Section 1 cited three broad types of aim in the study of sentence perception: linguistic, conceptual, and communicative. During the first few years of the reviewed period, the linguistic aim was the dominant one. Two causes may have contributed to this state of affairs. Firstly, there was still an echo sounding from the linguistic revolution of the nineteen-sixties. Secondly, the range of research methods developed during the nineteen-sixties belonged mostly to the class of successive measurement. These methods are particularly inapt for disproving the stage-like character of the models which had been developed within the linguistic framework. More specifically, it is hard to reject the notion that syntactic analysis of the clause precedes semantic analysis, that semantic analysis precedes the search for referents in long-term memory, and so on. Therefore, one could always maintain that in comprehending a sentence a listener first takes a general-purpose linguistic (and probably syntactic) step, and only then resorts to specific inferential activities which are tailored to the conceptual and communicative requirements of the particular task. This, moreover, would make the different types of aim compatible, and in fact complementary.

Two other causes, however, have badly undermined this picture during the second half of the reviewed period. Firstly, the development of simultaneous-measurement techniques has made it possible to demonstrate the highly inter-active nature of sentence-understanding processes: semantic decisions which can take place quite early in the sentence can affect syntactic and phonetic decisions, and it is not quite clear any more what occurs prior to what. Secondly, developments in artificial intelligence and related fields became increasingly influential in psycholinguistic theory construction. Goal-oriented parsing is most effectively realized in a heterarchical system where control is distributed.

It would be wrong, however, to replace one pet theory by another. Not undermined, for instance, is the notion that syntax plays an important role in sentence understanding. It will take much and thorough experimentation to determine how syntactic operations interact with semantic and conceptual decisions as the listener infers the intentions of the speaker. This type of research might profit from theories which are more local than full-size computer models of language understanding but more inclusive and more structured than a mere list of understanding strategies. Augmented transition networks form one example of such a level of theorizing, but other types of models should not be excluded.

ACKNOWLEDGEMENTS

The author is very grateful to Trudy Las, who assisted in searching the library, and in categorizing and summarizing materials. Gerard Kempen and William Marslen-Wilson were helpful in giving comments on earlier drafts of this paper. The author's gratitude also goes to the Institute for Perception Research, Eindhoven, where he wrote, as a guest, a major part of this chapter.

5. REFERENCES

1. Aaronson, D. Stimulus factors and listening strategies in auditory memory: An experimental demonstration. *Cognitive Psychology*, 1974, **6**, 133–158.
2. Abelson, R. P. The structure of belief systems. In R. C. Schank and K. M. Colby (Eds.), *Computer models of thought and language*. San Francisco: Freeman, 1973.
3. Abrams, K. and Bever, T. G. Syntactic structure modifies attention during speech perception and recognition. *Quarterly Journal of Experimental Psychology*, 1969, **21**, 280–290.
4. Amnon, P. R., Ostrowski, B., and Alward, K. Effects of task on the perceptual organization of sentences. *Perception and Psychophysics*, 1971, **10**, 361–363.
5. Anderson, J. R., Verbatim and propositional representation of sentences in immediate and long-term memory. *Journal of Verbal Learning and Verbal Behavior*, 1974, **13**, 149–162.
6. Anderson, J. R. *Language, memory and thought*. Hillsdale, N. J.: Lawrence Erlbaum Associates, 1976.
7. Anderson, J. R. and Bower, G. H. *Human associative memory*. Washington, D.C.: Winston, 1973.
8. Anisfeld, M. and Klenbort, I. On the functions of structural paraphrase: the view from the passive voice. *Psychological Bulletin*, 1973, **79**, 117–126.
9. Baddeley, A. D. *The psychology of memory*. New York: Harper & Row, 1976.
10. Baddeley, A. D. and Hitch, G. Working memory. In G. H. Bower (Ed.), *The psychology of learning and motivation*. New York: Academic Press, 1974.
11. Baird, R. and Koslick, J. D. Recall of grammatical relations within clause-containing sentences. *Journal of Psycholinguistic Research*, 1974, **3**, 165–171.
12. Baker, C. L. Double negatives. *Linguistic Inquiry*, 1970, **1**, 169–186.
13. Banks, W. P., Clark, H. H., and Lucy, P. The locus of the semantic congruity effect in comparative judgments. *Journal of Experimental Psychology: Human Perception and Performance*, 1975, **104**, 35–47.
14. Barclay, J. R. The role of context in remembering sentences. *Cognitive Psychology*, 1973, **4**, 229–254.
15. Bertelson, P. Listening from left to right versus right to left. *Perception*, 1972, **1**, 161–165.
16. Bertelson, P. and Tisseyre, F. Perceiving the sequence of speech and non-speech stimuli. *Quarterly Journal of Experimental Psychology*, 1970, **22**, 653–662.
17. Bertelson, P. and Tisseyre, F. Lateral asymmetry in the perceived sequence of speech and non-speech stimuli. *Perception and Psychophysics*, 1972, **11**, 356–362.
18. Bertelson, P. and Tisseyre, F. Lateral asymmetry in judgments of click location: Not an artifact of reporting mode. *Perceptual and Motor Skills*, 1973, **36**, 849–850.
19. Bever, T. G. The comprehension and memory of sentences with temporal relations. In G. B. Flores d'Arcais and W. J. M. Levelt (Eds.), *Advances in psycholinguistics*. Amsterdam: North-Holland, 1970.
20. Bever, T. G. The cognitive basis for linguistic structures. In J. R. Hayes (Ed.), *Cognition and the development of language*. New York: Wiley, 1970.
21. Bever, T. G. Serial position and response biases do not account for the effect of syntactic structure on the location of brief noises during sentences. *Journal of Psycholinguistic Research*, 1973, **2**, 287–288.
22. Bever, T. G., Garrett, M. F., and Hurtig, R. The interaction of perceptual processes and ambiguous sentences. *Memory and Cognition*, 1973, **1**, 277–286.
23. Bever, T. G., Hurtig, R. R., and Handel, A. B. Response biases do not account for the effect of clause structure on the perception of non-linguistic stimuli. *Research Bulletin Educational Testing Service*, RB–75–30, 1975.

24. Bever, T. G. and Hurtig, R. R. Detection of a non linguistic stimulus is poorest at the end of a clause. *Journal of Psycholinguistic Research*, 1975, **4**, 1–7.
25. Bever, T. G., Lackner, J. R., and Kirk, R. The underlying structures of sentences are the primary units of immediate speech processing. *Perception and Psychophysics*, 1969, **5**, 225–234.
26. Bever, T. G., Lackner, J. R., and Stolz, W. Transitional probability is not a general mechanism for the segmentation of speech. *Journal of Experimental Psychology*, 1969, **79**, 387–394.
27. Blaubergs, M. S. and Braine, M. D. S. Short-term memory limitations on decoding self-embedded sentences. *Journal of Experimental Psychology*, 1974, **102**, 745–748.
28. Bobrow, S. A. and Bell, S. M. On catching on to idiomatic expressions. *Memory and Cognition*, 1973, **1**, 343–346.
29. Bobrow, D. and Fraser, B. An augmented state transition network analysis procedure. In D. Walker and L. Norton (Eds.), *Proceedings of the International Joint Conference on Artificial Intelligence*. Washington D.C., 1969.
30. Bransford, J. D., Barclay, J. R., and Franks, J. J. Sentence memory: A constructive versus interpretive approach. *Cognitive Psychology*, 1972, **3**, 193–209.
31. Bransford, J. D. and Franks, J. J. The abstraction of linguistic ideas. *Cognitive Psychology*, 1971, **2**, 331–350.
32. Bransford, J. D. and Johnson, M. K. Contextual prerequisites for understanding: Some investigations of comprehension and recall. *Journal of Verbal Learning and Verbal Behavior*, 1972, **11**, 717–726.
33. Bransford, J. D. and Johnson, M. K. Considerations of some problems of comprehension. In W. G. Chase (Ed.), *Visual information processing*. New York: Academic Press, 1973.
34. Bransford, J. D. and McCarrell, N. S. A sketch of a cognitive approach to comprehension: Some thoughts about understanding what it means to comprehend. In W. B. Weimer and D. S. Palermo (Eds.), *Cognition and the symbolic processes*. Hillsdale, N.J.: Lawrence Erlbaum Associates, 1974.
35. Cairns, H. S. Effects of bias on processing and reprocessing of lexically ambiguous sentences. *Journal of Experimental Psychology*, 1973, **97**, 337–343.
36. Cairns, H. S. and Foss, J. Falsification of the hypothesis that word frequency is a unified variable in sentence processing. *Journal of Verbal Learning and Verbal Behavior*, 1971, **10**, 41–43.
37. Cairns, H. S. and Kamerman, J. Lexical information processing during sentence comprehension. *Journal of Verbal Learning and Verbal Behavior*, 1975, **14**, 170–179.
38. Caplan, D. Clause boundaries and recognition latencies for words in sentences. *Perception and Psychophysics*, 1972, **12**, 73–76.
39. Carey, P. W., Mehler, J., and Bever, T. G. When do we compute all the interpretations of an ambiguous sentence? In G. B. Flores d'Arcais and W. J. M. Levelt (Eds.), *Advances in psycholinguistics*. Amsterdam: North-Holland, 1970.
40. Carey, P. W., Mehler, J., and Bever, T. G. Judging the veracity of ambiguous sentences. *Journal of Verbal Learning and Verbal Behavior*, 1970, **9**, 243–254.
41. Carey, S. T. and Lockhart, R. S. Encoding differences in recognition and recall. *Memory and Cognition*, 1973, **1**, 297–300.
42. Carpenter, P. A. Extracting information from counterfactual clauses. *Journal of Verbal Learning and Verbal Behavior*, 1973, **12**, 512–521.
43. Carpenter, P. A. On the comprehension, storage, and retrieval of comparative sentences. *Journal of Verbal Learning and Verbal Behavior*, 1974, **13**, 401–411.

44. Carpenter, P. A. and Just, M. A. Semantic control of eye movements in picture scanning during sentence-picture verification. *Perception and Psychophysics*, 1972, **12**, 61–64.

45. Carpenter, P. A. and Just, M. A. Sentence comprehension: A psycholinguistic model of sentence verification. *Psychological Review*, 1975, **82**, 45–73.

46. Carpenter, P. A. and Just M. A. Models of sentence verification and linguistic comprehension. *Psychological Review*, 1976, **83**, 318–322.

47. Carroll, J. M. and Bever, T. G. Sentence comprehension: case study in the relation of knowledge and perception. In E. C. Carterette and M. P. Friedman (Eds.), *Handbook of perception. Vol. 7: Language and speech*. New York: Academic Press, 1976.

48. Chapin, P. G., Smith, T. S. and Abrahamson, A. A. Two factors in perceptual segmentation of speech. *Journal of Verbal Learning and Verbal Behavior*, 1972, **11**, 164–173.

49. Chase, W. G. and Clark, H. H. Semantics in the perception of verticality. *British Journal of Psychology*, 1971, **62**, 311–326.

50. Chase, W. G. and Clark, H. H. Mental operations in the comparison of sentences and pictures. In L. W. Gregg (Ed.), *Cognition in learning and memory*. New York: Wiley, 1972.

51. Clark, H. H. Linguistic processes in deductive reasoning. *Psychological Review*, 1969, **76**, 387–404.

52. Clark, H. H. Difficulties people have in answering the question 'Where is it?' *Journal of Verbal Learning and Verbal Behavior*, 1972, **11**, 265–277.

53. Clark, H. H. The language-as-fixed-effect fallacy: A critique of language statistics in psychological research. *Journal of Verbal Learning and Verbal Behavior*, 1973, **12**, 335–359.

54. Clark, H. H. Semantics and comprehension. In T. A. Sebeok (Ed.), *Current trends in linguistics*. Vol. 12: *Linguistics and adjacent arts and sciences*. The Hague: Mouton, 1974.

55. Clark, H. H. and Begun, J. S. The semantics of sentence subjects. *Language and Speech*, 1971, **14**, 34–46.

56. Clark, H. H., Carpenter, A., and Just, M. A. On the meeting of semantics and perception. In W. G. Chase (Ed.), *Visual information processing*. New York: Academic Press, 1973.

57. Clark, H. H. and Chase, W. G. On the process of comparing sentences against pictures. *Cognitive Psychology*, 1972, **3**, 472–517.

58. Clark, H. H. and Chase, W. G. Perceptual coding strategies in the formation and verification of descriptions. *Memory and Cognition*, 1974, **2**, 101–111.

59. Clark, H. H. and Haviland, S. Comprehension and the given-new contract. In R. O. Freedle (Ed.), *Discourse comprehension and production*. Norwood, N.J.: Ablex Publishing, 1977.

60. Clark, H. H. and Lucy, P. Understanding what is meant from what is said: A study in conversationally conveyed requests. *Journal of Verbal Learning and Verbal Behavior*, 1975, **14**, 56–72.

61. Cohen, A. and 't Hart, J. On the anatomy of intonation. *Lingua*, 1967, **19**, 177–192.

62. Collier, R. and 't Hart, J. The role of intonation in speech perception. In A. Cohen and S. G. Nooteboom (Eds.), *Structure and process in speech perception*. Berlin, Heidelberg, New York: Springer Verlag, 1975.

63. Collins, A. M. and Quillian, M. R. Experiments on semantic memory and language comprehension. In L. W. Gregg (Ed.), *Cognition in learning and memory*. New York: Wiley, 1972.

64. Conrad, C. Context effects in sentence comprehension: A study of the subjective lexicon. *Memory and Cognition*, 1974, **2**, 130–138.

65. Cornish, E. R. Pragmatic aspects of negation in sentence evaluation and completion tasks. *British Journal of Psychology*, 1971, **62**, 505–511.
66. Craik, F. I. and Lockhart, R. S. Levels of processing: A framework for memory research. *Journal of Verbal Learning and Verbal Behavior*, 1972, **11**, 671–684.
67. Cutler, A. Phoneme-monitoring reaction time as a function of preceding intonation contour. *Perception and Psychophysics*, 1976, **20**, 55–60.
68. Cutler, A. Beyond parsing and lexical look-up: an enriched description of auditory sentence comprehension. In R. J. Wales and E. Walker (Eds.), *New approaches to language mechanism*. Amsterdam: North-Holland, 1976.
69. Darwin, C. J. On the dynamic use of prosody in speech perception. In A. Cohen and S. G. Nooteboom (Eds.), *Structure and process in speech perception*. Berlin, Heidelberg, New York: Springer Verlag, 1975.
70. Davies, D. and Isard, S. D. Utterances as programs. In D. Michie (Ed.), *Machine Intelligence 7*. Edinburgh: Edinburgh University Press, 1972.
71. Donders, F. C. *Over de snelheid van psychische processen*. Onderzoekingen gedaan in het Psychologisch Laboratium der Utrechtse Hoogeschool, 1868–1869, Tweede reeks, II, 92–120.
72. Dooling, D. J. Rhythm and syntax in sentence perception. *Journal of Verbal Learning and Verbal Behavior*, 1974, **13**, 255–264.
73. Dooling, D. J. and Christiaansen, R. E. Context effects in sentence comprehension: A reply to Doll and Lapinski. *Bulletin of the Psychonomic Society*, 1975, **5**, 261–262.
74. Fillenbaum, S. Inducements: on the phrasing and logic of conditional promises, threats, and warnings. *Psychological Research*, 1976, **38**, 231–250.
75. Flores d'Arcais, G. B. Semantic and perceptual factors in the processing of comparative sentences. *Italian Journal of Psychology*, 1974, **1**, 267–303.
76. Flores d'Arcais, G. B. Some perceptual determinants of sentence construction. In G. B. Flores d'Arcais, (Ed.), *Studies in perception*. Milano: Martello, 1975.
77. Flores d'Arcais, G. B. The perception of complex sentences. This volume.
78. Fodor, J. A. *The language of thought*. Hassocks: Harvester Press, 1976.
79. Fodor, J. A. and Bever, T. G. The psychological reality of linguistic segments. *Journal of Verbal Learning and Verbal Behavior*, 1965, **4**, 414–420.
80. Fodor, J. A., Bever, T. G., and Garrett, M. F. *The psychology of language. An introduction to psycholinguistics and generative grammar*. New York: McGraw-Hill, 1974.
81. Fodor, J. D., Fodor, J. A., and Garrett, M. F. The psychological unreality of semantic representations. *Linguistic Inquiry*, 1975, **6**, 515–531.
82. Fodor, J. A. and Garrett, M. F. Some syntactic determinants of sentential complexity. *Perception and Psychophysics*, 1967, **2**, 289–296.
83. Fodor, J. A., Garrett, M. F., and Bever, T. G. Some syntactic determinants of sentential complexity II: Verb structure. *Perception and Psychophysics*, 1968, **3**, 453–461.
84. Forster, K. I. Visual perception of rapidly presented word sequences of varying complexity. *Perception and Psychophysics*, 1970, **8**, 215–221.
85. Forster, K. I. and Olbrei, I. Semantic heuristics and syntactic analysis. *Cognition*, 1973, **2**, 319–347.
86. Forster, K. I. and Ryder, L. A. Perceiving the structure and meaning of sentences. *Journal of Verbal Learning and Verbal Behavior*, 1971, **10**, 285–296.
87. Foss, D. J. Decision processes during sentence comprehension: Effects of lexical item difficulty and position upon decision times. *Journal of Verbal Learning and Verbal Behavior*, 1969, **8**, 457–462.
88. Foss, D. J. Some effects of ambiguity upon sentence comprehension. *Journal of Verbal Learning and Verbal Behavior*, 1970, **9**, 699–706.

89. Foss, D. J., Bever, T. G., and Silver, M. The comprehension and verification of ambiguous sentences. *Perception and Psychophysics*, 1968, **4**, 304–306.

90. Foss, D. J. and Cairns, H. S. Some effects of memory limitation upon sentence comprehension and recall. *Journal of Verbal Learning and Verbal Behavior*, 1970, **9**, 541–547.

91. Foss, D. J. and Jenkins, C. M. Some effects of context on the comprehension of ambiguous sentences. *Journal of Verbal Learning and Verbal Behavior*, 1973, **12**, 577–589.

92. Foss, D. J. and Lynch, R. H. Decision processes during sentence comprehension: effects of surface structure on decision times. *Perception and Psychophysics*, 1969, **5**, 145–148.

93. Foss, D. J. and Swinney, D. A. On the psychological reality of the phoneme: Perception, identification and consciousness. *Journal of Verbal Learning and Verbal Behavior*, 1973, **12**, 246–257.

94. Franks, J. J. Toward understanding understanding. In W. B. Weimer and D. S. Palermo (Eds.), *Cognition and the symbolic processes*. Hillsdale, N.J.: Lawrence Erlbaum Associates, 1974.

95. Frederikson, C. H. Effects of task-induced cognitive operations on comprehension and memory processes. In R. O. Freedle and J. B. Carroll (Eds.), *Language comprehension and the acquisition of knowledge*. New York: Winston, 1972.

96. Frederikson, C. H. Effects of context-induced processing operations on semantic information acquired from discourse. *Cognitive Psychology*, 1975, **7**, 139–166.

97. Freedle, R. O. and Craun, M. Observations with self-embedded sentences using written aids. *Perception and Psychophysics*, 1970, **7**, 247–249.

98. Friend, K. E. Perceptual encoding in comparative judgments of race. *Memory and Cognition*, 1973, **1**, 80–84.

99. Gamlin, P. J. Level of listening comprehension as a function of two process variables: Syntax and meaningfulness. *Language and Speech*, 1972, **15**, 232–261.

100. Garrett, M. F. Syntactic structures and judgments of auditory events. Unpublished Ph.D. Dissertation, University of Illinois, 1965.

101. Garrett, M. F. Does ambiguity complicate the perception of sentences? In G. B. Flores d'Arcais and W. J. M. Levelt (Eds.), *Advances in psycholinguistics*. Amsterdam: North-Holland, 1970.

102. Garrett, M. F. Experimental issues in sentence comprehension: Complexity and segmentation. In C. Cherry (Ed.), *Pragmatic aspects of human communication*. Dordrecht: Reidel, 1974.

103. Garrett, M. F. Syntactic processes in sentence production. In R. J. Wales and E. Walker (Eds.), *New approaches to language mechanisms*. Amsterdam: North-Holland, 1976.

104. Garrett, M. F., Bever, T. G., and Fodor, J. A. The active use of grammar in speech perception. *Perception and Psychophysics*, 1966, **1**, 30–32.

105. Garrod, S. and Trabasso, T. A dual-memory information processing interpretation of sentence comprehension. *Journal of Verbal Learning and Verbal Behavior*, 1973, **12**, 155–167.

106. Glass, A. L. and Holyoak, K. J. The effect of *some* and *all* on reaction time for semantic decisions. *Memory and Cognition*, 1974, **2**, 436–440.

107. Glass, A. L., Holyoak, K. J., and O'Dell, C. Production frequency and the verification of quantified statements. *Journal of Verbal Learning and Verbal Behavior*, 1974, **13**, 237–254.

108. Glucksberg, S., Trabasso, T., and Wald, J. Linguistic structures and mental operations. *Cognitive Psychology*, 1973, **5**, 338–370.

109. Gough, P. B. Experimental psycholinguistics. In W. O. Dingwall (Ed.), *A survey of linguistic science*. College Park, Md.: Linguistic Program University of Maryland, 1971.

110. Green, D. W. The effects of task on the representation of sentences. *Journal of Verbal Learning and Verbal Behavior*, 1975, **14**, 275–283.

111. Greene, J. M. Syntactic form and semantic function. *Quarterly Journal of Experimental Psychology*, 1970, **22**, 14–27.

112. Greene, J. M. The semantic function of negatives and positives. *British Journal of Psychology*, 1970, **61**, 17–22.

113. Greene, J. M. and Wason, P. C. Negation: A rejoinder to Wales and Grieve. *Perception and Psychophysics*, 1970, **8**, 238–239.

114. Grice, H. P. Logic and conversation. In P. Cole and J. L. Morgan (Eds.), *Syntax and semantics*. Vol. 3: *Speech acts*. New York: Seminar Press, 1975.

115. Grieve, R. and Wales, R. J. Passives and topicalization. *British Journal of Psychology*, 1973, **64**, 173–182.

116. Haggard, M. Understanding speech understanding. In A. Cohen and S. G. Nooteboom (Eds.), *Structure and process in speech perception*. Berlin, Heidelberg, New York: Springer Verlag, 1975.

117. Hakes, D. T. Does verb structure affect sentence comprehension? *Perception and Psychophysics*, 1971, **10**, 229–232.

118. Hakes, D. T. Effects of reducing complement constructions on sentence comprehension. *Journal of Verbal Learning and Verbal Behavior*, 1972, **11**, 278–286.

119. Hakes, D. T. and Cairns, H. S. Sentence comprehension and relative pronouns. *Perception and Psychophysics*, 1970, **8**, 5–8.

120. Hakes, D. T. and Foss, D. J. Decisions processes during sentence comprehension: Effects of surface structure reconsidered. *Perception and Psychophysics*, 1970, **8**, 413–416.

121. Hakes, D. T., Evans, J. S., and Brannon, L. L. Understanding sentences with relative clauses. *Memory and Cognition*, 1976, **4**, 283–290.

122. Halle, M. and Stevens, K. N. Speech recognition: A model and a program for research. In J. A. Fodor and J. J. Katz (Eds.), *Readings in the philosophy of language*. Englewood-Cliffs: Prentice Hall, 1964.

123. Hamilton, H. W. and Deese, J. Comprehensibility and subject-verb relations in complex sentences. *Journal of Verbal Learning and Verbal Behavior*, 1971, **10**, 163–170.

124. t'Hart, J. and Cohen, A. Intonation by rule: A perceptual quest. *Journal of Phonetics*, 1973, **1**, 309–327.

125. 't Hart, J. and Collier, R. Integrating different levels of intonation analysis. *Journal of Phonetics*, 1975, **3**, 235–255.

126. Haviland, S. E. and Clark, H. H. What's new? Acquiring new information as a process in comprehension. *Journal of Verbal Learning and Verbal Behavior*, 1974, **13**, 512–521.

127. Healy, A. F. and Miller, G. A. The relative contribution of nouns and verbs to sentence acceptability and comprehensibility. *Psychonomic Science*, 1971, **4**, 94–96.

128. Hogaboam, T. W. and Perfetti, C. A. Lexical ambiguity and sentence comprehension. *Journal of Verbal Learning and Verbal Behavior*, 1975, **14**, 265–274.

129. Holmes, V. M. Order of main and subordinate clauses in sentence perception. *Journal of Verbal Learning and Verbal Behavior*, 1973, **12**, 285–293.

130. Holmes, V. M. and Forster, K. I. Detection of extraneous signals during sentence recognition. *Perception and Psychophysics*, 1970, **7**, 297–301.

131. Holmes, V. M. and Forster, K. I. Click localization and syntactic structure. *Perception and Psychophysics*, 1972, **12**, 9–15.
132. Holmes, V. M. and Forster, K. I. Perceptual complexity and underlying sentence structure. *Journal of Verbal Learning and Verbal Behavior*, 1972, **11**, 148–156.
133. Holyoak, K. J. The role of imagery in the evaluation of sentences: imagery or semantic factors? *Journal of Verbal Learning and Verbal Behavior*, 1974, **13**, 163–166.
134. Holyoak, K. J. and Glass, A. L. The role of contradictions and counterexamples in the rejection of false sentences. *Journal of Verbal Learning and Verbal Behavior*, 1975, **14**, 215–239.
135. Hörmann, H. The concept of sense constancy. Paper for the XXIth International Congress of Psychology, Paris, July 1976.
136. Hörmann, H. *Meinen und Verstehen. Grundzüge einer psychologischen Semantik*. Frankfurt: Suhrkamp, 1976.
137. Hornby, P. A. Surface structure and presupposition. *Journal of Verbal Learning and Verbal Behavior*, 1974, **13**, 530–538.
138. Hupet, M. and Le Bouedec, B. Definiteness and voice in the interpretation of active and passive sentences. *Quarterly Journal of Experimental Psychology*, 1975, **27**, 323–330.
139. Huttenlocher, J., Higgins, E. T., Milligan, C., and Kauffman, B. The mystery of the 'negative equative' construction. *Journal of Verbal Learning and Verbal Behavior*, 1970, **9**, 334–341.
140. Jarvella, R. J. Effects of syntax on running memory span for connected discourse. *Psychonomic Science*, 1970, **19**, 235–236.
141. Jarvella, R. J. Syntactic processing of connected speech. *Journal of Verbal Learning and Verbal Behavior*, 1971, **10**, 409–416.
142. Jarvella, R. J. and Herman, S. J. Clause structure of sentences and speech processing. *Perception and Psychophysics*, 1972, **11**, 381–384.
143. Johnson-Laird, P. N. Experimental psycholinguistics. *Annual Review of Psychology*, 1974, **25**, 135–160.
144. Johnson-Laird, P. N. The three term-series problem. *Cognition*, 1972, **1**, 57–82.
145. Johnson-Laird, P. N. and Tridgell, J. N. When negation is easier than affirmation. *Quarterly Journal of Experimental Psychology*, 1972, **24**, 87–91.
146. Jones, S. Visual and verbal processes in problem-solving. *Cognitive Psychology*, 1970, **1**, 201–214.
147. Jorgensen, C. C. and Kintsch, W. The role of imagery in the evaluation of sentences. *Cognitive Psychology*, 1973, **4**, 110–116.
148. Just, M. A. Comprehending quantified sentences: The relation between sentence-picture and semantic memory verification. *Cognitive Psychology*, 1974, **6**, 216–236.
149. Just, M. A. and Carpenter, P. A. Comprehension of negation with quantification. *Journal of Verbal Learning and Verbal Behavior*, 1971, **10**, 244–253.
150. Just, M. A. and Carpenter, P. A. The relation between comprehending and remembering some complex sentences. *Memory and Cognition*, 1976, **4**, 318–322.
151. Just, M. A. and Clark, H. H. Drawing inferences from the presuppositions and implications of affirmative and negative sentences. *Journal of Verbal Learning and Verbal Behavior*, 1973, **12**, 21–31.
152. Kaplan, R. M. Augmented transition networks as psychological models of sentence comprehension. *Artificial Intelligence*, 1972, **3**, 77–100.
153. Kaplan, R. M. On process models for sentence analysis. In D. A. Norman and D. E. Rumelhart (Eds.), *Explorations in cognition*. San Francisco: Freeman, 1975.
154. Katwijk, A. van. *Accentuation in Dutch*. Eindhoven: I.P.O., 1974.

155. Kempen, G. Syntactic constructions as retrieval plans. *British Journal of Psychology*, 1976, **67**, 149–160.
156. Kimball, J. P. Seven principles of surface structure parsing in natural language. *Cognition*, 1973, **2**, 15–47.
157. Kintsch, W. *The representation of meaning in memory*. Hillsdale, N.J.: Lawrence Erlbaum Associates, 1974.
158. Kintsch, W., Kozminsky, E., Streby, W. J., McKoon, G., and Keenan, J. M. Comprehension and recall of text as a function of content variables. *Journal of Verbal Learning and Verbal Behavior*, 1975, **14**, 196–214.
159. Klee, H. and Eysenck, M. W. Comprehension of abstract and concrete sentences. *Journal of Verbal Learning and Verbal Behavior*, 1973, **12**, 522–529.
160. Klenbort, I. and Anisfeld, M. Markedness and perspective in the interpretation of the active and passive voice. *Quarterly Journal of Experimental Psychology*, 1974, **26**, 189–195.
161. Kornfeld, J. R. Clause boundary and dominance effects on sentence perception. *M.I.T. Research Laboratory of Electronics, Quarterly Progress Report*, 1973, **110**, 177–181.
162. Krueger, L. E. Sentence-picture comparison: A test of additivity and processing time for feature matching and negation coding. *Journal of Experimental Psychology*, 1972, **95**, 275–284.
163. Krulee, G. K. and Schwartz, H. R. Scanning processes and sentence recognition. *Journal of Psycholinguistic Research*, 1975, **4**, 141–158.
164. Lackner, J. R. and Garrett, M. F. Resolving ambiguity: Effects of biasing contexts in the unattended ear. *Cognition*, 1972, **1**, 359–372.
165. Ladefoged, P. *Three areas of experimental phonetics*. London: Oxford University Press, 1967.
166. Ladefoged, P. and Broadbent, D. E. Perception of sequence in auditory events. *Quarterly Journal of Experimental Psychology*, 1960, **13**, 162–170.
167. Lashley, K. S. The problem of serial order in behavior. In L. A. Jeffress (Ed.), *Cerebral mechanisms in behavior*, New York: Wiley, 1951.
168. Levelt, W. J. M. Generative grammatica en psycholinguistiek. II Psycholinguistisch onderzoek. *Nederlands Tijdschrift voor de Psychologie*, 1966, **21**, 367–400.
169. Levelt, W. J. M. Hierarchical chunking in sentence processing. *Perception and Psychophysics*, 1970, **8**, 99–103.
170. Levelt, W. J. M. *Formal grammars in linguistics and psycholinguistics*. Vol. I: *An introduction to the theory of formal languages and automata*. Vol. II: *Applications in linguistic theory*. Vol. III: *Psycholinguistic applications*. The Hague: Mouton, 1974.
171. Levelt, W. J. M. *What became of LAD?* Lisse: Peter de Ridder Press, 1975.
172. Levelt, W. J. M. and Kempen, G. Semantic and syntactic aspects of remembering sentences: A review of some recent continental research. In A. Kennedy and A. Wilkes (Eds.), *Studies in long term memory*. New York: Wiley, 1975.
173. Levelt, W. J. M. and Ouweneel, G. R. E. The perception of French sentences with a surface structure ambiguity. *Nederlands Tijdschrift voor de Psychologie*, 1969, **24**, 245–248.
174. Levelt, W. J. M., Schreuder, R., and Hoenkamp, E. Structure and use of verbs of motion. In R. N. Campbell and P. T. Smith (Eds.), *Recent advances in the psychology of language: Formal and experimental approaches*. New York: Plenum Press, 1978.
175. Levelt, W. J. M., Zwanenburg, W., and Ouweneel, G. R. Ambiguous surface structure and phonetic form in French. *Foundations of Language*, 1970, **6**, 260–273.
176. Lewis, J. L. Semantic processing of unattended messages using dichotic listening, *Journal of Experimental Psychology*, 1970, **85**, 225–228.

177. Lippman, M. Z. The influence of grammatical transform in a syllogistic reasoning task. *Journal of Verbal Learning and Verbal Behavior*, 1972, **11**, 424–430.
178. Locatelli, F. Le rôle des oppositions temporelles dans la compréhension de la succession. *L'Année Psychologique*, 1973, **73**, 493–506.
179. Loosen, F. Cognitive organisatie van zinnen in het geheugen. Unpublished Ph. Dissertation, Louvain, 1972.
180. MacKay, D. G. To end ambiguous sentences. *Perception and Psychophysics*, 1966, **3**, 426–436.
181. MacKay, D. G. Mental diplopia: Towards a model of speech perception at the semantic level. In G. B. Flores d'Arcais and W. J. M. Levelt (Eds.), *Advances in psycholinguistics*. Amsterdam: North-Holland, 1970.
182. MacKay, D. G. Aspects of the theory of comprehension, memory and attention. *Quarterly Journal of Experimental Psychology*, 1973, **25**, 22–40.
183. MacKay, D. G. and Bever, T. G. In search of ambiguity. *Perception and Psychophysics*, 1967, **2**, 193–200.
184. Marslen-Wilson, W. D. Linguistic structure and speech shadowing at very short latencies. *Nature*, 1973, **244**, 522–523.
185. Marslen-Wilson, W. D. Sentence perception as an interactive parallel process. *Science*, 1975, **189**, 226–228.
186. Marslen-Wilson, W. D. Linguistic descriptions and psychological assumptions in the study of sentence perception. In R. J. Wales and E. Walker (Eds.), *New approaches to language mechanisms*. Amsterdam: North-Holland, 1976.
187. Marslen-Wilson, W. D. and Tyler, L. K. Processing structure of sentence perception. *Nature*, 1975, **257**, 784–786.
188. Marslen-Wilson, W. D. and Tyler, L. K. Memory and levels of processing in a psycholinguistic context. *Journal of Experimental Psychology: Human Learning and Memory*, 1976, **2**, 112–119.
189. Martin, J. G. Rhythmic (hierarchical) versus serial structure in speech and other behavior. *Psychological Review*, 1972, **79**, 487–509.
190. Martin, J. G. Rhythmic expectancy in continuous speech perception. In A. Cohen and S. G. Nooteboom (Eds.), *Structure and process in speech perception*. Berlin, Heidelberg, New York: Springer Verlag, 1975.
191. McNeill, D. and Lindig, K. The perceptual reality of phonemes, syllables, words and sentences. *Journal of Verbal Learning and Verbal Behavior*, 1973, **12**, 419–430.
192. Meyer, D. E. On the representation and retrieval of stored semantic information. *Cognitive Psychology*, 1970, **1**, 242–300.
193. Miller, G. A. Toward a third metaphor for psycholinguistics. In W. B. Weimer and D. S. Palermo (Eds.), *Cognition and the symbolic processes*. Hillsdale, N.J.: Lawrence Erlbaum Associates, 1974.
194. Miller, G. A. and Johnson-Laird, P. N. *Language and perception*. Cambridge, Mass.: Harvard University Press, 1976.
195. Minsky, M. A framework for representing knowledge. In P. H. Winston (Ed.), *The psychology of computer vision*. New York: McGraw Hill, 1975.
196. Miron, M. S. and Brown, E. The comprehension of rate-incremented aural coding. *Journal of Psycholinguistic Research*, 1971, **1**, 65–76.
197. Mistler-Lachman, J. L. Levels of comprehension in processing of normal and ambiguous sentences. *Journal of Verbal Learning and Verbal Behavior*, 1972, **11**, 614–623.
198. Mistler-Lachman, J. L. Depth of comprehension and sentence memory. *Journal of Verbal Learning and Verbal Behaviour*, 1974, **13**, 98–106.
199. Mistler-Lachman, J. L. Queer sentences, ambiguity, and levels of processing. *Memory and Cognition*, 1975, **3**, 395–400.

200. Morton, J. A functional model for memory. In D. A. Norman (Ed.), *Models of human memory*. New York: Academic Press, 1970.
201. Morton, J. and Long, J. Effect of word transitional probability on phoneme identification. *Journal of Verbal Learning and Verbal Behavior*, 1976, **15**, 43–51.
202. Noordman, L. G. M. Foreground and background information in reasoning. In R. N. Campbell and P. T. Smith (Eds.), *Recent advances in the psychology of language: Formal and experimental approaches*. New York: Plenum Press, 1978.
203. Norman, D. A. and Rumelhart, D. E. *Explorations in cognition*. San Francisco: Freeman, 1975.
204. Olson, D. R. and Filby, N. On the comprehension of active and passive sentences. *Cognitive Psychology*, 1972, **3**, 361–381.
205. Olson, G. M. and Clark, H. H. Research methods in psycholinguistics. In E. C. Carterette and M. P. Friedman (Eds.), *Handbook of perception*. Vol. 7: *Language and speech*. New York: Academic Press, 1976.
206. Olson, J. N. and McKay, D. G. Completion and verification of ambiguous sentences. *Journal of Verbal Learning and Verbal Behavior*, 1974, **13**, 457–470.
207. Paivio, A. and Begg, I. Imagery and comprehension latencies as a function of sentence concreteness and structure. *Perception and Psychophysics*, 1971, **10**, 408–412.
208. Petrick, S. R. *A recognition procedure for transformational grammars*. Dept. of Modern Languages, M.I.T., 1965.
209. Reber, A. S. Locating clicks in sentences: Left, center and right. *Perception and Psychophysics*, 1973, **13**, 133–138.
210. Reber, A. S. and Anderson, J. R. The perception of clicks in linguistic and non-linguistic messages. *Perception and Psychophysics*, 1970, **8**, 81–89.
211. Riding, R. J. A method for investigating the perceptual segmentation of speech. *Language and Speech*, 1975, **18**, 153–157.
212. Riesbeck, C. K. Conceptual analysis. In R. C. Schank (Ed.), *Conceptual information processing*. Amsterdam: North-Holland, 1975.
213. Rips, L. J. Qualification and semantic memory. *Cognitive Psychology*, 1975, **7**, 307–340.
214. Rips, L. J., Shoben, E. J., and Smith, E. E. Semantic distance and the verification of semantic relations. *Journal of Verbal Learning and Verbal Behavior*, 1973, **12**, 1–20.
215. Roncato, S. and Sonino, M. On some strategies of comparing sentences against pictures. *Italian Journal of Psychology*, 1976, **3**, 165–186.
216. Rosenberg, S. and Jarvella, R. J. Semantic integration as a variable in sentence perception, memory and production. In G. B. Flores d'Arcais and W. J. M. Levelt (Eds.), *Advances in psycholinguistics*. Amsterdam: North-Holland, 1970.
217. Rosenberg, S. and Jarvella, R. J. Semantic integration and sentence perception. *Journal of Verbal Learning and Verbal Behavior*, 1970, **9**, 548–553.
218. Rubenstein, H., Garfield, L., and Millikan, J. A. Homographic entries in the internal lexicon. *Journal of Verbal Learning and Verbal Behavior*, 1970, **9**, 487–494.
219. Rubenstein, H., Lewis, S. S., and Rubenstein, M. A. Homographic entries in the internal lexicon: Effects of systematicity and relative frequency of meanings. *Journal of Verbal Learning and Verbal Behavior*, 1971, **10**, 57–62.
220. Russell, B. *Human knowledge: Its scope and limits*. Allen and Unwin, 1948.
221. Sachs, J. Recognition memory for syntactic and semantic aspects of connected discourse. *Perception and Psychophysics*, 1967, **2**, 437–442.
222. Savin, H. B. and Bever, T. G. The non perceptual reality of the phoneme. *Journal of Verbal Learning and Verbal Behavior*, 1970, **9**, 295–302.
223. Savin, H. B. and Perchonock, E. Grammatical structure and the immediate recall of

English sentences. *Journal of Verbal Learning and Verbal Behavior*, 1965, **4**, 348–353.

224. Schank, R. C. Conceptual dependency: A theory of natural language understanding. *Cognitive Psychology*, 1972, **3**, 552–631.
225. Schank, R. C. Identification of conceptualizations underlying natural language. In R. C. Schank and K. M. Colby (Eds.), *Computer models of thought and language*. San Francisco: Freeman, 1973.
226. Schank, R. C. *Conceptual information processing*. Amsterdam: North-Holland, 1975.
227. Schvaneveldt, R. W. and Meyer, D. E. Retrieval and comparison processes in semantic memory. In S. Kornblum (Ed.), *Attention and Performance IV*. New York: Academic Press, 1973.
228. Schwartz, D., Sparkman, J. P., and Deese, J. The process of understanding and judgment of comprehensibility. *Journal of Verbal Learning and Verbal Behavior*, 1970, **9**, 87–93.
229. Seitz, M. R. and Weber, B. A. Effects of response requirements on the location of clicks superimposed on sentences. *Memory and Cognition*, 1974, **2**, 43–46.
230. Shanon, B. The two meanings of a homophone. *Perception and Psychophysics*, 1974, **16**, 571–574.
231. Sherman, M. A. Bound to be easier? The negative prefix and sentence comprehension. *Journal of Verbal Learning and Verbal Behavior*, 1973, **12**, 76–84.
232. Sherman, M. A. Adjectival negation and the comprehension of multiply negated sentences. *Journal of Verbal Learning and Verbal Behavior*, 1976, **15**, 143–157.
233. Shields, J. L., McHugh, A., and Martin, J. G. Reaction time to phoneme targets as a function of rhythmic cues in continuous speech. *Journal of Experimental Psychology*, 1974, **102**, 250–255.
234. Smith, K. H. and McMahon, L. E. Understanding order information in sentences: Some recent work at Bell Laboratories. In G. B. Flores d'Arcais and W. J. M. Levelt (Eds.), *Advances in psycholinguistics*. Amsterdam: North-Holland, 1970.
235. Soli, S. D. and Balch, W. R. Performance biases and recognition memory for semantic and formal changes in connected discourse. *Memory and Cognition*, 1976, **4**, 673–676.
236. Springston, F. J. Some cognitive aspects of presupposed coreferential anaphora. Unpublished Ph.D. Dissertation, Stanford University, 1975.
237. Springston, F. J. and Clark H. H. *And* and *or*, or the comprehension of pseudo-imperatives. *Journal of Verbal Learning and Verbal Behavior*, 1973, **12**, 258–272.
238. Sternberg, S. The discovery of processing stages: Extensions of Donder's method. *Acta Psychologica*, 1969, **30**, 276–316.
239. Stevens, A. L. and Rumelhart, D. E. Errors in reading: An analysis using an augmented transition network model of grammar. In D. A. Norman and D. E. Rumelhart (Eds.), *Explorations in cognition*. San Francisco: Freeman, 1975.
240. Stillings, N. A. Meaning rules and systems of inference for verbs of transfer and possession. *Journal of Verbal Learning and Verbal Behavior*, 1975, **14**, 453–470.
241. Streeter, L. A. and Bever, T. G. The effects on the detection of linguistic and non-linguistic stimuli are opposite at the beginning and end of a clause. Mimeographed, Columbia University, 1975.
242. Sturges, P. T. and Martin, J. G. Rhythmic structure in auditory pattern perception and immediate memory. *Journal of Experimental Psychology*, 1974, **102**, 377–383.
243. Tanenhaus, M. K. and Carroll, J. M. The clausal processing hierarchy and nouniness. In R. Grossman, J. San, and T. Vance (Eds.), *Papers from the parasession on functionalism*. Chicago: Chicago Linguistic Society, 1975.
244. Tanenhaus, M. K., Carroll, J. M., and Bever, T. G. Sentence-picture verification

models as theories of sentence comprehension: A critique of Carpenter and Just. *Psychological Review*, 1976, **83**, 310–317.

245. Thorne, J. P., Bratley, P., and Dewar, H. The syntactic analysis of English by machine. In D. Michie (Ed.), *Machine Intelligence 3*. New York: American Elsevier, 1968.

246. Toppino, T. C. The underlying structures of sentences are not the primary units of speech processing: A reinterpretation of Bever, Lackner, and Kirk's findings. *Perception and Psychophysics*, 1974, **15**, 517–518.

247. Trabasso, T. Mental operations in language comprehension. In R. O. Freedle and J. B. Carroll (Eds.), *Language comprehension and the acquisition of knowledge*. New York: Winston, 1972.

248. Trabasso, T., Rollins, H., and Shaughnessy, E. Storage and verification stages in processing concepts. *Cognitive Psychology*, 1971, **2**, 239–289.

249. Treisman, A. M. and Squire, R. Listening to speech at two levels at once. *Quarterly Journal of Experimental Psychology*, 1974, **26**, 82–97.

250. Treisman, A. M., Squire, R., and Green, J. Semantic processing in dichotic listening? A replication. *Memory and Cognition*, 1974, **2**, 641–646.

251. Tversky, B. Encoding processes in recognition and recall. *Cognitive Psychology*, 1973, **5**, 275–287.

252. Tversky, B. Pictorial encoding of sentences in sentence picture comparisons. *Quarterly Journal of Experimental Psychology*, 1975, **27**, 405–410.

253. Wales, R. and Grieve, R. What is so difficult about negation? *Perception and Psychophysics*, 1969, **6**, 327–332.

254. Wang, M. D. Influence of linguistic structure on comprehensibility and recognition. *Journal of Experimental Psychology*, 1970, **85**, 83–89.

255. Wang, M. D. The role of syntactic complexity as a determiner of comprehensibility. *Journal of Verbal Learning and Verbal Behavior*, 1970, **9**, 398–404.

256. Wannemacher, J. T. Processing strategies in picture-sentence verification tasks. *Memory and Cognition*, 1974, **2**, 554–560.

257. Wannemacher, J. T. Processing strategies in sentence comprehension. *Memory and Cognition*, 1976, **4**, 48–52.

258. Wanner, E. Review of Fodor, J. A., Bever, T. G., and Garrett, M. F. *The psychology of language*. New York: McGraw-Hill, 1974. *Journal of Psycholinguistic Research*, 1977, **3**, 261–270.

259. Wanner, E., Kaplan, R., and Shiner, S. Garden paths in relative clauses. Mimeographed. Harvard University, Cambridge, Mass., 1975.

260. Wanner, E. and Maratsos, H. An augmented transition network model of relative clause comprehension. Mimeographed. Harvard University, Cambridge, Mass., 1975.

261. Wanner, E. and Shiner, S. Measuring transient memory load. *Journal of Verbal Learning and Verbal Behavior*, 1976, **15**, 159–167.

262. Wanner, E. and Shiner, S. Ambiguities in relative clauses. Mimeographed. Harvard University, Cambridge, Mass., 1975.

263. Wason, P. C. and Johnson-Laird, P. N. *Psychology of reasoning*. London: Batsford, 1972.

264. Wickelgren, W. A. The long and the short of memory. *Psychological Bulletin*, 1973, **80**, 425–438.

264. Wilks, Y. An artificial intelligence approach to machine translation. In R. C. Schank and K. M. Colby (Eds.), *Computer models of thought and language*. San Francisco: Freeman, 1973.

266. Wingfield, A. The intonation-syntax interaction: Prosodic features in perceptual processing of sentences. In A. Cohen and S. G. Nooteboom (Eds.), *Structure and process in speech perception*. Berlin, Heidelberg, New York: Springer Verlag, 1975.

267. Wingfield, A. and Klein, J. F. Syntactic structure and acoustic pattern in speech perception. *Perception and Psychophysics*, 1971, **9**, 23–25.
268. Winograd, T. Understanding natural language. *Cognitive Psychology*, 1972, **3**, 1–191.
269. Winograd, T. A procedural model of language understanding. In R. C. Schank and K. M. Colby (Eds.), *Computer models of thought and language*. San Francisco: Freeman, 1973.
270. Woods, W. A. Transition network grammars for natural language analysis. *Communications of the ACM*, 1970, **13**, 591–606.
271. Wright, P. Some observations on how people answer questions about sentences. *Journal of Verbal Learning and Verbal Behavior*, 1972, **11**, 188–195.
272. Wright, P., Holloway, C. M., and Aldrich, A. R. Attending to visual or auditory verbal information while performing other concurrent tasks. *Quarterly Journal of Experimental Psychology*, 1974, **26**, 454–463.
273. Wright, P. and Kahneman, D. Evidence for alternative strategies of sentence retention. *Quarterly Journal of Experimental Psychology*, 1971, **23**, 197–213.
274. Zwanenburg, W., Ouweneel, G. R., and Levelt, W. J. M., La frontière du mot en français. *Studies in Language*, 1977, **1**, 209–221.

CONTENTS

Chapter 2

Contributions of Prosody to Speech Perception

Sibout G. Nooteboom, Johannes P. L. Brokx, and Jacobus J. de Rooij

INTRODUCTION

In contemporary speech research many investigators seem to assume that if only we understand how acoustic and phonetic features are extracted from the acoustic wave and combined into recognized phonemes or syllables, then we may describe all further processing in terms of devices which take their recognized phonemes or syllables as their input. This was the basic assumption underlying such older proposals as the analysis-by-synthesis model (Halle and Stevens, 1962; Stevens and Halle, 1967) and the motor theory of speech perception (Liberman, Cooper, Shankweiler, and Studdert-Kennedy, 1967). More recent proposals, in the line of the information-processing approach, while still based on these old assumptions, now acknowledge the potential contribution of 'speech prosody' to perceptual segmentation (e.g. Pisoni and Sawusch, 1975; Massaro, 1975; Massaro and Cohen, 1975).

Further examples of the emphasis on the phoneme or syllable as the basic units of speech perception abound in the current literature. Common types of experiments in this area include the evocation of phonemic identifications of systematically varied speech-like sounds in optimal listening conditions, in noise conditions, in dichotic listening situations, after selective adaptation by repeated stimulation with a particular stimulus, and under conditions of backward masking. Eliciting similarity judgments, measuring reaction times, or studying errors in short-term recall are also much-used methods in experimental studies. These experiments are designed to provide information on such diverse topics as coding strategies in sensory store and short-term memory, the existence of acoustic and phonetic feature detectors, the hemispheric lateralization of speech, and the uniqueness of speech perception in comparison with other auditory processes. (For a discussion of this field of research see Studdert-Kennedy, 1975a, 1975b).

As a result of these research efforts we now have a reasonable understanding of the relation between the acoustic structure of phonemes and syllables spoken in isolation and their perception. However, our understanding of the relation between the acoustic structure of connected speech and its perception is much less satisfactory. There is, of course, a considerable psycholinguistic literature dealing with the perception of both visually and auditorily presented sentences; in this literature the structure of the physical stimulus is in most cases treated not as an interesting source of information but rather as an unwanted experimental variable. Experimental tasks in studies of sentence perception have included the following: the subjective localization of an audible click in one ear at the same time that an audible sentence is presented to the other; the pushing of a button in fast reaction to the appearance of every perceived specific phoneme, syllable, or word in the attended speech or in reaction to a tone burst presented simultaneously with the presented speech; the verification of the accuracy of an auditorily presented sentence purporting to describe correctly a visually presented picture; the verification of the truth value of an auditorily presented sentence; and verbatim recall of auditorily presented sentences. Such experiments are designed to throw light on such issues as the perceptual segmentation of sentences, coding strategies in sentence perception and in short-term memory, the psychological reality of rules of transformational grammar, the relation between syntactic structure and presuppositional structure, and the flow of information in mental verification procedures.

Despite the fact that in all experiments in which sentences are presented auditorily the acoustic structure of speech may be a major determinant of the subject's behaviour, this is only rarely acknowledged by investigators, and even more rarely is it made the object of systematic study. (For a survey of the literature on sentence perception see Levelt's paper in this volume.) In contrast to what we know about phoneme, syllable, and sentence perception, our knowledge of the acoustic structure and the perception of auditorily presented sentences is relatively small. This is in part due to the traditional emphasis on phonemes and syllables as the perceptual units of speech, and in part to the extreme complexity of the acoustic structure of speech, which makes its analysis and any attempt to describe the relation of the acoustic structure to what is perceived a laborious task. It is, however, a task which it is nonetheless worthwhile to undertake. For if we ever want to reach even a fair understanding of our ability to perceive and understand connected speech, then it is merely reasonable to take as our starting point a description of the nature and function of speech perception; that is, of the relation between the acoustic structure of speech and what is actually perceived. From here one may logically proceed to an investigation of the organization of speech perception.

In this paper we shall give a few examples to illustrate the relationship between acoustic and perceived aspects of both connected speech and speech-like sound sequences. The examples have been selected in order to make it clear that the acoustic structure of speech carries parallel information on a number of different perceived aspects of the attended speech, which vary from the awareness that the sequence of sounds one is listening to is actually a coherent stream of speech, to the perception of the syntactic aspects of the message expressed by the sound sequence. The first example, presented in the next section, concerns the perceived prosodic continuity of the attended voice. If sequences of words or syllables lack such prosodic continuity, recognition of the message may be hampered. We are interested in determining which acoustic properties of speech provide this necessary prosodic continuity.

The second example, presented in the third section, is related to one effect of a prosodic aspect of speech, i.e. local speech rate, on the identification of vowels. It will be shown that the acoustic durations of the segments immediately following the vowel segments concerned contribute to its perception. The third example, which is presented in the fourth section, concerns acoustic cues to such perceived prosodic properties of speech as the relative prominences of syllables and prosodic boundaries. These prosodic properties of speech may in turn carry information on the lexical and syntactic structure of the message.

All these examples concern aspects of speech which are generally considered to belong to what is known as *speech prosody*, which relates to a number of perceivable aspects of connected speech, most particularly those which cannot be assigned to individual speech sounds but rather are attributes of whole words and word sequences. Pitch contours (intonation) and temporal organization (relative lengthening of individual syllables, speech rate) are the most studied prosodic aspects of speech. In linguistics, experimental phonetics, and psycholinguistics, speech prosody and its acoustic basis has thus far been allowed only marginal attention; in this paper we will present data and observations to support our conviction that speech prosody — far from being of minor significance — is in fact central to speech communication.

ACOUSTIC ASPECTS OF PROSODIC CONTINUITY

Prosodic continuity in speech perception

Ever since the original observations and experiments by Cherry (1953), the 'cocktail party problem' has challenged theorists of speech perception.

How do we recognize what one person is saying when others are speaking at the same time? Possible facilitating factors mentioned by Cherry are directional hearing, visual information, the presence of numerous different voices and accents, and transition probabilities (Cherry, 1953). A recent experiment by Darwin (1975) suggests that an important factor may be 'prosodic continuity'. Darwin presented listeners simultaneously with two different passages of speech spoken by the same speaker, one on each ear. These passages of about 50 words each were constructed from pairs of passages of normal connected prose.

From each pair of passages four recordings were made: two were of the original passages and two were made by smoothly combining the first part of one passage with the second part of the other. On the basis of these four original recordings, four different dichotic conditions were made, which were as follows: (a) a *normal* condition, in which the two original passages were paired together; (b) a *semantic change* condition, created by pairing together the other two original recordings; (c) an *intonation change* condition, created by switching the latter pair of passages after the first part of the passage, so that the signal on the left ear continued on the right and vice-versa; and finally (d) a condition in which both *semantics and intonation changed*, created by switching the two original passages after the first part.

The listeners were instructed to shadow the message presented to one ear. The main feature of the results is that 'switching' the prosody (called intonation by Darwin) from the attended to the unattended ear resulted in a high percentage of intrusions from the unattended ear, whereas switching the signal in such a way as to break semantic continuity (but not the prosody) resulted mainly in omissions. Apparently prosodic continuity helps a listener to attend to a particular speaker, and when this continuity is switched from one ear to the other, the subject's urge to follow the stream of prosody may override the instruction to attend to one ear only.

It is of some interest to know which acoustic factors contribute to this prosodic continuity. We may find some clues in the difficulties we encounter when we attempt to synthesize speech by concatenation of prerecorded syllables or words. If, for example, one records syllables or words spoken in isolation by a single speaker and assembles them in the correct order to obtain a syntactically and semantically acceptable sentence, the resulting speech is unacceptable, and often unintelligible: the speech sounds garbled. Listeners may report hearing the speech coming from different directions and hearing more than one speaker; perception of temporal order is sometimes disturbed. However, when pauses are introduced between the concatenated fragments, the perceptual disturbance is reduced. Apparently listeners need some form of prosodic continuity in speech, which is lacking in concatenated speech. It seems reasonable to assume that the perceptual disturbance in concatenated speech is in some way related to the acoustic discontinuities on the boundaries of the concatenated fragments, such as discontinuities in pitch, spectral composition, and amplitude. Incorrect segment durations of the concatenated speech may also contribute to the effect. In the following section we will discuss some data related to the possible contribution of spectral information and pitch to perceived prosodic continuity.

Spectral continuity, perceived temporal order, and primary auditory stream segregation

When unpractised listeners are presented with sequences of concatenated vowels of less than some 125 msec duration each, they may have difficulty in

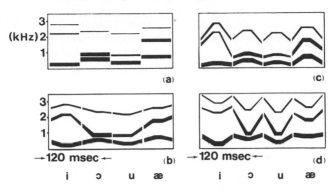

Figure 2.1. Spectrographic representations of four stimulus types used by Dorman *et al.* (1974). (a) steady-state vowels; (b) vowels connected by diphthong-like formant transitions; (c) vowels connected by /b/-like formant transitions; (d) vowels connected by phonetically impossible formant transitions

determining the order of the vowels (Thomas, Hill, Carrol, and Garcia, 1970). This observation was the starting point for perceptual measurements made by Dorman, Cutting, and Raphael (1975). They prepared stimuli of sequences of four concatenated vowel sounds, each of 120 msec duration presented in four conditions: (a) with steady-state vowels; (b) with diphthong-like transitions from one vowel to the next; (c) with transitions for /b/-vowel-/b/ sequences and (d) with phonetically impossible transitions. Examples of these stimuli are presented in Figure 2.1.

Listeners were asked to report the temporal order of the vowels. The percentage of correct vowels was 30% for the steady-state vowels, 65% for the diphthongized sequences, 61% for /b/-vowel-/b/ sequences, and 13% for the phonetically impossible sequences. The low percentage for phonetically impossible sequences resulted from the listeners' inability to recognize the vowels at all. Although this may be an interesting effect of phonetically impossible formant transitions, it is not necessarily an effect on temporal order perception. The difference between steady-state vowels and the other two conditions seems to reflect an effect of spectral continuity on perception. Spectral continuity apparently helps the listeners to identify the stimulus as a single auditory pattern which is perceived as an ordered sequence of vowels or consonant-vowel syllables.

The effect of spectral continuity on speech perception has also been demonstrated in similar experiments using sequences of four consonant noises, of transitionless CV-syllables, and of CV-syllables with vowel transitions. Perception of temporal order was least successful for consonant noises and most successful for CV-syllables with transitions. The sequences of transitionless syllables result in perceptual segregation into separate auditory streams consisting of consonants and vowels (Cole and Scott, 1973). The stream segregation may, however, be only partly due to the lack of formant transitions; it could also be caused by the unnaturalness of repetitive listening to exactly the same stimulus pattern, a condition which was typical of these experiments in which the acoustic stimulus is endlessly repeated with no silent intervals between repetitions.

Pitch continuity, spectral transitions, and auditory stream segregation

It has been observed that if one is presented with a repetitive sequence of the same CV-syllable, pronounced alternately by male and female voices, one will segregate the male and female voices into two auditory streams (Lackner and Goldstein, 1974). This suggests that extreme changes in pitch may disturb prosodic continuity, although differences in timbre between male and female voices may also be involved. We have attempted to investigate the contribution of pitch continuity to perceived prosodic continuity or, alternatively, the contribution of discontinuity in pitch to auditory stream segregation.

We speak of prosodic continuity when a sequence of speech sounds is perceived as one on-going auditory stream of sound, produced by a single voice. We have constructed sequences of nine synthesized, monotonous, steady-state vowels in the order /a, u, i, a, u, i, a, u, i/, with each vowel having a duration of 100 msec. Within each such vowel sequence, the silent intervals separating vowels were of equal and constant length having one of the following values: 0, 25, 50, 75, 100, 150, 200, 300 and 400 msec. The vowels were characterized by alternating low and high pitch, as follows:

    high: /   u   a   i   u   /
    low: / a   i   u   a   i /

Pitch intervals per sequence comprised approximately 0, 2.5, 5, 7.5, 10, 12.5, 15, 17.5, or 20 semitones. Listening to the vowel sequences with no pitch intervals and silent-interval durations shorter than 50 msec, we were able to observe that the sequences are difficult to follow perceptually under such conditions. One hears only one stream of speech sounds, but it is difficult to report the precise components it consists of. With silent intervals of 50 msec or longer, and still no pitch jumps, one hears a single stream of vowels sung by a single speaker. If pitch jumps of sufficient size are introduced, one hears two streams of vowels, each sung by a different speaker. The size of the pitch jump necessary to produce two perceptually distinct streams of vowels depends on the silent-interval duration. When hearing two streams of vowels, one may focus attention on either of these at will, and thus hear /a, i, u, a, i/ or /u, a, i, u/. In between the areas where only one speaker is heard and where two speakers are heard, there is an area where one may hear either one or two speakers, depending on the attentional set. Two listeners presented with these sequences were asked to report for each stimulus

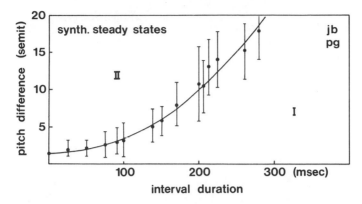

Figure 2.2. Fifty per cent transition points and standard deviations for hearing one or two streams of vowels in sequences of nine vowels, alternating between low and high pitch. Each vowel had 100 msec duration, silent intervals between vowels were varied in duration between 0 and 400 msec. Results are averaged over two listeners. I: The observers definitely hear one stream of vowels. II: The observers definitely hear two streams of vowels

sequence whether they heard one stream of vowels (one speaker) or two streams of vowels (two speakers). There were no systematic differences between the two listeners. The results are presented in Figure 2.2. The independent variables were silent-interval duration (horizontal axis) and pitch jump (vertical axis) between successive vowels. The dependent variable was the 50% transition point determining whether one hears one or two speakers. The spread in the data is indicated.

The data in Figure 2.2 suggest that pitch continuity is a powerful instrument either for holding the speech stream together or for breaking it up into separate streams. If we want to consider the relevance of these data to the perception of normal connected speech the effect of pitch jumps in those situations where silent intervals are shorter than, say, 150 msec is most interesting: the duration of voiceless consonants and consonant clusters in normal connected speech will generally not exceed 150 msec. In this region relatively small pitch jumps, of the order of 2–5 semitones, are sufficient to bring about stream segregation. The standard deviations were also relatively small.

To see whether the measured effect of the temporal characteristics of the vowel sequences on stream segregation depends on silent-interval durations alone — as hitherto assumed — or whether it also depends on scheduling of onset times, we have compared the effect of interval duration, varied from 50 to 150 msec, in two conditions: one in which vowel durations were kept constant at 100 msec (and thus onset to onset times varied from 150 to 250 msec) and another in which onset to onset times were kept constant at 250 msec (and thus

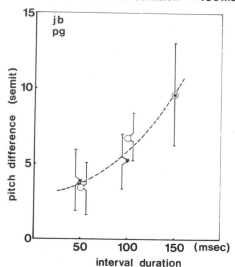

Figure 2.3. Fifty per cent transition points and standard deviations for hearing one or two streams of vowels in sequences of nine vowels, alternating between low and high pitch. Silent intervals between vowels had a duration of 50, 100, or 150 msec. Either the onset to onset time from one vowel to the next was kept constant at 250 msec, and thus vowel durations were 200, 150 or 100 msec, or the vowel durations were kept constant at 100 msec, and thus onset times were 50, 100, and 200 msec

vowel durations varied from 100 to 200 msec). That the results of not more than two listeners are presented has been caused by our inability hitherto to persuade more listeners to undergo the many hours of exhausting and boring listening which are needed to obtain these data.

Listeners were the same as those for the earlier measurements. The results are given in Figure 2.3. The dependent variable is again the 50% transition point which separates the hearing of one from the hearing of two speakers. It may be seen that there is no effect of vowel duration. Within the domain of our stimulus variables, the only temporal factor affecting stream segregation appears to be silent-interval duration. This is an indication that the stream segregation depends mainly on the steepness of the pitch jump from one vowel to the next.

A further question we asked is whether, and if so how, stream segregation, brought about by pitch jumps, is affected by consonant-like transitions in the

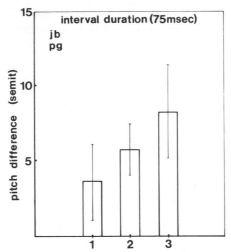

Figure 2.4. Fifty per cent transition points and standard deviations for hearing one or two streams of vowels in sequences of nine vowels, alternating between low and high pitch. Silent intervals between vowels were always 75 msec. (1) steady-state vowels; (2) vowels with a /b/-like transition at the beginning; (3) vowels with a /b/-like transition at both beginning and end

vowel sequences. In a first attempt to study this question we prepared stimulus sequences similar to those used for the earlier measurements. Silent-interval durations were kept constant at 75 msec. In condition (1) vowels were steady-state; in condition (2), /b/-like transitions were made in the beginning of all vowels; in condition (3), /b/-like transitions were made in the beginnings and endings of all vowels. Fifty per cent transition points for hearing one or two speakers were measured with the same two listeners, and results are presented in Figure 2.4. It may be seen that the presence of /b/-like spectral transitions increases the area where one speaker is heard. Apparently pitch continuity and consonant-like spectral transitions combine in holding the speech stream together. It seems reasonable to assume that they both favour a listener's ability to perceive a vowel sequence as a single auditory pattern.

Speech and non-speech

The perceptual measurements of vowel sequences presented above may be considered an extension of earlier research on auditory streaming in sequences of non-speech signals. Bregman and Campbell (1971) described the following phenomenon, denoted by them as primary auditory stream segregation. When listening to sequences of concatenated pure tones each of 100 msec duration, with alternation between low and high frequencies, listeners report hearing two independent streams of tones, one with low and one with high pitch. Temporal order cannot be correctly perceived between streams (Bregman and Campbell, 1971). Stream segregation may be inhibited by introducing frequency 'ramps' from one tone to the next (Bregman and Dannenbring, 1973). For this phenomenon Van Noorden (1975) used the term *fission* as opposed to *temporal coherence*. He also described a third perceptual phenomenon denoted as *fusion*. This occurs when one listens to a fast sequence of concatenated tones with small-frequency intervals. Such a sequence is heard as a continuous tone with some modulation of pitch and loudness. Van Noorden also demonstrated that, at least for fast sequences of tones of the duration of 40 msec and with onset intervals of 100 msec, temporal coherence does not depend on pitch but rather on the spectral continuity of successive tones: sequences of complex tones differing one octave in pitch but composed of harmonics in the same spectral region can be heard as temporally coherent, while sequences of complex tones having the same pitch but being composed of harmonics from different spectral regions lead to perceptual fission. With the latter type of stimulus material one may restore temporal coherence by increasing the onset intervals to about 150 msec or more (Van Noorden, 1975).

Van Noorden's observations, combined with our own, suggest that for onset intervals shorter than 150 msec, spectral continuity is probably a major determinant of temporal coherence — or, in the case of speech-like signals, of prosodic continuity — whereas for longer onset intervals continuity of pitch is the major factor. Apparently the disturbing effect of spectral discontinuity (or, on the other hand, the favourable effect of spectral continuity) between successive segments will rather rapidly decay upon increasing the time intervals between these segments. This is in line with results obtained by Huggins (1975a), who showed that the intelligibility of connected speech is largely unaffected by introducing silent intervals after each 60 msec of speech if the duration of the silent intervals is smaller than 60 msec. By increasing the silent-interval durations beyond 60 msec, we may rapidly decrease intelligibility, possibly because of the rapid decay of spectral information available, thus making it more difficult for the listener to combine the information in successive segments.

On the other hand, the information on pitch seems to deteriorate much less rapidly. The size of pitch jumps between successive segments can still make a decisive difference between the hearing of one or of two streams of sounds when silent intervals are of the order of 200 msec. In listening to temporally segmented speech, such as used by Huggins, one observes that while the stream of speech is in some sense broken up, disintegrated, by the silent gaps, one can still easily recognize the original pitch contour. This indicates that the information on the pitch of each segment has been preserved long enough to be combined with the pitch of the following segment.

In our own attempts to study the specific acoustic variables which contribute to the perceived continuity of speech, we have taken only very small steps in the direction of understanding ordinary speech. More research is needed to specify which acoustic properties of speech contribute to its perceptual integrity. However, within the framework of this paper — the contributions of prosody to speech perception — we may conclude that one of the major functions of continuity of pitch in speech is the preservation of the perceptual integrity of the attended voice. This may become particularly important in noisy communication situations, such as the famous 'cocktail party', when we are hearing more than one speaker simultaneously. This particular perceptual function of speech prosody may be rather basic to speech perception and is, in a general way, important to all further perceptual processing. In the following section, we will give a specific example of how a prosodic aspect of speech may contribute to the perception of phonemes.

PERCEPTUAL NORMALIZATION ON 'LOCAL SPEECH RATE'

Perceptual normalization in speech perception

In this section we will present data providing a specific example of *perceptual normalization*, which is the term we used to describe the phenomenon which occurs when an observer adjusts his categorical perception of a particular stimulus to its environment.

A simple example will explain. In English the perception of the vowel /æ/ (as in *bad*) as opposed to the vowel /ɛ/ (as in *bed*) depends, among other things, on its physical duration. By shortening an /æ/-like sound we can evoke /ɛ/ responses. We may refer to the vowel duration which results in 50% /ae/ responses and 50% /ɛ/ responses in a binary forced-choice experiment as the *phoneme boundary* between /ae/ and /ɛ/. We may embed the test vowels used for measuring this phoneme boundary in a sequence of vowel segments. It has been shown that the measured value for phoneme boundary depends on the rhythm of the vowel sequence: the faster the rhythm, the shorter the value for the phoneme boundary (Ainsworth, 1972). It is this type of phenomenon which we call *perceptual normalization*. Considerable evidence now exists of the occurrence of normalization in the categorical perception of spectral properties of vowels, consonant-like spectral transitions, voice onset time as a cue to the voiced-voiceless distinction, and segment duration (Ladefoged and Broadbent, 1957; Thompson and Hollien, 1970; Fourcin, 1972; Ainsworth 1972, 1975; Summerfield, 1975; Fujisaki, Nakamura, and Imoto, 1975).

Perceptual normalization on speech rate

Several investigators have presented evidence for perceptual normalization on speech rate. As described above, it has been shown that the phonemic perception of vowel duration in the identification of English vowel phonemes can be affected by changing the rhythm of a sequence of synthetic vowels in which the test vowel is embedded (Ainsworth, 1972). Likewise, the point of transition of the voiced-voiceless distinction in English prevocalic stop consonants shifts as a function of the speech rate in the preceding part of the utterance (Summerfield, 1975). The phoneme boundary between Japanese long and short phonemes appears to be a linear function of the speech rate of the utterance of which the test segment is a part (Fujisaki, Nakamura, and Imoto, 1975).

Local speech rate and backward perceptual normalization

In all the above cases, different overall speech rates in utterances were compared to ascertain their effects on phoneme identification. Speech rate (i.e. the rapidity with which consonant-like and vowel-like acoustic segments follow each other in time) may, however, vary within utterances from one part of the utterance to the next. In such cases we will speak of *local speech rate.* Changes in local speech rate often result from systematic contextual variation in syllable durations. Such contextual variation is in most cases anticipatory. For example, an initially stressed syllable of a word, other things being equal, will be physically shortened as a function of the number of syllables coming later in the word (Roudet, 1910; Nooteboom, 1972; Lindblom, 1975). The same is true of the stressed initial syllable of a phrase (Lindblom, 1975; Nooteboom and Cohen, 1975). Syllables which immediately precede major syntactic breaks are often physically lengthened, whether or not the syntactic break is marked by a speech pause (Klatt, 1975; Huggins, 1975b).

In these cases the local context affecting the spoken duration of a particular syllable, and of the segments constituting that syllable, comes after the syllable concerned. If a listener is to use this context in perceptual normalization he will have to delay his phonemic perception of the segment duration until the arrival of the acoustic information which follows. We shall refer to this fact as *backward perceptual normalization.*

Backward perceptual normalization in isolated words

Evidence for backward perceptual normalization, both within a syllable and over more than one syllable, has been obtained in a binary, forced-choice listening test in which response percentages of identification of Dutch short /a/ and long /a:/ were measured as a function of acoustic vowel duration (Nooteboom, 1975). The same set of test stimuli, consisting of spectrally homogeneous and monotonous vowel segments with durations varying in steps of 5 msec, from 60 to 130 msec, was embedded in six different contexts; as shown in Figure 2.5.

The context frames were obtained by removing an initial vowel /aː/ from recordings of naturally spoken words. The stop closure duration of /t/ in conditions (3) to (6) was kept constant at 80 msec.

On the basis of acoustic measurements of similar speech material it was predicted that if backward perceptual normalization were to take place, response distributions would shift towards shorter durations from context condition (1) to (6) in the order given. The results are presented in Figure 2.5.

We calculated separately the standard deviations in milliseconds of the distributions of phoneme boundaries (50% points) for the ten subjects in each context condition. The mean values found for mean phoneme boundaries and their standard deviations (in parentheses) in conditions (1) to (6) are respectively $\bar{X} = 100$ (s = 8.4); 97 (6.7); 91 (6.9); 88 (5.8); 85 (5.5); and 83 (4.3) msec. It is of interest that differences between subjects decrease considerably as more context becomes available.

From the results presented in Figure 2.5 we may conclude that the perception of vowel duration, at least if the vowel segment is ambiguous as to its phonemic perception, is systematically affected by some aspect of the local context which follows. It is noteworthy that in conditions (3) to (6) the acoustic information following the test vowel differs only after the /t/- closure: the phoneme

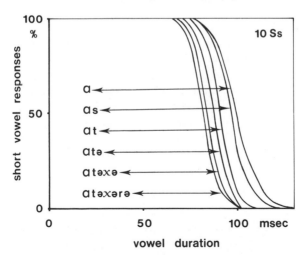

Figure 2.5. Percentage of short vowel responses as a function of vowel duration in six different context conditions. Response distributions of individual subjects were averaged after normalization on the mean of individual 50% transition points

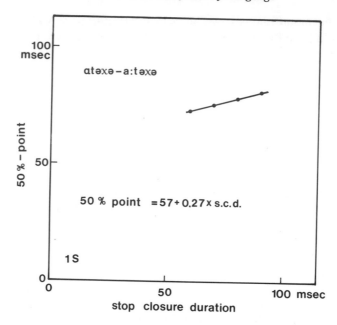

Figure 2.6. Fifty per cent crossover points in milliseconds of short versus long vowel responses as a function of the stop closure duration immediately following the stimulus vowel

identification in these cases appears to be based on the acoustic information distributed over the syllable containing the test vowel plus the following syllable. The effect of the /t/- stop closure duration was investigated separately in a nonsense word (cf. Figure 2.6). The phoneme boundary between /a/ and /a:/ in this frame word was measured in four conditions, viz. with /t/ - stop closure durations of 60, 70, 80, and 90 msec. Results are presented in Figure 2.6. The positive linear relationship between the duration of the postvocalic silent interval and the phoneme boundary confirms our hypothesis that local speech rate is a determining factor in backward perceptual normalization.

Backward perceptual normalization in sentences

In a further experiment we attempted to show that perceptual normalization may reflect contextual regularities due to the syntactic position of a word in a sentence. We measured response distributions of the vowels in the Dutch words /tak/ (branch) and /ta:k/ (task).

The following two frame sentences were used:

(1) *Kees kreeg een nieuwe t-k*
    (Kees got a new --)

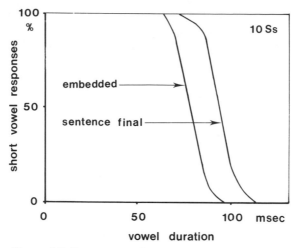

Figure 2.7. Percentage of short vowel responses as a function of vowel duration in two context conditions, viz. sentence final and embedded. Response distributions of individual subjects were averaged after normalization on the mean of individual 50% transition points

(2) *Kees kreeg een nieuwe t-k op zijn schouders*
    (Kees got a new -- on his shoulders)

The acoustic realization of the first frame sentence was obtained by removing the final phrase of a recording of the second sentence. The latter was spoken by a male speaker in a normal voice with rather unobtrusive intonation. Both frame sentences sounded like perfectly normal speech. We thus ensured that the speech material preceding the test vowel was identical in both conditions. Let us call the first frame sentence the *final condition*, and the second the *embedded condition*.

An identical set of /a/-like vowel segments was used for constructing stimulus sentences by inserting each vowel segment between /t/ and /k/ in both frame sentences. This was done by means of a computer facility for editing the speech-wave form. Figure 2.7 presents identification functions in both context conditions.

The average values of phoneme boundaries and the standard deviations in milliseconds of the distributions of these phoneme boundaries over ten listeners were, (a) final condition $\overline{X} = 94$ (s = 6.7) msec; (b) embedded condition: $\overline{X} = 79$ (s = 3.4) msec. It could be argued that the shift in phoneme boundary is caused by a difference in semantic probability of the words 'taak' and 'tak' in the two sentences. Alternatively, it is possible that the shift is brought about by an adjustment to the acoustic information which follows; that is, a rather long /k/

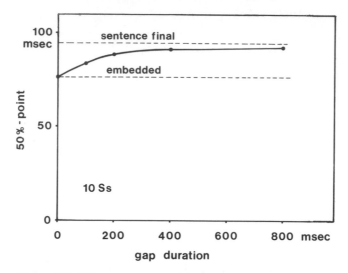

Figure 2.8. Fifty per cent transition points in milliseconds of short vowel responses in the words /tak/ versus /ta:k/ embedded in a sentence as a function of the duration of a gap introduced after the /k/ — noise burst. The interrupted lines indicate the values of 50% transition points in the two conditions of Figure 2.7

plus silence in the sentence final condition, and a short /k/ plus a rather brief syllable /op/ in the embedded condition.

If the latter hypothesis is correct we expect that a shift in phoneme boundary might be obtained by changing temporal aspects of the immediate environment without changing the recognition of the frame sentence and its meaning. In the frame sentence used for the embedded condition we introduced a silent gap between the /k/ of /t-k/ and the rest of the sentence. The silent gap could have one of the following durations: 0, 100, 200, 400, and 800 msec. The /a/-/a:/ phoneme boundary was measured for each of these five silent-gap durations. Results are presented in Figure 2.8. It may be seen that a silent-gap duration of approximately 200 msec is sufficient to obtain a phoneme boundary which is nearly identical to the one measured in sentence final condition. From the onset of the test vowel to the end of the 200 msec gap, a time interval of about 350 msec elapses. Thus the time-span over which perceptual normalization can take place comprises at least this much.

Conclusions

The above data show that a listener's phonemic perception of vowel duration can be systematically affected by the acoustic structure of the sound environment which follows the vowel segment. We have called this phenomenon backward perceptual normalization. We do not know the size of the time-span over which such perceptual normalization may take place, but it appears to be at least of the order of 350 msec. Within the aims of this chapter we are satisfied to show that one particular aspect of speech prosody, namely local speech rate, can contribute to recognition of segmental information. Apparently phonemic perception may depend on temporal aspects of the surrounding speech which derive from speech prosody. This may be a marginal contribution of prosody to speech perception. In the next section we will discuss some possibly more important contributions of prosody to recognition of lexical and syntactical information.

PROSODIC CUES TO LEXICAL AND SYNTACTIC STRUCTURES

Prosody in speech synthesis by rule

An important source of data concerning the perceptual relevance of prosodic structures is provided by work on systems for *speech synthesis by rule*. Such systems accept a discrete representation of utterances in the form of sequences of phonemic symbols plus some additional symbols at their input and generate speech wave-forms at their output. It appears that the 'naturalness' or 'acceptability' of the resulting speech is improved considerably by applying prosodic rules. In itself this is not enough to show that prosodic information contributes essentially to perception of lexical and syntactic information.

However, since the prosodic structures which appear to be necessary in synthesized speech reflect aspects of the lexical and syntactic structure of the messages, an analysis of some of the factors of such structures may give some indication of the contribution of prosody to the processing of lexical and syntactic information in the perception of sentences. Therefore, it seems worthwhile to indicate briefly what aspects of lexical and syntactic structure are reflected in the temporal organization and pitch contours of synthetically generated connected speech.

Rule systems for the temporal organization of speech

One of the results of work on speech synthesis has been that speech scientists have begun to realize that one cannot synthesize acceptable connected speech without carefully shaping the temporal organization of speech by an intricate set of rules generating correct durations for all acoustic segments. Most of the finer details covered by these rules relate to the segmental structure of the message. There are also a number of rather gross and perceptually fairly conspicuous effects which must be dealt with by prosodic rules (Mattingly, 1966; Allen, 1968; Flanagan, Coker, Rabiner, Schafer, and Umeda, 1970; Klatt, 1975; Barnwell,

1971; Slis, 1971; Nooteboom, Slis, and Willems, 1973; Carlson and Granström, 1973, 1975; Lindblom, 1975). For example, the acoustic segments, particularly the vowels, of lexically stressed syllables have to be made considerably longer than acoustic segments of unstressed syllables, other things being equal. Segments belonging to syllables immediately preceding a prosodic boundary have to be physically lengthened. A prosodic boundary is perceived as a 'break' or 'rest' in the flow of speech, signalled by syllable lengthening, which can be, but is not necessarily, followed by a speech pause. An additional cue to the prosodic boundary is often provided by the pitch contour. Prosodic boundaries are generally made to coincide with major syntactic boundaries: adequate temporal organization of speech can only be achieved when the rules have access to the syntactic surface structure of the messages to be synthesized (cf. Klatt, 1975; Lindblom, 1975); however, there appears to be a certain amount of freedom in choosing which syntactic boundaries are prosodically marked and which are not

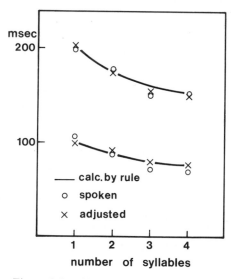

Figure 2.9. Effect of number of syllables in the word on the duration of the vowel in the stressed word's initial syllable, in existing Dutch words. The vowel was either long (/a:/) or short (/a/). The solid lines refer to durations calculated by rule; the open circles to average durations in versions of the words spoken by three Dutch speakers, the crosses to average durations preferred by the same three subjects and found in an adjustment experiment with synthesized versions of the same words (cf. Nooteboom, 1972)

(Klatt, 1975; Collier and 't Hart, 1975). Apparently, in normal speech, syntactic boundaries can be perceived in the absence of prosodic boundaries, and prosodic boundaries do not always coincide with syntactic boundaries.

In addition to these effects there are durational rules for physical shortening of segments, most conspicuously of stressed vowels, as a function of the number of syllables preceding and following within the word and within the phrase. Especially, the number of syllables coming later in the word or phrase has a decreasing effect on segment durations (Klatt, 1975, Lindblom, 1975).

For American English it has also been felt necessary to include rules which lengthen syllables immediately preceding morpheme boundaries (Barnwell, 1971). In some rule systems all segment durations in words which are felt to be semantically important are lengthened (e.g. Slis, 1971). All rule systems described in the literature referred to in this section generate speech wave-forms which conspicuously reflect lexical and syntactic aspects of the message. The data on which the rules are based mainly stem from measurements of real speech and informal evaluation of the perceptual results of proposed rules for synthesized speech.

A more systematic evaluation of the rules can be obtained by asking naïve listeners to adjust the control settings for speech-segment duration in a synthesized utterance until the resulting speech sounds acceptable to them. An example of the results of such a test on the duration of the vowel in the stressed initial syllable of Dutch words with different numbers of syllables is provided in Figure 2.9. The referred durations are averaged over ten trials of each of three subjects and presented together with the durations measured in spoken realizations, and with those generated by rule.

Rule systems for pitch contours

We will restrict our discussion of rule systems for pitch contours to such so-called intonation languages as the Germanic and Romanic languages and Japanese. In one way, the derivation of satisfactory rule systems for generating pitch contours is more difficult than developing systems for the temporal organization of speech. In normal speech, pitch is often hard to measure, and in those cases where it can be realiably measured we often find capricious fluctuations which are not easy to relate to perceived intonation or 'speech melody'.

Fortunately, however, it can be shown that most of the actual pitch fluctuations found in real speech are not relevant to the perception of speech melody. If the actual pitch of an utterance is replaced by a highly sylized pitch contour, the perceived speech melody is not changed (Collier and 't Hart, 1972). An example of a measured and a stylized pitch contour of a Dutch sentence, perceptually equivalent as far as speech melody is concerned, is presented in Figure 2.10. This perceptual equivalence between actual pitch fluctuations and stylized pitch contours has made it feasible to describe the intonation patterns of

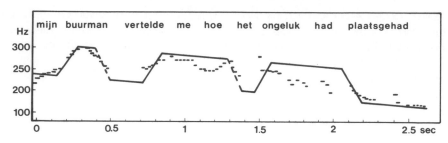

Figure 2.10. An actual pitch contour of a Dutch sentence, spoken by a female, as measured by a method of perceptual pitch matching (cf. Cohen and 't Hart, 1967), and a stylized pitch contour giving the same melodic impression

Dutch by means of a limited set of perceptually relevant pitch movements, mainly differing in direction and timing within the syllable, and in most cases superimposed on a gradually declining pitch (Cohen and 't Hart, 1967; 't Hart and Cohen, 1973; 't Hart and Collier, 1975). A basically similar approach has been or is being applied to a number of other languages, such as Swedish (Carlson and Granström, 1973; Lindblom, 1975), Japanese (Fujisaki and Sudo, 1971), American English (Maeda, 1974), and French (Vaissière, 1974).

Once a 'basic intonation pattern' (cf. Collier and 't Hart, 1972) has been chosen, the information which has to be forwarded to the system of rules for generating correct pitch contours consists of the number and location of accents and the location of prosodic boundaries. Pitch accents always fall on lexically stressed syllables, but not all stressed syllables receive a pitch accent. The rules for determining which do and which do not have not yet been formulated. We will return to this problem in the final section of the chapter.

We may safely say that proper pitch contours, like proper temporal organization, reflect lexical and syntactic properties of the message. Whether this prosodic information actually contributes to perception will be considered separately.

Prosodic cues to the perception of lexical stress and accent

A number of investigations have been directed towards the relative contribution of intensity, duration, and pitch to perceived stress. A general conclusion is that whereas intensity is not a very powerful cue to stress, vowel duration and pitch height or pitch movement can easily result in stress perception, pitch being the stronger of the two (e.g. Fry, 1958; Rigault, 1962; Jassem, Morton and Steffen-Batóg, 1968; Janota, 1970). A problem with these results is that lexical stress and accent are not distinguished. As early as 1958 Bolinger emphasized the need for a distinction between these two. In languages such as English and Dutch the general cue to lexical stress appears to be either syllable or vowel duration.

The most powerful cue to the perception of accent appears to be not an increase in pitch level, as often believed, but rather a rapid pitch rise, pitch fall, or combination of the two (Bolinger, 1958; Cohen and 't Hart, 1967; 't Hart and Cohen, 1973). It has also been shown that the timing of pitch movement with respect to vowel onset and end is particularly important to accent perception. For instance a rise has to be early in the vowel, a fall late in the vowel (Collier, 1972; Van Katwijk, 1974). The perception of a particular pitch movement in an utterance as an accent can be influenced by its position in the overall pitch contour (Van Katwijk, 1974).

Prosodic cues to syntactic boundary perception

We earlier mentioned that prosodic boundaries, which often coincide with syntactic boundaries, can be marked by syllable lengthening, speech pauses, and particular pitch contours. These cues often occur at the same time in normal speech. It may be of interest to see whether one of these cues alone is sufficient to bring about detection of a syntactic boundary. It has been shown that Dutch listeners, when presented with synthesized and carefully intonated auditory patterns consisting of sequences of 13 or 15 identical vowel-like signals of 200 msec, separated by pauses of 50 msec, can reliably hear a drop in pitch occurring early in one of the vowel sounds as a cue to syntactic boundary perception. The listeners' task was to think of sentences which would fit the pitch contour. In the great majority of cases the position of the major syntactic boundary in these sentences immediately preceded the fall in pitch (Collier and 't Hart, 1975).

Because we know that in normal speech a perceived prosodic boundary does not always coincide with a syntactic boundary, we can best interpret the results of Collier and 't Hart as follows. Apparently listeners are, in the absence of other prosodic cues, willing to perceive particular pitch movements as prosodic boundary markers. In the absence of lexical and syntactic information in the stimulus they prefer to think of sentences which have a syntactic boundary in the same position as the perceived prosodic boundary.

In further attempts to specify the relationship between acoustic attributes of speech and the perception of prosodic boundaries, we have recently made a few perceptual experiments to investigate the relative contribution of different types of acoustic cues to prosodic boundary perception. We used an ambiguous Dutch sentence, analogous to the following English sentence:

(3) The queen said the knight is a monster

which, depending on the location of prosodic boundaries, can be perceived as meaning either that the knight calls the queen or that the queen calls the knight a monster.

Reading 1: 'The queen', said the knight, 'is a monster.'
Reading 2: The queen said, 'the knight is a monster'.

A spoken version of a similar sentence was processed by means of a computer-controlled channel vocoder, which enabled us to vary both pitch contour and segmental durations at will (Willems and De Jong, 1974).

In informal listening we observed that introducing acoustic pauses without physical lengthening of the preceding syllables results in unacceptable speech. The perceptual effect is much like listening to someone with a speech handicap. We therefore decided that it was not meaningful to study the independent effect of acoustic pause and concentrated on the relative importance of pitch movements and syllable lengthening, which could be varied independently without unacceptable results. Acoustic pauses were not used at all.

In a first experiment we removed fluctations in pitch to study the effect of syllable lengthening alone. We constructed seven versions of the utterance, the first and seventh version having, with respect to the vowel duration in the three preboundary syllables, the durational organization of normally spoken

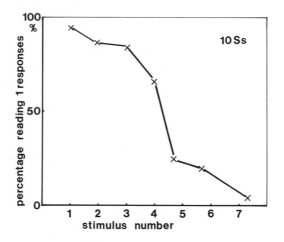

Figure 2.11. Percentage of reading 1 responses as a function of the vowel durations in the potential preboundary syllables in an ambiguous Dutch word sequence 'Daan zei de baas is te laat'. Reading 1: 'Daan, zei de baas, is te laat'; Reading 2: 'Daan zei, de baas is te laat'. Stimulus number 1: 1st vowel 258, 2nd vowel 130, 3rd vowel 230 msec; Stimulus number 7: 1st vowel 165, 2nd vowel 178, 3rd vowel 175 msec. Other stimulus numbers had in-between values for these three vowel durations. All other segment durations were equal in all stimuli

realizations of the two sentence readings and the others having intermediate values of the three relevant vowel durations. These stimulus sentences were presented to ten listeners in random order, ten times each, for identification of the sentence meaning. The results are presented in Figure 2.11. We see that changing the durations of only the three preboundary vowels in the utterance may reliably alter its perception. In a second experiment, we investigated the relative contribution of each of the three vowel durations to sentence perception by varying only one of the vowel durations at a time, keeping the other two at a value corresponding to the 50% transition point in Figure 2.11. The results are presented in Figure 2.12. It may be seen that the first and the second of the three preboundary vowels are equally effective. The third has no effect at all, possibly because by the time the subject hears the third vowel, his perception has already been fully determined by the other two.

In a third experiment we gave all three vowels durations corresponding to the 50% transition point in Figure 2.11, thus obtaining a durational structure containing no information on the intended sentence reading. We then introduced pitch contours corresponding to several types of normal intonation of the two readings. Two types of pitch movement were investigated as to their effect on sentence perception: a pitch fall immediately following a potential boundary, and a pitch rise immediately preceding a potential boundary. Both types of pitch movement equally affected sentence perception, but no stimulus sentence gave a better score of predicted responses than 80%.

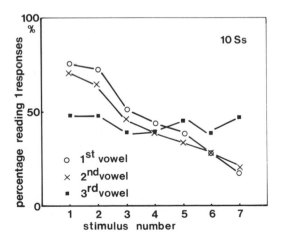

Figure 2.12. As Figure 2.11, but here vowel durations in the potential preboundary syllables were varied one at a time, the other two having values corresponding to the estimated 50% transition point in Figure 2.11

This suggests that the pitch movements we used are less effective than syllable lengthening as prosodic boundary markers. This was confirmed in a subsequent fourth experiment in which we introduced conflicting cues, namely the syllable lengthening of one reading and pitch cues of the other. In this experiment syllable lengthening gave a correct score of 90%, thus easily overriding the cue value of the pitch movements.

We have no reason to believe that there are other types of pitch movements in Dutch intonation which specifically serve as cues to prosodic boundaries and are more effective than the ones we studied. However, this may not be the whole story of the relative contribution of temporal cues and pitch cues to perceptual sentence segmentation. It seems possible to us that the location of accents, which in perception is determined by the pitch contours, may favour a particular segmentation of the sentence. In a sentence such as (3)

(3) The queen said the knight is a monster

pitch accents on *queen* and *monster* and absence of pitch accents on *said* and *knight* seem to favour a monster-queen. This has still to be tested.

Prosody and perceptual confusions

Another type of data bearing on the lexical and syntactic information listeners may extract from speech prosody stems from perceptual confusions in recognition tasks with distorted speech or speech-like auditory patterns. Kozhevnikov and Chistovich (1965) presented listeners with utterances of 3 to 12 syllables. The utterances were spectrally distorted by narrowband filtering, and were therefore difficult to understand. This resulted in perceptual confusions. It was found that in these confusions the correct number of syllables and the correct stress placements were often preserved.

The perceptual relevance of such prosodic variables is demonstrated in misperceptions occurring in the reading aloud of English by Indian speakers. When in these realizations stress placement was wrong, this prosodic feature tended to override segmental information in recognition by native speakers of English (Bansal, 1966 cited by Huggins, 1972). Kozhevnikov and Chistovich also observed that word boundaries were often not preserved in perceptual confusions. This is supported by the difficulty in discrimination between pairs like 'the grey tie' versus 'the great eye' (O'Connor and Tooley, 1964). Apparently word boundaries are often not acoustically marked by the speaker. In perceptual confusions occurring in recognition of connected speech distorted by spectral rotation, the distinction between grammatical function words and content words is often retained, probably because function words differ acoustically from content words by having shorter segment durations and lower intensity due to lack of word stress (Blesser, 1969). Similar results have been reported on the perception of hummed phrases (Svensson, 1974).

Some data of our own indicate that major syntactic boundaries more often than not are correctly perceived in spectrally scrambled utterances containing no speech pauses. Accents are nearly always correctly perceived in such distorted speech (de Rooij, 1975). These data indicate that speech prosody puts heavy constraints on the perception of speech with a low degree of intelligibility, by carrying information on lexical and syntactic aspects of the intended messages.

Conclusion

In this section we have presented data bearing on the relationship between prosodic attributes of speech and the perceived lexical and syntactic structure of messages. It has been shown that the pitch contour carries information on the location of accents and major syntactic boundaries. The temporal organization of speech is relevant to the perception of the number of syllables in words and phrases, the location of lexical stresses, and the location of major syntactic boundaries.

We have not discussed the degree in which such prosodic information is relevant to normal spontaneous speech perception. Nor have we dealt with the ways in which listeners can profit from speech prosody in perception. We will return to these issues in the next section.

DISCUSSION

In the preceding sections we have presented three types of experimental data relating to possible contributions of speech prosody to speech perception, dealing with prosodic continuity, perceptual normalization, and prosodic cues to lexical and syntactic structures respectively. In this final section we will attempt to outline some implications of these data for a better understanding of the perception of connected speech.

The primacy of prosodic continuity

Speech prosody is a conveniently broad term, covering a number of perceived aspects of connected speech. It traditionally includes the following:

(a) the *temporal segmentation* of speech in segments, often corresponding to whole word groups, separated by pauses or 'rests' in the flow of speech;

(b) the *intonation* or melody of speech;

(c) speech *rhythm*, that is the subjective grouping of syllables owing to differences in perceptual prominences of successive syllables;

(d) the *rate* of speech, that is the rapidity with which syllables follow each other in time;

(e) fluctuations in overall *loudness* of speech; and

(f) the *subjective quality* of the speaker's voice.

All these perceptual aspects of speech presuppose that the auditory events which together form the speech we listen to are perceived as belonging together, forming coherent auditory patterns suitable for further processing. Prosodic aspects of speech are then specific perceptual properties of such coherent auditory patterns. If sequences of speech-like auditory events are perceived as coherent auditory events, we say that they exhibit *prosodic continuity*. Prosodic continuity is a *conditio sine qua non* for the perception of speech prosody.

As we have shown in the second section of this paper, the presence or absence of prosodic continuity in syllable sequences is determined by the acoustic structure of sequences of syllables. The most important variable appears to be the jump in pitch from one syllable to the next. It seems reasonable to conclude that the relatively smooth fluctuations in pitch that we find in normal speech contribute to the perceived prosodic continuity.

A listener's ability to hear sequences of speech-like auditory events as either having or not having prosodic continuity is probably essential to his ability to perceive speech at all, for at least two reasons. It helps him in the perceptual integration of different speech sounds into meaningful patterns, and it enables him to sort out speech sounds emitted by different speakers simultaneously: if one were to perceive each sequence of speech sounds as prosodically continuous, it would probably be very difficult to attend to one voice in the presence of other voices. The sounds from different voices would fuse into an unintelligible stream of sound.

The relationship between our perceptual data on rather simple sound sequences and normal perception of speech masked by speech should be further explored. Particularly, data on the perception of simultaneous speech sounds are lacking. One may note, however, that our data show that if the successive sounds follow one other with no silent gaps in between, then only a small jump in pitch is sufficient to bring about stream segregation. This suggests that if we listen to two speakers simultaneously slight differences in pitch are sufficient to permit us to separate the voices.

Interactions between prosody and phoneme perception

Once a sequence of speech sounds is heard as prosodically continuous, these speech sounds can be perceptually integrated into patterns, perceived on the one hand as ordered sequences of discrete units such as phonemes, morphemes, and words, and on the other as non-discrete prosodic structures such as intonation, rhythm, and speech rate.

These two layers of perceptual aspects of speech appear not to be independent. In the third section we presented some data showing that phoneme perception can be systematically affected by the immediate prosodic environment. It seems to us particularly interesting that the effect of prosody or phoneme perception in our data is backward, that is from later to earlier, although the time-span involved is not necessarily much longer than a few hundred milliseconds. Apparently the perception of an ambiguous phoneme segment can be delayed somewhat and affected by prosodic information coming later in time. In this case the perception of a prosodic aspect of speech, local speech rate, seems to precede phonemic perception in the perceptual process. We do not imply that this is necessarily always the case. We would predict that it is possible to construct experimental situations in which phonemic perception would affect prosodic perception, thereby suggesting an inverse ordering of perceptual decisions.

Lexical, syntactic, and semantic cues from prosody

The contribution of specific prosodic aspects of speech to phoneme perception is possibly only marginal. Prosodic patterning may be more important to the perception of lexical and syntactic aspects of the messages. Connected speech appears to be perceptually segmented in coherent groups of syllables of limited length. The number of syllables and the alternation between more and less prominent syllables are conspicuous aspects of such groups. Prominent syllables are fairly consistently heard as lexically stressed syllables; and although word boundaries often appear not to be prosodically marked, the location of stressed syllables plus the number of syllables puts heavy constraints on the perception of lexical units within the syllable group.

Prominence of a syllable leading to the perception of lexical stress is mainly brought about by syllable lengthening. Some of the prominent syllables are additionally marked by a conspicuous pitch movement, perceived as accent. While it may be an additional cue to lexical stress, the main perceptual function of accent seems not so much to be its contribution to word recognition. Unfortunately, the relation between the location of accents and the linguistic aspects of the message has not yet been studied systematically. Our present guess is that it serves to indicate both syntactic grouping and, perhaps more importantly, semantic aspects of the message, particularly the opposition between 'given' and 'new' information (cf. Chafe, 1974). The absence of accents on content words seems to indicate that the speaker presupposes the semantic information contained in these words to be known by the listener ('given information'). The presence of an accent indicates presupposedly 'new' semantic information.

Prosodic boundaries and a perceptual strategy

The segmentation of the speech stream into the syllable groups discussed above is brought about by prosodic boundaries signalled by speech pauses, lengthening of the preboundary syllable, and particular pitch movements. There appear to be two main types of prosodic boundaries, those indicating the end of a message and those indicating that the message will continue in the next syllable grouping. These continuation boundaries often coincide with major syntactic boundaries. However, the location of prosodic boundaries in normal speech appears not to be fully predictable from the syntactic structure of the message.

Firstly 'major syntactic boundaries' is not a well-defined concept; secondly, we find that the prosodic marking of syntactic boundaries in speech is often optional; and thirdly, one may often observe prosodic boundaries which clearly do not correspond to major syntactic boundaries. The regularities in speech behaviour leading to the production of prosodic boundaries need further study. It seems likely to us that the production of prosodic boundaries depends on syntactic, semantic, and short-term memory factors. On the perception side we may ask how listeners operate with prosodic boundaries.

If prosodic boundaries contribute to perception of syntactic surface structure in speech perception, we may expect that recognition can be hampered when prosodic boundaries occur in the wrong places. It has been shown that if prosodic boundaries are misplaced with respect to syntactic boundaries, recognition may suffer, at least in artificially speeded-up speech (Wingfield, 1975). In recognizing sentences with conflicting prosodic and syntactic boundaries, listeners make more perceptual errors within one word on either side of the prosodically suggested boundary when this boundary precedes the major syntactic boundary than when it follows it (Darwin, 1975). A possible explanation of this finding is that prosody is constantly used in the on-going perception of the sentences searching for the expected syntactic boundary. When this syntactic boundary has been found, with or without prosodic aids, prosodic boundary markers are further discarded by the listeners. This strategy would easily lead to finding two conflicting boundaries when the prosodic boundary precedes the syntactic one, but not in the reverse case. This may be related to the finding of Collier and 't Hart that their subjects, asked to think of sentences fitting a particular pitch contour, often placed the major syntactic boundary earlier in the sentence than the intonationally suggested boundary, but very rarely later (Collier and 't Hart, 1975).

Speech rhythm and anticipation of lexical items

In this discussion we have hitherto dealt only with specific contributions of prosodic patterns to speech perception. We will now briefly discuss a more general, potentially important contribution of prosody to speech perception, relating to the general effect of speech rhythm on word recognition in connected speech. It has been suggested that the major role of rhythmic patterns in speech is to optimize the analysis of the more informative parts of the signals, the stressed syllables, by anticipation of their arrival time on the basis of the immediately preceding elements of the rhythmic pattern (Martin, 1972). A problem with Martin's rather abstract model of rhythmical patterning is that it is hard to relate to what we know about temporal patterns in speech. We would suggest that anticipation of relative arrival times of stressed syllables, or any other syllables, is only possible when two conditions are fulfilled: firstly, the listener should have anticipated the lexical items about to be said by the speaker; and secondly, he should have anticipated the particular time-course of the speaker's realization of these lexical items. It has recently been shown that listeners do indeed anticipate lexical items on the basis of an on-line analysis of preceding lexical, syntactic, and semantic information (Marslen-Wilson and Tyler, 1975). It is yet to be investigated whether listeners also use prosodic, and in particular rhythmic, information in the preceding speech mateial in order to facilitate recognition of anticipated lexical items. If this could be demonstrated, it would be an indication that the auditory image of the anticipated material is adjusted to the particular rhythmic pattern of the attended speech utterance.

CONCLUSION

This chapter is empirically rather than theoretically oriented. We have presented experimental data on the relation between the acoustic structure of speech and speech-like signals, on the one hand, and a number of perceived properties of speech on the other. We have also attempted to relate these data to the normal perception of connected speech. The picture of speech perception arising from the observations and speculations in this paper may be briefly summarized as follows: (a) The presence of prosodic continuity is a precondition for speech perception; (b) prosodic patterns contribute to the on-line perception of phonemic, lexical, syntactic, and semantic information. We have not discussed the potential contribution of speech prosody to the perception of individual traits of the speaker, attitudinal information (including questions, statements, and exclamations), regional dialect, and foreign accent. Our data and considerations do not go beyond inter-individual aspects of the perception of neutral descriptive messages in the standard language. Within these limits we feel safe to conclude that (a) theories of speech perception limiting the role of the acoustic wave-form of speech to supplying cues for phoneme perception will not be very successful; and (b) theories of sentence perception not taking into account the contributions of speech prosody are bound to fail with respect to auditorily presented sentences.

SUMMARY

In this chapter three types of empirical data illustrating contributions of prosody to speech perception were presented and discussed. The first type of data was concerned with the perception of the prosodic continuity of the attended voice. A sequence of speech sounds may or may not be heard as a continuous stream of speech produced by a single voice. It was shown that both continuity in periodicity pitch and continuity in spectral composition contribute to perceived prosodic continuity.

The second type of data relates to the contribution of speech rate in the immediate contextual environment of a test segment to the phonemic perception of this segment as a short or a long phoneme. The results can be explained by assuming the existence of backward perceptual normalization of segment duration to the temporal structure of auditory information, which comes later in time.

The third type of evidence relates to the relevance of prosody to the perception of specific linguistic information. Speech prosody potentially carries information on lexical, syntactic, and semantic aspects of the message. A number of investigations in addition to our own show that listeners may actually use this information if it is useful for linguistic processing.

ACKNOWLEDGEMENTS

We gratefully acknowledge the assistance of Mr G. Doodeman in running the experiments on backward perceptual normalization.

Thanks are also due to those of our colleagues in the IPO who read an earlier version of this paper and suggested many improvements. We are particularly grateful to Professor B. H. Leshowitz for his critical comments. Part of the work reported in this paper was supported by the Netherlands Organization for the Advancement of Pure Research (ZWO).

REFERENCES

Ainsworth, W. A. Duration as a cue in the recognition of synthetic vowels. *Journal of the Acoustical Society of America*, 1972, **51**, 648–651.

Ainsworth, W. A. Intrinsic and extrinsic factors in vowel judgments. In G. Fant and M. A. A. Tatham (Eds.), *Auditory analysis and perception of speech*. New York: Academic Press, 1975.

Allen, J. A study of the specification of prosodic features of speech from a grammatical analysis of printed text. Unpublished Ph.D. Dissertation, M.I.T., Cambridge, Mass., 1968.

Bansal, R. K. The intelligibility of Indian English: measurements of the intelligibility of connected speech, and sentence and word material presented to listeners of different nationalities. Unpublished Ph.D. Dissertation, London University, 1966.

Barnwell, T. P. An algorithm for segment duration in a reading machine context. *Research Laboratory of Electronics, M.I.T. Cambridge, Mass. Technical Report No. 479*, 1971.

Blesser, B. Perception of spectrally rotated speech. Unpublished Ph.D. Dissertation, M.I.T., Cambridge, Mass., 1969.

Bolinger, D. L. A theory of pitch accent in English. *Word*, 1958, **14**, 109–149.

Bregman, A. S. and Campbell, J. Primary auditory stream segregation and perception of order in rapid sequences of tones. *Journal of Experimental Psychology*, 1971, **89**, 244–249.

Bregman, A. S. and Dannenbring, G. L. The effect of continuity on auditory stream segregation. *Perception and Psychophysics*, 1973, **13**, 308–312.

Carlson, R. and Granström, B. Word accent, emphatic stress, and syntax in a synthesis by rule scheme for Swedish. *Speech Transmission Laboratory Stockholm, Quarterly Progress Report*, 1973, **2-3**, 31–36.

Carlson, R. and Granström, B. A phonetically oriented programming language for rule description of speech. *Speech Communication*, Vol. 2. Stockholm: Almqvist & Wiksell, 1975.

Chafe, W. L. Language and consciousness. *Language*, 1974, **50**, 111–133.

Cherry, E. C. Some experiments on the recognition of speech, with one and with two ears. *Journal of the Acoustical Society of America*, 1953, **25**, 975–979.

Cohen, A. and 't Hart, J. On the anatomy of intonation. *Lingua*, 1967, **19**, 177–192.

Cole, R. A. and Scott, B. Perception of temporal order in speech: The role of vowel transitions. *Canadian Journal of Psychology*, 1973, **27**, 441–449.

Collier, R. From pitch to intonation. Unpublished Ph.D. Dissertation, University of Louvain, 1972.

Collier, R. and 't Hart, J. Perceptual experiments on Dutch intonation. In A. Rigault and R. Charbonneau (Eds.), *Proceedings of the VIIth International Congress of Phonetic Sciences*. Montreal 1971. The Hague: Mouton, 1972.

Collier, R. and 't Hart, J. The role of intonation in speech perception. In A. Cohen and S. G. Nooteboom (Eds.), *Structure and process in speech perception*. Berlin, Heidelberg, New York: Springer Verlag, 1975.

Darwin, C. J. On the dynamic use of prosody in speech perception. In A. Cohen and S. G. Nooteboom (Eds.), *Structure and process in speech perception*. Berlin, Heidelberg New York: Springer Verlag, 1975.

De Rooij, J. J. Prosody and the perception of syntactic boundaries. *Institute for Perception Research, Eindhoven, Annual Progress Report*, 1975, **10**, 36–39.

Dorman, M. F., Cutting, J., and Raphael, L. J. Perception of temporal order in vowel sequences with and without formant transitions. *Journal of Experimental Psychology: Human Perception and Performance*, 1975, **1**, 121–129.

Flanagan, J. L., Coker, C. H., Rabiner, L. R., Schafer, R. W., and Umeda, N. Synthetic voices for computers. *I.E.E.E. Spectrum 7*, 1970, **10**, 22–45.

Fourcin, A. J. Perceptual mechanisms at the first level of speech processing. In A. Rigault and R. Charbonneau (Eds.), *Proceedings of the VIIth International Congress of Phonetic Sciences. Montreal*, 1971, The Hague: Mouton, 1972.

Fry, D. H. Experiments in the perception of stress. *Language and Speech*, 1958, **1**, 126–152.

Fujisaki, H., Nakamua, K., and Imoto, J. Auditory perception of duration of speech and non-speech stimuli. In G. Fant and M. A. A. Tatham (Eds.), *Auditory analysis and perception of speech*. New York: Academic Press, 1975.

Halle, M. and Stevens, K. N. Speech recognition: A model and a program for research. *IRE Transactions PGIT,* IT-8, 1962, 155–159.

Hart, J. 't and Cohen, A. Intonation by rule: A perceptual quest. *Journal of Phonetics*, 1973, **1**, 309–327.

Hart, J. 't and Collier, R. Integrating different levels of intonation analysis. *Journal of Phonetics*, 1975, **3**, 235–255.

Huggins, A. W. F. On the perception of temporal phenomena in speech. *Journal of the Acoustical Society of America*, 1972, **51**, 1279–1290.

Huggins, A. W. F. Temporally segmented speech and 'echoic' storage. In A. Cohen and S. G. Nooteboom (Eds.), *Structure and process in speech perception*. Berlin, Heidelberg, New York: Springer Verlag, 1975(a).

Huggins, A. W. F. On isochrony and syntax. In G. Fant and M. A. A. Tatham (Eds.), *Auditory analysis and perception of speech*. New York: Academic Press, 1975(b).

Janota, P. Perception of stress by Czech listeners. *Proceedings of the VIth International Congress of Phonetic Sciences.* Prague, 1967. Prague: Academia, 1970.

Jassem, W., Morton, J., and Steffen-Batóg, M. The perception of stress in synthetic speech-like stimuli by Polish listeners. In W. Jassem (Ed.), *Speech Analysis I*. Warsaw: *Panstwowe Wydawnictwo Naukowe*, 1968.

Katwijk, A. F. V. van. *Accentuation in Dutch*. Assen: Van Gorcum, 1974.

Klatt, D. H. Vowel lengthening is syntactically determined in a connected discourse. *Journal of Phonetics*, 1975, **3**, 129–140.

Kozhenikov, V. and Chistovich, L. *A Speech: Articulation and perception*. Washington D.C.: US Department of Commerce Translation, IPRS 30, 1965, 543.

Lackner, J. R. and Goldstein, L. M. Primary auditory stream segregation of repeated consonant-vowel sequences. *Journal of the Acoustical Society of America*, 1974, **56**, 1651–1652.

Ladefoged P. and Broadbent, D. E. Information conveyed by vowels. *Journal of the Acoustical Society of America*, 1957, **29**, 98–104.

Liberman, A. M., Cooper, F. S., Shankweiler, D. S., and Studdert-Kennedy, M. Perception of the speech code. *Psychological Review*, 1967, **74**, 431–461.

Lindblom, B. Some temporal regularities of spoken Swedish. In G. Fant and M. A. A. Tatham (Eds.), *Auditory analysis and perception of speech*. New York: Academic Press, 1975.

Maeda, S. A characterization of fundamental frequency contours of speech. *Quarterly Progress Report. Research Laboratory of Electronics, M.I.T.* 1974, **114**, 193–211.

Marslen-Wilson, W. D. and Tyler, L. K. Processing structure of sentence perception. *Nature*, 1975, **257**, 784–786.

Martin, J. G. Rhythmic (hierarchical) versus serial structure in speech and other behavior. *Psychological Review*, 1972, **79**, 487–509.

Massaro, D. W. *Experimental psychology and information processing*. Chicago: Rand McNally, 1975.

Massaro, D. W. and Cohen, M. M. Preperceptual auditory storage in speech recognition. In A. Cohen and S. G. Nooteboom (Eds.), *Structure and process in speech perception*. Berlin, Heidelberg, New York: Springer Verlag, 1975.

Mattingly, I. G. Synthesis by rule of prosodic features, *Language and Speech*, 1966, **9**, 1–13.

Noorden, L. P. A. S. van. Temporal coherence in the perception of tone sequences. Ph.D. Dissertation Polytechniek, Eindhoven, 1975.

Nooteboom, S. G. Production and perception of vowel duration. Unpublished Ph.D. Dissertation, University of Utrecht, 1972.

Nooteboom, S. G. Context effects in the perception of phonemic vowel length. Paper presented at the VIIIth International Congress of Phonetic Sciences, Leeds, August 17–23, 1975.

Nooteboom, S. G. and Cohen, A. Anticipation in speech production and its implications for perception. In A. Cohen and S. G. Nooteboom (Eds.), *Structure and process in speech perception*. Berlin, Heidelberg, New York: Springer Verlag, 1975

Nooteboom, S. G., Slis, I. H., and Willems, L. F. Speech synthesis by rule: why, what and how? *Institute for Perception Research, Eindhoven, Annual Progress Report*, 1973, **8**, 3–13.

O'Connor, J. D. and Tooley, O. M. The perceptibility of certain word-boundaries. In D. Abercrombie, D. B. Fry, P. A. D. MacCarthy, C. Scott, and J. L. M. Trim (Eds.), *In honour of Daniel Jones*. London: Longmans, 1964.

Pisoni, D. B. and Sawusch, J. R. Some stages of processing in speech perception. In A. Cohen and S. G. Nooteboom (Eds.), *Structure and process in speech perception*. Berlin, Heidelberg, New York: Springer Verlag, 1975.

Rigault, A. Rôle de la fréquence, de l'intensité et de la durée vocaliques dans la perception de l'accent en français. In *Proceedings of the IVth International Congress of Phonetic Sciences*, Helsinki 1961. The Hague: Mouton, 1962.

Roudet, L. *Eléments de phonétique générale*. Paris: Librairie Universitaire. H. Welter, 1910.

Slis, I. H. Rules for the synthesis of speech. *Institute for Perception Research, Eindhoven, Annual Progress Report*, 1971, **6**, 28–31.

Stevens, K. N. and Halle, M. Remarks on analysis by synthesis and distinctive features. In W. Wathen-Dunn (Ed.), *Models for the perception of speech and visual form*. Cambridge, Mass.: M.I.T. Press, 1967.

Studdert-Kennedy, M. From continuous signal to discrete message: syllable to phoneme. In J.F. Kavanagh and J. E. Cutting (Eds.), *The role of speech in language*. Cambridge, Mass.: M.I.T. Press, 1975(a).

Studdert-Kennedy, M. The nature and function of phonetic categories. In F. Restle, R. M. Shiffrin, N. J. Castellan, H. R. Lindman, and D. B. Pisoni (Eds.), *Cognitive Theory*, Vol 1. Hillsdale, N.J.: Lawrence Erlbaum Associates, 1975(b).

Summerfield, Q. How a full account of segmental perception depends on prosody and vice versa. In A. Cohen and S. G. Nooteboom (Eds.), *Structure and process in speech perception*. Berlin, Heidelberg, New York: Springer Verlag, 1975.

Svensson, S. Prosody and grammar in speech perception. MILUS 2, Monographs from the Institute of Linguistics, University of Stockholm, 1974.

Thomas, I. D., Hill, P. B., Carrol, F. S., and Garcia, B. Temporal order in the perception of vowels. *Journal of the Acoustical Society of America*, 1970, **48**, 1010–1013.

Thompson, C. L. and Hollien, H. Some contextual effects on the perception of synthetic vowels. *Language and Speech*, 1970, **13**, 1–13.

Vaissière, J. On French prosody. *Quarterly Progress Report. Research Laboratory of Electronics, M.I.T.*, 1974, **114**, 212–223.

Willems, L. F. W. and De Jong. Research tools for speech perception studies. *Institute for Perception Research, Eindhoven, Annual Progress Report*, 1974, **9**, 77–81.

Wingfield, A. The intonation-syntax interaction: prosodic features in perceptual processing of sentences. In A. Cohen and S. G. Nooteboom (Eds.), *Structure and process in speech perception*. Berlin, Heidelberg, New York: Springer Verlag, 1975.

Chapter 3

The Intra-clausal Syntactic Processing of Ambiguous Sentences

Joël Pynte

This chapter deals with the processes which take place during the perception of ambiguous sentences. An attempt will be made to show at which point during sentence processing disambiguation might take place.

There is ample experimental evidence, scattered throughout the literature and widely quoted in this book, to show that the clause is an important level of perceptual segmentation in the processing of sentences. An important question can be asked with regard to this point. How does the listener segment speech signals into clausal units? How much of the processing needs to be done at the same time that the linguistic information is being received, and how much can be left to process after the end of the clause?

Three possibilities have been suggested. First, that 'active' processing takes place at the end of the clause; second, that some underlying relations can be assigned immediately but most are not determined until the end of the clause; and third, that the deep structure of linguistic information is processed entirely *during* the perception of that information.

Much of the evidence in favour of the notion of clausal segmentation comes from experiments carried out with the well-known technique of click location. These experiments (e.g. Fodor and Bever, 1965; Garrett, Bever, and Fodor, 1966) have shown that one of the 'initial' strategies involved in the perception of sentences 'is the isolation of those adjacent phrases in the surface order which together could correspond to sentences at the level of internal structure' (Bever, 1970, p. 290).

It seems worthwhile to investigate the processes which intervene *during* the perception of each clause. It is likely that the minimum amount of processing which will enable the listener to mark off clauses as he identifies the words consists of the attribution of a lexical category to each word (cf. the role of noun-verb-noun (NVN) structures as emphasized by Bever). Reference to an internal lexicon could also inform the listener, at this level, about the *relationship* which a given item can hold with its neighbours (i.e. the grammatical context and structure in which the item can be found). The importance of lexical analysis, particularly in the case of verbs, was stressed by Fodor, Garrett, and Bever (1968). Using the same technique of click location, Bever, Lackner, and Kirk (1969) have also presented evidence which suggests that lexical analysis plays a part in the segmentation of utterances.

However, one of the problems with the click technique which several authors have pointed out is that the localizing response is normally given after the identification; that is, after the segmentation has already taken place. Some authors have devised variants of this technique which bring the experimental paradigm closer to the level of the perceptual process. For example, Abrams and Bever (1969) asked their subjects to press a key as soon as they heard a click, while Bever and Hurtig (1975) asked them to detect the presence of a click that was very slightly above the auditory threshold. In the first case, the dependent variable was the reaction time (RT), and in the second, the frequency of correct detections. In both situations, differences of performance were found depending on the position of the click in the sentence, detection apparently being easier at the beginning rather than at the end of a clause.

This confirms the preceding findings, namely that clauses seem to constitute privileged units. The underlying processes are, however, difficult to specify since even the significance of the phenomena observed has been debatable. For Bever *et al.*, the drop in performance observed at the end of clauses corresponds to a drop in the attention directed towards the stimulus; this interpretation relies on the distinction between sensory and perceptual processing and the assumption that the two types of processes occur alternately during the perception of a complex sentence. The listener's attention, it is claimed, is directed now 'outwards', now 'inwards', and the end of clauses is thus marked by a predominance of the second (perceptual) level over the first (sensory) level. It is therefore necessary to assume a model of speech perception according to which 'listeners are passively accumulating the external signal at the beginning of a clause, while at the end of a clause, they are actively organizing an internal representation of what they have just heard. . . .' (Bever and Hurtig, 1975, p. 6).

Another possible interpretation of these results would be that the subject cannot direct his attention to the linguistic signal while he is simultaneously remaining sufficiently vigilant to carry out the detection task correctly. (This analysis, which presupposes a double sensory channel, linguistic on the one hand and non-linguistic on the other, was hypothesized but finally rejected by Abrams and Bever, 1969.) From this point of view, a drop in detection performance would signify an *increase* in the level of attention paid to the linguistic stimulus. While the ends of clauses are marked by an increase in perceptual activity, the difference in intensity of activity would be merely one of degree, since the nature of the perceptual mechanisms would be identical throughout the perceptual process. The subject's strategy might, for example, consist of assigning all the underlying relations which he can during the presentation of the clause, leaving those which cannot immediately be identified for processing only after completion of the sentence.

It should be noted that Bever *et al.*'s hypothesis that drops in performance correspond to drops in the level of attention directed to the linguistic stimulus is not incompatible with a model of speech perception in which underlying relations are assigned during the process of word identification. It is quite possible that such fluctuations are simply linked to the nature of the sensory mechanisms, which might extract only fragmentary information from the stimulus. Why should the 'perceptual' activity be restricted only to periods when the 'sensory' processing is interrupted? Why could the two levels not operate simultaneously? From this point of view the listener would not *need* to pay attention to the end of clauses since the majority of the underlying relations would already have been assigned.

MacKay and Bever (1967) adopted a different approach to the problem. The procedure they used consists of introducing different types of ambiguity into the stimulus sentences, which, it is assumed, will be removed at different levels of processing. The subjects were asked to press a key as soon as they had discovered the two possible interpretations. The main difficulty with this type of approach arises from the fact that the majority of ambiguous sentences are ambiguous at several levels simultaneously. MacKay and Bever were consequently obliged to select extremely strict criteria in order to isolate three distinct levels. A sentence was considered ambiguous at the *lexical* level if one or more words had several different meanings 'and no difference at the other grammatical levels'. *Surface ambiguity* was defined by the possibility of 'grouping' adjacent words in different ways. *Deep ambiguity* concerned the logical relationships between words but did not involve 'a change in meaning of individual words ... nor a change in the apparent grouping of words' (p. 193). Sentences (1) to (3) are examples of these three levels of ambiguity:

(1) The soldiers like the port.
(2) Small boys and girls are frightened easily.
(3) The mayor will ask the police to stop drinking.

One of the most interesting findings of MacKay and Bever's study was the fact that the reaction time varied depending on the location of the ambiguity in the sentence when the ambiguity was lexical or surface, but not in the case of deep-structural ambiguities. This suggests that the processing of sentences can, at least in certain circumstances and at some level, be carried out 'from left to right'. Deep structure, however, seems to be processed in some other way (which the authors do not specify).

Using MacKay's (1966) technique of completing ambiguous sentences, Bever, Garrett, and Hurtig (1973) obtained results which seem to confirm this interpretation. They showed that more time is needed to complete an unfinished clause which is ambiguous than to complete an unfinished clause which is not ambiguous. When a subject was asked to add a continuation to a *complete* clause there was no difference dependent upon ambiguity—there was even a slight difference in the opposite direction with deep-structural ambiguity. On the basis of these results, the following notion can be proposed for the perception of complex sentences. Lexical analysis, which takes place *during* the presentation of each clause, is used to make hypotheses; the underlying relationships, however, are not assigned *definitively* until the *end* of the clauses (see also Garrett, 1970).

It can be objected that all these studies assume that the same processes are involved in resolving ambiguities as are involved in the perception of unambiguous sentences. In the following examples, the first sentence (4) is partially ambiguous, since one of the elements (the word *light*) can belong to several different lexical categories (cf. Bever, Fodor, and Garrett, 1966, cited by Bever, 1970):

(4) They watched the light. . .
(5) They watched the light turn green.
(6) They watched the light green car.

Are we to assume, as Garrett (1970) suggests, that the listener who hears the word *light* considers both the alternative structures represented by examples (5) and (6)? Are the different lexical categories to which such an ambiguous item can belong perceived by the subject in the same way as the different lexical patterns into which a non-ambiguous item could fit? Should we not, rather, distinguish two levels of lexical analysis, one responsible for the assignment of isolated meanings and the other for the exploration of grammatical patterns? This view seems to be shared by several authors, although the reasons given by each of them for such support are sometimes contradictory. Thus, according to MacKay (1970), the context of the sentence makes it possible to resolve ambiguities during a preliminary passive phase of identification. During a 'short period of time', consequently, no meaning at all is envisaged. It is only during a final phase of activation that one of the two meanings is 'boosted to threshold' (p. 92).

An entirely different point of view would be that perceptual hypotheses concerning deep structure are formulated right from the beginning of the sentence and that the attribution of meaning to words is therefore dependent on syntactic processing. Interpretations which are not compatible with the accepted hypotheses would in this case simply not be envisaged. In support of this point of view, we may mention the results obtained by Carey, Mehler, and Bever (1970) by means of the technique of 'syntax-setting' (Mehler and Carey, 1967, 1968). Carey *et al.* showed that subjects who have been accustomed to hearing a given syntactic structure by means of a presentation of a series of unambiguous sentences will generally not notice the ambiguity of a new sentence if one of its interpretations coincides with the structure of the previously presented unambiguous sentences. Moreover, subjects who claimed to have perceived the ambiguity took longer to verify the truth of such a sentence by comparison with a picture, while the reaction time for subjects who admitted they had not noticed any ambiguity was identical for ambiguous sentences and non-ambiguous control sentences.

The model for the perception of sentences proposed by Garrett (1970) and Bever, Garrett, and Hurtig (1973), based on results obtained with ambiguous sentences, must be considered with some caution. The works of MacKay (1970) on the one hand, and those of Carey, Mehler and Bever (1970) on the other, suggest in fact that ambiguous sentences present specific difficulties, which complicate, rather than facilitate, the study of perception.

In this chapter, no attempt will be made to review the several psycholinguistic studies on processing of ambiguous sentences. In this context, it will be enough to say that the experiments on the processing of ambiguous sentences scattered throughout the psycholinguistic literature have tried to test one of the following possible alternatives—or a combination of them. A first question is the following. When presented with ambiguous sentences, do people normally perceive the ambiguity, or do they only assign one interpretation to the sentence? The two alternatives are (a) that only one interpretation is assigned to the sentence or (b) that two interpretations are assigned. In this second case there are also two alternatives: (a) that the two interpretations are actively and explicitly envisaged during sentence processing, or (b) they are available only potentially. This is obviously also possible when only one interpretation is assigned. Finally, a third question concerns the moment at which an interpretation is assigned to the sentence. One alternative is (a) that the interpretation is assigned from the beginning of processing (as Carey *et al.*, 1970, imply). The other is (b) that an interpretation is assigned only towards the end of the sentence (as suggested by MacKay, 1970).

In the present study, an attempt was made to answer the question: At which point is a sentence disambiguated? An additional question faced in the study was whether both interpretations are explicitly envisaged during processing or are only potentially available.

In our experiments, we used as stimuli ambiguous French sentences, each word of which could belong to one of two lexical categories. The advantage of such sentences is that possible hypotheses concerning the deep structure are narrowly dependent on the analysis carried out on the lexical level. The beginning of sentence (7) for example, can be understood to mean either (8) or (9), depending on whether the word *méchant* is assumed to be a noun or an adjective:

(7) Le méchant juge le fait.
(8) The wicked person judges the act.

(9) The wicked judge does it.

(10) Le méchant procureur vous fera condamner.

The two alternative structures which can be imposed on (7) are therefore the following:

(7_1) Article-Noun-Verb-Article-Noun

(7_2) Article-Adjective-Noun-Pronoun-Verb

The point of disambiguation was varied by allowing a non-ambiguous word to appear at each position in the sentence, starting from the second. Thus, for example, in (10) the ambiguity is resolved (with meaning as in (9) above) as soon as the third word is presented, since it can be interpreted only as a noun.

In order to check whether the same strategies can be assumed to apply independently of the sensory mode employed (the experiments reported in Bever *et al.*, 1973, made use of a visual presentation) we carried out two experiments, one visual and the other aural. In both experimental situations a word-by-word presentation was made at a speed determined by the subjects themselves, who caused each successive word to appear by pressing a key. This technique reproduces fairly faithfully the natural conditions of reading as described in current research, which suggests that the eye fixates on each word separately with the exception of certain short and predictable words such as articles. When the eye falls on the beginning of a long word, a short saccade shifts the fixation point to the centre of the word (O'Regan, 1975). This technique was used successfully by Aaronson and Scarborough (1976), who obtained a longer latency time for words appearing at the end of clauses (the stimuli consisted of unambiguous, complex sentences), in a situation in which the subject's task was to memorize the stimulus sentence. No difference has been found, however, in a control situation which did not require mnemonic activity on the part of the subject.

A number of objections could be levelled against the use of such a technique with an aural presentation. Indeed, in normal listening conditions a listener does not have to solicit the production of each word. Furthermore, he is not in a position to prolong at will the duration of each clause. Such a procedure, however, should make it possible, at least more than the procedures used by Abrams and Bever (1969) or by Bever and Hurtig (1975), to separate 'perceptual' from 'sensory' processing. Imagine, for example, that a subject marks a pause in the sequence of presentation. This 'interruption' of sensory processing could then be interpreted as an indication of an alternative process which when operative displaces the sensory process. In a normal situation, such a drop in attention can always be attributed to fluctuations occurring at the sensory level.

If ambiguity is resolved only at the end of the sentence, then the subject should spend about the same amount of time on each word until the end of the sentence is reached; on the other hand, if the ambiguity is resolved as soon as possible during clausal processing, then the point at which disambiguation takes place should demand more time from the subject. The experimental paradigms chosen, and the type of sentence used, have allowed a test of these two possibilities which relates to the hypotheses previously formulated.

EXPERIMENT I

The technique used in the first experiment was similar to the one developed by Aaronson (Aaronson and Scarborough, 1976). But in order to simulate more closely the natural reading situation, each word appeared to the right of the preceding ones, which remained visible on the line. Sentences were to be read silently by subjects, and at the end of the sentence the subject was asked to give the meaning of what he had read, rather than a literal rendition. Furthermore, since each stimulus consisted of only a single clause, there was no mnemonic difficulty for the subject. The only reason, in fact, that the subjects were asked to give an account of what they had read was to ensure that the sentences were in fact read by the subject. Errors were very infrequent and have not been taken into account in the analysis.

Method

Apparatus. The subject was placed in front of an AFTEL 2048 display connected to a Télémécanique Electrique T 1600 computer. Each time the spacing bar was pressed, a word appeared on the screen; the end of a sentence was signalled by three dots appearing on the screen. An external clock linked to the computer made it possible to measure the time which elapsed between two pressings of the bar. The data were stored on a magnetic disc. (See Pynte, 1974, 1975, for more information on this method.)

Stimuli. Each sentence was composed of six words. The following five ambiguous sentences were taken as the basis for fifty stimulus sentences:

(11) Le nouveau garde la porte.
(12) Le vieux livre la montre.
(13) La petite brise la glace.
(14) La belle ferme le voile.
(15) Le méchant juge le fait.

Each word in these sentences, with the exception of the first word, can be understood in two different ways and assigned to two different lexical categories. Two different structures can be assigned to each sentence:

Structure 1: (Article-Noun) (Verb-Article-Noun)
Structure 2: (Article-Adjective-Noun) (Pronoun-Verb)

Design. Table 3.1 shows how ten stimulus sentences were built from each original ambiguous sentence by removal of the ambiguity (with either the first or second structure) at five different positions in the sentence. It should be noted that the sentences which were 'disambiguated' in position 2 did not, in fact, contain any ambiguity; they were used as a control in the data analysis.

The disambiguation procedure consisted of replacing an ambiguous element by a non-ambiguous one. For example, in the case of a structure 2 disambiguation in position 4, the critical word had to be a non-ambiguous pronoun. Disambiguation in position 6 consisted of *adding* a non-ambiguous word which was either an adjective (structure 1) or a verb or adverb (structure 2).

It goes without saying that any given subject did not see all the sentences given in Table 3.1: only one sentence from the ten constructed on the basis of each of the five original ambiguous sentences was presented to each subject, who therefore received five stimulus sentences, each based on a different original ambiguous sentence and each duplicating the syntactic structure of the model sentence. Ten groups of subjects were used, giving five subjects for each syntactic structure. This set of five was organized in the form of a Latin square with the five disambiguation positions and the five original ambiguous sentences.

Subjects. Each group comprised four subjects. Forty secretaries of the Université de Provence participated as subjects; all were native speakers of French, and their participation was voluntary and remunerated.

Procedure. The session began with the presentation of six training sentences identical to all the groups. The subjects then saw the five sentences attributed to their group. Two different orders of presentation were used. Each pair of stimulus sentences was separated by a dummy sentence. These dummy sentences were not identical for all subjects; their function was to counteract any possible habit-forming effects.

Results

We recorded 1200 durations (4 subjects × 10 groups × 5 sentences × 6 positions in the sentence). Table 3.2 summarizes these data, pointing out the two main independent variables—the place of disambiguation and the direction of disambiguation. Each value represents an average of 20 measurements (5 groups × 4 subjects). Table 3.3 groups the results of both types of disambiguation; each value represents the average of more than 40 measurements (10 groups × 4 subjects).

Table 3.1   Design of Experiment I. (The ten stimulus sentences built from one original ambiguous sentence)

Sentence structure	Place of disambiguation	Place of the words in the sentence						
		1	2	3	4	5	6	7
Structure 1	6	le	nouveau	garde	la	porte	GOTHIQUE	...
	5	le	nouveau	garde	la	FENETRE	GOTHIQUE	...
	4	le	nouveau	garde	CETTE	FENETRE	GOTHIQUE	...
	3	le	nouveau	REGARDE	CETTE	FENETRE	GOTHIQUE	...
	2	le	TOURISTE	REGARDE	CETTE	FENETRE	GOTHIQUE	...
Structure 2	6	le	nouveau	garde	la	porte	LOIN	...
	5	le	nouveau	garde	la	CONDUIT	LOIN	...
	4	le	nouveau	garde	NOUS	CONDUIT	LOIN	...
	3	le	nouveau	SURVEILLANT	NOUS	CONDUIT	LOIN	...
	2	le	FACETIEUX	SURVEILLANT	NOUS	CONDUIT	LOIN	...

Table 3.2   Experiment I. Mean reading times (milliseconds)

Sentence structure	Place of disambigu-ation	Place of the words in the sentence						
		1	2	3	4	5	6	7
Structure 1	6	—	711	658	762	831	1048	1586
	5	—	700	749	733	754	1100	1064
	4	—	697	709	786	794	941	1001
	3	—	655	756	745	697	809	951
	2	—	779	762	696	708	757	845
Structure 2	6	—	691	633	714	676	808	902
	5	—	701	702	739	953	788	902
	4	—	758	686	734	707	719	892
	3	—	682	737	712	751	755	832
	2	—	836	782	703	712	704	974

Table 3.3   Experiment I. Mean viewing times (both structures combined) (milliseconds)

Sentence structure	Place of disambigu-ation	Place of the words in the sentence						
		1	2	3	4	5	6	7
Both structures	6	—	701	645	738	753	928	1244
	5	—	700	725	736	854	944	983
	4	—	728	697	760	751	830	947
	3	—	669	747	729	724	782	892
	2	—	807	772	699	710	731	910

An examination of Tables 3.2 and 3.3 allows a number of comments. First, in each column, the highest value is situated on the right-to-left diagonal of the table. Secondly, the only exceptions are values immediately below this diagonal (see especially values corresponding to structure 1). Third, the values decrease the further they are away from this diagonal and towards the bottom of the table. Finally, values tend to increase from left to right across the table. It is difficult to say whether such an increase reflects effects of sentence processing or differences in word processing, since times relate to durations for different classes of words (cf. Table 3.1).

This set of tendencies suggests the following interpretations: (a) the subjects spent the most time on the word which removed the ambiguity of the sentence; (b) when the disambiguation provoked the apparition of a structure of type 1, there was also a pause on the word following; (c) after removal of ambiguity, the time spent on successive words decreased as the disambiguation became further away; and (d) if we take into account the serial effect mentioned above, we should say that the *increase* in latencies at the end of the sentence was *less marked* when the ambiguity was resolved earlier in the sentence.

A series of comparisons was carried out with information contained in the data. In no case, however, did we compare durations measured on different words, and we did not make use of the means situated above the diagonal. Furthermore, we made use only of columns 4, 5, 6, and 7, which contain more than one value below the diagonal. The following comparisons were made.

1. We compared the mean duration of words situated at the moment of disambiguation with the mean duration obtained on the same words when they appeared in unambiguous sentences. This corresponds to the set of underlined values on the diagonal in Table 3.3, on the one hand, and with the set of underlined values on the last line, on the other. According to the analysis of variance, the difference is significant: ($F = 12.16$; d.f. $= 1,30; p < .01$). The interaction with the type of disambiguation is not significant ($F < 1$).

2. We next compared the mean value of viewing times for word position immediately after the disambiguation (see the values underlined with a dotted line in Table 3.3) with the mean value of the times for the same word positions in non-ambiguous sentences. Once more, the difference is significant: $F = 6.14$; d.f. $= 1,30; p < .025$). This difference, however, is greater when the sentences have a structure of type 1 than when they have a structure of type 2. The interaction is significant ($F = 5.85$; d.f. $= 1,30; p < .025$).

3. We further calculated the regression line within each column of Table 3.3 (not taking into account, as we mentioned earlier, the figures situated above the diagonal). In each column, it is not possible to reject the null hypothesis according to which the population means fit a regression line (the F values are < 1 in columns corresponding to positions 4, 5, and 6 in the sentence, $F = 1.84$; d.f. $= 3,120$ in column 7), but in each column it is possible to reject the null hypothesis according to which the slope of the line is zero ($F = 5.71$; d.f. $= 1,60$; $p < .025$; $F = 4,73$; d.f. $= 1,90$, $p < .05$; $F = 5.46$; d.f. $= 1,120$; $p < .025$ and $F = 12.94$; d.f. $= 1,120$; $p < .001$; for columns 4, 5, 6, and 7, respectively).

We conclude, then, that the duration of the viewing time which occurred at a given point in a sentence varied as a linear function of the number of words presented since the moment of disambiguation.

Discussion

The results showed that there was an increase in viewing time for the word which removed the ambiguity from the sentence. This suggests that the subjects resolved the ambiguity *before the end of the clause*. We have not, however,

elucidated the nature of the process which intervened at the time that the disambiguating word was presented. Two interpretations are possible: first, that
the subjects made a choice between the two meanings, and second, that at that
moment the subjects rejected a previously made choice.

According to the first interpretation, we may distinguish two variants. We
may assume that the two possibilities were either *actively* envisaged by the
subject, or that they were perceived as *potential* solutions to the sentence. In
both cases, it is necessary to assume that the subjects 'perceived' the ambiguity,
consciously or not, since the place of removal of ambiguity had an effect on
processing. The second position corresponds, indeed, to one of the alternatives
mentioned in the introduction, according to which only one interpretation was
actively envisaged.

If the first interpretation is correct, we should find a similar increase in
viewing time for both types of disambiguation. The results, however, show that
this phenomenon is more pronounced (increasing viewing time on the following
word) in the case of structure 1. This result alone, however, is insufficient
evidence to indicate that the second interpretation might be the correct one. A
further experiment was necessary to test these two interpretations (see below
Experiment II) in order to obtain more evidence in favour of one or the other.

It should be noted that the main result of this first experiment, namely, that
the subjects did not wait until the end of the clause to assign one of the two
structures to the sentence (it would be assigned at the point of disambiguation,
according to the first interpretation, or at the beginning of the sentence,
according to the second interpretation) must be qualified in the light of the
surprising fact that the viewing times for words which followed the disambiguation apparently depended (among other things) on the distance from
the point of disambiguation. This suggests that the structure assigned when the
critical word was presented could have remained a 'hypothesis' which each
subsequent word had to confirm. The more material the subjects received after
the critical word, the more confident they would have become and the less time
they would consequently have had to spend on the following words in the
sentence.

EXPERIMENT II

The second experiment created a situation in which the two interpretations
could be compared. The rationale was that if the first interpretation of disambiguation were correct, then the 'pause' would occur for all subjects regardless of the type of disambiguation involved. This second experiment also aimed
at comparing the results obtained in Experiment I, featuring a visual
presentation of the sentences, with the corresponding results of an experimental
situation in which sentences were presented auditorily.

Method

Apparatus. The subject was seated in front of a table in a room adjoining the computer room. The index finger of his preferred hand rested on a very sensitive push-button. Each time he pressed the button, he heard a word which was relayed through earphones by means of an analogic converter connected to an amplifier. A loudspeaker, situated in front of the subject (connected to a binary output from the computer) gave out a 150 msec signal (a pure sound of 500 Hz) at the beginning and at the end of each sentence, which the subject could hear despite the earphones. The external clock permitted the measurement of the time which elapsed between the *end of a word* and the moment when the subject pressed the button to hear the next word. 'Listening' time was therefore not included, while in the first experiment latencies included reading time.

Stimuli. Thirty-two stimulus sentences were used in this experiment, each composed of five monosyllabic words which had previously been digitalized and stored in magnetic disc files. Their duration, which had been reduced by suppressing a certain number of vowel-periods (6–9, depending on the word), varied from 100 to 250 msec, depending on the original length of the words.

This procedure is fairly laborious: once the signal has been numerized and then visualized, the different phonemes have to be distinguished on sight. It does, however, give better results than the technique which consists of 'compressing' the signal with a constant ratio. It makes it possible to remove the most redundant parts of a signal, the steady states of vowels, and at the same time to preserve the parts which carry the most information, namely the *transitions* between phonemes. The words were consequently of a duration shorter than that of normal speech, but they contained all the information necessary for their identification (Gray, 1942, showed that isolated vowels of a duration less than one complete period, i.e. of about 10 msec, were easily recognizable). The purpose of such a procedure was to force the subject, *after* the word had been presented, to carry out the part of the processing which normally takes place *during* the perception of a word of normal duration. In this way, we intended to 'occupy' the subject during the time between two presentations, and the latencies measured would consequently reflect, at least in part, the actual perceptual activity and not only a motor RT. All the stimulus-sentences were based on the following four incomplete ambiguous clauses:

(16) La bonne brise le...
(17) Le vieux livre le ...
(18) La belle voix(t) le ...
(19) Les jeunes gardes(nt) les ...

Design. The design was similar to that of the first experiment. The differences arise from the number of levels of independent variables. There were only five

Table 3.4   Design of Experiment II. (The eight stimulus sentences built from one original incomplete ambiguous sentence)

Sentence structure	Place of disambigu-ation	Place of the words in the sentence				
		1	2	3	4	5
Structure 1	5	la	bonne	brise	le	VASE
	4	la	bonne	brise	UN	VASE
	3	la	bonne	CASSE	UN	VASE
	2	la	FILLE	CASSE	UN	VASE
Structure 2	5	la	bonne	brise	le	FROLE
	4	la	bonne	brise	ME	FROLE
	3	la	bonne	PLUIE	ME	FROLE
	2	la	DOUCE	PLUIE	ME	FROLE

words in each sentence and consequently four disambiguation positions (instead of five as in Experiment I). However, the variable 'type of disambiguation' kept its two values (cf. the example in Table 3.4).

Two out of the eight sentences constructed from each incomplete ambiguous clause were presented to each subject (one as structure 1, and the other as structure 2). Subjects therefore heard a total of eight stimulus sentences. Four groups of subjects were formed; the set of groups was organized in a Latin square design with the four disambiguation positions and the four original incomplete ambiguous clauses.

Subjects. Each group was composed of seven subjects. Twenty-eight students, native speakers of French, participated on a voluntary basis and received remuneration.

Procedure. The procedure was similar to that of Experiment I. The session began with the presentation of fifteen training sentences identical for all groups and constructed with the same classes of words as the stimulus sentences. The experimenter, placed behind the subject, collected the responses, given orally, and gave the signal announcing the beginning of a sentence. Upon hearing this signal the subject pressed a button to receive the first word of the sentence, and so on, thus controlling the speed at which the stimulus sentence was presented. The subject was obliged to continue with this procedure until he heard the signal announcing the end—even if at one moment he had the impression that he had reached the end of the sentence. Only after he had heard the ending signal was he to reproduce the sentence which he had heard. All responses which did not reproduce the *meaning* of the stimulus sentence were counted as errors.

Results

Table 3.5 summarizes the data collected and may be compared with Table 3.2. The number of durations recorded was 1120 (7 subjects $\times$ 4 groups $\times$ 2 structures $\times$ 4 sentences $\times$ 5 words). The mean values corresponding to the portion of the data which was used for analysis of variance are underlined in the table.

Results indicate that the subjects waited longer before pressing the push-button just after hearing a word which removed the ambiguity from the sentence. (The duration is greater than in the case of the same word presented in a non-ambiguous sentence: $F = 5.19$; d.f. $= 1,24$; $p < .05$.)

Furthermore, Table 3.5 shows that the effect is not more pronounced when the disambiguation intervenes later in the sentence. The tendency is, in fact, the opposite, but the differences are not significant ($F = 1.32$; d.f. $= 2,48$). An examination of the errors made when the subjects reproduced the sentences they had heard, however, shows that in this case the identification is more difficult (cf. Table 3.6).

Contrary to what we might have expected, the effect seems to be more pronounced for one of the two syntactic structures. (In the case of structure 1, it does not appear for positions 3 and 4.) This seems to indicate a preference on the part of the subjects for one of the two interpretations. This interaction did not turn out to be significant ($F < 1$).

Table 3.5   Experiment II. Mean interval durations before request of following word (milliseconds)

Sentence structure	Place of disambigu- ation	Place of the words in the sentence					
		1	2	3	4	5	Means
Structure 1	5	187	176	143	170	<u>156</u>	<u>193</u>
	4	611	164	236	<u>166</u>	177	
	3	239	167	<u>256</u>	182	160	
	2	283	180	<u>173</u>	<u>179</u>	<u>161</u>	<u>171</u>
Structure 2	5	287	169	163	216	<u>172</u>	<u>220</u>
	4	526	144	234	<u>290</u>	157	
	3	426	178	<u>197</u>	173	159	
	2	940	153	<u>182</u>	<u>222</u>	<u>152</u>	<u>185</u>

Table 3.6   Experiment II. Proportion of errors made in reproduction of the sentences. (Each value corresponds to a given cell in the experimental design)

Sentence structure	Position of disambiguation			
	5	4	3	2
Structure 1	.39	.25	.03	.11
Structure 2	.32	.21	.14	.11

As a result of the foregoing, we calculated for each subject the mean waiting time on critical words and on the same words in a non-ambiguous sentence. The subjects were classified into four categories: (1) for thirteen subjects, there was a difference (in the predicted direction) between these two means for both structures; (2) for six subjects, there was only a difference in the structure 1 case; (3) for seven subjects, the difference was only in the structure 2 case; and (4) for two subjects there was no difference at all (or only a slight difference in the unpredicted direction). The subjects of the first three categories can consequently be divided into two equal groups: (1) one, comprising thirteen subjects for whom an increase in listening time occurred for both types of disambiguation; and (2) another, comprising thirteen subjects for whom the phenomenon occurred for one type of disambiguation only.

Discussion

On the basis of the data obtained, it was not possible to choose between the two interpretations which had been proposed to account for the results of Experiment I. The subjects apparently made use of two different strategies. Some seem to have envisaged both possible structures and to have made their choice when the critical word was presented; others, on the contrary, seemed to have preferred one of the two structures (and therefore had to go back on their original choice about 50% of the time when the ambiguity was resolved).

In order to discover the motivation behind these two strategies, we decided to compare the overall mean value of the waiting time recorded on every word during the experiment (except those included in training sentences) for each of the two groups of subjects distinguished above. The values obtained were respectively 192 msec for the subjects who apparently envisaged both structures, and 271 msec for those who apparently envisaged only one structure. In the analysis of variance, this difference turned out to be significant ($F = 4.33$; d.f. $= 1,24$; $p < .05$).

This comparison, established *a posteriori*, has to be interpreted with caution. At most it can give us a few indications on what the subjects could be doing.

Those who did not perceive the ambiguity from the very beginning were perhaps engaged in extra processing. Such processing could have consisted, for example, of the construction of a more elaborate perceptual representation. Subjects who apparently perceived, consciously or not, the ambiguity of the sentences, were perhaps satisfied to keep the words in an unorganized form as they were presented (until the presentation of the critical word). It is, however, difficult to say whether the 'perception' of the ambiguity was the consequence of this strategy or whether the reverse is true.

It is also not possible to exclude the possibility that one or both of these two strategies was the consequence of the experimental technique used, which imposed a segmentation into words different from segmentation in natural speech or reading conditions.

CONCLUSION

The procedure we employed in these experiments can be compared with that used by Lashley (cited by Garrett, 1970, and MacKay, 1970), who interpreted the reactions of a group of listeners to a partially ambiguous sentence at the moment when the ambiguity was resolved. Just like the facial expressions observed by Lashley, the effects we obtained can be interpreted in one of two ways: (a) as a manifestation of surprise at an interpretation which had not been envisaged or (b) as a manifestation of hesitation when confronting a heretofore unexpected choice (cf. Thorne, cited by MacKay, 1970).

On the basis of our results it is not possible to decide in favour of one or the other of these two interpretations. During the aural experiment, certain subjects seemed to have perceived the ambiguity of the stimuli while the rest, on the other hand, seem to have considered only one structure.

For most of the subjects, however, there was an increase in viewing-listening time on the critical word for at least one of the two structures. It seems that whatever the strategy adopted, ambiguity can be resolved by either a choice or a change of interpretation *at any point in the sentence and not only at the end of clauses*. This does not necessarily imply that the structure of the sentence is definitively assigned at the moment of disambiguation. As emphasized in the introduction, the processes occurring during the resolution of ambiguities are not necessarily the same as those taking place during the perception of unambiguous sentences.

SUMMARY

Two experiments, one visual and one auditory, were conducted in order to test the model for the perception of sentences proposed by Bever, Garrett, and Hurtig (1973). The technique used consisted of a word-by-word presentation, either appearing on a screen or relayed through earphones, of ambiguous sentences. The amount of time spent by the subjects on processing each word was measured. Results of both experiments show that more time was spent on the words which remove the ambiguity of the sentence. In the auditory experiment, furthermore, two categories of subjects were differentiated on the basis of speed of processing. The group which processed the sentences more quickly were apparently more aware of alternative meanings of ambiguous sentences from the beginning of the presentation, while the slower group seems to have perceived only one meaning of the sentence or clause.

REFERENCES

Aaronson, D. and Scarborough, H. S. Performance theories for sentence coding: Some quantitative evidence. *Journal of Experimental Psychology: Human Perception and Performance*, 1976, **2**, 56–70.

Abrams, K. and Bever, T. G. Syntactic structure modifies attention during speech perception and recognition. *Quarterly Journal of Experimental Psychology*, 1960, **21**, 280–290.

Bever, T. G. The cognitive basis for linguistic structures. In J. R. Hayes (Ed.), *Cognition and the development of language*. New York: Wiley, 1970.

Bever, T. G., Garrett, M. F., and Hurtig, R. The interaction of perceptual processes and ambiguous sentences. *Memory and Cognition*, 1973, **1**, 277–286.

Bever, T. G. and Hurtig, R. Detection of a nonlinguistic stimulus is poorest at the end of a clause. *Journal of Psycholinguistic Research*, 1975, **4**, 1–7.

Bever, T. G., Kirk, R., and Lackner, J. R. An automatic reflection of syntactic structure. *Neuropsychologia*, 1968, **6**, 81–85.

Bever, T. G., Lackner, J. R., and Kirk, R. The underlying structures of sentences are the primary units of speech perception. *Perception and Psychophysics*, 1969, **5**, 225–234.

Bever, T. G., Lackner, J. R., and Solty, W. Transitional probability is not a general mechanism for the segmentation of speech. *Journal of Experimental Psychology*, 1969, **79**, 387–394.

Carey, P. W., Mehler, J., and Bever, T. G. When do we compute all the interpretations of an ambiguous sentence? In G. B. Flores d'Arcais and W. J. M. Levelt (Eds.), *Advances in psycholinguistics*. Amsterdam: North-Holland, 1970.

Fodor, J. A. and Bever, T. G. The psychological reality of linguistic segments. *Journal of Verbal Learning and Verbal Behavior*, 1965, **4**, 414–420.

Fodor, J. A., Garrett, M. F., and Bever, T. G. Some syntactic determinants of sentential complexity, II: Verb structure. *Perception and Psychophysics*, 1968, **3**, 453–461.

Garrett, M. F. Does ambiguity complicate the perception of sentences? In G. B. Flores d'Arcais and W. J. M. Levelt (Eds.), *Advances in psycholinguistics*. Amsterdam: North-Holland, 1970.

Garrett, M. F., Bever, T. G., and Fodor, J. A. The active use of grammar in speech perception. *Perception and Psychophysics*, 1966, **1**, 30–32.

Gray, G. W. Phonemic microtomy: The minimum duration of perceptible speech sounds. *Speech Monographs*, 1962, **17**, 75–90.

MacKay, D. G. To end ambiguous sentences. *Perception and Psychophysics*, 1966, **1**, 426–436.

MacKay, D.G. Mental diplopia: towards a model of speech perception at the semantic level. In G. B. Flores d'Arcais and W. J. M. Levelt (Eds.), *Advances in psycholinguistics*. Amsterdam: North-Holland, 1970.

MacKay, D. G. and Bever, T. G. In search of ambiguity. *Perception and Psychophysics*, 1967, **2**, 193–200.

Mehler, J. and Carey, P. Role of surface and base structure in the perception of sentences. *Journal of Verbal Learning and Verbal Behavior*, 1967, **6**, 335–338.

Mehler, J. and Carey, P. The interactions of veracity and syntax in the processing of sentences. *Perception and Psychophysics*, 1968, **3**, 109–111.

O'Regan, J. K. Constraints on eye movements in reading (part A). A computer controlled real-time tracking system (part B). Travaux du centre d'étude des processus cognitifs et du langage, Paris, 1975, **6**.

Pynte, J. Une expérience automatisée en psycholinguistique. *Informatique et Sciences Humaines*, 1974, **22**, 45–46.

Pynte, J. Programmation d'une expérience de psycholinguistique. *Cahiers de Psychologie*, 1975, **18**, 65–74.

Chapter 4

Following Instructions: An Exploratory Trisection of Imperatives

Patricia Wright and Penelope Wilcox

INTRODUCTION

Although there have been many studies of sentence comprehension, relatively few have been concerned with imperatives. A recent review by Clark and Clark (1977) suggests that only Huttenlocher and Strauss (1968) have had people actually carrying out simple instructions. Other studies of imperatives have either asked people whether a sentence matched a picture (e.g. Clark and Lucy, 1975) or have used retention techniques (e.g. Fillenbaum, 1975). Do such differences in experimental procedure matter? Tanenhaus, Carroll, and Bever (1976) have questioned the generality of models of comprehension based on asking people whether a sentence matches a picture. Fillenbaum (1970) has shown that it can be hazardous to use retention techniques to explore language processes. Aaronson and Scarborough (1976) have shown that the distribution of pauses when reading will vary depending on whether the material is being read for recall or for a quiz. Clearly the problem of the generality of psycholinguistic findings and of the models of comprehension based on those findings is a very real one.

The present interest in the comprehension of imperatives arises because it bypasses many of the difficulties of devising a technique for assessing the comprehension of declarative statements. There is considerable face validity in assessing the comprehension of imperatives through having people carry out the instructions. Certainly this may enlarge the definition of comprehension to include the preparation of executive plans. If such enlargement is felt to do violence to the term itself, other criteria may be adopted. Consequently it becomes useful to consider the temporal subdivision of the overall process of reading and following an instruction. If successful, this would make it possible to examine comprehension processes prior to the execution of the instruction. Such subdivisions have been found to yield useful insights in the sentence-picture matching task. Factors which affect the time to encode the sentence may have no effect on the subsequent verification time (e.g. Clark, 1971).

The following experiments will draw heavily on research by Seymour (1974) which was not primarily a study of imperatives at all. Seymour was interested in imagery processes. Nevertheless his interest led him to make comparisons between people's ability to match a sentence against a picture and to create the picture itself. Seymour's data suggest that variations in the surface form of a sentence influence the way the sentences are instantiated. This appears to contrast with the findings of Clark and Lucy (1975) who showed that the deep structure of an instruction was the critical determinant of performance, not the surface form of the sentence. Of course there are many differences between the two studies, differences both in procedure and in materials. Nevertheless, it establishes the need to clarify just what kinds of processing operations people utilize when they correctly carry out written instructions.

Such a large question has to be broken into smaller pieces in order to make it amenable to investigation. The present experiments will focus on two much smaller questions both concerned with how people comprehend verbal instructions such as '*Draw a circle above a square*'. The two questions to be studied are separate but related. The first question asks whether performance when reading and carrying out such an instruction can be meaningfully examined at successive time intervals after the instruction has been presented. If the answer to this question is affirmative then the next question is to determine what are the dominant processes during these successive time intervals.

There is every reason for expecting an affirmative answer to the first question. As has already been noted, it has been found useful to divide other sentence-comprehension tasks into initial encoding stages and subsequent verification stages (e.g. Clark, 1971). It should be noted that serial measures of performance, although consistent with, do not necessitate serial stages of processing. A variety of processing operations might start together, but if some finish sooner than others, then different processing operations would appear to dominate performance during successive time intervals.

The first three experiments to be reported will consider dividing the performance of following written instructions into three time periods: the first is the time spent reading the instruction, the second is the time spent thinking about the instruction and planning its execution, the third is the time spent making the drawing itself. Information about this third time period is necessary because some people may continue to plan while they are drawing, perhaps pausing between the two shapes to work out where the second shape had to be located. These three time periods will be labelled *reading*, *thinking*, and *drawing periods* respectively.

In order to examine whether this trisection of performance is meaningful or arbitrary, a transfer paradigm will be used. The effects of repeating different elements from the instructions will be monitored for each of the three time intervals. The elements to be repeated include lexical items, either nouns or prepositions, and the sentence form itself. Seymour (1974) showed that sentences such as *Above a circle is the square* were read more quickly than *The circle has the square above*. It has also been shown by Mehler and Carey (1967) that subjects who have encountered sentences such as *They are singing songs* are biased in their interpretation of sentences such as *They are eating apples*. The repetition of the sentence form affects the subsequent segmentation of the sentence surface structure to give (They) (are eating) (apples) rather than (They) (are) (eating apples). Consequently one might expect that repetition of the sentence form of an instruction would affect the first time interval during which the instruction is read.

Seymour (1974) suggested that following instructions such as *Draw a circle above a square* involved the formation of a plan specifying shape and location, e.g. *Draw X at L_1; Draw Y at L_2*. Decisions about the order of X and Y may well be made during the period here labelled thinking. So too may the processing that generates L_1 and L_2. Repetition of the locative information might therefore be expected to reduce this time interval. If relational terms such as prepositions are stored as procedures (e.g. Winograd, 1972), then repeating these procedures could take less time than executing new procedures.

However, it must be noted that the locative interpretation of prepositions is determined in part by the form of the sentence. An instruction such as *Draw a circle above a square* has the circle at the top, but when the preposition occurs at the end of the sentence *Draw a circle with a square above it* the square is on top. Therefore the reduction of the thinking period may occur only when both sentence form and the preposition are repeated. The first two experiments will examine the effects of repeating sentence forms and repeating prepositions.

A distinction needs to be drawn between two kinds of repetition effect. On the one hand there are the specific word recognition components which might influence reading times. On the other hand there are procedural components of the meanings of the lexical items. Nouns and prepositions have both components, but the word-recognition component would be comparable for nouns and prepositions, affecting performance during initial encoding, i.e. during the reading period. However, the procedural component would be rather different. Whereas for the reasons just outlined the procedural component of the preposition might be expected to influence the duration of the thinking period, the noun *square* is associated with a procedural routine for actually drawing a square. Thus repetition of the noun in successive instructions might be expected to reduce the time spent drawing. Moreover a square is always a square, so no interaction with the surface form of the sentence is to be expected.

The first three experiments will be concerned with whether such differential repetition effects can be found in the three time periods being called *reading, thinking,* and *drawing.* Evidence for such differential effects will be taken as validation of the performance measures.

EXPERIMENT I

This experiment grew out of an earlier study in which it was noticed that repetition effects could shorten the duration of the complete performance of reading and carrying out a written instruction (Wright, 1974). Although in Experiment I it will be possible to measure only two time periods, the data are reported here since they afford a replication of the effects obtained for the reading period. The two time intervals being measured will be termed reading and executing. The executing period will be a composite of thinking and drawing times.

The aim of the experiment is to compare the effects of repeating the sentence form with the effects of repeating the preposition. It is predicted that repetition of the sentence form will shorten the reading period, whereas repetition of the preposition will shorten the executing time, particularly when sentence form is also repeated.

Method

Design and materials. A 2×2 within-subject design was used, one of the factors being the repetition or non-repetition of the sentence form, the other factor being the repetition or non-repetition of the preposition. In all cases repetition was achieved across a sequence of three consecutive instructions. These sets of three instructions were denoted as 'a message' that had to be transmitted by subjects. The paper on which the drawings were made was divided into three vertical columns so that a complete message meant a pair of shapes in each column across the page. The shapes to be drawn varied throughout the message. The following are examples of messages within each of the four treatments.

1. *Sentence form repeated, preposition repeated*
   (a) Draw a circle above a cross.
   (b) Draw a tick above a square.
   (c) Draw a triangle above a diamond.
2. *Sentence form repeated, preposition varied*
   (a) Draw a circle above a cross.
   (b) Draw a tick to the left of a square.
   (c) Draw a triangle inside a diamond.
3. *Sentence form varied, preposition repeated*
   (a) Draw a circle above a cross.
   (b) Above a tick draw a square.
   (c) Draw a triangle with a diamond above it.
4. *Sentence form varied, preposition varied*
   (a) Draw a circle above a cross.
   (b) To the left of a tick draw a square.
   (c) Draw a triangle with a diamond inside it.

In order to equate for any guessing that subjects might do before reading the instruction the prepositions and the sentence forms were each selected from a set of three. The three prepositions were *above, left, inside*. The three sentence forms differed in whereabouts within the sentence the preposition occurred. It could be in front of both nouns (e.g. *Above a circle draw a square*). It could be in the middle of the sentence between the nouns (e.g. *Draw a circle above a square*). It could occur at the end of the sentence after both nouns (e.g. *Draw a circle with a square above it*). The terms *Front, Middle*, and *End* will be used to refer to these three sentence forms.

The shapes to be drawn were selected from a set of nine: circle, cross, diamond, equals, horseshoe, minus, square, tick, triangle. A card listing these shapes in both words and pictures was on view througout the experiment. All shapes occurred equally often with each sentence form and with each pre-position.

A scrambled sequence of 84 three-part messages was prepared (i.e. 252 instructions). Of these 84 messages, the first 12 were treated as practice and discarded from the analysis. They included three examples of each message type (i.e. each repetition condition). The remaining 72 messages included 18 messages within each of the four repetition conditions.

Procedure. Each instruction was typewritten and mounted in a purpose-built presentation device. The instructions appeared one at a time in a window that was covered by a metal flap. In order to read the instruction, subjects pressed a button which raised this flap. As soon as the button was released the flap dropped. Subjects carried out the instruction then pressed another button to indicate that they had finished drawing. This second button advanced the display to the next instruction. An 'end-of-message' button was pressed after the third pair of shapes had been drawn.

The presentation apparatus was linked to a Modular One computer which recorded how long the window flap was open and the time interval between closing the flap and pressing the button to indicate that the drawing was finished.

Subjects. Sixteen women from the panel of adult volunteers of the Applied Psychology Unit were paid for taking part in the experiment.

Results

The repetition effects of interest occur within messages on the second and third instructions. Therefore the analysis is confined to these instructions. The mean durations of the reading and executing periods are shown in Table 4.1 for the four repetition conditions.

An analysis of variance was carried out on a logarithmic transformation of

Table 4.1   Experiment I. Mean duration (seconds) of the reading and executing periods for the second and third instructions (N = 16)

Reading period

		Sentence form		
		Repeated	Not repeated	Mean
Preposition	Repeated	1.72	1.84	1.78
	Not repeated	1.72	1.78	1.75
	Mean	1.72	1.81	

Executing period

		Sentence form		
		Repeated	Not repeated	Mean
Preposition	Repeated	3.27	3.38	3.33
	Not repeated	3.28	3.34	3.31
	Mean	3.27	3.36	

the data. This showed that repetition of sentence form significantly shortened the reading period ($F = 18.0$; d.f. $= 1,15$; $p < 0.01$). Repetition of the preposition had no significant effect ($F = 3.23$; d.f. $= 1,15$; $p > 0.05$), nor was there a significant interaction ($F = 3.47$; d.f. $= 1,15$; $p > 0.05$).

The duration of the executing period was not significantly affected by any of the repetition conditions. The largest F ratio was obtained with repetition of sentence form ($F = 2.41$; d.f. $= 1,15$; $p > 0.05$).

DISCUSSION

The data have confirmed only one of the initial predictions. The duration of the reading period, which has been found sensitive to surface structure differences elsewhere (e.g. Seymour, 1974), is shorter when successive sentences have the same surface structure. It therefore would seem that the designation of a 'reading period' is not an arbitrary time slice through performance, but reflects a period during which the dominant psychological processes differ from those occurring subsequently.

The lack of any significant effects on the duration of the executing period is contrary to the earlier prediction about the effects of repeating the preposition. However, Table 4.1 shows that the mean duration of the executing period is almost twice that of the reading period. There may be too many processes occurring during this interval for the effect of repeating the preposition to be apparent. In particular the drawing activity, itself a relatively slow process, may swamp other effects. Therefore Experiment II repeats the comparison between the four repetition conditions, but divides the executing interval into thinking and drawing periods.

EXPERIMENT II

This experiment will repeat the comparisons made in Experiment I but with the performance measures being taken for reading, thinking, and drawing periods. The predictions being made are that repetition of sentence form will shorten the duration of the reading period. Repetition of the preposition will shorten the thinking period, particularly when sentence form is also repeated. There is no reason to expect any effects of repetition on the drawing period.

Method

Materials and procedure. The only changes made to the materials and procedure of Experiment I were to alter the instructions given to subjects. The instructions now encouraged subjects (a) to have the window flap open for as brief a time as possible; (b) to have a definite thinking and preplanning period prior to carrying out the instruction; (c) to carry out the instruction as rapidly as possible, pressing one button just before starting to draw and another button as soon as the drawing was complete.

To help subjects remember where to hurry and where they could take more time, the experiment was set in the fictitious context of sending and receiving coded messages in enemy territory. Subjects were told that although they were vulnerable to detection at any time during each three-part message, detection was most likely while they were receiving messages (i.e. when they had the window flap raised) or sending messages (i.e. when actually drawing). A buzzer sounded as soon as the 'start drawing' button was pressed. This was intended to remind subjects of their vulnerability during this phase. The buzzer continued until the 'stop drawing' button was pressed. Subjects were advised to be sure they knew what they were going to draw before they started. It was also emphasized that the only totally safe periods were between completed messages. Subjects were told that they could pause at the end of a three-part message whenever they wished but should consider themselves committed to an entire message once they had started reading the first instruction.

Subjects. Sixteen women from the panel of adult volunteers who had not participated in the previous study were paid for taking part in the experiment.

Table 4.2   Experiment II. Mean duration (seconds) of the reading, thinking, and drawing periods for the second and third instructions (N = 16)

Reading period

		Sentence form		
		Repeated	Not repeated	Mean
Preposition	Repeated	1.43	1.50	1.47
	Not repeated	1.44	1.48	1.46
	Mean	1.44	1.49	

Thinking period

		Sentence form		
		Repeated	Not repeated	Mean
Preposition	Repeated	1.55	1.59	1.57
	Not repeated	1.65	1.69	1.67
	Mean	1.60	1.64	

Drawing period

		Sentence form		
		Repeated	Not repeated	Mean
Preposition	Repeated	2.74	2.75	2.75
	Not repeated	2.82	2.77	2.80
	Mean	2.78	2.78	

Results

Table 4.2 shows the duration of the reading, thinking, and drawing periods for each of the four repetition conditions. Again the times shown are the means of the times for the second and third instruction in each message.

An analysis of variance was carried out on a logarithmic transformation of the data. This analysis showed that repetition of the sentence form resulted in a significantly shorter reading period ($F = 13.7$; d.f. $= 1,15$; $p < 0.01$). This was the only significant effect within the reading period and is consistent with the results of Experiment I.

Repetition of the preposition resulted in a significantly shorter thinking period ($F = 10.0$; d.f. $= 1,15$; $p < 0.01$). This was the only significant effect within the thinking period. There were no significant differences among the drawing periods. The largest F ratio was for repeating the preposition ($F = 2.34$; d.f. $= 1,15$; $p > 0.05$).

Discussion

The data from Experiment II confirm both predictions made at the outset. The reading period is shortened when the sentence form is repeated and the thinking period is shortened when the preposition is repeated. This effect of repeating the preposition did not appear dependent upon the repetition of the sentence form. This might imply that subjects formulate a plan for executing the drawings which is independent of the surface structure of the sentence. The lack of any significant differences within the drawing period would be consistent with this.

However, the possibility must also be considered that the drawing period is simply an insensitive measure. Table 4.2 shows that the mean length of the drawing period (2.8 sec) is 75% longer than the mean length of the thinking period (1.6 sec). Perhaps there are a number of quite different processes occurring during this interval which are not cleanly captured by the repetition conditions studied in Experiment II.

In the Introduction it was suggested that the drawing period was most likely to be affected by the repetition of the nouns. This possibility is examined in the next experiment.

EXPERIMENT III

The primary aim of this experiment is to examine the prediction that repetition of the shapes to be drawn will reduce the drawing period. However, it is also of interest to know how repetition of the nouns compares with the effects observed in Experiments I and II for repetition of the sentence form and preposition. Processes associated with lexical access might well reduce the reading period. No effects during the reading period have been observed for repeating the preposition. However, each instruction has two nouns but only one preposition. This may make it easier to detect repetition effects for nouns than for prepositions during the early stages of sentence encoding.

In order to compare noun repetition with other repetition effects within a single experiment of comparable length to Experiments I and II, the sentence form and preposition were treated as a single factor that was either held constant throughout a message or varied randomly (i.e. both sentence form and preposition varied) throughout the message. A second factor of repeating or not repeating the nouns was superimposed to yield a 2×2 factorial design similar to that used in Experiments I and II.

Method

Materials and procedure. The presentation device with its noisy window-flap operation was replaced by a quieter back-projection system, but the button-pushing sequence remained the same as that used in Experiment II. The sequence of 252 typewritten instructions, corresponding to 84 messages each of three instructions, was photographed onto a 8 mm film cassette which was viewed through a Philips 'Programmed Individual Presentation' cassetscope. The legibility of these typed instructions was felt by the experimenters to be rather less than that of the directly viewed typescript used in Experiments I and II. Nevertheless, ambient light conditions were so arranged that there were no legibility problems as such.

The time of each button-press was recorded on magnetic tape via a purpose-built digital tape-recorder. This tape was later analysed through the computer.

Subjects. Twenty women from the panel of adult volunteers were paid for taking part, none of whom had taken part in Experiments I and II.

Results

The mean durations of the reading, thinking, and drawing periods are shown in Table 4.3. For three repetition conditions these means are taken from performance on the second and third instructions, as they were in the previous experiments. However, when the factor of repetition of the sentence form and preposition was combined with the factor of repetition of the nouns, this meant that all three instructions in the message were verbatim repetitions of the first instruction. Therefore in this condition the data are reported from the second instruction only. Subjects had no need to read or think about the third instruction in such messages, so performance on that third instruction would not meaningfully reflect repetition effects of the kind being examined here. Because of a slight overall tendency of subjects to gather speed throughout the message, confining the analysis of one condition to the second message in the instruction will tend to reduce the magnitude of the repetition effects observed for that condition.

As previously, an analysis of variance was carried out on a logarithmic transformation of the data. This analysis suggested that during the reading period there was a significant effect of repeating the sentence form plus pre-position ($F = 40.47$; d.f. $= 1,19$; $p < 0.001$), a significant effect of repeating the nouns ($F = 7.96$; d.f. $= 1,19$; $p < 0.025$) and a significant interaction ($F = 32.56$; d.f. $= 1,19$; $p < 0.001$). Inspection of Table 4.3 suggests that these effects are primarily due to the very short duration of the reading period when the second instruction was a verbatim repetition of the first. A Newman–Keuls analysis confirmed that when both factors were repeated the duration of the reading

Table 4.3   Experiment III. Mean duration (seconds) of reading, thinking, and drawing periods for the second and third instruction*. (N = 20).

Reading period		Sentence form		
		Repeated	Not repeated	Mean
Nouns	Repeated	1.42	1.64	1.53
	Not repeated	1.56	1.61	1.59
	Mean	1.49	1.63	

Thinking period		Sentence form and preposition		
		Repeated	Not repeated	Mean
Nouns	Repeated	1.35	1.86	1.61
	Not repeated	1.88	1.94	1.91
	Mean	1.62	1.90	

Drawing period		Sentence form and preposition		
		Repeated	Not repeated	Mean
Nouns	Repeated	3.20	3.43	3.32
	Not repeated	3.50	3.44	3.47
	Means	3.35	3.44	

*Data are from second instruction only when sentence form, preposition, and nouns are all repeated.

period was significantly shorter than in each of the other three repetition conditions ($p < 0.01$, for all comparisons).

The second row of the reading data in Table 4.3 affords yet another replication of the earlier effects of repeating sentence form. A Newman–Keuls analysis confirmed that this difference was statistically significant ($p < 0.05$). Repeating the sentence form shortens the reading period.

Analysis of the data from the thinking period again showed many significant effects. Repeating the sentence form and preposition appeared to shorten the thinking period ($F = 26.77$; d.f. $= 1,19$; $p < 0.01$). Repeating the nouns appeared to shorten the thinking period ($F = 35.42$; d.f. $= 1,19$; $p < 0.01$). There was also a significant interaction between these two factors ($F = 26.04$; d.f. $= 1,19$; $p < 0.01$). However, Newman-Keuls tests showed that both apparent main effects were attributable entirely to the very short duration of the thinking period when the instruction was a verbatim repetition ($p < 0.01$ for comparison with each other condition). No other differences were significant.

It should be noted that the second row of the thinking data in Table 4.3 affords a replication of the effect of repeating the preposition, as was done in Experiment II. Table 4.3 shows that the mean differences are in the predicted direction although the difference itself was not significant on the Newman–Keuls analysis. In the present experiment this comparison is based on data from only half the number of observations that were included in the analysis of Experiment II. This probably accounts for the failure of the difference to reach conventional levels of statistical significance.

The analysis of the duration of the drawing period also suggested a number of highly significant effects. Repetition of sentence form plus preposition appeared to shorten the drawing period ($F = 6.46$; d.f. $= 1,19$; $p < 0.025$). Repetition of the nouns appeared to shorten the drawing period ($F = 10.37$; d.f. $= 1,19$; $p < 0.01$). Again there was a highly significant interaction ($F = 12.33$; d.f. $= 1,19$; $p < 0.01$). The Newman–Keuls analysis showed that both the apparent main effects were entirely due to the short duration of the drawing period when the instruction was repeated verbatim ($p < 0.01$ for comparison with each other condition). As Table 4.3 shows, repeating the nouns when sentence form and preposition varied had no effect on the duration of the drawing period.

Discussion

The primary aim of this experiment had been to examine whether the drawing period was too insensitive to detect repetition effects. The data show clearly that it is not. People can and do draw more rapidly under certain repetition conditions. The present study suggests that verbatim repetition may be necessary. However, it is possible that if there were repetition of nouns and prepositions but not word order, this might be sufficient. Thus the critical factor might be the repeated execution of an identical response sequence rather than the repetition of an instruction per se. The present data do not permit these alternatives to be distinguished. The critical test would be whether Front sentence forms could shorten the drawing period of subsequent End sentence forms, or vice versa. This cannot be examined with the present materials since a change in sentence form within the message was always accompanied by a change in preposition. Consequently identical responses were not made.

The aim of Experiments I, II, and III has been to explore the meaningfulness of trisecting the performance of following a written instruction into three successive time periods. The data suggest that these are meaningful divisions because different variables can be found which influence the duration of each period. Processes associated with sentence form affect the duration of the reading period. Processes associated with the preposition affect the duration of the thinking period. Processes associated with the nouns affect the drawing period. As was mentioned in the Introduction, the next question is to specify what these processes are. This is the problem addressed in Experiment IV.

EXPERIMENT IV

Seymour's suggestion for an output plan of the form X at L_1 and Y at L_2 has served well enough so far, but there are clearly some unanswered questions about the assignment of L_1 and L_2. L_1 might be the preposition specifically mentioned in the sentence, in which case X and Y would vary with the form of the sentence. X would be the first noun mentioned (N_1) in instructions having the middle sentence form, whereas X would be the second noun mentioned (N_2) in instructions having the Front and End sentence forms.

Data on which shape people draw first would be one means of answering this question. Seymour (1974) reported such data for six subjects. Consistency across subjects was found only for Middle sentences, where all subjects drew first the shape that was mentioned first in the sentence. This is also the shape whose spatial location is given explicitly by the preposition. So this data does not enable the possibilities to be distinguished. With End sentences only three subjects showed a strong tendency to draw first the shape in the location indicated by the preposition (i.e. N_2). With Front sentences only two subjects showed such a tendency, another two showed a strong tendency to draw first the shape that was mentioned first in the sentence. It is therefore unclear whether it is the preposition or the order of mention which usually determines how the elements are entered in an output plan.

Another way of examining the problem of how the output plan is determined is to consider the effect of sentence form on the three periods of reading, thinking, and drawing. Experiment II showed that the effects of repeating the preposition can be observed during the thinking period. Therefore it is in this time interval that one could expect to see differences in the time being taken with the different sentence forms. If the spatial features at L_1 are derived directly from the preposition specified in the instruction, then End sentences should have a shorter thinking period than Front sentences, because the preposition is adjacent to the appropriate noun in End but not in Front sentences. On the other hand, if X is the first noun in the sentence, then no such expectation holds.

Indeed, if the preposition's adjacency to a noun facilitates the derivation of locative information for that noun, then Front sentences may have shorter thinking periods than End sentences.

It will also be possible to extend Seymour's study to include other prepositions and other nouns. Seymour used only the prepositions *inside* and *outside*, and only the shapes *circle* and *square*. There is always a possibility that binary sets may enable subjects to adopt special strategies that are not generally available. The following experiment will therefore use six prepositions and twelve different shapes. The concern is no longer with repetition effects as such. Successive instructions within a message will vary in sentence form, in preposition and in nouns. The predictions are that the reading period will replicate the differences found by Seymour (1974): i.e. Middle < Front < End. The thinking period will be shorter for End than for Front sentence forms. The drawing period will be unaffected by sentence form since the output plan will by then be comparable for all sentences.

Method

Design. A within-subject design was used to compare performance on the three sentence forms, Front, Middle, and End. Message length was extended from three to six instructions, thus giving two examples of each sentence form and one instance of each preposition within a message. Across messages each sentence form occurred equally often with each preposition, with each pair of nouns, and at each of the six serial positions within a message. The first-order transitional probabilities between sentence forms were also balanced.

Materials and procedure. The sentences were back projected via the casset-scope as in Experiment III, but the originals were made from letraset instead of typescript, which enhanced the legibility of the instructions. As in Experiment III, there were 216 instructions in the experimental series, but now they were divided into 36 messages each six instructions long. Within a message the nouns were all different from each other.

The button-pushing sequence and the event-recording procedure were the same as in Experiment III. The response sheet was divided into six columns, rather than three as previously. These columns were then horizontally divided to give an 'answer box' for each instruction.

Subjects. Twenty-four women from the panel of adult volunteers were paid for taking part in the experiment. None had participated in any of the three previous experiments.

Table 4.4   Experiment IV. Percentage of subjects who drew N_1 first. (N = 19). (The subscripts in parenthesis in each cell shows the location of N_1)

| Preposition | Sentence form | | | Mean % drawing N_1 first |
	Front	Middle	End	
Above	$89\%_{(B)}$*	$89\%_{(A)}$*	$89\%_{(B)}$*	82%
Below	$100^*_{(A)}$	$26_{(B)}$	$100^*_{(A)}$	
Inside	$95^*_{(S)}$	$32_{(I)}$	$100^*_{(S)}$	75%
Surrounding	$68_{(I)}$	$63_{(S)}$	$89^*_{(I)}$	
Left	$47_{(R)}$	$79^*_{(L)}$	$68_{(R)}$	71%
Right	$95^*_{(L)}$	$42_{(R)}$	$95^*_{(L)}$	

$*P < 0.02$ for percentage greater than 79, binomial test, two-tailed.

Results

For technical reasons it was possible to collect data on the order in which the shapes were drawn for only 19 of the 24 subjects. Table 4.4 shows the consistency across subjects as a function of both sentence form and the preposition used in the instruction.

Table 4.4 shows that consistency across prepositions was greatest for End sentences, where five of the six prepositions yielded significant agreement that people drew first the noun that was first mentioned in the instruction. Consistency across prepositions was lowest for Middle sentences where only two of the six prepositions, *above* and *left*, yielded significant agreement across subjects. Indeed the data in Table 4.4 show that for Middle sentences there was a tendency for the order of output to be constant for a given spatial dimension. Subjects tended to draw first the shape in the *above* position irrespective of the preposition used in the instruction. Similarly the shapes in the *surrounding* and *left* locations tended to be drawn first.

Table 4.5 summarizes the data from Table 4.4 and shows how consistent the data are with three alternative hypotheses about the determinants of X and L_1. Table 4.5 shows that Front and End sentences fit the hypothesis that X is filled by N_1. Consequently for these sentence forms L_1 must be derived since it is not

Table 4.5   Experiment IV. Percentage of drawings in which the order of the shapes drawn was consistent with the hypothesis shown on the left

Hypothesis: That the shape drawn first is . . .	Sentence form		
	Front	Middle	End
(1) the shape mentioned first in the instruction	82%	55%	90%
(2) the shape to which the preposition refers	18	55	10
(3) a shape consistent with a constant drawing order (i.e. above, surrounding, left)	65	72	59

given explicitly in the instruction. This should be reflected in the duration of the thinking period.

Table 4.5 also shows that for none of the sentence forms does the L_1 slot in the output plan appear to be filled with the locative features of the preposition mentioned in the instruction. However, Middle sentences, as has already been seen, are best fitted by the hypothesis that subjects predetermine L_1 for a given spatial dimension. This difference between Middle sentences and the other sentence forms may make it difficult to interpret the data from Middle sentences for the reading, thinking, and drawing intervals, since such interpretation is most easily based on different times taken to achieve comparable levels of response.

Table 4.6 shows the mean duration of the reading period for each sentence form. Because repetition effects are not being examined here, the data are pooled from all six instructions within each message. As an indication of the internal consistency of the data, the times are given for each of the three spatial dimensions.

An analysis of variance was carried out on a logarithmic transformation of the data. This showed that there were significant main effects of word order

Table 4.6   Experiment IV. Mean duration (seconds) of reading period

Preposition	Sentence form		
	Front	Middle	End
Above/below	1.41	1.33	1.54
Inside/surrounding	1.57	1.32	1.63
Left/right	1.55	1.57	1.88
Mean	1.51	1.41	1.68

($F = 42.29$; d.f. $= 2,46$; $p < 0.01$) and spatial dimension ($F = 67.56$; d.f. $= 2,46$; $p < 0.01$) and also a significant interaction ($F = 6.19$; d.f. $= 4,92$; $p < 0.01$). A Newman–Keuls test showed that all sentence forms differed significantly in the duration of the reading period ($p < 0.01$). These data are consistent with the earlier prediction derived from Seymour's data, that the reading period would be shorter for Middle than for Front sentences and shorter for Front than for End sentences.

The mean duration of the thinking period is shown in Table 4.7. Because of the differences in drawing orders which have already been noted for Middle sentence forms, the main interest is in the comparison of Front and End sentences. Again the data are shown for each of the spatial dimensions.

An analysis of variance was carried out on the logarithmic transformation of the data. This analysis showed that there were significant differences among the sentence forms ($F = 7.86$; d.f. $= 2,46$; $p < 0.01$) and among the spatial terms ($F = 27.37$; d.f. $= 2,46$; $p < 0.001$) but no significant interaction ($F = 0.72$; d.f. $= 4,92$; $p > 0.1$). Inspection of Table 4.7 shows that the significant effect of sentence form is due to the duration of the thinking period being longer for Front sentences than for either of the other sentence forms. Since the drawing data suggest that subjects draw N_1 first, the longer thinking period for Front sentences suggests that the determination of L_1 is more complex in Front than in End sentences. The details of this complexity will be discussed below.

Table 4.8 shows the mean duration of the drawing periods. It is noticeable that here there is less consistency in the rank order of sentence forms for the three spatial dimensions than was found in the reading and thinking data.

An analysis of variance was carried out on the logarithmic transformation of the data. This analysis showed that there was a marginal effect of sentence form ($F = 2.92$; d.f. $= 2,46$; $0.10 > p > 0.05$) and a strong effect of spatial dimension ($F = 11.26$; d.f. $= 2,46$; $p < 0.001$) and there was also a significant interaction ($F = 3.47$; d.f. $= 4,92$; $p < 0.05$).

The marginal effect of sentence form was further explored by returning to the raw data. Of the 24 subjects tested, 19 had shorter drawing periods with End

Table 4.7   Experiment IV. Mean duration (seconds) of thinking period

Preposition	Sentence form		
	Front	Middle	End
Above/below	2.26	2.21	2.22
Inside/surrounding	2.69	2.40	2.39
Left/right	2.83	2.68	2.71
Mean	2.59	2.43	2.44

Table 4.8   Experiment IV. Mean duration (seconds) of drawing period

Preposition	Sentence form		
	Front	Middle	End
Above/below	3.27	3.40	3.16
Inside/surrounding	3.45	3.39	3.31
Left/right	3.23	3.19	3.24
Mean	3.32	3.33	3.24

than with Front sentences ($p < 0.01$, two-tailed). Seventeen had shorter drawing periods with End than with Middle sentences ($p = 0.064$, two-tailed). 14 had shorter drawing periods with Middle than with Front sentences ($p = 0.54$, two-tailed). It therefore seems that End sentences were drawn more rapidly than the other two sentence forms. These data are not consistent with the earlier prediction that sentence form would not affect the duration of the drawing period.

Discussion

This experiment had twin objectives. One was to gain further information about the way the output plan is constructed when people follow simple verbal instructions such as those used here. The other objective was to explore what processes might be occurring during the reading, thinking, and drawing periods.

The first point to emerge from the data is that the details of the output plans vary across different sentence forms. This is evident from the order in which the shapes are drawn (Tables 4.4 and 4.5). With Front and End sentences, subjects start by drawing the shape mentioned first in the instruction. This is not the shape referred to by the preposition. Middle sentences also showed no tendency for the output plan to be dominated by the preposition. In this respect the data contrast with those obtained by Seymour (1974). Even when one considers only the prepositions *inside* and *surrounding*, which was the spatial dimension used by Seymour, the strongest tendency observed there is to draw the surrounding shape first (66%) rather than to be influenced by the nouns or prepositions in the instructions (Table 4.4).

It is not at all clear why performance on Middle sentences should be so out of line with that of the other sentence forms. The discrepancy between the present data and those of Seymour might be explained by the wider range of shapes used in the present study. Seymour's subjects could afford to work out the spatial locations of just one term. Everything else in the output plan was then fully determined. In the present study both shapes needed to be represented in the output plan, although it is possible that L_2 might not have been needed explicitly. If X has been drawn at L_1, then the only space left in the answer box has to be L_2. But such reasoning applies to all sentence forms. It cannot account for the discrepancy between the drawing orders for Middle sentences and the N_1 dominated drawing order of Front and End sentences.

From Experiments I, II, and III it is known that the reading period can be shortened by the repetition of sentence forms. From Experiment IV it is known that the reading period is shorter for Middle sentences than for Front sentences, and longest for End sentences. The longer reading period for End sentences may be trivial. The imperatives used here had two extra lexical items *with* and *it* in the End sentence forms (e.g. *Draw a circle with a square above it*). Seymour, using declarative statements, was able to equate sentence length in terms of the number of words, but his equivalents of the present Front and Middle sentence forms used the verb *is* (e.g. *The circle is inside the square*) whereas End sentence forms used the verb *has* (e.g. *The circle has the square inside*). It therefore remains possible that the longer reading with End sentences in both studies is due to content differences among the sentences.

However, no such explanation can be applied to the difference between Front and Middle sentences. For 19 of the 24 subjects the reading period was longer for Front than for Middle sentences ($p < 0.01$). There are no content differences between the two sentence forms, so an explanation has to be found in terms of the structure of the sentences. In Front instructions the locative phrase is in a sense embedded. Such sentence structures have been found to give poorer performance in studies of temporal adverbs (e.g. Clark and Clark, 1968). People more easily remember sentences having the main clause first, as in Middle sentences. However, this consistency does not amplify the reasons for the reading period being longer for Front sentences.

One possibility is that these early reading processes are associated with the segmentation of the sentence into functional groupings, typically via the assignment of phrase markers (but see Martin, Kolodziej, and Genay, 1971). There are probably two such groupings within all the sentences used in Experiment IV. Nevertheless the assignment of an appropriate segmentation pattern might well be easier in some instances than others. The first segment of Middle sentences '*Draw a circle*' is a well-formed sentence. This is not true of Front sentences. *Above a circle* is not itself a sentence. It would not be surprising if people have more readily available procedures for inserting segmentation boundaries at the ends of sentences than at the ends of phrases.

Another possibility is that, given the repetitive nature of the experiment, subjects try deleting the redundant information during the reading period. The verb *draw* need not be encoded nor need the determiners. It is then possible that Middle sentences could be 'read in' as a single chunk *circle above square* whereas two such chunks might be needed for Front and End sentences—e.g. (*above circle*) (*square*) and (*circle*) (*square above*). Such a suggestion would be consistent with the findings of Manelis and Yekovich (1976) that reading time varies as a function of the number of propositions in a sentence. One implication of this suggestion is that the thinking period should be shorter for Middle sentences since the hypothesized chunk is already in the form X at L_1 plus Y. However, the suggestion also implies that for Middle sentences the first item drawn would be the first item mentioned. Table 4.4 showed that this was not so.

The significantly longer duration of the thinking period for Front sentences suggests that more complex processes are necessary in order to derive L_1. One possibility is that subjects first assign the locative features of the preposition to its reference noun, which is N_2. This gives an internal representation for Front sentences that is similar in form to that of End sentences with L_2 specified. The derivation of L_1 could then proceed as for End sentences. This processing sequence is schematically represented in Table 4.9.

If this line of thinking is correct, then it follows that the duration of the drawing period should be comparable for Front and End sentences. Middle sentences may be different because the order of execution is different there. However, for 19 of the 24 subjects the duration of the drawing period was shorter for End than for Front sentences ($p < 0.01$). Two classes of explanation can be put forward. One class would suggest that the processes schematized in Table 4.9 are incorrect, the specification of L_1 in Front sentences may instead be derived from operations applied within the first noun phrase. People may be able to utilize rules that deal with preposed prepositions—e.g. (preposition + noun)→(noun + opposite preposition). The longer duration of the thinking period for Front sentences would simply be a fortuitous consequence of different operations underlying the derivation of L_1 in Front and in End sentences. Because the use of such rules for Front sentences would no longer involve the second noun phrase, this leaves L_2 unspecified. This could be what causes the longer duration of the drawing period. However, the acceptance of such an explanation might lead to the expectation that repetition of the preposition shortened the drawing period, since the routines for deriving L_2 could be rerun. No such effects were found in Experiment II.

An alternative class of explanation accepts the suggestions of Table 4.9 and accounts for the difference in drawing times by reference to additional processes occurring during the drawing period. For example, people may monitor the accuracy of their drawings against some earlier internal representation of the sentence. The second noun in End sentences when drawn in the 'Above' locations matches the remembered (*square above*) for a sentence such as *Draw a circle with a square above*. Whereas a similarly located N_2 in Front sentences may appear incongruent (Clark, 1969) with a remembered (*above a circle*) for sentences such as *Above a circle draw a square*. Such a suggestion implies that people generate an internal representation which is used for some purposes, in particular for the generation of a motor programme, but which does not eradicate or overwrite certain earlier representations. Intuition supports this. If

Table 4.9   Schematic representation of processes for deriving an output plan for Front sentences

Phase	Result of process
Sentence as presented	'*Above a circle draw a square*'
Segmentation	(Above a circle) (Draw a square)
Assign preposition* to its referrent noun	(Circle) (Square above)
Derive L_1	(Circle below) (Square above)

*It is only necessary to assume that adequate locative features of the preposition are assigned, not the preposition itself in a lexical or phonological representation.

one gets confused trying to decide whether it is true that an ounce is not heavier than a pound, there usually remains the option of returing to the original surface structure form and starting again even if that form is no longer physically present.

These two alternative classes of explanation cannot be unequivocally distinguished on the basis of the present data. However, the availability of L_2 might be examined directly by experimentally constraining the order in which the shapes were drawn, or even by asking questions about which item goes where. The relative ease of monitoring the drawings might be examined by seeing how quickly mistaken executions could be detected. Studies designed to explore these alternative are already under way.

A third class of explanation can be dismissed more easily. It might be suggested that since End sentences had longer reading periods but shorter thinking and drawing periods, then the total time taken was comparable for all sentence forms and the distribution of this total time across the measurement periods was simply fortuitous. This seems highly unlikely, given the data for Experiments I, II, and III. Even the suggestion that in the earlier experiments the repetition effects were responsible for generating the apparent meaningfulness of the trisection is inadequate. When a retrospective analysis of the effects of sentence form is carried out on the earlier studies, then differences such as those found in Experiment IV are obtained. For example, in Experiment I in the two conditions involving the repetition of sentence form, there were significant differences in the duration of the reading period ($F = 6.12$; d.f. $= 2,30$; $p < 0.01$) with Middle instructions having the shortest time, and also significant differences in the duration of the executing period ($F = 9.96$; d.f. $= 2,30$; $p < 0.01$) with End sentences having the shortest time. Not too much weight should be attached to such retrospective analyses since these materials were counterbalanced for repetition effects, not for effects of sentence form. Nevertheless, the data give no support to explanations of the differences observed in

Experiment IV being due to the arbitrariness of the performance measures. Instead, cogent explanations of the processing operations taking place within each period are needed.

GENERAL CONCLUSIONS

The present series of studies have shown that psychological processes underlying reading and following written instructions can be examined during at least three successive temporal intervals. Different processing operations appear to dominate the different periods. This was evident both from the repetition effects observed in Experiments I, II, and III and also from the way that variations in sentence form influenced the durations of these intervals in Experiment IV.

From the outset this study of the comprehension of imperatives has been acknowledged as explanatory. It has not been possible on the basis of the present data alone confidently to distinguish between alternative explanations of which processing operations might be occurring during the different periods. Nevertheless, the data are consistent with the suggestion that there may be six major categories of processing operations. These are summarized in Table 4.10.

At this stage in the exploration of the comprehension of imperatives, the importance of Table 4.10 does not lie in the accuracy of the details shown. These can easily be sorted out by further experimentation. The importance lies in the contrast between the kinds of operations depicted in Table 4.10 and the processing operations which typify other models of sentence comprehension (e.g. Carpeneter and Just, 1975). Whereas models of the comprehension

Table 4.10   Tentative outline of processing operations in following written instruction

Measurement interval	Operation
Reading	(1) Assign surface structure segmentation
Thinking	(2) Assign the locative features of the preposition to the referent noun
	(3) Derive the locative features for the other noun
	(4) Plan the order of output
Drawing	(5) Execute the output plan
	(6) Monitor the correspondence between (5) and (1)

processes derived from the sentence-picture verification task are concerned with comparison processes, such comparisons appear to play a much smaller part in the comprehension of imperatives (e.g. category (6) in Table 4.10), if indeed they occur at all. Such differences in the kinds of processes mediating comprehension inevitably raise questions about the generality of the findings from particular experimental paradigms used by psycholinguists. This is not the appropriate place to explore such questions. They have been considered in detail elsewhere (e.g. Fillenbaum, 1970; Aaronson, 1976; Wright, in press). Here the need is only to emphasize that the notion of 'comprehension' may benefit from sharper definition. An apparently straightforward question such as 'What happens when we understand sentences?' (e.g. Johnson-Laird, 1974) may turn out to be as inappropriate as asking 'What happens when we learn?'

SUMMARY

Four studies are reported, all concerned with the comprehension processes underlying people's ability to read and carry out a written instruction such as *Draw a circle above a square*. The first three experiments explore whether such performances can be meaningfully divided into successive time periods which for convenience are labelled reading, thinking, and drawing. The technique used is to look for differential repetition effects within the three different time periods. Experiment I shows that repetition of the sentence form shortens only the reading period. Experiment II shows that repetition of the preposition shortens only the thinking period. Experiment III shows that the drawing period is shortened by verbatim repetition of the entire instruction. It is concluded that the three intervals being examined are not arbitrary time-slices through performance but reflect the dominance of different psychological processing operations at different periods after the instructions have been presented.

Experiment IV explores what these processing operations might be. It uses the technique of trisecting performance into reading, thinking, and drawing periods and examines the effects that different sentence forms have on the durations of these periods. The reading period is found to be shorter for *Draw a circle above a square* than for *Above a square draw a circle*. It is suggested that this may reflect the relative ease of assigning surface structure segmentation to the two sentence forms. Both the thinking period and the drawing period are shorter for *Draw a square with a circle above it* than for *Above a square draw a circle*. It is suggested that the shorter thinking period may arise from the differential ease of assigning locative information to the first noun, *square*, whereas the shorter drawing period may arise from monitoring processes which occur during drawing. The need for further experimental support for these suggestions is recognized, but the suggestions appear to point towards a model of the processes underlying the comprehension of imperatives that differs in many respects from models of comprehension derived from the sentence-picture verification paradigm.

ACKNOWLEDGEMENTS

The authors would like to acknowledge their indebtedness to Mr Raymond Bloomfield. It was his skill and expertise in providing both the online and the offline computer-interfacing facilities that made this series of experiments possible. We are also very appreciative of the detailed, helpful comments made by Professor G. B. Flores d'Arcais on an earlier version of this paper.

REFERENCES

Aaronson, D. Performance theories for sentence coding: Some qualitative observations. *Journal of Experimental Psychology: Human Perception and Performance*, 1976, **2**, 42–55.

Aaronson, D. and Scarborough, H. S. Performance theories for sentence coding: Some quantitative evidence. *Journal of Experimental Psychology: Human Perception and Performance*, 1976, **2**, 56–70.

Carpenter, P. A. and Just, M. Sentence comprehension: A psycholinguistic processing model of verification. *Psychological Review*, 1975, **82**, 45–73.

Clark, H. H. The influence of language on solving three-term series problems. *Journal of Experimental Psychology*, 1969, **82**, 205–215.

Clark, H. H. The chronometric study of meaning components. Paper presented at the Colloque International sur les Problèmes Actuels—Psycholinguistique, C.N.R.S., Paris, December 1971.

Clark, H. H. and Clark, E. V. Semantic distinctions and memory for complex sentences. *Quarterly Journal of Experimental Psychology*, 1968, **20**, 129–138.

Clark, H. H. and Clark, E. V. *Psychology and language. An introduction to psycholinguistics.* New York: Harcourt, Brace, Jovanovich, 1977.

Clark, H. H. and Lucy, P. Understanding what is meant from what is said: A study of conversationally conveyed requests. *Journal of Verbal Learning and Verbal Behavior*, 1975, **14**, 56–72.

Fillenbaum, S. On the use of memorial techniques to assess syntactic structures. *Psychological Bulletin*, 1970, **73**, 231–237.

Fillenbaum, S. A note on memory for sense: Incidental recognition of warnings phrased as conditional, disjunctives, and conjunctives. *Bulletin of the Psychonomic Society*, 1975, **6**, 293–294.

Huttenlocher, J. and Strauss, S. Comprehension and a statement's relation to the situation it describes. *Journal of Verbal Learning and Verbal Behavior*, 1968, **7**, 527–530.

Johnson-Laird, P. N. Experimental psycholinguistics. *Annual Review of Psychology*, 1974, **25**, 135–160.

Manelis, L. and Yekovich, F. R. Repetition of propositional arguments in sentences. *Journal of Verbal Learning and Verbal Behavior*, 1976, **15**, 301–312.

Martin, J. E., Kolodziej, B., and Genay, J. Segmentation of sentences into phonological phrases as a function of constituent length. *Journal of Verbal Learning and Verbal Behavior*, 1971, **10**, 226–233.

Mehler, J. and Carey, P. Role of surface and base structure in the perception of sentences. *Journal of Verbal Learning and Verbal Behavior*, 1967, **6**, 335-338.

Seymour, P. H. K. Generation of a pictorial code. *Memory and Cognition*, 1974, **2**, 224-232.

Tanenhaus, M. K., Carroll, J. M., and Bever, T.G. Sentence-picture verification models as theories of sentence comprehension: A critique of Carpenter and Just. *Psychological Review*, 1976, **83**, 310-317.

Wright, P. Processing imperatives: Some transfer effects when following a sequence of verbal instructions. Paper presented at the British Psychological Society, London, December 1974.

Wright, P. Feeding the information eaters: Suggestions for integrating pure and applied research on language comprehension. *Instructional Science* (in press).

Winograd, T. *Understanding natural language*. New York: Academic Press, 1972.

Chapter 5

The Perception of Complex Sentences

Giovanni B. Flores d'Arcais

PERCEPTUAL DECISIONS IN LANGUAGE SEGMENTATION

There are several usages of the word 'perception' in psycholinguistic literature. In some studies, for example, the term is used to indicate the process of detection of certain linguistic elements, from the phoneme to the syllable to the word. In other studies the term is used for typical tasks involving judgments about the structure or the grammaticality of sentences. In other contexts perception means the process of perceptual segmentation of the speech segment into meaningful units.

In this chapter the term will be used primarily in the latter sense, to indicate the assignment of a certain structure to the incoming speech signal. Perception then means the process by which the incoming signal is segmented into units which can be given a meaningful interpretation. For example, the perception of a word in a sentence implies the isolation of a particular word unit out of the sequence of sound elements present in the linguistic signal. We are not concerned here with the correct identification of the speech signal as intended by the speaker, but with the process through which a perceptual structure is imposed on the incoming signal, be it 'correct' or not.

The exposure to a totally unfamiliar and remote language offers a dramatic example of a non-segmented event, characterized by a lack of perceptual breaks capable of signalling the end of units, be these words or phrases. In the same situation, the knowledge of one or a few words in an otherwise totally unknown language might result in a radical perceptual change, the known words being perceptually isolated as clear units within a non-structured sequence of sounds.

The idea on which this work is based is that the perceptual process consists of attributing a structure to the incoming signal by isolating several units at different levels. This process requires a series of *perceptual decisions*, on the basis of which the hearer decides that a word is completed or that a particular break between two syllables marks the end of a sentence, and so forth. We would like to propose that there are several levels of such perceptual decisions about which elements of the incoming signal have to be segmented and given an appropriate interpretation: these levels may be represented by the phoneme, the syllable, the morpheme, the constituent, or the clause. Notice that it is by no means suggested that the process of perceptual segmentation starts at the 'lowest' of such levels (for example the level of the phoneme), from which it proceeds 'upward' to the other levels. A perceptual decision made at one level has a certain influence on the decision-making process at the other levels, both 'above' and 'below' (for example, detecting a phoneme which is part of a meaningful word might be, under certain conditions, easier than detecting the same phoneme in a meaningless syllable).

The general idea which we favour is that the isolation of a linguistic unit is an active process undertaken by the listener, for whom the acoustic information represents only the raw material to be used in the production of a perceptual response. This process requires use of the following components: (a) the knowledge of the phonological, morphological, and syntactic rules of the language; (b) some knowledge of the lexicon of the language, as a tool to isolate certain word units when making perceptual decisions; (c) the awareness of the information carried by prosodic features in the language; and (d) the use of certain heuristics or perceptual strategies as a means of encoding certain elements of the incoming signal in a given sequence, and of making hypotheses about a possible break between word units, constituent units, or clause units, etc.

In this chapter we are concerned with the process of perceptual segmentation when the incoming signal is a *complex sentence*, that is, a sentence composed of a main clause and of one or more subordinate clauses. Three main arguments will be developed concerning this process. First, it is proposed that among the different levels of perceptual decisions, the *clause* represents an important level of perceptual segmentation. According to this notion, perceptual assignment of an interpretable structure would be made clause by clause. This proposal is consistent with the idea that sentence processing involves a level of syntactic processing at which syntactic information is fully available in working memory for computation for a brief period of time: after this period, most syntactic information will either be 'abandoned' and subject to rapid decay, or substituted by the information coming next in sequence. The 'unit' within which syntactic processing would take place in order to extract semantic interpretation would normally correspond to the clause. Once a speech segment has been perceptually isolated as a clause, processed and understood, its information is stored in memory and processing of the next segment can take place.

Second, it is suggested that the processing of different types of clauses within a complex sentence may impose different loads on the processor, and that subordinate clauses, which are less canonical and usually marked with sub-ordinate conjunctions, will require more 'work' in order to be given an appro-priate perceptual structure. Furthermore, such a structure would be less stable, and this perceptual instability could result in perceptual or mnestic trans-formation into a more 'regular' or standard form.

Third, it is proposed that, depending on the strength of the relationship between the clauses, surface information of one clause might still be used when processing the next: the perceptual decisions taken at the end of one clause might have to leave some surface material available for processing the following clause unit.

In the first part of the chapter we will briefly review some evidence for the suggestion that decoding a complex sentence may involve, at some level, the processing of the clauses as units. We will present some results in favour of the hypothesis that sentences are processed clause by clause. We shall then consider some experimental support for the hypothesis that there is a difference between processing main and subordinate clauses, and we will see whether the order of main and subordinate within a complex sentence has some effect on processing. In the second part of the chapter, the results of four experiments on the perception and processing of complex sentences will be presented and discussed.

THE CLAUSE AS A LEVEL OF PERCEPTUAL ORGANIZATION

We have hypothesized that an important perceptual and processing unit within a long sentence is the clause. Information about the surface linguistic structure would be retained only for the time necessary to process one clause. Once this clause has been isolated, interpreted, and its meaning stored in memory, surface syntactic information would undergo a rapid decay. In this section we will briefly review some experimental evidence bearing on this point: we will examine the psycholinguistic literature for results capable of supporting the notion that the clause represents an important level of perceptual decision in sentence processing.

How can we obtain evidence on the perceptual organization of units such as the clause? Unlike visual perception studies, subjects' reports about the perceptual organization of speech signals are a rather weak source of evidence. We have to rely either on responses under particularly difficult or limited presentation conditions, or on some non-direct indicator of perceptual organization. Let us have a very quick look at some classes of possible methods useful for our problem (for a more complete presentation of these methods, see Levelt's review in this book).

One possibility consists of requiring quick processing of sentences, at a faster than normal processing rate, which is therefore probably more difficult and vulnerable to errors. Such a 'restricted' presentation might consist of a rapid visual exposure to the successive parts of the sentence, as with a rapid exposure of the individual words of a sentence, which was the method adopted by Forster (1970, and in several other papers), the task being to recall as much as possible of the material presented. Another procedure might consist of the presentation of the sentences together with *noise*, or in the form of *time-compressed* speech. This last method has been used rather infrequently in studies of language perception (Foulke, 1971; Wingfield, 1975), yet it seems rather a good method because of the possibility of producing an increase in processing speed in a very fine and controlled way.

In the search for indicators of perceptual segmentation, one possibility is to look for some 'natural' indices, such as the reports on the perceived duration of pauses between 'parts of speech': one can assume that such pauses can be perceived as longer—independently of their real duration—when they fall between 'natural' units of language perception. However, while *measurements* of pauses have been widely used in the study of speech production, the use of reports on pause duration made while listening to speech is probably a rather weak indicator, given the extremely short durations of the events which must be discriminated for their phenomenal length.

A better alternative is to look for the phenomenal action of events external to the linguistic signal during sentence processing, and to see the extent to which some particular units, such as the word, the immediate constituent, or the clause, are vulnerable or resistant to the intrusion of such events, much in the same way that resistance to figural intrusion has been used in visual perception studies to 'measure' the structural qualities of figures.

A further possibility consists of using evidence from short-term memory, under the assumption that the availability of material in STM can be used as evidence for perceptual organization. Finally, data on recall of sentences can also be used as a basis for inferences on perceptual organization, in much the same way as students of visual perception have used reproductions of figures to make inferences not only on mnestic structural transformations, but also on the action of principles of organization in the perception of figures.

The largest amount of available data, among the different paradigms just described, comes from a series of 'click' studies carried out by Fodor, Bever, and Garrett (Fodor and Bever, 1965; Garrett, 1965; Garrett, Bever, and Fodor, 1966; Bever, Garrett, and Hurtig, 1973). The experimental paradigm is well known and does not need a presentation here.

While the first click studies were intended to test the 'psychological reality' of surface linguistic constructs such as the immediate constituents, and click displacements were in fact repeatedly found to go towards constituent breaks, these studies also showed a clear tendency for the clicks to be attracted to clause boundaries: the click-displacement effects seem to be particularly evident at surface clause boundaries.

Stronger evidence for clausal segmentation comes from click data which did not consist of judgments on the localization, but of other 'on-line' responses to the extraneous events. Clicks superimposed on or near to major clausal boundaries are responded to much faster in a reaction-time task than are clicks within major constituents (Holmes and Forster, 1970). According to the results of Abrams and Bever (1969), a click superimposed towards the end of a clause (before interclausal break) requires a longer RT than clicks located at the beginning of the clause. This result suggests the interpretation that processing load increases towards the end of the clause, and that at the beginning of it the 'processor' is still in a condition to devote more attention to such extraneous events as the click.

Clear effects of interest also emerge when other variations on the basic 'click' method are introduced. In a study by Wingfield and Klein (1971), instead of localization of extraneous clicks, source localization was used as the dependent variable: the sentences were presented over dichotic earphones and switched at a certain moment from one ear to the other, and subjects were asked to report the sentences and indicate where switching had occurred. Source localization was much more accurate when ear switch occurred at the main syntactic boundaries marking the interval between two clauses.

Another source of evidence about the notion of perceptual segmentation of linguistic material at the level of the clause is to be found in experiments on the immediate recall of sentences. If spoken discourse is interrupted during presentation and subjects are tested for immediate recall of the material presented just before the interruption, then the amount of material which a subject can recall verbatim can be used as an indication of syntactic processing: or in other words, recall of the terminal portion of the speech just presented might offer some information about the size of the units still being processed (Jarvella, 1970, 1971). In a series of experiments based on this paradigm, verbatim recall was highest for words within the last clause presented before interruption, and much lower for all segments presented prior to the last clause (Jarvella, 1971). These recall data can be interpreted as indications that speech processing units tend to correspond to surface clause units. According to these results, then, it may be concluded that sentences are processed and organized in memory clause by clause (Jarvella, 1970, 1971; Jarvella and Herman, 1972).

If target words are given after a sentence, or part of it, has been presented, and subjects are asked to decide as quickly as possible whether the target word was presented within the given sentence material, it has been demonstrated that with two-clause sentences listeners respond faster to probe words taken from the second rather than the first clause, even when both words are equidistant from the end of the sentences and are acoustically the same (Caplan, 1972), as in the following example:

(1) Now that artists are working in *oil*, prints are rare.
(2) Now that artists are working fewer hours, *oil* prints are rare.

The probe word was in both cases *oil*. With sentences of type (2) RT were shorter than with sentences of type (1).

It is interesting to note that perceptual segmentation based on clausal boundaries might be made in the absence of intonational cues (Abrams and Bever, 1969). However, prosodic features may offer additional information for the determination of clause boundaries (Wingfield, 1975).

Evidence for the idea of sentence segmentation at the level of the clause also comes from data on language production: it is, nonetheless, an open question as to what extent such results can be relevant for conclusions on language perception. In speech production, *filled pauses* seem more frequent before and at the beginning of longer clauses (Cook, Smith, and Lalljee, 1974), thus perhaps indicating some kind of 'span of planning' at the level of the clause. Also Boomer's data (1965) on filled pauses can be interpreted as evidence for a segmentation of speech production clause by clause.

PERCEPTUAL DECISIONS FOR THE MAIN AND THE SUBORDINATE CLAUSE

So far we have tried to examine evidence in favour of the idea that an important level of perceptual segmentation is the clause. We have not yet considered, however, the question whether there might be differences in the perceptual organization for different types of clauses. Let us limit our attention to complex sentences consisting of a main and one or more subordinate clauses, joined by a subordinating conjunction. The evidence so far reviewed and the arguments discussed do not allow us to decide whether all clauses are processed in the same way or whether in terms of perceptual complexity there are some differences. A typical subordinate clause, as it is less canonical in its form, could be more resistant to perceptual aggregation: the listener could be waiting for additional linguistic data before making a decision about the clausal unit, or he could make hypotheses about a different structure before deciding on the form of the subordination. All this would mean that a greater amount of perceptual work is involved in the process of structuring a subordinate clause, and a larger perceptual instability. In Gestalt terminology, we could suggest that the subordinate clause is a less 'good form' and therefore also less stable. If this argument is valid, then we should find some differences in the case of perceptual organization of a main and of a subordinate clause.

Another question, related to the preceding one, is the possible effect of the order of main and subordinate clauses on perceptual organization. According to linguistic analysis (at least in terms of transformational grammar) a sentence with the main clause in first position is derivationally simpler. Also, the main clause, since it is the more natural result of a perceptual strategy which constructs a 'canonical' clausal unit out of the first string of words which can potentially be organized as an SVO (or of a similar strategy), would, as the *theme* of the sentence, be strongly preferred in processing with the remaining subordinate clause then assigned to a dependent position (Bever, 1970). If these arguments are correct, we should expect a higher perceptual simplicity of the order main/subordinate as opposed to the order subordinate/main.

The experimental evidence on both questions is, however, rather scarce. In Kornfeld's study (1973a,b), latencies in deciding whether a probe word was present in a sentence previously given were shorter when the target word was in the main than when it was in the subordinate clause, thereby indicating a different 'perceptual load' for the two types of clauses, with fewer processing difficulties in the main clause. This point definitely needs more direct experimental testing.

Some evidence also exists that the order of the two clauses within the sentence has an effect on processing. In the same experiment by Kornfeld (1973a), probe latencies were shorter for the main/subordinate order than for subordinate/main. Holmes (1973) found that two-clause sentences are easier to perceive when the main clause occurs first. This effect was limited to adverbial and noun-phrase complements, while the reverse effect was obtained for relative clauses. Jarvella and Herman (1972) found that sentences with main/subordinate clause order were recalled significantly *less well* than those with subordinate/main order. They interpret this result as due to the fact that listeners delay the interpretation of the material in sentences with subordinate/main clause order.

Nominals in subject position as in 'That Mary was happy surprised Max' were rated for ease of comprehension as harder to comprehend than nominals in object position, and preposed adverbials ('When Mary left, Max was happy') were rated as more difficult to comprehend than postponed adverbials (Weksel and Bever, 1966).

THE PROBLEM

The experiments reviewed thus far allow us to make the following conclusions:

(a) There is definite evidence that the clause represents an important level of perceptual segmentation and of processing.

(b) There is some, but still very little evidence for the hypothesis that processing the main clause is easier than processing the subordinate clause.

(c) There is some evidence that the order of the main and of the subordinate with a two-clause sentence has an effect on processing: sentences with the order main/subordinate seem to be easier to process than sentences with the order subordinate/main.

As we have seen, the experimental evidence is still rather weak: the main bulk comes from click studies which, as has been pointed out by several authors (see Levelt, this book) are not without serious methodological weaknesses.

Alternative procedures designed to avoid or reduce possible response biases made use of direct indicators of the detection of the non-linguistic event: measuring latencies in detecting the clicks, which does obviously require a response *during* sentence processing, is a method which has been used with success by Holmes and Forster (1972). Another attempt to overcome response-biases and to obtain a more direct indication of perceptual segmentation has been the use of a 'phoneme-monitor task' adopted by Foss and his associates (Foss, 1969; Foss and Lynch, 1969; Hakes and Foss, 1970; etc.). The method yielded a rather sensitive indicator of differences in syntactic processing; for example, in the comprehension of right-branching or self-embedded sentences (Foss and Lynch, 1969), or pronoun complementization, and so forth. However, the method also has a serious weakness. The nature of the task, detecting a phoneme within an organized sequence of meaningful words, does not allow the experimenter to control for possible expectation sets. Phoneme distributions within meaningful sentences are by no means random distributions, and the morphological, syntactic, and semantic characteristics of a language do impose several constraints on the type of phonemes which may appear at a certain position in the sentence. The subject of a phoneme-monitor experiment may therefore develop certain expectations for a given word, and anticipate his reaction. Another source of bias might be dependent on the information about a given sound which is already present in the syllable that precedes the target consonant, or even a few syllables before, as recent work in the perception of speech has shown (see, for example, Nooteboom and Cohen, 1975).

The procedures used to obtain indicators of perceptual segmentation in our experiments were chosen with consideration of the methodological short-comings already discussed. The reasoning underlying our work has been the same: when the listener is making hypotheses about the incoming message, and is assigning some structure to it, his attention is less available for the processing of other sensory information. In models of contemporary cognitive literature this idea has become so common since Broadbent's filter model (1958), that no reference is necessary here. Delays in detecting a very brief event superimposed on the linguistic material can be used as an indication of the difficulty of the primary processing task, and as an indication of the points where perceptual segmentation has been possible: at these points detection should be easier, that is, more accurate. In other words, if we superimpose an extraneous signal on the linguistic material being processed, or if we produce some brief event, or supply an extra target which is difficult to detect, and if we look for some measure of the accuracy of ease of detection or of processing the extraneous event, then the more accurate or the better the detection is at a given point, the more likely it is that the same point represents a 'natural' break between units with higher cohesion or with a stronger internal structure. Certain portions of the linguistic event have been isolated and given some perceptual structure, and the points which mark the interval between such perceptual units are more valnerable to penetration and more available for quick and precise processing of events extraneous to the linguistic material.

The methods used in our experiments were (a) measuring latencies in detecting ear switching; and (b) measuring latencies in detecting a brief non-speech sound during the presentation of complex sentences. In both cases, comprehension of the sentences was tested to ensure adequate linguistic processing as the primary task of the subjects.

The questions asked in the present study were related to the notions of perceptual segmentation stated at the beginning of the chapter, and can be summarized as follows:

(a) Can we speak of perceptual segmentation at the level of the clause in processing complex sentences?

(b) Is there a difference in processing difficulty between the main and the subordinate clause? Is a higher perceptual load required by the subordinate clause, which is marked by a conjunction, and which in some languages, such as Dutch, the language which we used in our experiments I and II, demands post-position of the verb?

(c) Does the order main/subordinate clause in a two-clause sentence make a difference in perceptual segmentation?

DETECTION OF EAR SWITCHING: EXPERIMENT I

The experimental technique which we have used was based on the previously mentioned method introduced by Wingfield and Klein (1971). In their study, the experimental sentences were presented to one ear and switched to the other ear either between or within major linguistic constituents: subjects were requested to write down the sentences and to indicate where ear switching had occurred. In our experiment the dependent variable used was *latency in detecting ear switching*. The sentence was presented to both ears with an attenuation of about 3–5 dB in one ear. The paradigm was, therefore, a 'dichotic' presentation, with the same message presented in the two ears at two different intensity levels. Switching only had the effect of interchanging the physical dominance of the two messages, (one loud and the other attenuated). Phenomenally, this kind of dichotic presentation results in a localization of the signal 'somewhere within the head' in the direction of the 'louder' messages, while switching has the effect of producing a kind of dislocation of the signal 'within the head' from one side of the head to the other. Notice that by manipulating the difference in intensity level it should to some extent be possible to control the difficulty of the task: when both ears receive an identical signal, under good switching conditions, with the same intensity level, switching should not be noticed since the two ears are stimulated in an identical way. When the difference in intensity is very small, localization of the louder signal is difficult and detection of ear switch is also difficult and might take longer, although so far we have not explored this question. From our preliminary and very partial observations, we can conclude that it seems possible to some extent to control response latencies of subjects through manipulation of the difference in intensity between the two messages. This fact may be used as a possible way of increasing the sensitivity of the measure.

Method

Material and design. Twenty complex sentences were used as experimental material. They were all two-clause sentences, comprising a main and a subordinate clause, temporal or causal, with both clauses having approximately the same length as measured by the number of syllables. Half of the sentences had the structure main/subordinate, half the reverse order. The total number of sentences was based on the following. Ear switch was to occur (a) about three or four syllables before the end of the first clause; (b) at the main boundary between the two clauses (more exactly: on the first syllable of the first word of the second clause); (c) three or four syllables before the end of the second clause, that is, before the end of the sentence. In a fourth condition (d), no switch occurred. To decrease bias toward expectation of the switch (3:1), this last condition was put into effect twice (therefore producing a ratio of three sentences with switch to two without it). Since we had two orders of the clauses, the design so far required ten sentences. For each of the above switch conditions two sentences were used (four for the no-switch condition) thus yielding a total of 20 sentences (12 with switching, 8 without). Half were temporal, half causal sentences. Order of clause and the position of the switch were the main factors in a 2×3 design.

Subjects and procedure. Sixteen adult subjects, mostly university students, took part in the experiment, which was carried out individually with the sentences presented over high-fidelity earphones. Ear switching started a clock counter which was stopped when the subject pressed a response on a button on the instructions. Emphasis was given in the instructions to avoid false alarms: the subject had to be really sure before pressing the button. Immediately after the presentation of the sentence, subjects were requested, through the earphone, to answer a question about the sentence. The questions were of different types, depending on the sentence. The most typical were of the following forms: (a) Who has done something? (b) When did event A occur? (c) Did A occur before B? (d) Why did event A happen? (e) Why did X do Y? Questions of the type (b) and (c), were given only after temporal sentences, (d) and (e) only after causal sentences. The responses of the subjects were recorded on a tape. The criterion for correctness was the appropriateness of the response in relation to the input sentence.

The 20 experimental sentences were preceded by eight training sentences of a different syntactic form, half of them including ear switching.

Scoring. For each of the switching conditions, six scores were obtained for each subject, based on the mean between the two sentences presented in the same switch condition, as follows: (1) First score: main/subordinate with switch during the first clause; (2) Second score, main/subordinate with switch during the second clause, etc. The form of the clause (temporal or causal) was not considered in this computation. Latencies were also excluded for those few sentences for which subjects gave either a wrong or no answer to the question given after presentation. In some cases the data were missing due to failure in detecting ear switching. The following data were also excluded from computation: (a) in a few cases subjects 'anticipated' the real switching: this may be considered equivalent to the false alarms produced in the no-switching conditions, and as such these were obviously excluded from the computation; (b) in few cases extremely high latencies were measured (we arbitrarily set a criterion for an exceptionally high latency at 1500 msec); these were considered equivalent to no response and excluded from computation. All together, there were 23 cases of missing data, false alarms etc., out of a total of 192 possible measures. In all these 23 cases the latency score was based on one measure only (with the exception of two cases where both measures were lacking: two missing data were then given).

Results

The mean latencies for the six conditions are presented in Table 5.1. An analysis of variance was carried out on the results, followed by a comparison of the means for the three switch conditions. Order of clause did not have any significant effect on the latencies, but switch position showed a significant effect ($F = 3.62$; d.f. $= 2,15$; $p < .05$). Comparison of the three means showed that latencies in detecting ear switching are significantly lower ($t = 3.07$; $p < .01$) when switching is made at the main interclausal boundary, in correspondence with the beginning of the second clause. Latencies are longer when switching occurs during a subordinate rather than during the main clause, while for switching in the second clause the effect is neutralized and the main clauses turn out slightly, but not significantly, worse. This interaction effect between type of clause and position in the sentence is a most interesting fact. When switching occurs in the first part of the sentence, the main clause is favoured; when switching occurs in the second clause, the latencies are slightly shorter for the subordinate.

Table 5.1   Experiment I. Mean latencies (milliseconds) in detecting ear switch during presentation of two-clause sentences

| Order of clauses | Position of switch | | | Average |
	First clause	Interclause boundary	Second clause	
Main/Subordinate	447	393	521	454
Subordinate/Main	522	435	497	484
Both orders	484	414	507	

Discussion

The first clear result is the lower latency obtained for ear switching in correspondence with the beginning of the second clause. We could interpret the result by assuming that the listener has just finished processing the first clause and is now 'waiting for' the second to occur: since his attention is fully available, he may immediately notice the change of ear dominance and still have time to 'catch' the full clause. This interpretation is consistent with the idea of processing clause by clause. When switching occurs within clause units, it interrupts processing and is therefore somewhat delayed in reaction.

The interaction found seems at first glance to be inconsistent with the idea, put forward before, of a higher 'load' for the processing of the subordinate clause. However, it is possible to interpret the results in the following way: when a sentence begins with a main clause and switching occurs, then it should be relatively easy to detect the switch. When switching takes place during a first-position subordinate clause, the higher processing load required by it produces a higher latency. When, on the other hand, switching is made during presentation of the second clause, if this is the main clause, the hearer may still be 'carrying' the load of the first subordinate, and therefore be somewhat slower in detecting the switch. When, finally, the main clause is in the first position, its processing is more likely to have been completed without much 'residual load', and consequently processing of the subordinate clause may become easier. The two effects, namely the lower amount of difficulty involved in processing the main clause and the 'residual load' from the first clause, tend to cancel out in this situation.

Notice that this result neatly corresponds to the results obtained by Jarvella and Herman (1972).

DETECTION OF A TONE DURING SENTENCE PROCESSING: EXPERIMENT II

The main purpose of this experiment was to test, as a possible sensitive indicator of perceptual segmentation, the effectiveness of the method of measuring latencies in detecting an extraneous acoustic event presented while the subject was listening to complex sentences. The extraneous event was a 30 msec 1000 Hz tone superimposed on two-clause temporal sentences during either the first or the second clause, or at the boundary between the clauses.

Method, material, and subject

Sixty-four temporal sentences each comprising two clauses, a main and a subordinate introduced by the conjunction *voordat* (before) or *nadat* (after), were used as experimental sentences. The noise was a 30 msec 1000 Hz tone, with an intensity level corresponding to the average of the loudest 'peaks' of the sentences. The tone was recorded on the second track of a stereo tape whose first track contained the sentence. Precise localization of the points in which the tone had to appear was determined through a system of timers and gates which allowed localization of any point of the sentence with a precision to the millisecond. Determination of the points upon which the tone was to be superimposed was facilitated by visual inspection of the frequency spectrum of the sentences on an oscilloscope. The tone was superimposed on the first or last part of the clause, or at the boundary between the clauses, according to the following schema: (a) in the first clause, three syllables after the beginning of the sentence; (b) in the first clause, two syllables before the interclausal boundary; (c) at the interclausal boundary; (d) in the second clause, three syllables after the beginning of the clause; (e) two or three syllables before the end of the clause; and (f) no tone was presented. A total of 24 sentences without tone ('catch trials'), corresponding to condition (f)), were presented. The experimental material therefore included a total of 64 sentences with tone and 24 without tone.

The sentences and the tone were presented binaurally through an earphone to the subject, who was sitting in an isolated chamber. The experimental sentences were preceded by eight training, non-experimental sentences. The subject had to press a response key as soon as he heard the noise. Immediately after the sentence, a word was presented to the subject indicating whether he had to tell which event had occurred *first*, which had occurred *second*, or *both*, in order of occurrence. The responses were recorded on a tape for later control of their correctness.

Sixteen subjects, paid volunteer university students, took part in the experiment. Each subject received 32 sentences with tone and 12 sentences without tone. The latencies were recorded from onset of the tone to the responses of the subjects. When a wrong answer was given to the question presented after the sentence, the corresponding latencies were excluded from further analysis.

The following latency scores were obtained for analysis:

1. Individual scores for each sentence.

2. Combined scores for all sentences with the tone in the corresponding position: these were the median latencies for each individual subject over the sentences with the tone in the corresponding position.

3. Combined scores for all sentences with the tone in the first clause in both positions (conditions (a) and (b) above); for all sentences with the tone in the second clause in both positions (conditions (d) and (e)); and for the sentences with the tone at the interclausal boundary.

Results

The mean overall latency scores are presented in Table 5.2. An analysis of variance was carried out on these scores. Comparisons of means were made, whenever it was appropriate and interesting to our study, over these scores and the latency scores of the second type as specified above.

First, let us look at the overall difference in latency for tones superimposed on the clausal boundary or within the clauses. This difference is not significant. However, if we make a separate analysis of these latency scores for the two types of structures, we find that the latencies in detecting interclausal tones are longer when the tones come immediately after a subordinate than after a main clause ($p < .05$).

Second, consider the latencies for the tones within clauses for the two sentence structures main/subordinate and subordinate/main. When the subordinate precedes the main, the latencies in the second clause, both in initial and in final

Table 5.2a   Experiment II. Mean latency scores (milliseconds) in detecting tones superimposed within clauses on correctly interpreted sentences

| Order of clauses | Connective | | | |
	Before	After		
Main/Subordinate	345	395	380	Difference not significant
Subordinate/Main	366	352	359	
	356	374		
	Difference not significant			

Significant effects:
Difference 345 – 395 $p < 0.05$
            352 – 395 $p < 0.05$
Interaction type of connective/order of clause $p < 0.05$.

Table 5.2b   Experiment II. Mean latency scores (millisecond) in detecting tones superimposed within clauses on correctly interpreted sentences, partitioned by order of event

| Order of events | Connective | | | |
	Before	After		
S_1, S_2	345	352	349	Difference significant $p < 0.05$
S_2, S_1	366	395	381	
	356	374		

position, tend to be longer: as we shall see further on, this result is particularly clear for temporal sentences with the following general structure:

(3) Before S_2, S_1,

(in which S_1 and S_2 are the two clauses which refer to the two events in temporal succession). In this case the result may be an effect of order of mention. From several studies (e.g. Clark and Clark, 1968, and several others thereafter: for a brief review, see Flores d'Arcais, 1978) it is known that when the order of mention does not correspond to the order of events, as in the case we are considering, latencies tend to be longer.

Third, let us look at the overall effects for the sentences on which the tones have been superimposed within the clauses. The difference between sentences with *before* and those with *after*, shown in Table 5.2a and b, is not significant, nor is the overall difference between mains/subordinate and subordinate/main significant. The rank order of the mean latencies is the following (once again let S_1 indicate the clause expressing the first event in time, and S_2 the second event):

(4) S_1, before S_2: 345 msec
(5) After S_1, S_2: 352 msec
(6) Before S_2, S_1: 366 msec
(7) S_2 after S_1: 395 msec.

Individual comparisons between the means with the *t* test show only the differences between (4) and (7), and (5) and (7) to be significant (.01 and .05 level). Notice that the sentences in which the order of mention and the order of events are the same ((4) and (5)), show shorter latencies than the sentences with a mismatch between the two orders. This overall difference for the order-of-mention effect (349 versus 381 msec) is significant at the .05 level.

The data in Tables 5.2a and b also show an interesting and significant (.05 level) interaction between the type of conjunction and the order of the clauses: the sentences with *after* have the longest latency for the order main/subordinate.

Several interesting observations would also emerge from an analysis of the latency scores for the individual sentences. Given the low numerosity of our sample (16 subjects, with only 8 answering to any given sentence), to draw conclusions from such specific results would be too premature: further data are necessary before general conclusions can be attempted.

Discussion

A first important result is the lack of difference in processing difficulty between sentences with the conjunction *before* and *after*, as indicated by the latency in detecting a tone superimposed on the sentences. The second is the lack of difference found in the processing of main sentences with either of the two clausal orders, main/subordinate or subordinate/main. An interesting result is the significant effect of the order of mention: when the order of mention matches the order of the events, latencies tend to be shorter. Notice that this effect may be related to the form of the question-answering task: subjects have to pay close attention to the order of the events. When this matches the order of mention, the clauses may be easier to process. The effect is more marked in the second clause. When the two orders do not match, at the second clause the subjects might have to keep track of the 'mismatch' and this could impose an additional perceptual load.

PERCEPTUAL DECISIONS WITH DIFFERENT LEVELS OF SUBORDINATION: EXPERIMENT III

In the first part of this chapter we developed the suggestion that the clause represents an important level of perceptual decision-making and processing, and that surface information is more available while one is processing a clause than after the perceptual conclusion of it. How much surface information will still be available, once a clausal unit has been perceptually isolated and 'concluded'? We can think of different possibilities, from a complete 'clearing' of surface information immediately after completion of a clause, to a more or less rapid decay of such information, depending on the material and on the amount and type of new surface information contained in the next string of linguistic material. If we are dealing with a self-embedded sentence, for example, the completion of the main clause requires first the completion of the embedded clause. As Bever (1970), and Fodor, Bever, and Garrett (1974), among others, have argued, this fact might be one of the sources of the difficulty in processing self-embedded sentences. Even when a clause unit is completed, however, some 'links' to the new incoming unit could still be available.

Let us consider as examples two linguistic structures with different levels of subordination, and take as instances a sentence (8) composed of a main and a subordinate clause, and another sentence (9), with a main and two subordinates, the second of which is dependent on the first:

(8) Because John was tired, Mary prepared a cup of coffee;
(9) Because John was so tired, that he fell asleep, Mary prepared a cup of coffee.

(Probably in normal language usage we would prefer to relate the causal and the main clause more strictly with the introduction of a 'dative' pronoun, for example, in an expression such as ... 'Mary prepared him a cup of coffee'. However, we will not consider this point here.)

In both (8) and (9), the main clause can be processed in isolation and still be perfectly grammatical and understandable. On the other hand, the causal cannot be used alone. But if we compare the two causal clauses in (8) and (9) we find a difference. The causal in (9) is marked by a connective to the second subordinate, the consecutive clause. If we consider the events expressed in the two sentences, we might indicate them in the following way:

For (8) (a) John was tired;
For (8) (b) Mary made a cup of coffee.
For (9) (a) John was tired to an extent which had a consequence;
For (9) (b) John fell asleep (as a consequence of being tired);
For (9) (c) Mary made a cup of coffee.

If we consider the relation between the clauses in the two sentences, we might say that the two subordinate clauses in (9) are more related to each other than to the main clause. This notion of the 'strength' of relatedness is rather vague and far from being satisfactory, but intuitively it does make some sense; at any rate, it should correspond to the intuitions which speakers have about sentence structures. That this might be the case can be substantiated from a series of data collected in two studies on judgment of relatedness between clauses of complex sentences (Flores d'Arcais, unpublished data and a research report, 1970). In these studies, subjects were given complex sentences comprising several clauses, and were asked to judge on the relationship between the clauses by means of several methods, including forced choice of the two most closely related and the two least related clauses for each of the triads obtained with the $N(N-1)(N-2)/6$ combinations of the N clauses of each sentence. Cluster analysis applied to the typical similarity matrix obtained with such a procedure indicated certain clear and consistent 'groupings' of clauses with different 'levels' of perceptual relatedness: for example, a consecutive (such as in sentence (9)) was always judged as being very closely related to the clause which included the word *so*. Thus, speakers were able to offer consistent judgments of relatedness among clauses within complex sentences, which correspond to the notion we are trying to develop.

We might then propose that when two clauses are as strongly related and almost 'mutually supporting' as the two subordinate clauses in (9), this would be reflected in clausal processing. In sentence (9), part of the surface information of the causal clause might be kept 'available' until processing of the consecutive has taken place, while in (8) this would be less the case. In other words, we might expect different levels of perceptual elaboration within different sentence types.

Suppose, to further clarify our point, that we make the rather common analogy of clause processing with the processing of information in a computer. Let the working memory unit involved in keeping track of the parts of the clause be analogous to a register: as soon as words are identified they are put in this register, and once a clause unit has been isolated and processed, the information could be transmitted to an appropriate location in memory. In a computer the register could now be cleared for the processing of the following clause; in our system, however, we can think of part of the register as still occupied with some surface information of the previous clause, until processing of the following clause is completed.

At this point we can suggest a distinction within the relationship between clauses, with two labels for the poles of an underlying continuum. At one pole we would have a *strong dependency* between clauses, at the other pole the instances of *weak dependency*. An example of strong dependency would be the relationship between the consecutive and the causal in sentence (9), while the relationship between the causal and the main both in (8) and (9) would be somewhat weaker. Once more, this is a poorly defined distinction, and offered here only on intuitive grounds. We can expect that for a strongly dependent clause certain elements of the previous clause would be available more readily than for a weak dependent clause.

Let us reconsider sentence (9) and represent its structure through the symbols S_1, S_2, M (for first subordinate, second subordinate and main clause). According to our discussion, S_2 would have a strong dependency on S_1, while S_1 and M would have a weaker dependency relation. In order to make specific predictions about the processing of clauses with different strengths of dependency by keeping constant the position of the clauses, we can take the same three clauses of (9) in a different order, namely in the order MS_1S_2, as follows:

(9)a. Mary prepared a cup of coffee, because John was so tired, that he fell asleep.

Let us now take into consideration both for (9) and (9a) the last two clauses which are respectively S_2 and M, and S_1 and S_2, and suppose that they are equivalent with respect to length and number of words and syllables, and that they are not too different in terms of the accessibility of the semantic information. We can expect that after completion of the first of these last two clauses there will be less availability of surface information of S_2 when processing M, than of S_1 when processing S_2. Therefore, if during or immediately after processing of the second of the two we give a task which involves STM recovery of some surface material of the first of the two clauses, we might expect a difference in the recovery of the material under the two conditions. Namely we might expect the recovery from S_1 in the S_1S_2 combination to be better then the recovery from S_2 in the S_2M combination. This could be taken as an indication of a difference in the availability of the material of the preceding clause for perceptual decisions about the last clause.

The experimental paradigm chosen to test this notion was to ask subjects, after completion of a sentence, about the presence of a target word beginning with a given phoneme also specified immediately after sentence presentation. The task bears clear similarities to the method adopted by Jarvella (1971) or to the procedure employed by Caplan (1972). The search process, at any rate, requires some use of the surface information of the sentence: the more decay such surface information has undergone, the less easy it will be to produce a good performance in the task.

Method

Material. Twenty-four experimental sentences and 24 filler sentences of various length and syntactic types were used throughout the experiment. Of the experimental sentences, 12 had the form S_1S_2M, and 12 the form MS_1S_2. In 16 of the 24 experimental sentences there was a target, while in the other 8 no correct target was present. In half of the sentences the target was in the last clause (M or S_2); in the other half, in the second clause of the sentence (S_2 or S_1). The target word was never in the last two words of the sentence. The distribution of the positions of the target words within the two types of sentences was perfectly matched. For each sentence, half of the subjects were given as the target a word from the last clause, and the other half, a word from the second clause.

Procedure and subjects. The sentences were presented through a tape-recorder connected to a loudspeaker. Immediately after each sentence a question was presented on a screen by a slide projector. The questions were of several types and can be exemplified by the following: (a) Was there a word starting with *P*? (B) Was the word *dog* there? (c) Did John go home?

Notice that with such questions, sufficient attention should be expected for the meaning of the sentence, and not only attention for the first phoneme of all words. The type of question used for the 24 experimental sentences was (a), while questions of (b) and (c) type were used for the filler sentences. In the experimental sentences with a target word in the second or last clause, there was obviously only one word, namely the target, starting with the phoneme specified by a letter in the question. For the eight sentences with no correct target, no word started with the phoneme specified. The question remained on the screen for 5 sec, during which time the subject had to give an answer by marking a YES or a NO on a preprepared answer sheet. After each question, a 'ready' slide, with the identification number of the sentence to follow, to be matched on the answer sheet, appeared on the screen for 5 sec, and the cycle continued in this way with no interval: (a) Ready; (b) Sentence; (c) Question; (d) Ready. . . .

The subjects were 24 Italian students in education and psychology at the University of Padova, unpaid volunteers. The experiment was run individually or in small groups of two to four people, depending on the availability of subjects. The total duration of the experiment did not exceed 20 minutes, of which about 13 minutes were necessary for the presentation of the stimulus sentences and the responses of the subjects.

Scoring. The data consisted of the responses (YES or NO) to the questions about the target words; these responses were classified as correct or incorrect. The few missing answers were scored as incorrect. Separate frequency scores were computed for the 16 sentences with a correct target (for which the correct answer was YES) and for the eight sentences without a correct target (for which the correct answer was NO). Only the data on the 24 experimental sentences are reported.

Results

The proportion of correct responses is reported in Table 5.3. The clearest result is the difference between the two types of sentence for the detection of target words in the second, non-final clause: it is more difficult to retrieve a target word in a subordinate clause when the last clause is a main clause, less strongly related to the subordinate, than it is in the subordinate when a second-level subordinate is the last clause. The difference is significant beyond the .01 level (z for differences between the two proportions = 3.19). Second, there is a difference in the proportion of correct detections of the target word in the clause in the final position, and it seems easier to detect the target in a main clause. However, the difference found lacks significance. It also seems slightly easier to remember that there was no word beginning with a given letter when the clause in the last position is the main clause. Once more, the difference lacks significance. From the proportion of errors for the distractor trials (the sentence with no target) we might conclude that it is more difficult to find out that in a sentence there was no

Table 5.3   Experiment III. Proportion of correct detection of targets in the last two clauses. Proportions based on 16 target sentences and 8 non-target sentences, respectively. N = 24

Position of target	Sentence form[a]	
	MS_1S_2	S_1S_2M
Second clause	0.67	0.52
Third clause	0.80	0.89
No target[b]	0.49	0.55

[a]MS_1S_1 = Main, Subordinate$_1$, Subordinate$_2$.
  S_1S_2M = Subordinate$_1$, Subordinate$_2$, Main.
[b]The proportions indicate correct answer: 'No target'.

word starting with a given letter than to find out that there *was* a word with a given letter. However, to try to discuss and interpret this result would mean to try to propose a model for the possible searching strategies subjects would employ while looking back in memory for the target words, and the issue, however important it might be to information-processing theory, is not central to our discussion here.

Discussion

The results clearly show that surface aspects of the clause which precedes the final clause of a sentence seem more available in the case of a *strong dependency* subordinate relationship than in the case of *weak dependency*. In the first case the surface information is still more available for perceptual decisions than in the second. Notice that the distances of the target words from the end of the sentence were distributed in exactly the same way in the two sentence types, and this both in terms of number of words and number of immediate constituents, which were the same in the two conditions. In terms of simple serial position effect, therefore, we should not have expected a difference between the two conditions. The critical variable, then, seems to be the structure of the whole sentence. It is perhaps possible to state that processing a clause which is strongly dependent on a previous one requires a higher availability of surface aspects of the previous clause.

If we want to relate the present findings to the previous ones, we might suggest that if it is true that in language perception a clear segmentation is made clause by clause, in order to extract the meaning of a significant unit, it would be misleading to think of the process of segmentation of a clausal unit as a process advancing from one clause to the next after completely clearing the working memory and sending the semantic information contained in each clause to long-term storage units. While processing a new clause, certain surface elements of the previous clause or of previous clauses may be useful or necessary in order to make the right perceptual decision at any given point in the sentence.

The results of this experiment can be taken as an indication of different strengths in the perceptual organization of the clausal units. As always, one must be extremely cautious when making inferences on perceptual organization by using memory data. But differences in availability of surface aspects of a previous clause while processing another are probably not too weak as indicators of differences in perceptual organization.

SEGMENTATION OF CLAUSE UNITS IN SHORT-TERM RECALL IN CHILDREN: EXPERIMENT IV

In the introductory part of this chapter it was suggested that a strategy in language perception consists of the tendency to 'isolate' a unit by constructing it from the sound comprising the linguistic signal. When there are constraints on the use of linguistic information—for example as in a presentation of a sentence in noise, or when linguistic competence is still limited, as in the language of the child—we might expect segregation of linguistic units on the basis of 'incorrect' groupings of elements to make a noun phrase or a clause. For example, we might assume that among the strategies used in language perception a very important one would be the following:

Strategy 1: 'Isolate the first unit which can be given the structure NP_1VNP_2 (SVO) as the first clause of a complex sentence'.

A strategy of this type is suggested in the work of Bever (1970) and Fodor, Bever, and Garrett (1974).

We can present material which might (incorrectly) suggest a segmentation according to the above strategy and then test to see whether the strategy will be applied. We have in fact tried such a test in an experiment on short-term recall of complex sentences in children from 3.3 to 7 years old. The experimental paradigm was very simple: we presented the children with complex sentences and asked for immediate reproduction of the material presented. The sentences were constructed in such a way as to make an 'incorrect' reading possible according to Strategy 1: they were typically self-embedded sentences with an adverbial clause inserted.

Method

Material. Eighteen sentences composed of a main clause and an inserted dependent subject or adverbial clause were used throughout this experiment. The sentences were constructed according to the following basic structure:

(10) NP_1, Past Part. NP_2, V NP_3.

NP_1 V and NP_3 always made a simple main clause, with NP_3 being the direct object of a transitive V, or some complement. For the inserted unit Past Part NP_2, three basic structures were made;

(a) The inserted unit was a subjectal referring to NP_2, and NP_2 was a direct object, as in the following example:

(11) '*Il gatto, mangiato il topo, si leccar i baffi*' (The cat, having eaten the mouse, licks its whiskers).

(b) The inserted unit was a subjectal referring to NP_1 and having a passive form and an agent, as in the following example:

(12) '*Il bambino, sgridato dall'amico, corre via nel giardino*' (The boy, scolded by his friend, runs away in the garden).

Notice that the inserted passives were all *reversible* passives, so that a possible reversion would be semantically and pragmatically perfectly acceptable.

(c) A third type of sentence included an adverbial clause made with an intransitive verb and an NP_2 which was independent of the rest of the sentence, as in the following example:

(13) *'I bambini, finita la pioggia, giocarono un nuovo gioco'* (The boys, when it finished raining, played a new game).

The 12 sentences were presented individually to the subjects together with 12 other non-experimental sentences of various syntactic types. They were presented one at a time, and read to the subject with even intonation. The subjects were 56 children from 3.3 to 7 years old, either in Kindergarten or in first grade. For the purpose of analysis of the data, they were divided into three age groups as indicated in Table 5.4 as follows: group 1: $N = 17$; group 2: $N = 21$; group 3: $N = 18$. After the presentation of each sentence, the child had to repeat it back to the experimenter. The responses of the subject were recorded and transcribed for analysis.

Scoring. The responses were classified according to variations in repetition as related to intput. Let us consider the main types of the changes that emerged in the corpus of the answers.

(a) In some cases a clausal unit was made by joining together some of the words isolated at the beginning of the sentence, typically the first and the second NP and the past participle, which is transformed to a finite verb form. The result is normally a sequence of the form NP_1 V NP_2 with a SVO function, that is, a simple active sentence. These cases have been classified under the category 'First part as clause'.

(b) In some other cases the children made two explicit sentences in a typical coordinate form. Notice that this also implies the development of the implicit nominal or adverbial into an explicit clause.

(c) In some other cases only the main clause was given, leaving out the inserted form.

(d) The inserted adverbial could be made explicit in the form of a subordinate clause (e.g. sentence (11) could be reproduced as 'After having eaten the mouse, the cat licks at its whiskers').

The nominal categories reported in Table 5.4 correspond to these types of responses.

Results

The proportion of responses for the different categories is presented in Table 5.4. The main results are the following. First, and not surprisingly, there is an increase in the number of correct reproductions with age. Second, especially at the lower age level, a good proportion of the subjects make a clause out of the first elements which may be put together in an SVO sequence. We can have to types of this solution, as classified in Table 5.4. The first is to isolate the first NP, make the past partiple into a finite verb form and then make the second NP the

Table 5.4   Experiment IV. Proportions of the different sentence forms in children's reproductions

| | Form of reproduction | | | | | |
Type of subordinate clause	Same	Coord.	First part clause	Devel. subor.	Main only	Rest
(a) *Inserted subjectal*						
Age groups						
1 (3.3—4.6)	.24	.17	.37	—	.06	.16
2 (4.7—5.10)	.39	.10	.23	.08	.09	.11
3 (5.11—7)	.58	.11	.12	.06	.05	.08
(b) *Inserted passive*						
Age groups						
1 (3.3—4.6)	.20	.16	.27	.14	.14	.09
2 (4.7—5.10)	.34	.11	.16	.16	.17	.06
3 (5.11—7)	.53	.16	.09	.08	.09	.05
(c) *Inserted intr. adv.*						
Age groups						
1 (3.3—4.6)	.19	.09	.19	.10	.29	.15
2 (4.7—5.10)	.32	.04	.13	.15	.23	.13
3 (5.11—7)	.56	—	.03	.11	.16	.14

Response categories

Same: Reproduction identical to input sentences (minor changes allowed).
Coord.: Two coordinate clauses are given in reproduction (includes changes of original meaning).
First part clause: The first two NPs are joined together in a typical SVO structure.
Devel. subor.: The inserted adverbial is reproduced as an explicit subordinate preceded or followed by a main clause.
Main only: Only the main clause is reproduced, with exclusion of the inserted adverbial.
Rest: Rest category. It includes few cases in which only the inserted clause was reproduced.

direct object of the verb, and forget about the rest of the sentence. This solution can be exemplified by the following typical repetition of sentence (11):

(14) The cat eats the mouse.

A second solution is to make the first clause as just explained, and add the rest of the original main clause as a coordinate:

(15) The cat eats the mouse and licks his whiskers.

Notice that such a solution is rather difficult, both with the adverbial and with the passive nominal; in order to make an active clause out of these input sentences the children therefore do the following. For the passive, they can (a) either reverse the passive, by making the agent the surface subject of an active clause, or (b) make a clause which keeps the surface order but changes the meaning of the sentence. The first solution can be exemplified by the following:

(16) The friend scolds the boy,

while the second solution would be the following:

(17) The boy scolds the friend.

The second solution is by far the most frequent one resorted to by the younger children when they give a single explicit clause or when they make two coordinates. As for the adverbials, to make a single clause requires a radical change in the meaning of the input sentence—such solutions are not very frequent, and can be exemplified by the following repetitions of sentence (13):

(18) The children looked at the rain and played a game;
(19) The children were made wet by the rain.

The remaining categories of responses are rather clear and do not require further comments.

Discussion

Clearly the results indicate a strong tendency to try to make up a clause unit out of the first part of the input sentence. A strategy like *Strategy 1* therefore seems a clear operating principle in sentence processing. Another clear result is the tendency, shown by the youngest children, to keep the surface subject as much as possible: in the case of the passive nominals, there are more reproductions which keep the first NP as the subject of the output sentence, at the cost of violating the meaning of the original sentence, rather than make reproductions by inverting the surface structure in order to make the agent become the subject of the clause.

Even in this case, as in the previous experiment, it is an important question to what extent the results obtained in an experiment on short-term recall can be taken as indicative of segmentation at the perceptual level. Obviously an answer would require an experiment with a more specific perceptual task, which is certainly difficult to realize with small children. Also, one does not have to exclude the possibility of biases due to the processing load during sentence repetition: the child might start repeating back the sentence 'left to right' and during the time necessary for verbal encoding some structural changes might take place, as a result of limitation in output processing capacity. At any rate, the data are indicative of a tendency to construct clausal units from the beginning of the processing and before much elaboration can have taken place.

CONCLUSIONS

Let us briefly look at the most important results obtained in this study, beginning with the first two experiments. The methods used in these experiments seemed sensitive to small differences in the perceptual responses, and capable of yielding some interpretable results. The data obtained confirm the already available evidence cited in the first parts of this chapter. The clause seems to represent a linguistic level at which it is easy and natural for the perceiver to make perceptual decisions. The fact that events external to the linguistic signal tend to be processed more easily at interclausal boundaries than within clauses speak in favour of the hypothesis of perceptual segmentation of a complex sentence at the level of the single clauses. Also, the results point to some differences in the ease of processing main and subordinate clauses: the latter ones seem to require more attention from the listener. It is difficult to conclude, however, whether this difference is due to the syntactic form (the subordinate being somewhat 'deviant' from the most common SVO pattern which is typical of the active declarative sentences) or to the additional load required for processing the subordinating connective, or to the additional semantic information given by the subordinate, (which in our experiment was marked for *cause* or for *temporal* relation), or, finally, to some combination of these factors.

Some interesting results also emerged in relation to the conclusions on the processing of temporal sentences available in the literature (see a brief review in Flores d'Arcais, 1978). First, order of mention was again found to have a clear effect on sentence processing: when the order of mention of two events in a sentence matches the temporal order of the events, the sentence is easier to process. The order of the two clauses, which in some of the previous studies turned out to have a certain effect on sentence processing (main/subordinate being easier than subordinate/main), did not show any significant effect in the present study. Also, according to Clark and Clark (1968) and to Clark (1971), sentences with the connective *before* should be easier than sentences with *after*, because of the simpler semantic structure of the first conjunction. The small difference in the predicted direction obtained in the present study was not significant, however.

Another suggestion introduced in this chapter was that there might be different 'strengths' of perceptual organization in the isolation of the clause units: in some cases the clause would be perceptually more isolated, in other cases it would be more related to other clause units. Evidence for this has been obtained in the third experiment reported here, in which the level of surface material available for one clause when one is processing the following clause was measured by a task requiring a search in short-term memory for a given target. The results confirmed the hypothesis that when the dependency between two clauses is rather strong, there is more 'residual' availability of surface information of the first clause during processing of the second.

Finally, the last experiment on short-term recall of complex sentences in children indicated that children, when presented with a complex sentence, tend to construct clausal units from the beginning of the sentence, sometimes even at the cost of violating meaning. When dealing with difficult sentence material, then, children of 4 and 5 years tend to rely on a strategy of trying to 'make up' a sentence out of the input material 'as soon as possible'. These results are consistent with the idea that the perceiver may be working by making hypotheses about the structure of the incoming signal and will thus tentatively isolate successive clausal units.

It is interesting to observe that the same notion can be found in such contemporary simulation models of language understanding, as Winograd's (1972). In his model, a syntactic parser tries out a preliminary analysis on parts of the sentence and produces some syntactic structured output on which semantic analysis can be attempted. This check can in turn require some new attempts on grouping words, etc. The first level of analysis of a sentence would be at the surface level and would yield 'partial' syntactic structures. Much in a similar way to the children of our last experiment, Winograd's parser works with some heuristics which give some structure to a list of words and makes some hypotheses regarding such a structure, later to be tested for semantic properties.

In a way, this chapter is only a progress report, for more work is currently being carried out on the ways in which complex sentences with different levels of subordinating relations are organized perceptually.

As we proposed in the first part of the chapter, the general approach taken is to consider language perception as an active process of construction by using the incoming information as a basis for inferences about a possible structure. In addition to knowledge of the uses of language, and of the situational context, the perceiver is using several perceptual strategies as ways of quickly and economically organizing the input material into interpretable units. One of the main aims of this study and of the others in progress is to discover what kind of heuristics perceivers apply in giving structure to the incoming linguistic signals. The data so far collected and reported here are intended to represent a contribution in this direction.

SUMMARY

This paper deals with a series of four experiments on the perception and short-term processing of complex sentences; that is, sentences composed by a combination of a main clause with one or more subordinate clauses. Two basic notions underly the experiments. First, it was claimed that perception of complex sentences involves several levels of processing and decision-making, and that in the perceptual segmentation of the incoming signal the clause represents an important level: at this level, perceptual assignment of an interpretable structure is made clause by clause. Once a speech segment has been isolated as a clause, processed and understood, its information is stored in memory and processing of the next segment can take place. Second, it was suggested that the processing of different types of clauses within a complex sentence may impose different loads on the processor, and that subordinate clauses, which are less canonical in their form and usually marked by subordinate conjunctions, will require more work in order to be given an appropriate perceptual structure.

The first of the four experiments reported consisted of measuring latencies in the detection of ear switching during dichotic presentation of complex sentences presented in both ears at different intensity levels. The second study involved measuring latencies in the detection of a short tone superimposed on complex sentences in binaural presentation. The third experiment required memory search for a word beginning with a target phoneme specified only after the end of the sentence, and the fourth was an experiment on short-term recall of complex sentences in children. Among the results, the following are worth mentioning here:

(1) When the subordinate clause precedes the main, latencies in the detection of the tones superimposed at a given position are longer than those obtained with sentences in which the subordinate follows the main clause.

(2) Latencies for tones superimposed at the boundary between the two clauses are slightly longer after a subordinate clause than after the main clause, thus indicating a higher perceptual load for the first.

(3) Latencies in detecting ear switching are slightly longer during subordinate than during main clauses.

(4) The search for a target word in a clause followed by another clause (this being the last of the sentence) is more successful when the target is part of a clause which has a strong level of subordinating relationship to the last clause;

this is taken as an indication of different levels of availability of surface material within clauses during processing.

(5) Finally, a short-term recall of complex sentences by children indicates a strong tendency to segment the linguistic signal into clause units by joining together, from the very beginning of the sentence, whatever surface material can be used to make up a clausal unit.

The results are consistent with the idea of perceptual segmentation of complex sentences at the level of the clause, and with the suggestion that processing a subordinate clause imposes a higher perceptual load on the perceiver. The data obtained are also compatible with a substantial, if not a large, amount of evidence already available from recent experiments reported in the literature, which support the conclusion that the linguistic material in a long sentence tends to be perceptually organized into clausal units.

ACKNOWLEDGEMENTS

This chapter has been prepared at the N.I.A.S., Wassenaar, whose support is gratefully acknowledged. Experiment I was carried out by Mr G. de Boer and Mr P. Houten, as part of a special psycholinguistic minor at the University of Leiden. Experiment II was designed and carried out by Mr P. A. van der Steen, and full credit should be given to him for his kind cooperation. Substantial help for the organization of the experiment has been given by Drs. J. Joustra. This experiment has been completely supported by Z. W. O. Grant Nr. 35/24.

The help of Mr U. Toffano at the University of Padova in the preparation of the stimulus material and of the slides used in Experiment III is gratefully acknowledged. Experiments III and IV were carried out at the University of Padova in 1970 and 1971, and were supported by the C.N.R. (Italian Research Council).

REFERENCES

Abrams, K. and Bever, T. G. Syntactic structure modifies attention during speech perception and recognition. *Quarterly Journal of Experimental Psychology*, 1969, **21**, 280–290.

Bever, T. G. The cognitive basis for linguistic structures. In J. R. Hayes (Ed.), *Cognition and the development of language*. New York: Wiley, 1970.

Bever, T. G., Garrett, M. F., and Hurtig, R. The interaction of perceptual processes and ambiguous sentences. *Memory and Cognition*, 1973, **1**, 277–286.

Boomer, D. S. Hesitation and grammatical encoding. *Language and Speech*, 1965, **8**, 148–158.

Broadbent, D. E. *Perception and communication*. Oxford: Pergamon Press, 1958.

Caplan, D. Clause boundaries and recognition latencies for words in sentences. *Perception and Psychophysics*, 1972, **12**, 73–76.

Clark, E. V. On the acquisition of the meaning of *before* and *after*. *Journal of Verbal Learning and Verbal Behavior*, 1971, **10**, 266–275.

Clark, H. H., and Clark, E. V. Semantic distinctions and memory for complex sentences. *Quarterly Journal of Experimental Psychology*, 1968, **20**, 129–138.

Cook, M., Smith, J., and Lalljee, M. G. Filled pauses and syntactic complexity. *Language and Speech*, 1974, **17**, 11–16.

Flores d'Arcais, G. B. Ricerche sulla comprensione e produzione di frasi e studi sull'acquisizione e uso del linguaggio nel fanciullo. Relazione sul contratto C.N.R. 115/2750/05131. Mimeo, Padova, Istituto di Psicologia, 1970.

Flores d'Arcais, G. B. The acquisition of the subordinating construction in children's language. In R. N. Campbell and P. T. Smith (Eds.), *Recent advances in the psychology of language: Language development and mother–child interaction*. New York: Plenum Press, 1978.

Fodor, J. A., Bever, T. G., and Garrett, M. F. *The psychology of language. An introduction to psycholinguistics and generative grammar*. New York: McGraw-Hill, 1974.

Fodor, J. A. and Bever, T. G. The psychological reality of linguistic segments. *Journal of Verbal Learning and Verbal Behavior*, 1965, **4**, 414–420.

Forster, K. I. Visual perception of rapidly presented word sequences of varying complexity. *Perception and Psychophysics*, 1970, **8**, 215–221.

Foss, D. J. Decision processes during sentence comprehension: Effects of lexical item difficulty and position upon decision times. *Journal of Verbal Learning and Verbal Behavior*, 1969, **8**, 457–482.

Foss, D. J. and Lynch, R. H. Jr. Decision processes during sentence comprehension: Effects of surface structure on decision times. *Perception and Psychophysics*, 1969, **5**, 145–148.

Foulke, E. The perception of time compressed speech. In D. L. Horton and J. J. Jenkins (Eds.), *The perception of language*. Columbus, Ohio: Merrill, 1971.

Garrett, M. Syntactic structures and judgments of auditory events: A study of the perception of extraneous noise in sentences. Unpublished Ph.D. Dissertation, University of Illinois, 1965.

Garrett, M., Bever, T. G., and Fodor, J. A. The active use of grammar in speech perception. *Perception and Psychophysics*, 1966, **1**, 30–32.

Hakes, D. T. and Foss, D. J. Decision processes during sentence comprehension: Effects of surface structure revisited. *Perception and Psychophysics*, 1970, **8**, 413–416.

Holmes, V. M. Order of main and subordinate clauses in sentence perception. *Journal of Verbal Learning and Verbal Behavior*, 1973, **12**, 285–293.

Holmes, V. M. and Forster, K. I. Detection of extraneous signals during sentence recognition. *Perception and Psychophysics*, 1970, **7**, 297–301.

Holmes, V. M. and Forster, K. I. Perceptual complexity and underlying sentence structure. *Journal of Verbal Learning and Verbal Behavior*, 1972, **11**, 148–156.

Jarvella, R. J. Effects of syntax on running memory span for connected discourse. *Psychonomic Science*, 1970, **19**, 235–236.

Jarvella, R. J. Syntactic processing of connected speech. *Journal of Verbal Learning and Verbal Behavior*, 1971, **10**, 409–416.

Jarvella, R. J. and Herman, S. J. Clause structure of sentences and speech processing. *Perception and Psychophysics*, 1972, **11**, 381–384.

Kornfeld, J. R. Clause structure and the perceptual analysis of sentences. *Quarterly Progress Report, Research Laboratory of Electronics, M.I.T.*, 1973a, **108**, 277–280.

Kornfeld, J. R. Clause boundary and dominance effect in sentence perception. *Quarterly Progress Report, Research Laboratory of Electronics, M.I.T.*, 1973b, **110**, 177–181.

Nooteboom, S. G. and Cohen, A. Anticipation in speech production and its implications for perception. In A. Cohen and S. G. Nooteboom (Eds.), *Structure and process in speech perception*. Berlin, Heidelberg, New York: Springer Verlag, 1975.

Weksel, W. and Bever, T. G. In *Harvard Center for Cognitive Studies Progress Report*, Harvard University. Cambridge, Mass., 1966.

Wingfield, A. The intonation-syntax interaction: Prosodic features in perceptual processing of sentences. In A. Cohen and S. G. Nooteboom (Eds.), *Structure and process in speech perception*. Berlin, Heidelberg, New York: Springer Verlag, 1975.

Wingfield, A. and Klein, J. F. Syntactic structure and acoustic pattern in speech perception. *Perception and Psychophysics*, 1971, **9**, 23-25.

Winograd, T. *Understanding natural language*. New York: Academic Press, 1972.

Chapter 6

The Perception of Relations: The Interaction of Structural, Functional, and Contextual Factors in the Segmentation of Sentences

John M. Carroll, Michael K. Tanenhaus, and Thomas G. Bever

THE ORGANIZATION OF THE STIMULUS: FROM CHUNKING TO SENTENCE SEGMENTATION

Much theory and research in cognitive psychology is predicated on the assumption that human information-processing capacities are limited relative to the apparent complexity of human behaviour and experience. This is particularly clear if the limits of working memory capacity are contrasted with the length and complexity of the sequential stimuli that people are able to process without apparent difficulty. For example, recall memory for a sequence of random words is limited to about eight. However, this direct assessment of 'working memory' capacity does not jibe with actual human verbal performance. People readily produce and understand sentences containing many more than eight words. One fundamental task of cognitive theory is to describe a mechanism which organizes basic and limited processing capacities to create complex human behaviour and deal with ordinary experience.

Miller (1956) proposed such a mechanism in his 'chunking' analysis. He noticed that when items in a sequence are grouped, or chunked, together, subjects can successfully deal with more items. He inferred that these chunked items are recorded into higher order units, as schematized in (1).

(1) Input Sequence → Recoding Scheme → Chunks

A large number of unstructured items in the input sequence is distilled, as it were, into a smaller number of structured items. But such chunks can be chunked themselves. The hierarchical and iterative imposition of structure on sequences effectively allows for *unlimited* processing capacity. Thus, Miller's chunking proposal offers a potential framework in which to describe the organization of complex human information processing. (Of course, the application of chunking has to be restricted in some manner or else the chunking analysis will predict an infinite memory capacity.)

Miller reports an experiment by Sidney Smith that illustrates how chunking can increase processing capacity, in this case, short-term memory capacity. Smith presented subjects with sequences of binary digits, ones, and zeros, which they were to keep track of. Not surprisingly, he found that they were able to recall about eight digits. He then trained his subjects to recode pairs of binary digits into base four digits, thus: $00 \rightarrow 0$, $01 \rightarrow 1$, $10 \rightarrow 2$, $11 \rightarrow 3$. In this condition, recall performance goes up. When subjects were told to recode triples of binary digits into octal numbers (i.e. $000 \rightarrow 0$, $001 \rightarrow 1$, $010 \rightarrow 2$, $011 \rightarrow 3$, $100 \rightarrow 4$, $101 \rightarrow 5$, $110 \rightarrow 6$, $111 \rightarrow 7$), recall was even better. Smith's recording schemes are illustrated in (2).

(2) a. No Instructions

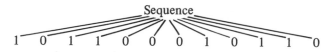

b. Base four Recording

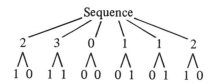

c. Octal Recording

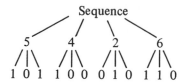

Lists of digits have very minimal intrinsic structure. In Smith's experiment, the recoding schemes, and therefore the nature of the chunking units, are defined by the experimenter. This is just the sort of example Smith and Miller needed to bring into relief the potential advantages of chunking to human processing: sequences that would otherwise exceed working memory capacity can be processed when structured by recoding schemes.

Miller's chunking analysis can be easily extended to the processing of *complex* stimuli, i.e. stimuli with apparent intrinsic structure. As items enter working memory, the processor groups or chunks them into higher order units.

However, the recoding schemes which define these units, unlike the recoding schemes Smith defined, must enable the processor to recover the intrinsic structure of the sequence, in addition to the literal items constituting the sequence. The relationships, for example, between the words and phrases of a sentence or the contours and objects in a visual scene have such intrinsic structure. In order to comprehend a sentence or a visual scene the perceiver must recover not only the components, but also the relations between them. The task of perceptual theory is to describe how the relations between items in a structured array are recovered given the limitations of the perceptual system.

Returning to Miller's analysis, one might expect there to be a rather close correspondence between the major structural units of the stimulus and the chunking units constructed by perceptual recoding schemes. The structural units of the stimulus are defined by the relations which the perceiver must recover in order to comprehend the stimulus. The linguistic constituents of a sentence enter into various grammatical relations like subject-of, object-of, and modifier-of. The constituent contours and objects in a visual scene enter into various spatial relations. Of course, the exact nature of this correspondence between structural and perceptual units will be determined by the extent to which the structural units of the stimulus can be used as effective chunking units by the perceptual system (i.e. can be constructed by perceptual recoding schemes). In order to study the nature of this correspondence, we need to consider the perception of a complex stimulus whose intrinsic structure is fairly well understood.

From this perspective, the psychological study of language provides an excellent case study. Language is clearly an intrinsically structured and complex human capacity. The science of linguistics is fundamentally concerned with describing the intrinsic structure of language. Indeed, one of the central concerns of the last 15 years of psycholinguistic research has been to describe the role of linguistic structures in behavioural theories of language.

In particular, several theorists have applied Miller's chunking analysis to the description of sentence perception. Basically, the hypothesis explored is that some particular structural unit in the linguistic description of the sentence functions as a chunking unit during sentence perception. (In the area of sentence perception these chunking units are often called *segmentation units*.) Bever, Lackner, and Kirk (1969) and Fodor, Bever, and Garrett (1974) have developed the claim that the listener treats the linguistic clause as a segmentation unit. Thus, on their model, sentence perception consists in part of isolating and segmenting together word sequences which correspond to linguistic clauses. Fodor and Bever (1965) and Chapin, Smith, and Abrahamson (1972) have also defined the segmentation unit in terms of a level of linguistic structure. They propose that major surface-structure constituents are segmentation units in sentence perception (see Carroll and Bever, 1976, for review).

Both of these hypotheses about the nature of the segmentation units of sentence perception are couched in purely *structural* terms. They describe a simple and straightforward relation between what we earlier referred to as intrinsic stimulus structure (in this case, syntactic structure) and the determination of recoding schemes for chunking (in this case, segmentation). But they purchase this simplicity at the price of overlooking potentially important *functional* segmentation variables. Recall that structural units should be expected to function as perceptual units just to the extent that they can be effectively organized by the perceptual system. Neither the clause nor the constituent satisfies this requirement.

First, consider the constituent theory. In its strongest form, this theory claims that major surface-structure constituents are the segmentation units of sentence perception. Thus, in the course of perceiving a sentence like (3), the listener is segmenting the initial eight words as a noun-phrase surface constituent and the final eight words as a verb phrase constituent.

(3) The big old worn and splintering carriage wheel rolled down the hill and across the road.

Thus, a sentence 16 words long is intermediately organized into two more manageable units of eight words each. Sentences like (4), however, present problems for this analysis.

(4) The big old worn and splintering heavy wooden carriage wheel with the rusted spokes is a genuine antique.

In sentence (4) the initial noun-phrase constituent is itself 14 words long. Indeed, noun-phrase constituents can be arbitrarily long and complex. Accordingly, there are cases, like (4), in which it is preposterous to claim that major constituents are segmentation units.

The clausal theory is no better off, although in many cases it too makes intuitively satisfying predictions. For example, in (5) a 16-word sentence is rendered as two clausal segmentation units of eight words each.

(5) After John hung up the clothes to dry he went inside to start cooking his supper.

However, surface-structure clauses, like noun-phrase surface constituents, can be arbitrarily long. The initial surface clause in (6) is 18 words long.

(6) After the long dry summer of our sorrow and utter discontent had finally come to a welcomed end we simply moved to Pittsburg.

Consequently, the limitations of processing capacity would be exceeded before segmentation could occur. If, as Bever *et al.* (1969) suggest, the pertinent notion of clause is actually the deep-structure clause, other problems appear. On a deep-clause segmentation theory, the initial sequence of nine gerunds in (7) would correspond to nine separate segmentation units since each corresponds to a deep-structure clause.

(7) Walking, talking, eating, drinking, hurrying, studying, listening, theorizing and sleeping were John's daily activities.

Here the number of segmentation units which would have to be integrated into a perceived sentence will exceed processing capacity. Instead of predicting too many words per hypothesized segmentation unit, the deep-clausal theory will predict too many hypothesized segmentation units per sentence.

The objections we have just raised regarding the clausal and constituent theories address issues of processing capacity. A second line of argument centres on whether clausal or constituent segmentation units enable the listener to recover the defining relations of the sentence. In sentence (7) each of the initial nine gerunds is a surface noun-phrase constituent which corresponds to a deep-structure clause. Each has the noun 'John' as its subject relation. However, this relation is not specified until the final three words of the sentence. It is not clear how these initially subjectless gerunds could be perceptually organized as complete clausal segmentation units. The deep-structure clause position encounters additional difficulties with sentences like (8a).

(8) a. *The tall* man ordered a Scotch.
    b. (the man(the man is tall) ordered a Scotch)
      S_1 S_2 S_2 S_1

In sentence (8a), the adjective 'tall' corresponds to the deep-structure clause S_2 in (8b), which presents a deep-structure bracketing of (8a). Thus, the deep-structure clause theory makes the unlikely prediction that the sequence 'the tall' should be segmented and recoded as a perceptual unit.

It is important to note that we have attacked the *strongest* versions of the two structural-linguistic segmentation theories (see Carroll, 1976, for discussion). However, it seems reasonable to proceed in this fashion if we want to bring into relief the directions in which the theory of sentence perception must now be elaborated. The structural-linguistic segmentation theories provide solid ground from which to begin this elaboration: comprehending a sentence necessarily involves representing the information contained in the sentence's linguistic structure (i.e. one cannot be said to have understood a sentence unless one tacitly knows which noun was the object of a given preposition, the subject of the main verb, etc.; see Fodor, 1968). Thus, whatever the segmentation units of sentence perception are like, they are logically entrained by linguistic structures.

In the remainder of this chapter we will present an initial functionalist elaboration of the linguistic-structural theories of segmentation. On this view, the segmentation structure of a sentence is determined by a variety of factors including, but not limited to, the intrinsic structure of the sentence (see Carroll, 1976; Tanenhaus and Carroll, 1975). Indeed, we will show that the strong versions of the linguistic-structural segmentation theories can be experimentally rejected. We adopt a perceptual cue approach; we ask 'what are the cues utilized by the listener to identify complete propositions reflected in good potential segmentation units?' and 'how do these cues interact to predict the segmentation structure of perceived sentences?'

FUNCTIONAL AND CONTEXTUAL FACTORS IN SEGMENTATION

According to the chunking analysis, sequences of items are recoded into higher order units in a way that conserves processing capacities, like working memory. From this it follows that a sequence of words will comprise a better segmentation unit if it is potentially recodable into an independent memory structure. Current views of memory have identified such memory units with propositional structures (e.g. Kintsch, 1974; Rumelhart, Lindsay, and Norman, 1972). Thus, we make the assumption that linguistic sequences which can be directly mapped onto complete propositional structures are the ideal segmentation units in sentence perception. We refer to such sequences as *functionally complete*.

Functionally complete sequences contain a complete, explicit, and coherent set of grammatical relations. Functionally incomplete sequences fail to meet this requirement. The two initial clauses in example (9) are both examples of functionally complete sequences.

(9) a. After John spilled the beans, everyone ignored him.
    b. The town's construction of a new school cost the taxpayers a mint.

In (9a), 'John' is the subject relation, 'spilled' is the verb and 'the beans' is the object. In (9b), 'the town' is the subject, 'construction' is the verb and 'a new school' is the object.

The initial three-word sequence in sentence (10a) is functionally incomplete in that it lacks an explicit verbal relation.

(10) a. The big dog bit me on the knee.
     b. Fleeing was John's alternative to fighting.

It corresponds to a proposition which can be glossed as 'the dog is big', but as it appears in sentence (10a), it lacks the copulative verb 'is' which relates the noun 'dog' to its adjectival modifier. Similarly, the sentence-initial gerund 'fleeing' in sentence (10b) provides the listener with a functionally incomplete sequence (recall sentence (7)). 'Fleeing' in sentence (10b) corresponds to the proposition 'John flee'. But the subject relation of this proposition is not present in the manifest initial sequence of the sentence. It is not specified until later in the sentence.

A possible elaboration of the functional completeness property concerns the *specificity* with which grammatical relations are represented in a sequence. Thus, the italicized noun phrases in (11a) through (11c) seem to be increasingly less specific (*qua* sentences out of context, see below). Indeed, unless the noun 'John' in (11d) is understood as referring to a particular person, it is quite abstract, and unspecific, for this listener.

(11) a. After *the little fellow with a moustache* left, we realized what a great guy he was.
    b. After *the man* left, we realized what a great guy he was.
    c. After *he* left, we realized what a great guy he was.
    d. After *John* left, we realized what a great guy he was.

Ceterus paribus, sequences with more specific grammatical relations may be better potential segmentation units than sequences with less specific grammatical relations. Similarly, the difference in specificity between the italicized object noun phrases in (12) may render the clause in (12a) a better potential segmentation unit than that in (12b).

(12) a. After he bought *some gum*, he went home.
    b. After he bought *some*, he went home.

(See Marslen-Wilson, Tyler, and Seidenberg, 1976; Tanenhaus and Seidenberg, 1978.) In this paper, we do not treat specificity, aside from specificity via context (see section on contextual cues).

In considering the role of the functional completeness property in structuring sentence segmentation, we will be concerned, first, with how functional completeness might be recognized in a word sequence during sentence perception, and, second, with how functional completeness might be compromised in the course of sentence segmentation. We will approach these questions by examining two sorts of perceptual segmentation cues: cues which describe the internal structure of sequences (specifically, whether or not given sequences are functionally complete) and cues which indicate how much processing resource a particular sequence requires.

There are quite clearly a variety of potential cues that can serve to inform the listener about the internal structure of a linguistic sequence. With particular regard to the property of functional completeness, the listener might be cued by a 'noun-verb-noun' configuration. Bever (1970) showed that listeners assume that a sequence whose lexical configuration is noun-verb-noun corresponds to a canonical set of propositional relations: subject-predicate-object. Thus, listeners apparently interpret noun-verb-noun configurations as potential functionally complete segmentation units. They use the 'noun-verb-noun' configuration as a cue to functional completeness.

But there are other potential cues available to the listener. Consider, for example, the information available by way of context and inference. As we have noted earlier, the sentence initial noun-phrase sequence in (10a) is functionally incomplete because the copulative verb relation between the noun 'dog' and the modifier 'big' is not explicitly present in the sequence.

The deletion of the copulative verb, however, is a regular and general syntactic process and hence the omitted relation can be recovered and 'filled in' by inference. Such inferential cues, if they are used by listeners in perceptually organizing sentences, could effectively render certain functionally incomplete sequences functionally complete. By assumption, this would make sentence comprehension an easier task for the listener.

Certain other functionally incomplete sequences can be effectively rendered functionally complete by way of contextual cues. For example, the initial word of sentence (10b) is a functionally incomplete sequence. However, if the deleted subject relation 'John' is provided somehow, then the incomplete sequence 'Fleeing' can be organized into the complete propositional segmentation unit 'John flee'. Context could help do this in several ways, either by prior discourse (i.e. the sentence occurs in a talk about John), ostension (i.e. John is there) or even by means of the information provided in the following clause of (10b).

Another class of cues that can inform the listener of a sequence's internal structure can be referred to as *local sign cues*. Lexical items, like nouns and verbs, are themselves local sign cues which denote functionally complete sequences: a sequence cannot be functionally complete unless it contains *some* nouns and verbs. Thus, quite aside from what configurational cues are present (e.g. noun-verb-noun), the simple fact that nouns and verbs occur cues the property of functional completeness. Clearly, these lexical local signs are not perfectly valid cues of functional completeness. The initial noun phrase of (10a) contains the noun 'dog' but is functionally incomplete (in that it contains no explicit verbal relation). And the initial headless nominalization of (10b) contains the verbal element 'fleeing' but is also functionally incomplete (in that it contains no subject noun).

There may be further local sign cues below the level of the word. Consider the tense morpheme component of verbs. Tense morphemes actually have a greater cue validity than their stems in signalling a functionally complete sequence: if a verbal element bears a tense morpheme then its surface-subject relation is always explicitly present in the word sequence. Conversely, as sentences like (10b) demonstrate, the occurrence of a verbal stem does not guarantee functional completeness. However, the occurrence of a tensed verbal element does indeed guarantee this. (Note though, that certain functionally complete sequences do *not* contain tensed verbal items, as in '*The men's refusing the offer cost the company a lot.*')

The classes of cues we have considered thus far provide information that the listener can use to recognize functional completeness in a sequence: they are cues to the internal structure of sequences. However, these cues interact with cues that indicate how much processing capacity a particular sequence requires. We assume that the listener's processing attempts to optimize the amount of processing capacity expended on each segmentation unit. If too much capacity is required per segmentation unit, processing breaks down. If too little is required, capacities go unused, and processing is less efficient than it could be.

Consider working memory. If a sequence is very long, working memory can become overtaxed. In order to avert breakdown, the processing capacity cue of sequence length can induce segmentation, perhaps compromising functional completeness. Thus, the sentence-initial noun phrase in (3) may indeed serve as a segmentation unit even though it is functionally incomplete. The initial eight words of sentence (4) 'The big, old, worn and splintering, heavy, wooden' might even serve as a segmentation unit of necessity, though this sequence has virtually no 'intrinsic' structure at all. In contrast, if a sequence is very short, it may fail to stimulate segmentation processing even if it *is* functionally complete. Thus, the first five words of sentence (13) may be segmented as one unit even though these five words comprise two distinct functionally complete sequences.

(13) *John returned and Mary arrived* just in time for both of them to meet the mayor of Utica.

Like sequence length, sequence complexity may act as a processing capacity cue. If a sequence becomes too complex, segmentation units may not be isomorphic with functionally complete sequences. (See Carroll, 1976, and Carroll and Bever, 1976, for further speculation and discussion of processing capacity cues.)

Before proceeding, we must make two disclaimers. First, we have certainly not presented an exhaustive catalogue of segmentation cues. Much remains to be done just to understand the role in sentence perception of the cues we have identified, but even with this work complete we would not have a comprehensive theory of segmentation cues. Second, we are not committed to an all-or-none model of segmentation. One may ultimately need to talk about amount or degree of segmentation, rather than simply about whether or not segmentation obtains.

We now turn to some experimental work-in-progress designed to provide experimental evidence against purely linguistic definitions of the segmentation units of sentence perception and to validate initially the role of our functional cues in sentence perception.

SOME EXPERIMENTS

The configurational N-V-N cue

The first two experiments we will present were designed to test the claim that the N-V-N configurational cue perceptually denotes the functional completeness property. Thus, our main prediction is that noun-verb-noun functionally complete sequences will be better segmentation units than functionally incomplete sequences. We used the location technique since the linguistic models of segmentation are fundamentally based on the results of research using this technique (see Fodor and Bever, 1965; Bever *et al.*, 1969; Chapin *et al.*, 1972).

Fodor and Bever observed that when a click is superimposed on a recorded sentence, listeners systematically mislocate the click with regard to the sentence sequence. Fodor and Bever account for this by arguing that clicks are phenomenally displaced towards a segmentation boundary: the relatively high perceptual coherence of a segmentation unit 'resists' interruption by the click.

We presented subjects with sentences which in most cases contained a brief tone (see Carroll, 1976; and Carroll and Tanenhaus, 1978; for details of method and procedure). In the experimental sentences there are two tone locations: just before the final word of the sentence-initial sequence and just after the first word of the sentence-final sequence. The four types of initial sequences we studied are listed in (14), with tone locations indicated by slashes.

(14) a. Main Clauses (Functionally Complete N-V-N):
    I felt very sorry for the old/bum so/I gave him a dime.
  b. Subordinate Clauses (Functionally Complete N-V-N):
    After the crook stole the woman's/bag he/ran for safety.
  c. Headless Nominalization (Functionally Incomplete):
    Meeting the pretty young/girl was/the highlight of Peter's trip.
  d. Noun Phrase (Functionally Incomplete):
    The old painted wooden/pipe was/on display at the local museum.

Our experimental sentences were divided evenly among the four sequence-type categories in (14). Thus, half of the sentences had functionally complete N-V-N initial sequences and half had functionally incomplete initial sequences. We also manipulated sequence length and varied it orthogonally with initial sequence-type. Half of our experimental sentences had 'long' initial sequences (eight words and ten syllables) and half had 'short' initial sequences (five words and seven syllables).

Following the Fodor and Bever procedure, subjects listened to the sentences through headphones and then wrote them out from memory in a booklet. If a tone had occurred in the sentence, the subject then marked the tone location with a slash in his written script. Tones were not placed in all sentences in order to avoid an increase in the probability of a tone with serial position in the sentence (Abrams, 1973).

We modified our location-scoring procedure from that of Fodor and Bever. Recent research indicates that the behavioural basis of the manifest location effect may be more complex than Fodor and Bever originally supposed. In particular, it may be that subjects tend to assume that interruptions of whose location they are actually uncertain occurred while they were busy processing. Abrams and Bever (1969), Bever and Hurtig (1975) and Seitz (1972) have shown that sensitivity to interruptions is lowest just at the end of a presumed segmentation boundary. Thus, part of the location effect may be due to a 'response bias' for locating interruptions at points of relatively high segmentation processing (see Bever, Hurtig, and Handel, in preparation).

To accommodate this possibility we count mislocations of tones into or towards the 'processing zone' implicated by the work of Abrams and Bever, Bever and Hurtig, and Seitz, namely the last word of the initial sequence and the sequence boundary itself, as confirming the hypothesis that the sequence boundary is a segmentation boundary. Any mislocation away from this processing zone is scored as disconfirming the segmentation hypothesis. Correct subjective locations and overshoots (mislocations which go towards the boundary and beyond it out of the processing zone) are not scored.

The results of Experiment I are summarized in Table 6.1 in percentages. A Friedman two-way analysis of variance by ranks for k correlated samples (see Ferguson, 1971, pages 331–335) reveals an overall difference in tone mislocation across the four sequence-types by-subject (i.e. taking subjects as the unit of analysis), $p < .05$. However, the Anova taking items, or sentences, as the unit of analysis (i.e. by-item) fails to reveal an overall difference (Kruskall-Wallis one-way Anova by ranks for k uncorrelated samples, see Ferguson, 1971, pages 331–335).

Since the functional completeness and sequence length contrasts were planned comparisons, further tests were performed. For functionally complete initial sequences 69% of the errors analysed were mislocated into or towards the processing zone. However, for functionally incomplete initial sequence-types this figure is only 56%. This difference is significant by subject, $p < .01$

Table 6.1   Experiment I. Percentages of tones mislocated into or towards the processing zone, for the different types of clauses

Functionally complete 69%		Functionally incomplete 56%	
Long 65%	Short 70%	Long 50%	Short 60%
Mains 74%	Subordinates 61%	Noun phrases 60%	Nominalizations 51%

(Wilcoxon signed ranks test, correlated samples) and by-item, $p < .005$ (Wilcoxon rank sums test, uncorrelated samples). The effect of sequence length is less encouraging. An overall Anova for the four functional completeness X sequence length possibilities (long functionally complete, short functionally complete, long functionally incomplete, short functionally incomplete) is non-significant. Internal paired comparisons and an overall long versus short contrast are also non-significant.

We draw several conclusions from this experiment. First, the results of Experiment I are fully consistent with our claim that functionally complete N-V-N sequences should be better segmentation units than functionally incomplete sequences. Thus, our approach is encouraged. However, on the basis of this experiment alone we cannot uniquely determine what sort of cue is responsible for this functional completeness effect. It appears that contextual/inferential cues are *not* responsible, since on the basis of context and inference the initial sequences of (14c) and (14d) would indeed be functionally complete.

The functionally complete experimental items in Experiment I clearly do differ from the functionally incomplete items in terms of the N-V-N configurational cue: only the former items provide the listener with an N-V-N cue. However, this differentiation confounds with other differences between the functionally complete and functionally incomplete items of Experiment I. Although both functionally complete and incomplete sequences contain lexical nouns (cf. 'bum', 'bag', 'girl', 'pipe' in 14), there are also local sign differences between the two classes. Main clauses and subordinate clauses always contain lexical verbs, and these verbs are always tensed verbs. In the functionally incomplete cases, only the nominalizations contain lexical verbs and these verbs bear a nominalizing morpheme (e.g. '-ing' in 14c) instead of tense. Also, functionally incomplete noun-phrase sequences, like (14d), tend to contain more lexical modifiers (e.g. 'old', 'painted', 'wooden'). Thus, while Experiment I establishes the pertinence of functional completeness to segmentation organization, it leaves open whether the efficient cue is a configuration (e.g. N-V-N) or a local sign (e.g. verb tense), or, perhaps more reasonably, some combination of the two. (It is not clear that any notion of configuration—such as a propositional segmentation structure—*can* be constructed out of purely local sign elements, Köhler, 1929.)

The apparent failure of Experiment I to reveal an effect of sequence length may simply indicate that the tone-location response measure is relatively insensitive to processing capacity cues. However, we must also consider the possibility that our hypothesized sequence-length cue has limited construct validity as a principle of sentence segmentation. In either case, of course, the only way to resolve this question is to study sequence length using other experimental response measures. Some of this research will be reported below.

A final conclusion we draw from Experiment I is that the two structural-linguistic segmentation theories are manifestly inadequate. First, consider the clausal model. In most theories of grammar *all* of the four initial sequence-types in (14) correspond to deep-structure clauses. (Nominalizations are formed by a transformational rule of Nominalization. Noun phrases are formed by Relative Clause Reduction followed by Adjective Preposing. And sentence-initial subordinate clauses are formed by a rule of Adverb Preposing. See Stockwell, Schachter, and Partee, 1973.) Thus, adopting the deep-clausal view offers no way of distinguishing nominalizations and noun phrases from main and subordinate clauses. Therefore, it cannot account for the results of Experiment I.

A surface-clausal view could distinguish noun phrases, which are not surface clauses, from the other three sequence-types, which are. However, it cannot distinguish nominalizations from main and subordinate clauses. This contrast is significant by-subject, $p < .05$ (Wilcoxon signed ranks test, correlated samples), and nearly so by-item, $p < .1$ (Wilcoxon rank sums test, uncorrelated samples).

Finally, consider the constituent theory of Fodor and Bever and Chapin *et al.* Both of our functionally incomplete sequence-types comprise major surface constituents (noun phrases and nominalizations) but neither of our functionally complete sequence-types do. Thus, the constituent theory predicts the obverse of what was found.

Experiment II was designed to confirm and elaborate the functional completeness result of Experiment I. First, it replicates the functionally complete versus incomplete difference discovered in Experiment I. In doing so, it also tries to control more thoroughly structural-linguistic variables, and thus to establish the independent importance of functional completeness in sentence segmentation. Finally, it attempts to unconfound the configurational cue to functional completeness (N-V-N) and the local sign cue (verb tense), and therefore to demonstrate the independent contribution of different cues. The four types of initial sequences we examined are listed in (15), with tone locations indicated by slashes.

(15) a. Relative Clause (Functionally Complete, Tensed Verb):
   The judge who resisted the l/arge bribe was q/uite well respected by his colleagues.
   b. Noun Phrase (Functionally Incomplete):
   The very pretty and talented b/londe girl was t/he runner-up in the Miss Wisconsin contest.
   c. Headed Nominalization (Functionally Complete, Nominalized Verb):
   Humphrey's refusal to take a f/irm stand caused h/im to lose the election.
   d. Headless Nominalization (Functionally Incomplete):
   The overall reaction to the n/ew play was m/ore positive than negative.

The experimental sentences for Experiment II were divided equally among the four categories in (15). (Stimulus preparation, procedure, and scoring are identical to that of Experiment I except that tones were placed in words rather than word boundaries. We found that tones could be placed more accurately and easily in words, since they are more integral acoustic events—for further discussion see Carroll, 1976, and Carroll and Tanenhaus, 1976, 1978.)

The results of Experiment II are summarized in Table 6.2 in terms of percentages. The Friedman two-way Anova by ranks for the four sequence categories is significant by-subject, $p < .05$. The Kruskall-Wallis one-way Anova by ranks is significant by-item, $p < .05$.

The main result for functional completeness is also summarized in Table 6.2. For functionally complete items (relative clauses and headed nominalizations), 78% of the errors analysed were mislocations into or towards the hypothesized processing zone. The corresponding figure for functionally incomplete sequences (noun phrases and headless nominalizations) is only 65%. This difference is significant by-subject, $p < .005$ (Wilcoxon Signed Ranks Test), and by-item, $p < .001$ (Wilcoxon rank sums test). Thus, Experiment II succeeds in replicating the functional completeness result of Experiment I.

A further issue, however, concerns just what sort of cue to functional completeness is the efficient experimental variable. Consider the differences between relative clauses and headed nominalizations. Both consist of N-V-N configurations (i.e. 'Judge resist bribe' and 'Humphrey refuse take—stand'), but they differ in terms of the local sign cues they provide. Relative clauses contain tensed verbs (e.g. 'resist*ed*') and relative pronouns (e.g. 'who'). Headed nominalizations contain the possessive morpheme (e.g. 'Humphrey'*s*') and nominalization morphemes (e.g. 'refus*al*'). We did not make predictions about all of these local sign differences, but we have noted earlier that tense morphemes, since they imply functional completeness, might serve as effective segmentation cues.

The results of Experiment II cannot distinguish between relative clause cases and headed nominalizations (see Table 6.2). Thus, we find no evidence for any of the above-mentioned local sign cues. On this basis, we conclude that the results of Experiment II implicate the configurational N-V-N cue. (We do not give up on local sign cues, however: see Experiment III below.)

Table 6.2   Experiment II. Percentages of tones mislocated into or towards the processing zone, for the different types of clauses

Functionally complete 78%		Functionally incomplete 65%	
Relative clauses 77%	Headed nominalizations 78%	Noun phrases 54%	Headless nominalizations 70%

As Experiment II provides further evidence for the functional completeness property and, in particular, for the N-V-N configurational cue, it also marshals further evidence against the linguistic-structural theories of the segmentation unit. Consider Relative Clauses and Noun Phrases. In standard accounts of English grammar (e.g. Chomsky, 1957) surface noun phrases with modifiers, like (15b), are *derived* from underlying relative clause structures. Thus, Relative Clauses and Noun Phrases, like (15a) and (15b), have a rather close linguistic relationship. They are both major surface-structure constituents (noun phrases) and both correspond to deep-structure clauses. However, for Relative Clauses 77% of the location errors in Experiment II were located into or towards the processing zone, while for noun phrases this figure is 54%. This difference is significant by-subject, $p < .005$ (Wilcoxon Signed Ranks Test), and by-item, $p < .001$ (Wilcoxon Rank Sums Test).

Relative Clauses and Noun Phrases, do, however, differ linguistically. Relative Clauses are surface-structure clauses where Noun Phrases are not. In this sense, the nominalizations of Experiment II provide a critical case: headed and headless nominalizations are syntactically identical with respect to their constituent analysis. They are deep clauses, surface clauses and, in our sentences, subject noun phrases. Neither structural-linguistic theory would predict a difference. Nevertheless, headed nominalizations, as predicted by functional completeness, seem to be better segmentation units. This difference is reliable by-subject, $p < .05$ (Wilcoxon Signed Ranks Test), but misses significance by-item, $p = .102$ (Wilcoxon Rank Sums Tests, one-tailed prediction).

To summarize, the results of Experiments I and II are inconsistent with the two structural-linguistic positions characterized in our first section. Since these positions predict no difference where differences in fact obtain, they are empirically rejected in just the sense that the statistical null hypothesis is rejected. In contrast, the functional completeness property is fully consistent with the data at hand and to that extent is therefore empirically confirmed. Finally, as argued under Experiment II, the evidence appears to show in particular that the configurational N-V-N cue is an efficient variable in organizing functionally complete segmentation units.

The local sign verb tense cue

The conclusions we can draw from Experiments I and II are limited in that only one experimental paradigm was used. Thus, our results confound the intended manipulation with possible idiosyncracies of the experimental procedure. Therefore, we decided to investigate functional completeness using other experimental tasks. Experiments III and IV make use of the Suci, Ammon, and Gamlin (1967) *next-word naming task.*

Suci *et al.* presented subjects with sentences like (16) followed by probe words from the sentence.

(16) The small black ant digs holes.

They measured the time required for subjects to utter the word that immediately followed a given probe word in the original sentence. Thus, if sentence (16) was followed by the word 'black' the subject would respond 'ant', etc. Suci *et al.* found that the largest next-word naming latencies obtain when the probe word is the final word in the noun phrase ('ant' in (16)) and the response word is the initial word in the verb phrase ('digs' in (16)).

Their interpretation of this, in the terms we have been using, is that major surface constituents are segmentation units and that a probe word is a poorer prompt for a response word which has been organized into a different segmentation unit than it is for one organized into the same segmentation unit. We can extend this interpretation to amount or degree of segmentation: the more segmentation that occurs at the juncture between the probe word and the response word in the sentence, the longer it should take to retrieve the latter given the former. (For further discussion of this logic, see Carroll, 1976.)

In Experiment III we studied sentence-paradigms like (17).

(17) a. Relative Clause (Functionally Complete, Tensed Verb):
     Howard who revised//the game-rules aggravated the old pros.
   b. Sentential Subject (Functionally Complete, Tensed Verb);
     That Howard revised//the game-rules aggravated the old pros.
   c. Headed Nominalization (Functionally Complete, Nominalized Verb):
     Howard's revision of the game-rules aggravated the old pros.
   d. Headless Nominalizations (Functionally Incomplete, Nominalized Verb)
     The revision of//the game-rules aggravated the old pros.

The probe word in each exemplar is 'game-rules', the response word is 'aggravated'. Each such sentence-paradigm was constructed by cross-splicing an acoustically identical copy of the sequence from the double slash through the completion of the probe-word presentation, beginning 200 msec after the end of the sentence. (The probe was read in the same voice, but with list intonation.) Each subject responded to only one member of each sentence-paradigm, but across subjects, this procedure allows us to use matched-pairs statistics by-item. (See Carroll, 1978, for further details of stimulus preparation, procedure, and scoring.)

Next-word naming latencies measure the interval from the probe onset to the beginning of the response, and are reported in Table 6.3. Analysis of variance

Table 6.3   Experiment III. Geometric mean latencies by-subject (milliseconds) for next-word naming

	Mode of verb		
Tensed		Nominalized	
Relative clause (Functionally complete)	1559	Headed nominalization (Functionally complete)	1394
Sentential subject (Functionally complete)	1438	Headless nominalization (Functionally incomplete)	1350
Means	1498		1371

reveals significant effects of initial sequence-type, by-subject, $p < .05$, and by-item, $p < .05$. These overall differences militate against the unelaborated structural-linguistic segmentation theories. *All* of the four sentence categories in (17) have similar linguistic descriptions. Their underlined initial sequences correspond to deep-structure clauses, surface-structure clauses and noun-phrase (major surface) constituents (see Chomsky, 1976; Stockwell *et al.* 1973). Thus, once again the structural-linguistic theories predict the null hypothesis, and are rejected by the data.

What is of greater interest to us, however, is how these overall differences bear on the validity of the segmentation cues we have proposed. In particular, we would like to test the validity of our hypothesized local sign segmentation cues. We were unable to find effects of local sign cues in the data of Experiments I and II. For the data of Experiment III we tested the prediction that tense on a verb stem acts as a perceptual cue identifying a potential functionally complete segmentation unit.

Two of the sequence-types studied in Experiment III contained tensed verbs (relative clauses and sentential subjects) and two contained nominalized verbs (the two nominalization types). The difference between tensed cases and nominalized cases is significant by-subject, $p < .005$, and by-item, $p < .05$. However, this overall contrast partially confounds the local sign tense cue with the configurational N-V-N cue: Both tensed sequence sequence-types comprise N-V-N configurations, however, only one of the nominalized sequence-types comprises N-V-N configurations (headed nominalizations are N-V-N, but headless nominalizations are not). Therefore, we contrasted the two tensed sequence-types with headed nominalization cases alone. This difference is significant by-subject, $p < .025$, and nearly significant by-item, $p = .077$.

We also examined the data of Experiment III for effects of the N-V-N cue. First, we contrasted the three sequence-types which comprise N-V-N configurations (relative clauses, sentential subjects, headed nominalizations) with the fourth which does not (headless nominalization). This difference is reliable by-subject, $p < .025$, and by-item, $p < .025$. However, this overall comparison confounds N-V-N with various local sign differences (e.g. relative clauses have relative pronouns 'who' and tense 'revis*ed*', sentential subjects have the complementizer 'that' and tense). Contrasting headless nominalization cases only with headed nominalizations minimizes these spurious differences. When we assessed the effects of the N-V-N cue by contrasting the two nominalization types, we found only a non-significant trend, ($p = .19$, by-subject; $p = .13$, by-item).

Post hoc we also examined the data of Experiment III for effects of sequence length. We correlated the length in words of the initial sequence for each of our experimental sentences within a sequence-type with the geometric mean next-word naming latency across subjects for each sentence (the overall range of sequence length was 4 to 11 words, $\overline{X} = 6.8$). Longer initial sequences should encourage segmentation to a greater extent than shorter initial sequences, since the former consume more processing capacity. For Relative Clauses, the correlation between sequence length and response latency is $r = .51$, $p < .01$. For Sentential Subjects, this correlation is $r = .56$, $p < .005$; for Headed Nominalizations, $r = .35$, $p < .05$; and for Headless Nominalizations, $r = .26$, n.s. These data suggest that the processing capacity cue of sequence length *does* influence segmentation organization. We elaborate this result in Experiment IV.

Experiment III provides more evidence against the structural-linguistic theories. Further, it provides some initial confirmatory evidence for our functional completeness cues of verb tense and N-V-N, as well as for the processing capacity cue of sequence length. The evidence concerning verb tense and N-V-N is somewhat paradoxical: recall that in Experiment II we were unable to find an effect of verb tense, when N-V-N configurational properties were controlled. Conversely in Experiment III the significant effect of N-V-N we found overall, reduces to a non-significant trend when verb morpheme (and other local sign) properties are controlled.

The difficulty we have had in separating configurational and local sign cues is in itself not surprising. These cues are ecologically very highly correlated. The ideal factorialized manipulations one would like to make, do not exist in English. But what is surprising, or at least intriguing, is the seeming asymmetry between the local sign cue and the configurational cue vis-à-vis the two response measures we used in Experiments II and III. We will return to this in our conclusion.

Sequence length as a processing capacity cue

Experiment III provided highly significant but indirect evidence of sequence length as a segmentation cue. Experiment IV was designed to test directly for an effect of the processing capacity cue of sequence length. We used sentence-pairs like the one in (18).

(18) a. Long:
The dark and dangerously empty//city park seemed to get more frightening by the minute.
b. Short:
The//city park seemed to get more frightening by the minute.

'Long' members of a pair had an initial noun-phrase sequence seven words long; 'Short' members had noun phrases three words long. The probe word was the final word of the noun phrase (e.g. 'park') and the response word was the verb (e.g. 'seemed'). Sentence-pairs were cross-spliced so that they were acoustically identical from before the original occurrence of the probe word in the sentence through its presentation beginning 200 msec after the sentence (in (18), from the double slash on).

We predicted that the 'long' cases would be better segmentation units than the 'shorts' and hence obtain longer naming latencies. However, this prediction is confounded with a non-segmentation 'sequence search' model: there are more words to search through in the long cases in order to find the probe word–response word sequence. We therefore included control sentences as in (19).

(19) a. *The very unusual but impractically shaped clay* dish sold for 75 dollars.
b. *The rowdy school* boys were punished for disrupting the assembly.

The italicized sequences are 'potential' noun phrases, but cannot be interpreted as such in the sentences of (19). We probed the same serial positions as in the experimental sentences, the seventh word (clay) or the third word (school).

In the control sentences, unlike the experimental sentences, a segmentation boundary does not intervene between probe word and response word. Thus, on the segmentation account of length differences, but not on the sequential search model, we predict, first, a long versus short difference for experimental but not control sentences and, second, an overall effect of longer latencies for experimental than for control due to segmentation effects in the former but not the latter. (For further details of design and procedure, see Carroll, 1976.)

Both of these predictions obtain; refer to Table 6.4 for summary statistics. Analysis of variance reveals an overall effect of condition (experimental versus control, $p < .05$. T-tests show a significant effect of sequence length by-subject, $p < .05$, and by-item, $p < .025$, for experimental sentences. However, no sequence-length effect obtains for control sentences. Thus, using the next-word technique we measure an effect of length but not 'mere length'. Length cannot

Table 6.4 Experiment IV. Geometric mean latencies by-subject (milliseconds) for next-word naming

		Sentences	
		Experimental	Control
Length of sequences	Long	1309	1074
	Short	1148	995
	Means	1225	1034

stimulate segmentation when that segmentation would constitute a misparsing (e.g. (the very unusual but impractically shaped clay) + (dish sold for 75 dollars) = (19a)).

Context as a segmentation cue

Processing capacity cues interact with cues to internal structure to define the potential segmentation units of the perceived sentence. 'Long' and 'short' experimental sentences both have similar internal structures (in the sense of functional completeness), but the 'long' cases consume more processing resource and therefore encourage segmentation more. On the other hand, while 'long' experimental and control exemplars are comparable in terms of the sequence length estimation of processing requirements, they differ in terms of internal structure and the experimental cases stimulate segmentation more than the control cases.

We now turn to the question of whether and, if so, how contextual cues help the listener to recognize and recode functionally complete sequences. In two experiments, we preceded sentences like (20a), which has functionally incomplete a first clause, with specifying contexts that provided the missing grammatical relations, (20b), or with neutral contexts that did not do so, (20c).

(20) a. After buying some he returned home.
   b. The boy went to the store to buy some gum.
   c. The store was around the corner.

If contextual cues can help the listener to recognize and recode good potential segmentation sequences, the functionally incomplete sequences preceded by specifying contexts should be better segmentation units than those preceded by neutral contexts. Only in the former case can the functionally incomplete sequence be 'completed'.

The first experiment used the next-word naming technique. The probe was the last word of the first clause and the correct response word was the first word of the second clause. No differences in probe latencies were found as a function of the two types of contexts used. The second experiment used the location technique. Tones were placed either before the last word of the first clause or after the first word of the second clause (see Experiment I). Context did not affect the pattern of tone locations.

These non-results led us to speculate that the initial recoding schemes of sentence processing operate independently of context. However, a disturbing aspect of these experiments is that both the location and next-word naming tasks require that the listener maintains aspects of the literal form of the test sentence in memory. It is possible that this actually discourages subjects from integrating the test sentence with the preceding context sentence. *Prima facie*, this does not seem to be what happens in ordinary sentence comprehension. As a result, we have recently conducted several additional experiments to determine whether context can influence the early stages of sentence perception and comprehension.

In Experiment V, subjects were presented with two-sentence discourses, like those in (21).

(21) a. Why did Smith resign?
   b. Smith who Ford asked to remain in Vermont, for political reasons, decided to resign his post.
   c. Why did Ford want Smith to remain in Vermont?
   d. Smith who Ford asked to remain in Vermont, for political reasons, decided to resign his post.

The context question, (21a) and (21c), was typed on an index card. The subject first read the question aloud. A tape-recorded version of the second sentence, (21b) and (21d), respectively, was then played to the subject. The second sentence was always ambiguous in that it contained an adverbial 'swing phrase' that could modify either the main clause or the embedded clause. In (21), the swing phrase is 'for political reasons'. The sentences were recorded using subdued intonation, with a brief pause, before and after the swing phrase. The same recording was used for both context question conditions.

After reading the context question and hearing the ambiguous sentence the subject first paraphrased the ambiguous sentence, then answered the context question. The question directed the subject's attention either to the main clause of the second sentence, as in (21a), or to the embedded clause of the second sentence, as in (21b). We used the subjects' paraphrase of the ambiguous second sentence to determine which organization was assigned to it. Subjects' paraphrases were overwhelmingly consistent with the assignment called for by the question-context. In addition, only one subject even noticed that some of the sentences were ambiguous. Thus, in a task for which discourse context must be held in memory (question-answering), apparent context effects on segmentation organization *do* obtain.

Experiment VI provides evidence indicating that contextual cues are actually used on-line during sentence processing. We have already discussed the N-V-N configurational cue, and the evidence for it in Experiments I, II, and III. Consider, from this perspective, sentences (22).

(22) a. *The girl who kissed the boy* blushed.
    b. *The girl whom the boy kissed* blushed.

The initial italic sequence in (22a) is an N-V-N functionally complete unit, while the corresponding sequence in (22b) is functionally complete but is not an N-V-N configuration. On this basis, we would predict that sentence (22a) would be easier to organize perceptually than sentence (22b). This prediction accords with a variety of evidence showing that subject relative-clause sentences, like (22a), are less difficult to process than object relative-clause sentences, like (22b) (see Wanner, 1976).

In a pilot study, subjects were presented with a series of sentences including subject and object relative clauses, like (22a) and (22b), respectively. Their task was to press a telegraph key as soon as they understood each sentence. Reaction times to understand subject-relative sentences were faster than reaction times to understand object-relative sentences.

Two types of context were then constructed for each pair of sentences containing subject and object relative clauses. The *congruent* context condition presented the information contained in the relative clause of the following sentence. For example, the congruent contexts for (22a) and (22b), were (23a) and (23b), respectively.

(23) a. One of the girls kissed the boy.
    b. A boy kissed one of the girls.
    c. The kids were playing spin the bottle.

The *neutral* context (23c), which did not specify anything about the information in the relative clause, was the same for both subject- and object-relative sentences. The two types of context and the two types of relative clauses were then varied factorially, resulting in four presentation versions. The versions were then recorded with normal intonation. Each subject heard only one version. The subject's task was to press a key as soon as he understood the second sentence of each pair. (For details of method, procedure, and results, see Tanenhaus, 1978.)

If the initial stages of sentence processing are independent of context, then the complexity difference between the subject and object relative clauses should not be affected by specifying versus neutral contexts. The results, which are presented in Figure 6.1, clearly do not support this prediction. Anova reveals a

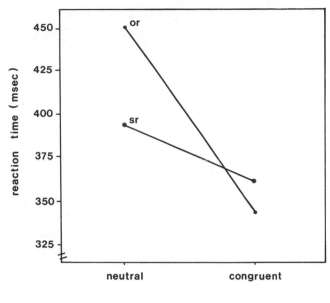

Figure 6.1. Reaction times to understand sentences containing subject (SR) and object (OR) relative clauses when preceded by neutral and congruent context sentences

main effect of context, $p < .001$ by-subject and $p < .025$ by-item, and an interaction between context and sentence type, $p < .001$ by-subject and $p < .025$ by-item. In the neutral context condition, reaction times to understand object-relative-clause sentences were significantly longer than reaction times to understand subject-relative clauses. This presumably reflects the difference between the two sentence types measured without any context manipulation. However, in the congruent context condition this object-relative versus subject-relative difference was completely eliminated. This pattern of results clearly suggests that intra-sentence syntactic-based processing strategies can be influenced by context.

Experiments V and VI suggest, contrary to our initial hypothesis, that listeners use context on-line as they are processing and organizing sentences. These results suggest that functionally incomplete sequences should become better processing units when they are preceded by contexts that clearly provide the information missing in the incomplete sequence. We are currently investigating this hypothesis, using paradigms that do not require the subject to hold the test sentences in memory.

CONCLUSIONS: THE PERCEPTION OF RELATIONS

Our conclusions divide into three sections. First, we summarize the specific points which have been discussed in the present chapter. Next, we consider some broader implications of this work for the study of sentence perception. We speculate on the relation of our cue constructs to levels of processing and representation in sentence perception. Finally, we attempt to place this research in the general context of the study of perception and comprehension.

Summary and specific conclusions

Early in this discussion, we raised an apparent paradox: human behaviour and experience are 'complex', while human processing resources are 'limited'. We reviewed the classic 'chunking' proposal of Miller (1956) concerning the deployment of limited resources. Miller and Smith's work shows that a saving in processing resource can be realized if stimuli are hierarchically and iteratively grouped, or 'chunked'. We then posed a further question: What are the principles that underlie chunking? In Smith's digit-recall experiments, recoding schemes were given by fiat of experimenter. Subjects were instructed as to how they should organize sequences. This work points out the potential advantages of chunking as a construct accounting for the manifest complexity of behaviour and experience. However, it suffers two limitations: first, digit lists are not intrinsically structured, in contrast to more natural stimuli; second, in ordinary behavioural situations people are usually not explicitly given recoding schemes to organize their processing capacity. General principles of chunking based exclusively on this work might overlook the implicit contribution of intrinsic stimulus structure to the organization of behaviour and experience.

Our own work has focused on a sequential stimulus which has a well-studied intrinsic structure. We have investigated how, if at all, the intrinsic structure of the stimulus determines the nature of the recoding schemes utilized in organizing the stimulus (e.g. perceptually). In particular, we have been concerned with the relation of linguistic structure and the recoding schemes that organize sentence perception. We reviewed two previous proposals to the effect that these recoding schemes pick out particular linguistic structures (clauses or major surface constituents). These proposals describe a simple and straightforward relation between stimulus structure and the recoding schemes that organize sentence perception: the latter must directly reconstruct the former (for further discussion, see Carroll, 1976). However, we were compelled to abandon this approach on both intuitive and experimental grounds. In the second section of this paper, we developed the claim that the recoding schemes of sentence perception are determined by an interaction of factors including, but not limited to, structural details of the stimulus.

We adopted a 'functionalist' perspective, and reapproached sentence perception from the viewpoint of the perceiving organism. We made the assumption that the organism attempts to organize perceptual input into optimally propositional units. However, we allowed, on the basis of the examples discussed in the first section, that these units might not always correspond to the propositions of the sentence's logical form. (Although, when comprehension succeeds, the 'logical' propositional structure of a sentence will always be recoverable from its 'perceived' propositional structure.) In the second section, we considered intuitively how listeners might recognize and assemble propositional (or grammatical) relations. In the third section, we experimentally tested some of these initial hypotheses.

The central property we have considered is functional completeness: the property of having a complete, coherent, and explicit set of grammatical relations. Functional completeness guarantees the listener a good propositional unit. But how can functional completeness be recognized? Can the listener always organize a sentence into functionally complete units? And, if not, how does the listener's processing compromise functional completeness when it must?

In approaching these questions we introduce a taxonomy of perceptual cues. We opposed cues to internal structure and processing-capacity cues. The former assist the listener in identifying good perceptual units (by hypothesis, functionally complete sequences). The latter restrict the processing of the former, and thereby can cause the listener to compromise functional completeness. Cues to internal structure were further divided into local sign, configurational and contextual/inferential cues.

In the third section, we presented six initial experimental studies designed to show that the sorts of cues we hypothesized could indeed influence the perceptual organization of sentences. In particular, we wanted to collect evidence indicating that local sign, configurational, and contextual/inferential cues influence segmentation and recoding to the extent that they inform the listener about the functional completeness of potential segmentation units. Additionally, we wanted to show that processing capacity cues influence perceptual organization in interaction with cues to internal structure.

Experiments I and II used the tone-location response measure. They showed that functionally complete sequences are better perceptual units than functionally incomplete sequences. Experiment I also manipulated sequence length, a presumed processing-capacity cue. However, no effect of sequence length obtained. Experiment II manipulated particular cues to internal structure in order to determine more specifically what accounted for the overall functional-completeness result. Contextual/inferential cues cannot provide the basis for the effect, since if contextual/inferential information were structuring the perceptual organization of the sequences we studied in Experiments I and II, *all* of them would effectively be functionally complete.

On our taxonomy, that leaves local sign and configurational cues. In Experiment II, we tried to separate these two cue classes and determined that the N-V-N configurational cue could account for our data. The additional assumption of local sign cues was not supported by the results of Experiment II.

Experiments III and IV used the next-word naming response measure. Experiment III replicated the main functional completeness result of Experiments I and II. Again, we tried to determine which functional completeness cue or cues accounted for the obtained effect. Contextual/inferential cues were not manipulated, but we were able to contrast the N-V-N configurational cue with the local sign cue of verb tense. The data suggest that the configurational cue has a somewhat marginal influence, and that the local sign cue provides a much better account of obtained differences.

Experiment III also revealed significant correlational effects of the processing-capacity cue of sequence length. Experiment IV directly manipulated sequence length, and replicated this finding. Additionally, Experiment IV showed that 'mere' length does not influence the suitability of sequences as recoding units, but that length in conjunction with internal structural properties does.

Experiments V and VI addressed the issue of contextual/inferential cues. Experiment V demonstrated that contextual information can, at least in part, determine which of two possible organizations a listener imposes on an ambiguous sentence. Experiment VI shows that context can render a sequence which is configurationally a relatively poor segmentation sequence (i.e. not N-V-N), as good a segmentation sequence as one which is configurationally N-V-N.

As should be clear, we find the previous structural-linguistic theories of sentence segmentation inadequate. Neither of these theories distinguishes functionally complete sequences from functionally incomplete sequences. Neither of these theories distinguishes sequences of differing lengths. Finally, neither of these theories characterized discourse context as a segmentation variable. As we argued in the first section, the logical basis of these theories is not sound. But more concretely, the data from the experiments presented in the third section reject these theories as null hypotheses. It seems beyond question that a new approach to sentence segmentation is required.

Speculation on segmentation cues and processing capacity

While the preceding statement of results and conclusions is as far as, and perhaps farther than, we can go at present, some of the apparent 'weaknesses' in the data we have presented suggest a possible further elaboration of our cue theory of sentence perception, a 'strengthening' of our claims. First, consider the intuitive trade-off of cue 'cost' and cue 'validity' among the three classes of cues to internal structure that we presented.

Contextual-inferential cues seem to be highly valid indicators of functional completeness. They pick out any sequence that *can* be represented by a well-formed proposition (i.e. subject-predicate-object). However, the cost of contextual-inferential cues seems to be quite high too. In order to recognize a headless nominalization as a potential functionally complete unit, for example, it is necessary to recall previous discourse context, or to inspect the following clause for a logically antecedent subject, etc.

In contrast, consider our class of configurational cues. At this level of analysis, there is a sharp distinction between sequences like headless nominalizations which are themselves functionally incomplete (even though context may complete them) and sequences which are themselves functionally complete, like headed nominalizations. Only the latter comprise a complete, coherent, and explicit *configuration* of grammatical relations.

In the sense that configurational cues pick out a smaller subset of potential functionally complete sequences, they are less valid cues of functional completeness than contextual/inferential cues, which pick out a larger set. On the other hand, configurational cues seem to have less cost, as well. In order to compute, recognize, or apprehend a configurational cue, the listener need not concern himself with preceding information, subsequent information, or concurrent extra-linguistic information.

In this regard, consider local sign cues. In this case, the listener need not even consider the sequence, in its entirety, in order to obtain some information about the suitability of the sequence as a recoding unit. The listener can limit the scope of processing to single lexical items, or even single morphemes. Thus, local sign cues seem to have even less cost than configuration cues. Of course, they also have less cue validity. Verb tense, for example, is a local sign cue of functional completeness, but fails to pick out headed nominalizations. Local sign cues pick out a smaller subset of potential functionally complete sequences than configurational cues. (See Brunswik, 1956, and Carroll, 1976, for further discussion of cue cost and cue validity trade-offs.)

The various experimental paradigms that we used can also be intuitively ordered in terms of their 'cost' in processing capacity to the listener. We used four tasks: tone location, next-word naming, paraphrasing, and comprehension time. Of these, the next-word naming task of Experiments III and IV seems to place the greatest load on the listener's processing capacities. The task requires, first, that the subject must maintain a relatively literal representation of the sentence, and second, that the subject must rapidly search this representation for two particular adjacent words.

The location task of Experiments I and II also requires that the subject must maintain the literal word sequence of the sentence. It further requires that the subject must remember the position of the tone in the sentence sequence. However, the subject is not under any time pressure to generate his recall and tone-position responses.

Neither the paraphrase task of Experiment V nor the comprehension task of Experiment VI requires the subject to retain any verbatim representation of the sentence. (However, in the latter task but not in the former, the subject's response is timed.)

Organizing our cue taxonomy and our experimental paradigms into 'cost' hierarchies suggests an account of the asymmetries in the data we have presented. Cue cost and task demands vis-à-vis processing capacity may trade off: higher cost cues can be used in lower cost experimental task environments. Conversely, lower cost cues will be relied on to a greater extent in higher cost task environments. Higher cost cues are preferable because they are more highly valid indicators of functional completeness. However, in relatively high-cost task environments, their cost in processing capacity may be prohibitive.

With this hypothesis in mind, reconsider the evidence from Experiments I to VI. Experiments V and VI made use of tasks relatively low in cost vis-à-vis processing capacity. These experiments provide evidence of contextual cues—relatively high in cost vis-à-vis processing capacity. Experiment VI, in particular, indicates that in the comprehension time task, contextual cues are more prepotent than configurational cues.

We have analysed the location task as being higher in cost than the paraphrase and comprehension tasks. In this task environment, we measured effects of the N-V-N configurational cue, but failed to find effects of the local sign verb tense cue or of context. This is consistent with the view that the listener does not have the processing capacity to make use of context. Being able, then, to use configurational and local sign information, he relies on the more highly valid configurational indicators of functional completeness.

Finally, consider the next-word naming task. In this relatively high-cost task environment, the listener must rely on the lowest-cost local sign type of cue. A trace effect of the N-V-N configurational cue is still found, but effects of context are not.

Somewhat more direct support for this analysis comes from our study of the processing-capacity cue of sequence length in Experiments I, III, and IV. In a relatively lower cost task environment (location), we find no effect of sequence length. However, in a higher cost task environment (next-word naming), we do find length effects.

Our 'cost' hierarchy hypothesis requires some conceptual elaboration. First, the notion of 'cost', while it has very much intuitive appeal, must be spelled out in far more detail. This necessitates an analysis of the micro-structure of sentence segmentation, and of the psycholinguistic research paradigms used to study segmentation, that has really only begun. Why and how, precisely, are configurational cues higher in cost than local sign cues? Why and how, precisely, is one task higher in cost than another? Would, for example, tone location, with some time pressure introduced, be higher in cost than next-word naming, with accuracy weighted far greater than speed? Without such an elaboration the cost-hierarchy hypothesis rests on very thin ice.

Second, we need to specify just what the cue hierarchy commits us to. We feel that while the effectiveness of local sign cues in segmentation processing may typically *precede* that of configurational cues, the former may not necessarily construct the input to the latter. Another way of putting this is to say that we doubt that the hierarchy of cues reflects a serially structured segmentation process. Again, we can only speculate on this matter in the absence of an analysis of the micro-processes of segmentation and recoding.

Finally, we need to investigate what relation exists between our task hierarchy and ordinary levels of processing in sentence perception. For instance, it is tempting to suggest that higher cost task environments (which tend to require the subject to maintain a nearly verbatim representation and to generate a response under time pressure), are actually tapping representations and processes of relatively early levels of sentence processing. Lower cost tasks might actually be more sensitive to later levels of perceptual processing. On the other hand, tasks may·artifactually deform 'ordinary' perceptual representations to the extent that there would be no interesting correspondence with our notion of task cost and isolable levels of processing. But again, these are matters for further research.

Recoding schemes and relations: General remarks

We have several times recalled Miller's chunking proposal and raised the question of whether there are any general properties of recoding schemes, and if so, of course, what these properties are. On the basis of our investigations thus far, we are encouraged to believe that there are general properties. Specifically, we propose that all recoding schemes have the common property that they construct coherent relational mental structures. In the context of the study of sentence segmentation, our claim is that recoding schemes construct linguistic propositions consisting of coherent sets of grammatical relations.

More follows from this, however. We have already noted that the propositions constructed by perceptual recoding schemes may not correspond isomorphically to the underlying syntactic propositions of the logical form of the sentence. Thus, we must distinguish between the structural relations intrinsic to the sentence and the functional relations which are jointly determined by the intrinsic structure of the sentence and the exigencies, heuristics, limitations, and contexts of perception. At any given stage or level of processing, in any given task-environment and in any discourse or extra-linguistic context we can only measure the consequences of functional relations and the propositional units they define. This does not alter the fact that functional propositions are entrained by logical structures, that functional relations are entrained by structural relations. From the former we must be able to recover the latter. If a perception/comprehension device cannot satisfy this requirement it is not general.

But recoding schemes must do even more than construct functional relations and map them into structural relations. Once a functionally complete unit has been isolated and recoded, it must be integrated with other similar units to recover the 'perceived sentence'. Similarly, the perceived structure of a sentence must be integrated with other similar units to recover the 'perceived discourse'.

Recoding schemes map from stimulus sequences onto relational structures, and from relational structures onto other relational structures. At relatively 'immediate' stages of perceptual organization these ideals or goals may be most severely compromised by limitations of processing capacity. But even at relatively later stages, functional limitations of the task-environment, motivations, other context, etc., compromise these mappings. In every case, we would claim, the output structures are 'better' mental units: more complete relational structures, more complete amalgamations of relational structures and relational structures more consistent with the intrinsic structure of the stimulus.

The fundamental question in the description of comprehension processes is how the defining relations of the stimulus are internally organized. The propositions of a sentence, the relations between them and the grammatical relations internal to them, *inhere* in the sentence (or, perhaps more precisely, in our knowledge of the sentence). A theory of sentence comprehension must describe a process that can recover and properly organize these relations.

This is, perhaps, not a unique property of the study of sentence comprehension. The objects of a visual display, the spatial relations between them (above, behind, within) and the relations of the contours, areas, and volumes (etc.) internal to them, *inhere* in the display. Comprehending a visual display entails recovering and properly organizing these defining relations. In both cases, however, various limitations of human processing capacity complicate comprehension. For example, an obvious limitation in visual information processing is the relatively small spatial extent of what can be foveally fixated. Resultingly, the comprehension of visual displays is intermediately structured by a sequence of foveal glances from which the relations underlying the entire display must be recovered (Hochberg, 1968).

From this perspective, the units or 'objects' of perception and comprehension are coherent relational structures. In order to study perception and comprehension, we must identify the relations intrinsic to the structure of the stimulus and the mechanisms and heuristics employed in recovering and organizing these defining relations. In the case of sentence perception, the science of linguistics provides a theory of the fundamental relations which define the stimulus. Similarly, the intrinsic structure of visual objects and events has been described (Carroll, 1977; Clowes, 1971; Winston, 1970). In both cases, the most formidable question is *how* these relational structures are recognized and integrated into percept and concept.

ACKNOWLEDGMENTS

This research was supported in part by NSF-BNS 76-04334. An earlier version was presented at the 1976 Annual Meetings of the Eastern Psychological Association (Carroll and Tanenhaus, 1976). We thank Ellen Perecman and David Tucker who helped with stimulus preparation and in administering the experiments.

REFERENCES

Abrams, K. Real-time sentence processing. Unpublished Ph.D Dissertation. University of Michigan, 1973.

Abrams, K. and Bever, T. G. Syntactic structure modifies attention during speech perception and recognition. *Quarterly Journal of Experimental Psychology*, 1969, **21**, 280–290.

Bever, T. G. The cognitive basis for linguistic structures. In J. R. Hayes (Ed.), *Cognition and the development of language*. New York: Wiley, 1970.

Bever, T. G. and Hurtig, R. Detectability of a non-linguistic stimulus is poorest at the end of a clause. *Journal of Psycholinguistic Research*, 1975, **4**, 1–7.

Bever, T. G., Hurtig, R. R., and Handel, A. B. Response bias does not account for the effect of clause structure on the perception of non-linguistic stimuli. In preparation (available as Research Bulletin, Educational Testing Service, RB–75–30, 1975).

Bever, T. G., Lackner, J. R. and Kirk, R. The underlying structures of sentences are the primary units of immediate speech processing. *Perception and Psychophysics*, 1969, **5**, 225–234.

Brunswick, E. *Perception and the representative design of psychological experiments*. Berkeley: University of California Press, 1956.

Carroll, J. M. The interaction of structural and functional variables in sentence perception: Some preliminary studies. Unpublished Ph.D. Dissertation, Columbia University, 1976.

Carroll, J. M. A program for cinema theory. *The Journal of Aesthetics and Art Criticism*, 1977, **35**, 337–351.

Carroll, J. Sentence perception units and levels of syntactic structure. *Perception and Psychophysics*, 1978, **23**, 506–514.

Carroll, J. M. and Bever, T. G. Sentence comprehension: A study in the relation of knowledge to perception. In E. C. Carterette and M. P. Friedman (Eds.), *The handbook of perception*. Vol. 5, *Language and speech*. New York: Academic Press, 1976.

Carroll, J. M. and Tanenhaus, M. K. Function clauses and sentence segmentation. *Journal of Speech and Hearing Research*, 1978, in press.

Carroll, J. M. and Tanenhaus, M. K. Functional completeness and sentence segmentation. Annual Meetings, Eastern Psychological Association, 1976.

Chapin, P., Smith, T., and Abrahamson, A. Two factors in perceptual segmentation of speech. *Journal of Verbal Learning and Verbal Behavior*, 1972, **11**, 164–173.

Chomsky, N. *Syntactic structures*. The Hague: Mouton, 1957.

Chomsky, N. *Reflections on language*. New York: Pantheon, 1976.

Clowes, M. On seeing things. *Artificial Intelligence*, 1971, **2**, 79–98.

Ferguson, G. *Statistical analysis in psychology and education*. New York: McGraw-Hill, 1971.

Fodor, J. A. *Psychological explanation*. New York: Random House, 1968.

Fodor, J. A. and Bever, T. G. The psychological reality of linguistic segments. *Journal of Verbal Learning and Verbal Behavior*, 1965, **4**, 414–420.

Fodor, J. A., Bever, T. G., and Garrett, M. *The psychology of language. An introduction to psycholinguistics and generative grammar*. New York: McGraw-Hill, 1974.

Hochberg, J. In the mind's eye. In R. Haber (Ed.), *Contemporary theory and research in visual perception*. New York: Holt, Rinehart and Winston, 1968.

Kintsch, W. *The representation of meaning of memory*. Hillsdale, N.J.: Lawrence Erlbaum Associates, 1974.

Köhler, W. *Gestalt Psychology*. New York: Liveright, 1929.

Marslen-Wilson, W. D., Tyler, L. K., and Seidenberg, M. The semantic control of sentence segmentation. Paper presented at the Annual Meetings, Midwestern Psychological Association, 1976.

Miller, G. A. The magical number seven plus or minus two: Some limits on our capacity for processing information. *Psychological Review*, 1956, **63**, 81–96.

Rumelhart, D. E., Lindsay, P. H., and Norman, D. A. A process model for long-term memory. In E. Tulving and W. Donaldson (Eds.), *Organization of memory*. New York: Academic Press, 1972.

Seitz, M. AER and the perception of speech. Unpublished Ph.D. Dissertation, University of Washington, 1972.

Stockwell, R., Schachter, P., and Partee, B. *The major syntactic structures of English*. New York: Holt, Rinehart and Winston, 1973.

Suci, G., Ammon, P., and Gamlin, P. The validity of the probe-latency technique for assessing structure in language. *Language and Speech*, 1967, **10**, 69–80.

Tanenhaus, M. K. Linguistic context and sentence perception. Ph.D. Dissertation, Columbia University, 1978.

Tanenhaus, M. K. and Carroll, J. M. The clausal processing hierarchy and ... nouniness. In R. Grossman, J. San, and T. Vance (Eds.), *Papers from the parasession on functionalism*. Chicago: Chicago Linguistic Society, 1975.

Tanenhaus, M. K. and Seidenberg, M. Informational determinants of the processing units in sentence perception. Annual Meetings, Midwestern Psychological Association, 1978.

Wanner, E. Paper presented at the Symposium on the Perception of Language. XXI International Congress of Psychology, Paris, July 1976.

Winston, P. Learning structural descriptions from examples. Unpublished Ph.D. Dissertation, M.I.T. Cambridge, Mass., 1970.

Chapter 7

Sentence Processing and the Clause Boundary

William Marslen-Wilson, Lorraine K. Tyler, and Mark Seidenberg

The identifying characteristic of most recent theorizing about sentence perception has been its emphasis on the role of the syntactic clause. This approach, known in general as the 'clausal hypothesis' (Carroll and Bever, 1976; Fodor, Bever, and Garrett, 1974), can in principle be separated into two main components. The first of these is the hypothesis that the speech input is segmented into relatively large processing units, which correspond to the syntactic clausal structure of the material (cf. Fodor and Bever, 1965; Garrett, Bever, and Fodor, 1966). We will refer to this as the clausal *structuring* hypothesis. The second main component is a theory about the order of processing events underlying the clausal organization of the input. This is an essentially serial theory, which argues that speech is not understood as it is heard, but rather that the major interpretative efforts of the processing system are focused around the syntactic clause boundary. We will label this the clausal-*processing* hypothesis.

The purpose of the arguments and the experiments to be presented in this chapter is to investigate the consequences for both these clausal hypotheses of a rather different approach to sentence perception, which we will refer to as the *on-line interactive* approach. This approach claims, in essence, that the listener attempts to interpret fully each utterance word-by-word as he hears it, from the first word of the input onwards (cf. Marslen-Wilson, 1976; Marslen-Wilson and Tyler, 1975). This claim, and the evidence supporting it, stand in obvious contrast to the clausal processing hypothesis. One of the experiments to be described here will include an additional test of the two approaches, focusing on the point in the processing of a sentence at which their predictions most clearly diverge: namely, as to whether or not there is an asymmetry in the availability of a semantic interpretation of the incoming material at the end of a clause as opposed to the beginning of a clause.

Secondly, we will examine the relationship between the on-line interactive approach and the clausal structuring hypothesis. Our purpose here will be, first, to show that the correctness of the claim that speech is structured into clause-like processing units does not necessarily depend on the correctness of the clausal processing hypothesis as well. We will then go on to propose a rationale for the clausal structuring hypothesis that is more compatible with the on-line interactive approach. In particular, we will try to show experimentally that to the extent that there is 'clausal' segmentation of the speech input, it is a function of what we will call the interpretative informational structure of the utterance, and not simply of its syntactic structure.

THEORIES OF CLAUSAL PROCESSING

The clausal processing hypothesis originally derived from the proposal that a transformational generative grammar could provide the guidelines for a psychological processing model (cf. Miller and Chomsky, 1963), and that the primary goal of the sentence-processing system was to derive a syntactic deep-structure representation of the input (Fodor, Bever, and Garrett, 1974; see also Levelt, this volume, for an extensive discussion of the issues and studies involved). This processing hypothesis is represented in the psychological literature in many different versions. According to the strongest versions of the hypothesis, the listener passively accumulates information during the clause about the lexical and surface syntactic properties of the input, and only at the end of the clause does he actively begin to develop a deep-structure syntactic and semantic interpretation of what he has heard (e.g. Bever and Hurtig, 1975; Forster, 1974).

The weaker versions of the hypothesis permit, to varying degrees, at least some preliminary structural hypotheses to be actively computed before the boundary is reached. This weakening is implicit, for example, in the conventional interpretation of syntactic structural ambiguity effects. Bever, Garrett, and Hurtig (1973), for example, argue that deep-structural ambiguity leads to the parallel computation of two or more deep-structure hypotheses during the clause, with the decision between them being made at the clause boundary. And an explicit statement of the weaker hypothesis is to be found in the concluding remarks of a recent review by Carroll and Bever: 'During clauses, listeners use local lexical and semantic information to develop hypotheses about the possible sentoid mappings onto elementary grammatical relations' (1976, p. 335). But note that however weak the clausal processing hypothesis becomes, it still requires the basic assumption that sentence understanding is a qualitatively discontinuous process; that at some points in a sentence (in particular, the beginnings of clauses) the listener is not developing a semantic interpretation. If the theory does not maintain this assumption of a serial relationship between the development of a deep syntactic representation and the subsequent semantic interpretation, then it loses any meaningful connection with the linguistic formalisms which motivated its postulation in the first place (cf. Marslen-Wilson, 1976; Tyler and Marslen-Wilson, in preparation).

The assumption of discontinuous interpretation, and the clausal processing hypothesis in general, are in conflict, however, with the results of some recent experiments which demonstrate, instead, that the listener can begin his structural interpretation from the first word of a sentence, without having to wait until a clausal unit has been completed (Marslen-Wilson, 1973a, 1973b; Marslen-Wilson and Tyler, 1975; Tyler and Marslen-Wilson, 1977). These results enable us, in particular, to rule out any of the stronger versions of the clausal processing hypothesis. Active interpretation of the input can clearly begin as soon as the sentence starts (see especially Marslen-Wilson and Tyler, 1975; Tyler and Marslen-Wilson, 1977). The evidence so far, however, does not directly enable us to counter the claims of the weaker versions of the clausal processing hypothesis for the existence of a discontinuity in semantic processing at points around the major clause boundary. The word-monitoring study of Marslen-Wilson and Tyler (1975) did test at several word positions in a large pool of sentences, but it did not make the necessary controlled contrasts between before- and after- clause-boundary locations.

In the first experiment to be reported here, therefore, we have used the word-monitoring task to ask directly the following question: Is the listener more likely to have available, on-line, a semantic interpretation of what he hears at the end of a clause but not of what he hears at the beginning of a clause? As far as we are aware, this is not a question that has previously been subjected to the appropriate on-line test.

The experiment used sentences of the following type (monitoring target-word emphasized):

(1)a. Although Mary very rarely cooks *trout*, when she does so it tastes delicious.
   b. Although Mary very rarely cooks, *trout* is one thing she prepares well.

The critical feature of this sentence pair is that exactly the same sequence of words precedes the target word in each case; the only difference is in the syntactic and hence prosodic structure assigned to each sequence. In sentence (1a) the target occurs at the end of the first clause, while in sentence (1b) it occurs at the beginning of the second clause. Under these conditions, any differences in reaction times to targets in the two locations can be ascribed to their different relationships to the clausal structure of the sentence.

A simple word-monitoring task, in which the subject is told in advance exactly which word to listen for, is inadequate for our purposes. Instead, we will contrast the *rhyme*- and *category*-monitoring tasks (Marslen-Wilson and Tyler, 1975; in preparation). In both tasks the subject listens to a sentence for a word target, but under different definitions of the target. In rhyme monitoring, the target is defined as a word that rhymes with a cue word given in advance, while in category monitoring the target is defined as a member of a particular semantic category, also specified in advance.

Earlier results show that these two tasks are differentially sensitive to the availability of a semantic interpretation of the material being processed. When a sentence is semantically uninterpretable, rhyme-monitoring latencies increase (relative to a normal sentence context) by an average of 44 msec, whereas category-monitory latencies increase by 100 msec in the same situation (Marslen-Wilson and Tyler, 1975). This pattern of results is best accounted for by assuming that the monitoring response requires a two-stage process, and that semantic context facilitates both stages in category monitoring and only one stage in rhyme monitoring.

Monitoring for words in sentence contexts requires first identifying the word in question, and then performing some kind of attribute-matching process to determine whether the word matches the semantic or phonetic properties specified for the target. The word-indentification stage in both tasks is facilitated in the same way by contextual constraints, in the manner outlined by Marslen-Wilson and Welsh (1978). But the attribute-matching stage in rhyme monitoring does not interact with semantic context, since the determination of a phonetic match is clearly independent of semantic variables. In category monitoring the process of attribute matching involves the determination of the semantic properties of the word being recognized. This is clearly a process that can be facilitated when the word in question is in any case being semantically analysed in order to determine its proper mapping into the on-going semantic interpretation of the sentence. But when the word occurs in a situation where a semantic interpretation is not being attempted, then the semantic attribute-matching process itself has to initiate and carry through the semantic analysis of the word. This produces the large increases in category-monitoring response latency that we observe when the subject monitors for words in sentences that have no coherent semantic interpretation (Marslen-Wilson and Tyler, 1975).

In the light of this analysis of the two monitoring tasks, the weak clausal processing hypothesis should predict that category-monitoring latencies will be faster to targets in the before-boundary position (as in sentence (1a)) than to after boundary targets (as in (1b)). This is because the theory states that a semantic interpretation should not be being attempted at the beginning of a clause, corresponding to the location of the after-boundary targets. The before-boundary targets, in contrast, occur at the end of a clause, at a point where the clausal-processing hypothesis does allow for semantic processing to be taking place. But rhyme-monitoring latencies should be considerably less affected by target location. Performance in this task is less sensitive to the presence of a sentential semantic level of interpretation, and more dependent on levels of analysis (phonetic and lexical) that should be equally available before and after the clause boundary, since the boundary does not reflect a discontinuity at these levels of analysis.

The on-line interactive hypothesis, in contrast, predicts that the two tasks should behave in the same ways. If the listener is at all points in a normal utterance attempting to map what he hears on to a structural syntactic and semantic interpretation, then the category-monitoring target will never occur in conditions where the attribute-matching process cannot benefit from the on-going semantic analysis of the words in the string. Thus although there may be an overall difference between rhyme- and category-monitoring latencies, the relationship between them should not vary as a function of target location. If the listener's on-going representation does not undergo qualitative changes during processing, then whatever factors affect rhyme and category monitoring at one point in a sentence should affect these latencies in the same way at any other point in the sentence.

Note, however, that these predictions leave open the possibility that overall monitoring latency (for both tasks taken together) may change as a function of target location. In fact, for sentences like (1a) and (1b), the interactive model predicts that after-boundary latencies (in both tasks) will be slower than before-boundary latencies. To establish the rationale for this prediction we will first have to show how the on-line interactive approach can account for the organization of connected speech into clause-like perceptual units. This in turn requires some consideration of the relationship between the interactive approach and the clausal-structuring hypothesis.

INFORMATIONAL STRUCTURE, PROCESSING STRUCTURE, AND CLAUSAL STRUCTURE

The second main aspect of the general clausal hypothesis, the clausal structuring hypothesis, has in the past been closely linked to the kinds of clausal processing hypotheses we described earlier. And, clearly, if the primary goal of the processing system is to compute deep-structure representations of the input, then it follows naturally that the perception of sentences will be organized into processing units that correspond to complete deep-structure sentences (or 'sentoids'), which themselves usually correspond in turn to surface-structure syntactic clauses. But, in fact, although there is considerable evidence that does favour some degree of clausal structuring of the input, none of this evidence necessarily implicates the clausal processing hypothesis as well.

The original, and probably the major source of evidence for the clausal structuring hypothesis is the click displacement effect (e.g. Fodor and Bever, 1965; Garrett *et al.*, 1966). This is the claim that when a subject hears an extraneous noise, such as a click, superimposed on a normal sentence, he will tend to displace the perceptual location of the click towards the boundaries of the major sentential processing units. Leaving aside the methodological controversies which have surrounded this task (cf. Levelt, this volume), the point of interest here is whether the click displacement data implicate the deep or the surface syntactic clause as the main segmentation unit. For the click data would only directly support the clausal processing hypothesis if they showed perceptual segmentation to be sensitive to deep-structure syntactic variables.

In fact, almost all of the click-location studies have used sentences in which surface- and deep-structure clause boundaries coincide in the surface structure, so that it was not possible to conclude that it was the deep rather than the surface unit which produced the effects. The main exception to this was a study by Bever, Lackner, and Kirk (1969), which specifically manipulated deep and surface boundaries, and claimed to show that it was the deep boundaries which attracted clicks. But subsequent research, as well as criticisms of the linguistic analysis upon which Bever *et al.*'s experimental contrasts were based, seriously undermine their conclusions (cf. Chapin, Smith, and Abrahamson, 1972; Fodor, 1974; Levelt, this volume).

The second main source of support for the clasual structuring hypothesis comes from some memory studies (e.g. Jarvella, 1971; Caplan, 1972). However, in all of these experiments the deep-structure boundaries coincided with surface-structure boundaries. Furthermore, none of them necessarily support the clausal processing hypothesis—even though they have usually been described as doing so. Testing several words after the end of a clause, these studies show that material within that clause is now represented in memory in a semantic format, whereas lower-level information is still available about a clause which is still in progress. These results are perfectly compatible with an on-line interactive analysis, since they do not show that semantic information is *not* available about the clause still in progress (cf. Marslen-Wilson and Tyler, 1976).

The standard evidence, then, for the clausal structuring of the speech input does not lend any special support to the clausal processing hypothesis. And as far as its relationship to any particular linguistic theory is concerned, the clausal structuring hypothesis appears to be compatible with any formalism which recognizes a level of immediate constituent structure similar to the surface syntactic clause.

However, given that the clausal structuring hypothesis itself remains more or less intact, the question arises of its relationship to the on-line interactive approach. For this approach not only rules out the clausal processing hypothesis as the mechanism underlying clausal structuring, but also provides no particular evidence for the existence of a computationally distinct level of syntactic representation as part of normal sentence processing (cf. Tyler and Marslen-Wilson, 1978). The significance of the latter suggestion is that clausal structuring effects are normally stated in terms of the strictly syntactic properties of sentences. But if it is possible that syntactic factors do not play an independent role in on-going sentence processing, then why should sentences appear to be organized during processing into segments that seem to be straightforwardly syntactically defined?

We can best develop our alternative rationale for clausal structuring effects by returning to the suggestion we made at the end of the previous section. Namely, that the on-line interactive hypothesis predicts that for sentences like (1a) and (1b) the after-boundary response latencies will be shorter than the before-boundary latencies.

The way we will motivate these predictions reflects the basic assumption of the on-line interactive hypothesis; that the listener attempts to fully interpret utterances word-by-word as he hears them. For if this is the case, then the primary constraint on the organization of on-going processing will be the order in which the processing information necessary for the complete interpretation of the input becomes available. The importance of syntactic clauses, in this framework, is that the syntactic clause will often (but not always) represent an informationally complete interpretative unit. In particular, it usually constitutes a complete subject-predicate structure, or, alternatively, a verb together with all its arguments (i.e. subject, object, indirect object, etc.).

This kind of concept can be illustrated by reference to the operations of a parsing device which builds interpretative structures left-to-right as it goes. For an example, we can refer to the routines that Riesbeck and Schank (this volume) describe for the interpretation of a sentence like (2) below.

(2) John was given a book by Mary

In particular, when the program encounters the word 'given' it sets up a preliminary structure in which somebody is transferring something to a man called John. This means that predictions are set up to look for the 'somebody' and the 'something' and these predictions are fulfilled by 'a book' and by 'Mary'. What is happening, then, is that the word 'given' is indeed being immediately mapped on to a structural interpretation (which includes more than just syntactic information), but this interpretation is in a real sense incomplete until more of the string has been heard. Note, of course, that not all of the arguments attached to a verb like 'give' are obligatory, so that, for example, the predicted slot corresponding to the donor ('Mary') need not have been filled.

Clearly, it is along these lines that we can develop a mechanism for the clause-like structuring of speech processing that is compatible with the on-line interactive hypothesis. There will indeed be a kind of periodicity to the speech perceptual process, with the processing units bounded at one end by the beginning of the utterance, and at the other by those points in the utterance at which the expectations triggered by the preceding elements of the string can be satisfactorily closed off (c.f. Ades, 1977). It is never the case that interpretative activity is not being attempted, but it will often be the case, as it were, that this activity will raise more questions than can be immediately answered—as, for example, with the word 'given' in the case just discussed.

But the crucial hypothesis here is that the on-line delimitation of these large-scale processing structures is not a simple function of the syntactic structure of the string. The on-line interactive hypothesis claims that the primary target of processing is not an intermediate and strictly syntactic level of representation, but rather a domain of much fuller semantic interpretation. Since this implies that syntactic variables alone do not determine processing structure, we need to develop an experimental situation which contrasts syntactic segmentational variables with what we can call interpretative informational variables—that is, the presence or absence of the necessary information for the complete interpretation of a sequence.

To do this, we need to look at informational relationships *between* clauses, since within clauses syntactic and interpretative variables seem to be perfectly confounded. These between-clause relationships can be illustrated by reference to the following pair of sentences:

(3)a. *Because he didn't like it*, John threw the book away.
   b. John threw the book away, *because he didn't like it*.

The italicized clausal segment in these sentences differs in the extent to which a full interpretation can be assigned to it by the time the end of the segment is reached. In sentence (3a) the listener cannot know at the end of the first clause who the principal agent is, nor what is the object of his actions. The interpretative representation that he has of that clause will not become fully fleshed out until he has heard the words 'John' and 'book' in the second clause. In contrast, the listener's on-line representation of the lexically identical segment in sentence (3b) can be fully interpreted within the clause. The processing information necessary for its complete interpretation had become available earlier in sentence (3b), in the first clause.

The important point about the informational relationships between clauses in (3a) and (3b) is that they do not involve strictly syntactic factors. As far as a syntactic representation is concerned, 'Because he didn't like it' is not informationally distinct, for example, from 'Because John didn't like the book'. In both cases the arguments associated with the verb have been filled with the appropriate syntactic elements, since a pronoun is as good a noun phrase as 'John' or 'the book'. But at the richer level of interpretation invoked by the on-line interactive hypothesis, there is a clear difference in the informational completeness of the two clauses, in the ways outlined above. Between clauses, therefore, we can manipulate informational dependencies in a way which separates syntactic from more interpretative informational variables.

We will exploit this separation by including in the first experiment a comparison between the effects of target location in sentences such as (1a) and (1b) with the effects in sentences such as (4a) and (4b) below:

(4)a. Even though they are quite small *cats*, they need a lot of living space.
   b. Even though they are quite small, *cats* need a lot of living space.

In sentence (4a) the first clause is relatively informationally complete. The referent for the pronoun 'they' is provided within the first clause, so that the clause can function as a self-sufficient interpretative processing sequence. The informational completeness of this clause is comparable to that of the first clause in sentence (1a)—'Although Mary very rarely cooks trout, . . .'.

The critical difference is between sentences (4b) and (1b). The first clause of (4b) contains the anaphoric pronoun 'they', the referent for which only becomes available in the second clause. But in sentence (1b) the first clause—'Although Mary very rarely cooks, . . .'—is relatively informationally complete. The clause contains no anaphoric pronouns, and the verb 'cooks' is used in its intransitive sense, so that it requires no object.

What this means is that the target words in the (1a/1b) sets will differ from the target words in the (4a/4b) sets in their relationships to the boundaries of inter-pretative processing sequences. In both (1a) and (1b) the syntactic segmentation unit corresponds to the interpretative segmentation unit, so that the target words occur either at the end point (in 1a) or at the starting point (in 1b) of a processing sequence. But this contrast is much weaker in the (4a/4b) set. The target word in (4a) does indeed occur at the end of a processing sequence. However, in (4b) the syntactic clause boundary does not, on the interpretative structuring hypothesis, mark the termination of a processing sequence. This means that the target word in (4b) will not occur at the starting point of a processing sequence, but, if anything, towards the end point of the sequence. In other words, the targets in (4a) and (4b) will occur under much more similar conditions than the targets in (1a) and (1b).

We now need to translate these differences between the target-word sets into predictions about monitoring reaction times. We can phrase these predictions in terms of the general claim that the location of a word in a processing sequence will affect the *determinacy* of the syntactic and semantic constraints operating at that point in the sequence. To the extent that these constraints are stronger (more determinate), recognition of the word will be facilitated. As we have demonstrated elsewhere (Marslen-Wilson and Tyler, 1975), the time it takes to recognize a spoken word in a sentential context is strongly determined by the strength of the structural constraints available at the point in the sequence at which it occurs. This, in brief, seems to be because these constraints operate on-line to reduce the size of the decision space within which the mapping of the acoustic input onto the correct entry in the mental lexicon has to be achieved (cf. Marslen-Wilson and Welsh, 1978).

Towards the end of a processing sequence, a word is more likely to occur under conditions where the preceding structural interpretation of the utterance has set up relatively determinate expectations. For example, in the Riesbeck and Schank case mentioned earlier (sentence (2)), the word 'Mary' occurs at a point where there are strong restrictions on the permissible syntactic function and on the plausible semantic properties of whatever element is to fill that slot in the sentence. Although the restrictions will not in general be as strong as this in the test sentences used here, the target words occurring at the ends of processing sequences will certainly tend to occur under conditions of relatively greater determinacy than the target words that occur at the beginnings of sequences.

Thus, on our interpretative structuring hypothesis, using predictions derived from some extensions of an on-line interactive processing hypothesis, there should be a significant increase in reaction time across the clause boundary in sentences like (1a) and (1b), with the before-boundary reaction times being faster than the after-boundary reaction times. Whereas in sentences like (4a) and (4b), where the syntactic clause boundary does not mark an interpretative processing boundary, the increase across the boundary should be significantly smaller. These predictions apply equally to the rhyme and to the category-monitoring tasks, since the effects operate at the word-identification stage, which is identical in both tasks.

The syntactic clausal structuring hypothesis does not make these predictions. Given that a clause is syntactically complete, the clause boundary will signal the completion of a perceptual processing unit. The theory contains no mechanism whereby this process can be modulated by the interpretative informational relationships between successive clauses. If there is a clause-boundary effect in any of the sentences used, it should remain constant across all degrees of interpretative informational dependency.

We should note at this point that a recent modification of the clausal structuring hypotheses to allow for variations in surface structure 'clausiness' (Carroll and Bever, 1976; Tanenhaus and Carroll, 1975) also does not predict differences between the sentences used here. These authors suggest that deep-structure clauses which do not correspond to full clauses in the surface structure are not 'functionally complete', and therefore produce less perceptual segmentation than full surface-structure clauses. But all the first clauses in this experiment are syntactically and functionally complete, by Carroll and Bever's (1976) definition, and so should not produce different effects across the mid-sentence clause boundary.

To summarize, then, the first experiment reported here will test two sets of hypotheses. The first of these involves a contrast between the predictions of the on-line interactive model and of the clausal processing hypothesis for the processing functions of the major syntactic clause boundary. If the claims of the on-line interactive model are correct, then the relationship between category- and rhyme-monitoring reaction times should remain the same on both sides of the clause boundary. If the clausal processing hypothesis is correct, and there are indeed systematic discontinuities in the listener's attempts to interpret the input semantically, then the semantically-based monitoring decisions should be more affected by target location than should the phonetically-based monitoring decisions.

The second set of hypotheses involves a contrast between two different claims about the factors underlying the clausal organization of sentence processing. If clausal structuring is simply a function of the syntactic structure of the material, then the mid-sentence clause boundary in all the sentences used will always mark the termination of a processing sequence. But if syntactic factors are secondary to what we have called interpretative organizational factors, then we will find a reduction in clause-boundary demarcation effects when the first clause of a test sentence is dependent on the second clause for its full interpretation.

We will also report a second experiment, which examines in more detail some of the variables contributing to the informational incompleteness of a potential interpretative processing sequence.

EXPERIMENT I

Method

Subjects. Thirty-two subjects were tested, all of whom had normal hearing and were native speakers of English. The subjects were recruited from the University of Chicago student population through newspaper advertisements, and were paid for their services.

Materials and design. The materials consisted of 24 sets of test sentences, embedded within a further 58 filler sentences. Each set of test sentences comprised a pair of sentences of the type described earlier (1a and 1b, 4a and 4b). The first seven words in each member of a pair (up to and including the target word) were the same, and were constructed so that when read with the appropriate intonation pattern the target word would occur either at the end of the first clause or at the beginning of the second clause. The target words were chosen so that they could function both as category and rhyme targets. The words, all monosyllables, were selected from the Battig and Montague (1969) category norms, and included members of 16 different categories. All words selected had at least four readily available rhymes.

The 24 pairs of test sentences were subdivided into two groups of 12 pairs, such that one group contained sentences with informationally complete first clauses, while the other 12 were judged informationally less complete—primarily because they contained anaphoric pronouns referring forward into the second clause. To validate these judgments, the relevant materials were rated by an additional group of 20 subjects. These subjects were given a list of the 24 first clauses corresponding to the after-boundary target conditions (for example, 'Even though they are quite small, . . .'). The subjects rated these clauses on a five-point scale, ranging from very complete (1) to very incomplete (5). The concept of completeness was defined to the subjects as follows:

The clauses (fragments) vary in the amount of information they present. Some of them may seem to express complete ideas, others less complete ideas.

In other words, some allow you to determine what the fragment is about more than others do. Please read the following fragments, and rate them in terms of the above dimension, which, for the sake of brevity, we will term 'completeness'.

The mean rating for the 12 incomplete sentences was 3.20, which differed significantly from the 2.13 rating for the 12 more complete first clauses ($t = 8.089$, d.f. $= 22$; $p < .001$). We will refer to the more complete group as the High-Completeness sentences, and to the others as the Low-Completeness sentences.

The 24 test sentences were then recorded in two versions, varying the location of the clause boundary relative to the target word, so that each tape contained 12 before-boundary test targets and 12 after-boundary test targets. The stress value of the target word was balanced across the two completeness groups. The test sentences were interspersed among a further 58 filler sentences. This large number of fillers was used to obscure the regularities in the test sentences. The fillers were all of a subordinate-main two-clause construction, but the target never occurred immediately adjacent to the mid-sentence clause boundary—for example: 'If you are able to salvage some, we could use a few *lamps* for the dining area'. A further 20 sentences, similar in structure to the fillers, were recorded for use as practice.

Two sets of instruction booklets were also constructed, each page of which specified the monitoring task for the next sentence, and gave the appropriate target definition. Thus, for sentences (1a) or (1b), the instructions would either read 'RHYME: DOUBT' or 'CATEGORY: FISH'. By crossing the two tapes with the two sets of instructions, four experimental conditions were created, such that across each group of four subjects each target word (such as *trout*) occurred in all combinations of target-location and monitoring tasks. No subject monitored for the same word in more than one of these four conditions. The monitoring tasks for the filler sentences were divided equally between rhyme and category.

To allow measurement of monitoring reaction times, timing pulses were placed on the second channel of each stimulus tape at the onset of the target word in a sentence. These timing pulses were located with an accuracy of ± 15 msec, as checked on a dual-trace storage oscilloscope. During testing the timing pulses started a digital millisecond clock, which was stopped by the subject's detection response (pressing a key).

Procedure. The subjects were first read a set of instructions, describing the experimental situation and the different types of monitoring tasks they would encounter. It was emphasized in the instructions, and during the practice session, that they should not try to guess the category or rhyme targets in advance. They were told to respond as quickly and accurately as they could.

Each subject was tested separately in a sound-treated room. They heard the stimulus materials over headphones as a binaural monophonic signal, and responded to the target words by pressing a telegraph key. There was a two-way voice communication channel open between the subject and the experimenter. To make sure that the subjects had read the instructions for each trial correctly, they were required to read aloud the contents of the relevant page of the instruction booklet before each trial started. For example, the subject would read aloud 'Rhyme: Doubt'. The subjects were told never to turn the page of the booklet on to the next set of instructions until the test sentence they were hearing was completed. Each experimental session lasted about 35 minutes, with a short break after every 30 trials to change instruction booklets.

Results

For purposes of analysis, eight subject groups were formed. Each group consisted of four subjects, with one selected from each of the four combinations of tapes and instruction booklets. This meant that within each group every cell of a fully factorial design was filled. One of the High-Completeness sentences was discarded from the analysis, because it apparently functioned as a 'garden-path' sentence, which led to a large number of missed responses and abnormally long reaction times. To balance the design, one of the Low-Completeness sentences was also discarded.

An analysis of variance was then performed on the raw monitoring latencies for the remaining 22 test sentences, with two random variables (groups and sentences) and three fixed factors. The factors were task (rhyme or category monitoring), target location (before or after the clause boundary), and informa-

Table 7.1   Experiment I. Mean monitoring reaction times (milliseconds)

	Target location	
Level of completeness of sentences	Before boundary	After boundary
High Completeness		
Rhyme	419	482
Category	399	481
Mean	409	481
Low completeness		
Rhyme	436	438
Category	437	451
Mean	437	445

tional completeness (high and low completeness of the first clause). Missing observations (due to errors and equipment failures) and extreme reaction times (those above 800 msec) were replaced according to the method recommended by Winer (1971). These amounted to 3% of the data set.

The overall means, collapsed across subjects and sentences, are given in Table 7.1. First, there was a significant main effect of target location ($F'' = 7.728$; d.f. $= 1,26$; $p < .025$), with before-boundary latencies (423 msec) being faster than after-boundary latencies (463 msec). This boundary effect interacted significantly with the informational incompleteness variable ($F'' = 6.210$; d.f. $= 1,27$; $p < .025$). In the High-Completeness conditions there is a mean increase across the clause boundary of 72 msec, from 409 msec before the boundary to 481 msec after the boundary. But in the Low-Completeness conditions the difference between the two locations is much smaller: mean reaction time was 437 msec before the boundary and 445 msec after the boundary. Pairwise comparisons between these means, using the Newman–Keuls statistic, showed only the difference across the boundary in the High-Completeness condition to be significant ($p < .01$).

There was no main effect of task ($F'' < 1$), with overall mean latencies of 444 msec for rhyme monitoring and 442 msec for category monitoring. Nor were there any interactions of task with the informational incompleteness variable ($F'' < 1$) or with target location ($F'' = 1.133$; d.f. $= 3,27$; $p > .10$). Planned comparisons showed that the rhyme and category means did not differ significantly in any of the four combinations of target location and informational completeness conditions. In particular, the differences between the boundary effects in the two informational incompleteness conditions were similar in both monitoring tasks. There was a 68 msec advantage for the High-Completeness condition in category monitoring and a 61 msec advantage in rhyme monitoring.

The third main effect, of informational incompleteness, was also not significant ($F'' < 1$), with overall mean latencies of 445 msec for High-Completeness sentences and of 441 msec for Low-Completeness sentences. There were, however, significant main effects of group ($F = 5.029$; d.f. $= 7,140$; $p < .001$) and of sentence ($F = 12.102$; d.f. $= 20,140$; $p < .001$). There was also a significant interaction between sentence and target location ($F = 3.229$; d.f. $= 20,140$; $p < .001$). This reflects variations in the size and the direction of the boundary effect for individual sentences. Possible sources for these variations will be taken up in Experiment II.

Errors (defined as failures to detect the target or as responses to the wrong word) were very infrequent. To the extent that any pattern can be detected, the majority of these errors occurred in the after-boundary conditions, where latencies were longest.

Discussion

The first question at issue in Experiment I concerned the nature of on-going processing immediately before and after the major syntactic clause boundary. Contrary to the predictions of the clausal processing hypothesis, there was no sign of any asymmetry in the kinds of processing information available on either side of the boundary. To the extent that monitoring latencies differed in the two target locations, the differences were the same for both rhyme and category monitoring. If, as even the weakest clausal processing hypothesis must propose, a semantic level of interpretation is more likely to be available at the end of a clause than at the beginning, then the boundary effects should have been larger for category than for rhyme monitoring.

The results, instead, support an analysis in which there is no qualitative change in the on-going processing representation as the sentence is heard. The on-line interactive hypothesis claims that at all points the listener has available a multi-faceted processing representation which includes syntactic and semantic as well as phonetic and lexical information. This representation does not vary in the type of processing information it includes, but rather (in so far as the present tasks are concerned) in what we have called its overall determinacy. When these variations in determinacy coincide, for reasons we outlined earlier, with the syntactic clause boundary, then monitoring performance will be affected. But any such effects do not vary as a function of the monitoring task.

The second issue we investigated concerned the effects of informational dependencies between clauses on the processing significance of the clause boundary. The results showed a large increase in monitoring latency across the boundary in the High-Completeness conditions, and a much smaller increase in the Low-Completeness conditions. This pattern of effects is consistent with the on-line interactive analysis of the processing segmentation of the speech stream, while a syntactically-based clausal structuring hypothesis appears to provide no basis for predicting these differences.

Experiment I does not, however, enable one to determine exactly which variables differentiate Low-Completeness sentences from High-Completeness sentences. The two sets of sentences were originally classified on the basis of the intuitions of ourselves and of a group of pre-test subjects as to their informational completeness. This leaves wide open the question of what determines such judgments. Detailed examination of the stimuli revealed that the High- and Low-Completeness sentences in fact differed in two ways. The most straightforward difference was in the presence or absence of a forward-referring anaphoric pronoun in the first clause. This clearly informational variable perfectly separates the two sets of sentences, since none of the High-Completeness sentences contained such a pronoun but all of the Low-Completeness sentences did.

The other systematic difference involved the distribution of different types of first clause, which we will refer to as the Adjective, Verb, and Quantifier Types. These labels refer to the kind of word that appeared at the end of the clause, immediately preceding the target word (see sentences 5–7 for examples). The Low-Completeness sentences were primarily of the Adjective and Quantifier Types, while the High-Completeness sentences contained mostly Verb-Type first clauses and very few of the other two types.

(5) If only they were more reliable, *trains* . . . (Adjective Type)
(6) Even though they haven't seen many, *bears* . . . (Quantifier Type)
(7) If a child will not eat, *cake* . . . (Verb Type)

These variations in the distribution of first-clause types in the two sets of sentences do not seem to bear any clear relationship to the informational variables we had intended to manipulate. The purpose of Experiment II, therefore, is to allow us to determine whether the strictly informational variable of the presence or absence of a forward-referring anaphoric pronoun did in fact produce the differences in clause-boundary effects between the High- and Low-Completeness sentences.

EXPERIMENT II

To avoid the interpretative problems caused by the use of a between-sentence design in Experiment I, the second experiment will contrast the effects of the presence or absence of an anaphoric pronoun in a within-sentence design, using sets of stimuli of the following kind:

(8)a. Even though Ron hasn't seen many *bears*, they are apparently his favorite animal.
  b. Even though Ron hasn't seen many, *bears* are apparently his favorite animal.
  c. Even though he hasn't seen many *bears*, they are apparently Ron's favorite animal.
  d. Even though he hasn't seen many, *bears* are apparently Ron's favorite animal.

The first clauses of sentences (8c) and (8d) differ from those of (8a) and (8b) along only one dimension; the presence or absence of a pronoun in the first clause. If this difference alone is adequate to produce informational dependency effects, then there should be a larger increase across the clause boundary for the (8a)/(8b) contrast than for the (8c)/(8d) contrast.

Since the type of processing information available before or after the clause boundary is not itself at issue in this experiment, only one monitoring task needs to be used. The rhyme task was chosen, since it allows more freedom in the choice of target words. As Experiment I has shown, rhyme monitoring is clearly sensitive to the variables we are testing, through their effects on the word-identification stage of the task.

Method

Subjects. Thirty-six subjects were tested, none of whom had participated in Experiment I. The subjects were recruited from the University of Chicago student population and were paid for their services.

Materials and design. The materials consisted of 36 sets of test sentences, embedded within 58 filler sentences (the same fillers as in Experiment I). Each set of test sentences consisted of four sentences, varying target location (before and after the clause boundary) and informational completeness of the first clause. Informational completeness was varied in the manner illustrated in sentences (8a–8d). The first clause of two members of a sentence quartet contained a full referent in subject position—for example, 'Ron', 'the men', 'a child', etc. In the other two sentences a forward-referring anaphoric pronoun was substituted into subject position—for example, 'he', 'they', etc. We will refer to these as the No-Pronoun and the Pronoun conditions, respectively. As an additional control, the 36 sets of test sentences were subdivided into three groups, each corresponding to one of the three first clause types (Adjective, Verb and Quantifier) used in Experiment I. Each group contained 12 quartets of test sentences.

Four experimental tapes were then recorded, at a normal speaking rate, with each tape containing one of the four versions of each test sentence. Thus each rhyme target word occurred, across tapes, in each of the four combinations of target location and informational completeness. To avoid the possibility that subjects might adopt the strategy of listening for the word with primary stress, the target words never received the primary stress in the clause in which they occurred. Only one set of instruction booklets was required, since the monitoring targets were the same in all tapes, and occurred in the same pseudo-randomized order in each tape.

These manipulations created a mixed between- and within-sentence and subject design. Sentences were nested within first-clause types, but were crossed with target location and informational completeness (Pronoun/No-Pronoun). Groups of four subjects were required to complete the design, and nine such groups were tested.

In all other respects Experiment II paralleled Experiment I, except for minor changes in the instructions to accommodate the use of only one monitoring task.

Results and discussion

Following the procedures used in Experiment I, nine subject groups were formed. An analysis of variance was then performed, with sentences and groups treated as random effects, together with three fixed factors. The factors were sentence type (Adjective, Verb, or Quantifier), target location (before or after the clause boundary), and informational completeness (presence or absence of an anaphoric pronoun in the first clause). The analysis was performed on the raw monitoring latencies, with missing observations and extreme reaction times (those above 800 msec) replaced (Winer, 1971).

The overall means are given in Table 7.2. First, there was a significant effect of target location ($F' = 5.030$; d.f. $= 1,32$; $p < .05$), with overall before-boundary latencies (414 msec) being faster than after-boundary latencies (437 msec). The main effects of sentence type ($F'' = 2.225$; d.f. $= 1,35$) and of informational completeness ($F'' < 1$) were not significant. More importantly, the interaction between informational completeness and target location fell well short of significance ($F'' = 1.524$; d.f. $= 2,48$), indicating that the Pronoun/No-Pronoun manipulation did not have an overall effect on monitoring latencies in different target locations. Instead, there was a significant interaction between sentence type and target location ($F'' = 4.844$; d.f. $= 2,48$; $p < .01$), and a marginally non-significant interaction between sentence type and informational completeness ($F'' = 2.673$; d.f. $= 3,48$; $p < .10$).

Inspection of Table 7.2 reveals that these interactions with sentence type are primarily due to the very long mean reaction times to monitoring targets in the Adjective before-boundary positions. This immediately raises the possibility that the informational completeness effects in Experiment I could be accounted for by the asymmetric distribution of Adjective-Type first clauses. But the Adjective-Type sentences in Experiment I do not seem to behave in the same way as in

Table 7.2   Experiment II. Mean monitoring reaction times (milliseconds)

	Target location	
Sentence type	Before boundary	After boundary
Verb		
Pronoun	402	421
No-Pronoun	373	420
Quantifier		
Pronoun	409	447
No-Pronoun	387	451
Adjective		
Pronoun	445	434
No-Pronoun	469	449

Experiment II. Removing the Adjective sentences from the Low-Completeness set in Experiment I only reduces the differences between the two completeness conditions by 12 msec, so that there is still a 52 msec greater increase across the boundary in the High-Completeness condition.

The Adjective effects in Experiment II in fact reflect a different problem, which derives from the within-sentence design we used in this experiment. In constructing the stimuli for the experiment, we had difficulty in finding sentences which sounded equally natural in all the four variations used in a quartet. This difficulty was apparently compounded, in recording the sentences, by the requirement that the target word should not receive primary stress. This particularly affected the Adjective-Type before-boundary sentences, such as (9) below, which seem most acceptable when the target word is given primary (and contrastive) stress. Whereas Quantifier and Verb-Type sentences, such as (10) and (11) below, seem quite acceptable whether or not the target word is given primary stress.

(9) Although the new door is very expensive *steel*, . . .
(10) Although the patient didn't want any *pills*, ...
(11) Ever since Alan started to drink *rum*, ...

This problem signals a more general issue in the evaluation of the results of Experiment II. The validity of the experimental contrasts we are making requires that all four sentences in a quartet sound equally natural to the subject. If any one of the four is in some way odd, then this will increase the monitoring latency for that sentence for reasons which invalidate the comparisons with the other members of the quartet.

Looking at the means for individual sentences, it became clear that all sentence types, though preponderantly the Adjective Type, contained some cases where one or more of the four versions in a quartet was associated with very long mean reaction times. If these perturbations were in fact obscuring the experimental contrasts we were trying to make, then it follows that the quartets containing them should tend not to show the experimental effects we had originally predicted. To evaluate this possibility, each quartet was assessed against a stringent criterion. We selected out all quartets in which any of the mean before- or after-boundary latencies was more than two standard errors above the mean for the whole ensemble of before- and after-boundary means. This meant that any before-boundary means above 453 msec and any after-boundary means above 489 msec would fail to meet the criterion.

Of the original 36 quartets, 22 had shown the predicted No-Pronoun advantage; that is, the increase across the clause boundary was larger for the No-Pronoun sentences than for the Pronoun sentences. The other 14 sentences showed the opposite pattern. The assessment procedure led to the rejection of 18 of the original 36. If the presence of deviant reaction times was not correlated with the absence of the predicted No-Pronoun effect, then we would expect about eleven of the rejected sentences to be among those that had showed the effect, while seven should not. We found the opposite pattern. Twelve of the 14 quartets not showing the No-Pronoun advantage were rejected, but only six of the 22 that had originally shown the predicted effect. This departure from the expected distribution is unlikely to have occurred by chance ($\chi^2 = 8.679$, $p < .01$), and supports the hypothesis that Experiment II originally failed to show a Pronoun/No-Pronoun effect because of problems with some of the stimuli. The claim that subjects did find some of the stimuli unnatural is corroborated by another feature distinguishing the 18 rejected quartets from the 18 that passed the criterion. The acceptable quartets were significantly more likely to occur later in the experimental tapes ($t = 2.237$; d.f. $= 34$; $p < .05$), suggesting that the subjects were finding the test sentences more acceptable as they became more familiar with their general format.

Breaking down the effects of the selection procedure according to sentence type, three of the Adjective quartets passed the criterion, seven of the Verb, and eight of the Quantifier. These differences between sentence types make the original experimental comparison between them quite uninterpretable. In general, sentence type seems to be correlated with difficulties in constructing quartets of natural sentences, rather than with processing effects at the clause boundary. However, given that the remaining 18 quartets have been screened for the presence of confounding variations in mean reaction time, it now becomes possible to test the main hypothesis at issue in Experiment II: whether or not the Pronoun/No-Pronoun variation is sufficient to produce informational-incompleteness effects across the clause boundary.

The scores for the 18 acceptable quartets were entered into a second analysis of variance, with the factor of sentence type omitted. The overall means for these quartets are given in Table 7.3. The analysis showed no main effects of target location ($F'' = 1.347$; d.f. $= 1,20$;) or of informational incompleteness ($F' < 1$), but did show the interaction between target location and informational incompleteness ($F' = 5.901$; d.f. $= 1,18$; $p < .05$). In the Pronoun condition, latencies across the clause boundary stay essentially unchanged, while the No-Pronoun condition shows an increase of 37 msec. In other words, the Pronoun/No-Pronoun variation produces a significant clause-boundary effect similar to—though slightly smaller than—the effect obtained in Experiment 1.

There are, of course, problems with the application of a *post hoc* selection procedure to the experimental stimuli—even when the procedure itself contains no intrinsic bias which would cause it to select cases that were consistent with our original hypotheses. However, given that there may be variations in the naturalness of the sentences within a comparison group in a within-sentence design, it is difficult to see how we could have excluded such variations in advance. A pretest in which subjects rated the different versions for naturalness gives no guarantee that this procedure would have picked out the precise

Table 7.3   Experiment II. Mean monitoring reaction times for the acceptable quartets of test sentences

	Target location	
Informational completeness	Before boundary	After boundary
Pronoun	390	385
No-Pronoun	358	395

variations that produce unusually long reaction times in the quite different situation of listening for a rhyme-monitoring target. In fact, Experiment II might quite reasonably be considered the appropriate pretest, with the 18 quartets of sentences that we ended up with being those that passed this preliminary screening.

A final question concerns the apparent differences between the sentences in Experiment I—especially those of the Adjective Type—and those originally used in Experiment II. As we have already noted, the Adjective sentences in Experiment I were generally not as anomalous as those in Experiment II. Secondly, when a cut-off based on the standard error of the means is applied to the Experiment I sentences, this has little effect on the pattern of results. The advantage of the High-Completeness clause-boundary effect increased by 8 msec to 72 msec.

The problem with the sentences in Experiment II seems to stem from the requirement that they allow for the interchange of pronouns and explicit referents in the first clause. Some first clauses, those of the Quantifier and Verb types, can work quite well in either the Pronoun or No-Pronoun version. Sentences such as (1a) and (1b), (8a–8d), (10), and (11), for example, seem equally natural under both conditions. The results of the selection procedure showed that most of the Quantifier and Verb quartets were in fact acceptable. But an Adjective-Type sentence that is acceptable in a pronoun version—for example, sentence (12)—cannot readily be converted to a No-Pronoun version.

(12) Although it is quite cheap *beer*, ...

The replacement of 'it' by something like 'the drink' makes the last word in the clause ('beer') seem out of place at that point in the sentence. Given that such a sentence is not read with contrastive stress on 'beer', the subject may simply not expect the clause to continue beyond the word 'cheap'. It was this kind of problem which resulted in the long before-boundary latencies in the Adjective sentences in Experiment II, and which was not an issue in Experiment I.

In conclusion, Experiment II can be seen as serving three principal functions. First, it provides further preliminary evidence for the importance of between-clause interpretative informational variables in on-going sentence processing. Second, it suggests that the partial confounding of sentence type with informational completeness in Experiment I did not in fact undermine the legitimacy of the informational contrasts there. The additional data that we obtained about the behaviour of these sentence types in Experiment II enabled us to apply further tests to the material in Experiment I, from which the informational completeness results escaped unscathed. It should be noted that the confounding with sentence type in Experiment I was never relevant to the rhyme and category contrasts, since the same sentences were used for both monitoring tasks. Thirdly, and somewhat involuntarily, Experiment II does provide a graphic illustration of the kinds of problems one can run into when trying to investigate the behaviour of complex structural variables during the perception of spoken language.

CONCLUSIONS AND OVERVIEW

The research described here has had two main functions. On the one hand, it represents the completion of a particular line of research, and on the other it helps to establish the importance of a new set of psycholinguistic processing variables.

First of all, then, the results fall into place in a sequence of on-line processing experiments. These experiments have demonstrated, with increasing specificity, that spoken sentence perception is best understood in an on-line interactive framework. The earliest results, involving speech shadowing at very short latencies (Marslen-Wilson, 1973a; 1973b; 1975; 1976), appeared to demonstrate that the subjects could syntactically and semantically interpret speech word-by-word as they heard it. Spontaneous shadowing errors, produced at 250 msec shadowing latencies, were almost always constrained by the structural semantic and syntactic context in which they occurred (Marslen-Wilson, 1973a). Similarly, when subjects were asked to shadow sentences containing errors deliberately inserted by the experimenter, these errors were only corrected when the outcome of the correction was both semantically and syntactically consistent with the preceding words in the string (Marslen-Wilson, 1975).

The results of these and other shadowing experiments (Marslen-Wilson, 1973b) led to the original formulaton of an on-line interactive hypothesis. To account for the shadowing data it seemed necessary to propose that utterances are indeed understood as they are heard; that the listener constructs a syntactic and semantic interpretation of the input word-by-word as he hears it, and that he actively uses this information to guide his processing of the subsequent words in the string (cf. Marslen-Wilson, 1973b). This proposal stood in obvious contrast to the clausal processing hypothesis (as stated, for example, in Fodor *et al.*, 1974), and subsequent experiments were devoted to testing the on-line interactive model at those points where it most strongly diverged from the clausal approach.

First, using a variety of word-monitoring techniques, we systematically tested for the availability of a semantic interpretation at different points in a sentence (Marslen-Wilson and Tyler,1975; in preparation). Subjects monitored for target words which occurred at serial positions ranging from the second to the tenth word position in three different types of test sentences (normal prose, semantically uninterpretable, and random word-order sentences). In all monitoring tasks the same pattern was found, with response latencies to targets in normal prose contexts diverging from those to targets in semantically uninterpretable and random word-order contexts in the manner predicted by the interactive hypothesis. In particular, normal prose responses were significantly facilitated (relative to the other two contexts) at even the earliest word positions. Further experiments, in which the test sentences were presented either with or without a preceding context sentence, showed that these effects were due not only to the presence of a semantic interpretation very early on in the sentence, but also to the contribution of the preceding context to the determinacy of this early interpretation (Marslen-Wilson and Tyler, in preparation).

These monitoring results were therefore inconsistent with the clausal processing hypothesis in two ways. First, by showing semantic facilitation effects very early in the sentence, and secondly, by demonstrating the immediate incorporation of contextual information into the interpretation of a subsequent sentence. On the clausal processing hypothesis, semantic effects should not have been detectable until later in the test sentences, and contextual information should not have been able to interact with the processing of the test sentence until the clause boundary has been reached.

The interaction of prior context with the immediate interpretation of subsequent inputs was investigated in more detail in a later experiment (Tyler and Marslen-Wilson, 1977), which focused in particular on the interactions of semantic context with syntactic processing decisions. Although the earlier research had shown that both syntactic and semantic information were available to the listener very early in sentence processing, the results did not necessarily require a reciprocal interaction between them. In particular, the claims of the clausal hypothesis for the 'autonomy of syntax' (e.g. Forster, 1976) could not be ruled out. The clausal processing claim here is that the syntactic analysis of a sentence is autonomous within the clause, so that syntactic processes cannot be affected by semantic variables until the clause boundary is reached.

In this further experiment, the subjects heard deep-structure syntactically ambiguous fragments (such as 'landing planes' or 'folding chairs') preceded by disambiguating context clauses which biased one or the other of the structural interpretations of these fragments. The subject's task was to name as rapidly as possible a visually presented probe word which immediately followed the offset of the ambiguous fragment. This verb probe (for example, either 'is' or 'are') was either compatible or incompatible with the syntactic reading of the ambiguous fragment that was biased by the context clause. The results showed that the subjects' responses were facilitated when the probe was an appropriate continuation of the contextually-biased reading. This preference, for a singular or plural verb probe, reflects the outcome of a syntactic processing decision. But this decision, given the design of the experiment, could only be the result of the on-line intervention of the preceding semantic context in the syntactic interpretation of the ambiguous fragment.

This evidence for within-clause interactions between syntactic and semantic information has consequences not only for the claim that 'syntax' is autonomous but also for the form of the interactive hypothesis itself. In earlier statements of the hypothesis (e.g. Marslen-Wilson, 1975; Marslen-Wilson and Tyler, 1975), it was assumed that two separate levels of structural analysis (syntactic and semantic) were being computed in parallel. But the available evidence about on-line sentence processing does not, in fact, seem to require the postulation of an intermediate strictly syntactic level. As we have argued in more detail elsewhere (Marslen-Wilson, 1976; Tyler and Marslen-Wilson, 1978), the postulate of a computationally distinct syntactic level of analysis is only properly motivated in a psychological processing theory if this level serves some demonstrable function in the system's on-going operations.

On the clausal processing hypothesis, a syntactic deep-structure representation is an essential step in the serial progression from the analysis of the surface properties of the input to the extraction of meaning. But the on-line evidence we have cited shows that this postulated serial relationship between syntactic and semantic analyses does not in fact hold. A semantic interpretation is being initiated at points in a sentence at which a deep-structure syntactic analysis (as classically defined) could not yet be available. But if this is the case, then the hypothesized deep-structure representation is not necesaary to fulfil the processing functions originally assigned to it.

Equally, it is not clear either what function a syntactic level of representation would serve in a truly interactive parallel processing system. If a distinct syntactic level is being computed, then the data show that it would run concurrently with a level of semantic interpretation with which it would be in continuous interaction. But if the listener can draw simultaneously on both syntactic and semantic knowledge to construct two such closely interdependent processing representations, then these two representations would hardly be functionally distinguishable, and the separation between them appears to serve no obvious purpose for the processing system (cf. Tyler and Marslen-Wilson, in preparation).

The Tyler and Marslen-Wilson (1977) results, therefore, taken together with the earlier on-line research, have led to the version of an on-line hypothesis put forward here. The listener is seen as attempting a direct word-by-word mapping of the input onto a single internal representation. In its most developed form, this representation could correspond to what we call comprehending a sentence, and would not be describable in strictly linguistic terms, since it would have to contain the products of inferences drawn from the listener's non-linguistic knowledge. So it would not, in itself, be either a syntactic or a semantic representation, although for its construction it would draw upon both syntactic and semantic aspects of the input.

Within this framework, a major gap in the on-line interactive approach was clearly its failure to accommodate the experimentally more robust aspects of the general clausal hypothesis—that is, the evidence for the clausal structuring of on-going sentence processing. Thus a major aspect of the research reported here, as we stressed in the introduction, was the attempt to develop a clausal structuring hypothesis that was consistent with an on-line interactive processing theory. But at the same time, it was also important to demonstrate that whatever did happen at the clause boundary, it did not involve the kind of shift from one mode of processing to another that was claimed in the clausal processing hypothesis. This demonstration was all the more necessary because there had been no previous on-line research which directly examined the qualitative properties of sentence-processing activities at and around the clause boundary.

The results of the rhyme- and category-monitoring contrasts confirm, then, that even in the immediate vicinity of the clause boundary there seem to be no qualitative discontinuities in on-going processing. The listener is at all points attempting a semantic interpretation of the input, and this holds across the mid-sentence clause boundary just as it does when other points in a sentence are sampled. It is this result that we see as completing a line of research, since it is at the clause boundary, if anywhere, that the claims of the clausal-processing hypothesis for a serial relationship between syntactic and semantic analyses would have to hold true.

More positively, the results of the manipulations of the informational incompleteness variables were inconsistent with a purely syntactic mechanism for on-line clausal structuring, and suggest instead that interpretative structuring variables also need to be taken into account. And it is in this kind of direction, we believe, that the future development of an on-line interactive hypothesis needs to be pushed. The crucial variable for a processing system that attempts to fully interpret its input word-by-word as it receives it, is clearly going to be the ordering of processing information in the input. The preliminary investigation reported here has touched upon just one aspect of ordering structure—the relationship between a pronoun and its referent in within- and between-clause contexts. But these ordering effects will also have to be dealt with as they occur between sentences, and, indeed, between the general linguistic and non-linguistic environments of the utterance.

Some of the monitoring research mentioned earlier (Marslen-Wilson and Tyler, in preparation) can be seen as tapping, in a non-specific manner, some of these between-sentence informational dependencies. Rather more specifically, some recent work by Harris (1977) demonstrates in detail the word-by-word fluctuations in processing complexity that result from differences in the informational relationships between successive sentences. His materials varied the 'given-new' structure of a test sentence relative to the information provided in a preceding context sentence. The results show how the complexity (and the determinacy) of the on-going representation of the test sentence vary as a direct function of these large-scale informational variables.

Similar concerns have emerged, for example, in the recent work of Flores d'Arcais (this volume), who stresses the importance of informational dependencies between clauses in determining the distribution of processing resources in the perception of complex, multi-clause sentences. Our approach here also seems to be compatible with the direction recently taken by Carroll and his coworkers (e.g. Carroll, Tanenhaus and Bever, this volume). Their work now places less emphasis on linguistic variables, and more emphasis on the role of surface perceptual cues used by the perceiver to construct 'functional propositional units'. In addition, their paper underlines the importance of informational dependencies between sentences, arguing that contextual information can be used on-line to fill in the gaps in otherwise functionally incomplete processing sequences.

Finally, we should acknowledge the probability that some of the most concrete inputs to the construction of an on-line interactive theory are likely to come from artificial intelligence research into natural language parsing systems. In this connection, the kind of system developed by Riesbeck (cf. Riesbeck and Schank, this volume) clearly has many of the properties that we have demonstrated that a psychological processing model needs to have. Riesbeck's ELI parser builds interpretative structures left-to-right as it goes through the string, and it generates structural expectations as it does so. In this respect it is closer to our approach than, for example, the parser proposed by Steedman and Johnson-Laird (1978). Their program—a 'semantically augmented transition network'—also builds interpretations word-by-word as it encounters the string, but it is not clear that it generates explicit structural expectations of the type that seem necessary to account for the on-line variations in determinacy that our results have demonstrated. But it is noteworthy that both the Steedman and Johnson-Laird and the Riesbeck parsers have in common with our approach an emphasis on semantic interpretation as the immediate goal of the processing system. In all cases a strictly syntactic level of representation is not a computationally necessary stage in the operation of the system.

ACKNOWLEDGEMENTS

The research reported in this chapter was carried out at the University of Chicago, with the support of NIMH grant MH 27465-01 to W. Marslen-Wilson.

We thank D. McNeill for the use of his laboratory, supported by NSF grant GB 31127X2.

We also thank A. E. Ades, W. J. M. Levelt, and, in particular, G. B. Flores d'Arcais, for their comments on the manuscript. We are also grateful to Hilde Kleine Schaars for secretarial assistance.

REFERENCES

Ades, A. E. Internal memorandum. Max-Planck-Gesellschaft, Projektgruppe für Psycholinguistik, Nijmegen, 1977.

Battig, W. F. and Montague, W. E. Category norms for verbal items in 56 categories: A replication and extension of the Connecticut Category Norms. *Journal of Experimental Psychology Monograph*, 1969, **80**, (3, pt. 2).

Bever, T. G., Garrett, M. F., and Hurtig, R. The interaction of perceptual processes and ambiguous sentences. *Memory and Cognition*, 1973, **1**, 277–286.

Bever, T. G. and Hurtig, R. R. Detection of a non-linguistic stimulus is poorest at the end of a clause. *Journal of Psycholinguistic Research*, 1975, **4**, 1–7.

Bever, T. G., Lackner, J. R., and Kirk, R. The underlying structures of sentences are the primary units of immediate speech processing. *Perception and Psychophysics*, 1969, **5**, 225–234.

Caplan, D. Clause boundaries and recognition latencies for words in sentences. *Perception and Psychophysics*, 1972, **12**, 73–76.

Carroll, J. M. and Bever, T. G. Sentence comprehension: A case study in the relation of knowledge and perception. In E. Carterette and J. Friedman (Eds.), *The handbook of perception*. Vol. 7: *Language and speech*. New York: Academic Press, 1976.

Carroll, J. M., Tanenhaus, M. K., and Bever, T. G. The perception of relations: The interaction of structural, functional, and contextual factors in the segmentation of sentences. This volume.

Chapin, P., Smith, T., and Abrahamson, A. Two factors in perceptual segmentation of speech. *Journal of Verbal Learning and Verbal Behavior*, 1972, **11**, 164–173.

Flores d'Arcais, G. B. The perception of complex sentences. This volume.

Fodor, J. A. and Bever, T. G. The psychological reality of linguistic segments. *Journal of Verbal Learning and Verbal Behavior*, 1965, **4**, 414–420.

Fodor, J. A., Bever, T. G., and Garrett, M. F. *The psychology of language*. An introduction to psycholinguistics and generative grammar. New York: McGraw-Hill, 1974.

Fodor, J. A., Fodor, J. D., Garrett, M. F., and Lackner, J. R. Effects of surface and underlying clausal structure on click location. *Quarterly Progress Report*, Research Laboratory of Electronics, M.I.T., 1974, 113.

Forster, K. I. The role of semantic hypotheses in sentence processing. In Colloques Internationaux du C.N.R.S., No. 206, *Problèmes actuels en psycholinguistique*. Paris, 1974.

Forster, K. I. The autonomy of syntax. Paper presented at the MIT-AT & T Convocation on Communications, Cambridge, Mass., March 1976.

Garrett, M. F., Bever, T. G., and Fodor, J. A The active use of grammar in speech perception. *Perception and Psychophysics*, 1966, **1**, 30–32.

Harris, J. W. Levels of speech processing and order of information. Unpublished Ph.D. Dissertation, University of Chicago, December, 1977.

Jarvella, R. J. Syntactic processing of connected speech. *Journal of Verbal Learning and Verbal Behavior*, 1971, **10**, 409–416.

Levelt, W. J. M. A survey of studies in sentence perception. This volume.

Marslen-Wilson, W. D. Linguistic structure and speech shadowing at very short latencies. *Nature* (London), 1973, **244**, 522–523(a).

Marslen-Wilson, W. D. Speech shadowing and speech perception. Unpublished Ph.D. Dissertation, Department of Psychology, M.I.T., June, 1973 (b).

Marslen-Wilson, W. D. Sentence perception as an interactive parallel process. *Science*, 1975, **189**, 226–228.

Marslen-Wilson, W. D. Linguistic descriptions and psychological assumptions in the study of sentence processing. In R. J. Wales and E. Walker (Eds.), *New approaches to language mechanisms.* Amsterdam: North-Holland, 1976.

Marslen-Wilson, W. D. and Tyler, L. K. Processing structure of sentence perception. *Nature* (London), 1975, **257**, 784–786.

Marslen-Wilson, W. D. and Tyler, L. K. Memory and levels of processing in a psycholinguistic context. *Journal of Experimental Psychology: Human Learning and Memory*, 1976, **2**, 112–119.

Marslen-Wilson, W. D. and Tyler, L. K. The time-course of sentence processing events: The perception of sentences and of words in sentences. Manuscript in preparation.

Marslen-Wilson, W. D. and Welsh, A. Processing interactions and lexical access during word-recognition in continuous speech. *Cognitive Psychology*, 1978, **10**, 29–63.

Miller, G. A. and Chomsky, N. Finitary models of language users. In R. D. Luce, R. R. Bush, and E. Galanter (Eds.), *Handbook of mathematical psychology*, Vol. 2. New York: Wiley, 1963.

Riesbeck, C. K. and Schank, R. C. Comprehension by computer: Expectation-based analysis of sentences in context. This volume.

Steedman, M. J. and Johnson-Laird, P. N. A programmatic theory of linguistic performance. In R. N. Campbell and P. T. Smith (Eds.), *Recent advances in the psychology of language: Formal and experimental approaches.* New York: Plenum Press, 1978.

Tanenhaus, M. K. and Carroll, J. M. The clausal processing hierarchy and nouniness. In R. Grossman, J. San, and T. Vance (Eds.), *Papers from the parasession on functionalism.* Chicago: Chicago Linguistics Society, 1975.

Tyler, L. K. and Marslen-Wilson, W. D. The on-line effects of semantic context on syntactic processing. *Journal of Verbal Learning and Verbal Behavior*, 1977, **16**, 683–692.

Tyler, L. K. and Marslen-Wilson, W. D. Serial and interactive approaches to on-line sentence processing. In J. Morton and J. C. Marshall (Eds.), *Psycholinguistics III.* (In preparation).

Winer, B. J. *Statistical principles in experimental design.* New York: McGraw-Hill, 1971.

Chapter 8

Comprehension by Computer: Expectation-based Analysis of Sentences in Context

Christopher K. Riesbeck and Roger C. Schank

INTRODUCTION

Language is the medium by which ideas, or meanings, are transmitted from one individual to another. The analysis of the medium itself is not of primary interest to a goal-oriented system. That is, speakers are concerned with getting their ideas across. They are concerned with the medium of language only in so far as better use of it will more effectively present their ideas. Similarly, a hearer is concerned with best approximating in his own mind the intended ideas of the speaker to whom he is listening. The hearer seeks to understand what is said to him.

Most of what we have said so far seems rather obvious on the surface. Yet it stands in contradiction to a great deal of research in linguistics, psycholinguistics, and computational linguistics. In these three fields, syntax has commanded a great deal of the time and energy spent on research. We might do well to question that approach. A goal-oriented system is primarily concerned with the best path to the goal. If our goal as understanders is to extract a meaning from its language-encoded form, then the question we must ask is this: What is the best possible process to decode natural language?

In answering this question we focus on the process itself. We will assume that the best process is the one that satisfies the two criteria of not doing unnecessary work (that is, being relatively efficient), and of closely mirroring the actual process that people employ. We will assume in this paper that Conceptual Dependency (CD) (Schank, 1972, 1973, 1975) will serve as an adequate meaning representation and we will have no more to say about that here.

In order to begin to find the best process, one must find at least one process. It should be stated at the outset that no such process actually exists in computer-implemented form to our knowledge at the time of writing. A great many natural language parsers exist, but few of them do more than assign syntactic structure to isolated English sentences. They do no meaning analysis and thus do not understand what they parse. Of the few parsers that do go beyond this level (i.e. to some level more meaning-like than syntactic structure), none can parse all the sentences that anyone would ever say. The reason for this is partially because we are at an early stage in the field of natural language parsing and there is very much more work to be done. But there is another more significant reason: in order to understand what someone says it is necessary to have a highly developed model of the kinds of things he could say. That is, in order to construct an adequate meaning representation from a spoken input, one must have a deep understanding of the context of the input. The hearer must have and use a great deal of knowledge about what things can happen in the world and their usual place and time for happening. No such complete or nearly complete model is at present available to aid our understanding of how we understand sentences. Without it we cannot expect to see a complete 'natural language to meaning representation' parser. But, as our knowledge of the entire process of understanding increases, so too will our ability to write computer programs to translate natural language sentences into meaning.

PARSING STORIES

We do not mean to convey by what we have written above, that we view the problem of parsing as far-off and hopeless. This is not at all the case. Rather we are arguing for a view of comprehension that looks at the process as a whole, as opposed to a view that considers the understanding process to consist of well-defined modules that function in linear sequence. The common linguistic model with a syntactic analysis phase followed by a semantic interpretation phase is a good example of what we are up against. The modules in the understanding process affect each other in both directions. Modules that see the input first are affected by the expectations of modules that operate later. For example, the perceptual module that moves the human eye across the page will skip forward and backward on the basis of expectations from the high-level module that says 'this is written like a children's fairy story, so expect (and do little processing for) phrases like "once upon a time" and "they lived happily ever after."'

The parser we will describe in this paper, ELI (English Language Interpreter), was written by the first author and an early version is described in Riesbeck (1975). The description given here is of a more recent version of that parser and supplants much of what was said in the earlier publications. ELI is a part of a larger understanding system called SAM. As such, it receives a great deal of information from SAM about what SAM expects to be sent by the parsing process. ELI is not limited to SAM, however. ELI is also used as a part of other natural language understanding programs at Yale (e.g. PAM described in Wilensky, 1976). But being mobile does not mean that ELI operates in independence of these systems. The predictions that these programs make, about where a story or conversation will lead, are converted by ELI into predictions about how the English text will look, and these predictions in turn help ELI to understand the text that it actually sees.

Below we present an example of the kind of understanding of which the current version of SAM is capable. As all the sentences in the story below, including the questions, were parsed by ELI, they also serve as examples of ELI's current capabilities. The story is an edited version of one that appeared in a local newspaper, the *New Haven Register*. The story is understood by the use of scripts (Schank and Abelson, 1975, 1977), and various principles of script application (Cullingford, 1975).

(3) Friday evening a car swerved off Route 69. The vehicle struck a tree. The passenger, a New Jersey man, was killed. David Hall, 27, was pronounced dead at the scene by Dr. Dana Blauchard, medical examiner. Frank Miller, 32, of 593 Foxon Rd, the driver, was taken to Milford Hospital by Flanagan Ambulance. He was treated and released. The passenger was extricated from the vehicle by the Branford Fire Department. No charges were made. Patrolman Robert Onofrio investigated the accident.

Question-Answering Output.

Q1: Was anyone killed?
A1: YES, DAVID HALL DIED.

Q2: Was anyone hurt?
A2: YES, FRANK MILLER WAS SLIGHTLY INJURED.

Q3: Why was Frank Miller hurt?
A3: BECAUSE THE AUTOMOBILE HIT A TREE.

Q4: Did Frank Miller go to the hospital?
A4: YES, HE WAS IN MILFORD HOSPITAL.

Q5: How did Frank Miller get to the hospital?
A5: AN AMBULANCE TOOK HIM TO MILFORD HOSPITAL.

Summary:
AN AUTOMOBILE HIT A TREE NEAR HIGHWAY 69 FOUR DAYS AGO. DAVID HALL, AGE 27 RESIDENCE IN NEW JERSEY, THE PASSENGER, DIED. FRANK MILLER, AGE 32, RESIDENCE AT 593 FOXON ROAD IN NEW HAVEN, CONNECTICUT, THE DRIVER, WAS SLIGHTLY INJURED. THE POLICE DEPARTMENT DID NOT FILE CHARGES.

SAM can understand a large variety of newspaper stories about car accidents as well as stories of a similar length and overall difficulty in other quite different domains. We will concentrate, in this paper, on how ELI does the parsing part of SAM.

PRINCIPLES OF NATURAL LANGUAGE ANALYSIS

ELI is not a parser in the ordinary sense of the word. It does not have an intermediate syntactic analysis stage. As we have argued, the process of understanding is one that can only superficially be broken down into separate parts. For the purpose of this paper we will talk about ELI as a conceptual analyser. That is, a program that maps English sentences into their conceptual representation. In doing so, it should be kept in mind that ELI talks to the other parts of SAM a great deal and that the division we make between the analysis, script application, and inference parts of SAM may turn out to be as superficial in the end as the original syntax-semantics distinction.

Any natural language analyser, we would claim, must conform to certain principles that we have come to believe typify how people parse.

I. A parse must be done in context only. This seems like a rather obvious principle, yet with a few exceptions (e.g. Wilks, 1973; Winograd, 1972), nearly everyone violates it. To talk about the meaning of a sentence out of context is a nice abstract linguistic exercise, but it has little to do with how people actually function. True, people can be given sentences out of context in experiments and they will make decisions, but these decisions need not bear a great deal of similarity to the ones that people employ when given context.

Consider sentence (1):

(1) I just came from New York.

Sentence (1) is not obviously ambiguous. However, its meaning is wildly different when placed in different contexts. Thus, consider sentence (1) again, this time assuming it had followed sentences (2), (3), (4) or (5):

(2) Would you like to go to New York today?
(3) Would you like to go to Boston today?
(4) Why do you seem so out of place?
(5) Why do you look so dirty and bedraggled?

After (2), (1) means something akin to 'No'. After (3) we have 'No, I'm tired of traveling'. After (4), (1) means, 'I'm lost and disoriented because I've only just arrived here'. After (5), (1) means 'New York can make you dirty and tire you out'. Notice that what we have done here is still out of context. As hearers we would like to know more, in order to understand fully what (1) means. Where is the speaker now? How long has he been in New York? What is his relationship to the questioner? These and other questions define the context. Without their answers we are disoriented understanders. That is, we cannot really understand without enough contextual knowledge. With enough context, ambiguity usually gives way and people can agree on what sentences mean. This leads us to principle II.

II. A parser should never notice ambiguity. Traditionally, researchers (e.g. Kuno and Oettinger, 1963) considered that one measure of the adequacy of their programs was the large number of ambiguities they could detect in a sentence. Sentence such as (6):

(6) Hunting dogs can be dangerous.

had multiple meaning representations because of their multiple possible syntactic representations. Programs that build a syntactic representation in order to do semantic interpretation must see these ambiguities in order to avoid missing the right meaning. Returning to principle I, if we place (6) in the context, making it a response to (7) or (8):

(7) Do you want to try shooting those dogs that have been pillaging the village?
(8) Let's take some dogs with us when we go to hunt moose.

then it seems obvious that a hearer would not notice any ambiguity to (6). Moreover, although (6) is thought of primarily as an example of syntactic ambiguity, sentences with identical syntactic structures are not at all ambiguous, even out of context. This can be seen by examining (9) and (10):

(9) Hunting dogs can be rabid.
(10) Eating octopus can be enjoyable.

The reason for the lack of ambiguity of (9) and (10) is that the alternative readings of (9) and (10) analogous to the alternatives of (6) do not make semantic sense. A syntactic parser could be written that used selectional restrictions to block these readings. The problem with such a parser is that it has to consider the alternative readings long enough to block them out by resorting to selectional restrictions, doing work that we have no reason to believe people do. People do not notice the potential ambiguity in (9) and (10) even out of context.

People have thus added to their syntactic parsers the capability of calling semantic routines to help them to decide between syntactic alternatives. To use this is a case of automatic *reductio ad absurdum*. To get the meaning a syntactic analysis is done, but to get the analysis the meaning must be found. It is like a man, locked out of his house, crawling in a window to get his keys, so that he can go outside again to come in by the door. This leads us to principle III.

III. A parser must take care of syntactic considerations only when required to do so by semantic considerations. For one reason or another, we have often been reported as advocating the abandonment of any syntactic analysis in a parser. This has really never been our position. Rather, we simply believe that syntactic considerations should be done only when they are needed, i.e. after other more highly ranked considerations are used. We have turned the syntactic approach of 'semantics only when needed' around, because it is meaning, not syntactic structures, that we need from a text.

For example, consider sentence (11):

(11) That mug of coffee was delicious.

An ordinary syntax-based parser will handle sentence (11) as a statement that the mug was delicious. It is assumed that a semantic interpreter will later see this to be an error and find the right referent to coffee. Here again we are left with the feeling that the order of processing is backwards. People simply do not notice such ambiguities.

IV. Parsing is expectation-based. People have a fair number of expectations about what they will hear before they actually hear it. These expectations become more and more precisely defined as the input information grows larger. Consequently, we would expect that an intelligent parser would be much faster towards the end of a sentence and be able to predict the last word of a sentence with a fair degree of accuracy. Consider sequences (12) and (13):

(12) John's car crashed into a guard-rail. When the ambulance came, it took John to the x.

(13) John read the menu. When the waitress came he x-ed a hamburger.

In (12) and (13) an understander presumably can fill in the x's with a high degree of accuracy. Note that in both cases the meaning of x is easier to fill in than its lexical realization. That is, in (12) we know that x is a place where John can get medical attention. We presume that x is 'the emergency room of a hospital'. Whether x is lexically 'hospital', 'emergency room', or 'doctor' is unknown and quite unimportant. People make mistakes in understanding and the above examples are typical of why people make errors. Often we are so busy making predictions that we do not notice that our expectations have been violated. Such errors point up two things: (i) people are expectation-based parsers; (ii) if a computer parser takes advantage of expectations, then it will necessarily make mistakes at times, thus reflecting problems humans have in understanding.

The same argument can be made with respect to (13). We do not know if x is 'order' or 'asked for' and there is a sense in which it really does not matter as their meanings are identical in this case.

An important point can be made here with respect to principle II. Notice that if 'order' were the word used in (13) there is no way anyone would consider the sense of 'order' as in 'order a corporal' to be possible. The fact that that sense of 'order' is never considered leads to principle V.

V. Words with multiple senses are ordered with respect to context. Linguists for years got a great deal of mileage out of organizing and counting all the senses of words, for example 'bachelor' (Katz and Fodor, 1963). A natural extension of such enterprises was to build parsers that carry along all possible meanings for a word. Far from being abandoned in artificial intelligence research, such an approach was used recently by Winograd (1972) in the parser for SHRDLU.

Such approaches, apart from doing too much work, can be faulted on the grounds that, in context at least, decisions about words with multiple senses seem to be made without carrying along alternatives, but rather as the words are encountered. This can easily be seen by examining sentence (14):

(14) The old man's glasses were filled with sherry.

It is the rare reader of (14) who does not do a double-take and have to back up to figure out the sentence. The context provided by the sentence itself is enough to cause the spectacles sense of 'glasses' to be chosen initially. Such decisions are normally made on the fly, rather than being saved until the end (whenever that might be). When the context provides the solution, then ambiguities are even more easily resolved:

(15) We went on a hunting expedition. We shot two bucks. That was all the money we had.

Here, 'bucks' gets a decidedly unusual hearing assignment from the understander. The last sentence forces the understander to undo what he has done (and, as a result, laugh).

The consequence of principle V is that the context must be set up in a parser beforehand so as to force the parser not to notice non-contextual senses of a word. Certain word senses, which are normally highly ranked due to frequent usage (as would be done for 'bachelor'), must not be noticed in certain contexts. This is difficult to do but ultimately necessary to prevent unwarranted back-up in the parser.

VI. Parsing is really a memory process. Is it really possible to divorce the parsing processes from the memory processes that reside above? The answer can be seen by examining some sentences whose parses cannot really be explained without reference to memory. Consider (16):

(16) John went to the store for Mother.

This sentence (see Hemphill, 1975; for fuller discussion of this) cannot really be parsed without recourse to information residing in memory. It presupposes that both speaker and hearer know Mother's present location. If she is at the store, then John went to get her; if she is elsewhere, he is going to the store to buy something that Mother wants. How can we hope to parse (16) without the ability to ask these questions about Mother's location?

The above argues that the parsing process cannot be complete in isolation, a position that, to our knowledge, is held by no other researchers who actually write parsers (with the possible exception of Wilks). Parsers are written as processes separate by themselves, and thus cannot really be reasonable in any long-term view of the problem.

Arguing that parsing depends on memory, however, does not argue that parsing itself is a memory process. To do this, we must show examples of memory processes and parsing processes and point out their similarity. Such a detailed discussion is beyond the scope of this paper. We can, however, give a sketch of the argument. Consider story (17):

> (17) When his truck carrying 100 penguins being shipped to the local zoo broke down, the driver hailed a passing truck and asked for help in getting the penguins to their destination. The second driver acquiesced and soon was on his way to the zoo with the penguins. Later that day, the driver of the truck that broke down spotted the other driver striding down the street hand-in-wing with a penguin and trailed by 99 other penguins.
> 'I thought I asked you to take those penguins to the zoo', screamed the first driver when he caught up with the column.
> 'I did', replied the second. 'They enjoyed it very much, and now we're headed for the ball game.'

Story (17) is a joke taken from a newspaper. It is funny because the parsing of the story initially makes use of expectations obtained from memory that later turn out to have been misunderstood. The joke is founded on a mis-parse, but it is not obvious what has been mis-parsed exactly. We could say that 'take to the zoo' is ambiguous and the wrong sense was chosen. But 'take to the zoo' is not really ambiguous in any natural parsing sense, and furthermore, it is not even present in the first paragraph of the story.

What is happening here is best explained by scripts. A script is a standard sequence of events that describes a situation. Our script applier program (SAM) and our parser (ELI) work in the same general fashion. They both have tests which look for certain conditions to be the case. When these conditions are recognized, new expectations about future inputs are brought in. These expectations are tests for conditions that are likely to occur next and so on.

In story (17) we have a DELIVERY script. Once this script is recognized, the context has been set for ELI to see all future events in terms of their relationship to that script. The phrase 'take to the zoo' refers unambiguously to one event (a PTRANS to the zoo), but refers ambiguously to what script that event plays a part in, i.e. what the intent of the PTRANS is. The fact that the ambiguity comes from the script applier and not from the parser should be quite irrelevant to an understanding system. Any reasonable understander will see 'take to the zoo' in the context of the DELIVERY script as unambiguous. However, the understander will see the ambiguity when a second script is invoked that could also have interpreted the phrase 'take to the zoo', namely the ENTERTAIN CHILDREN script. It is the realization that this script was erroneously invoked (and an equality made between children and penguins) by the second driver that makes this joke funny.

For our purposes, (17) is interesting because it looks like a parsing ambiguity problem but it is in fact a memory problem. It suggests that the same process is used in both memory and parsing. We believe that the basic memory process of testing for conditions and making predictions based on the results of those tests is fundamental to both parsing and higher level processes. Just as it was hard to imagine that the distinction between syntax and semantics would support totally separate programs doing the work, so also it is hard to imagine the distinction between parsing and memory supporting two separate programs. A parser is just one part of our active knowledge about what goes on in the world. As such it is expectation-oriented and context-dependent.

AN OVERVIEW OF ELI

ELI is an extension of the analyser used in the MARGIE system (Schank, Goldman, Rieger and Riesbeck, 1975). It now functions as a part of SAM, our story understanding system. The purpose of the MARGIE system was to show how three independently developing programs—a parser, an inferencer, and a generator—could communicate with each other using Conceptual Dependency meaning representations. The tasks of MARGIE were determined by the capabilities of these three programs. The purpose of the SAM system is to show natural language story understanding can be done. It is this system task that defines what the subprograms have to do. ELI exists to serve SAM and other such text-understanding programs.

Because there is a larger system, things are both easier and harder for ELI. Certain jobs that are often considered the concern of an analyser are delegated elsewhere in SAM. For example, pronominal reference in SAM is done by a program called MEMTOK that knows about the normal properties of people and objects, about names, about locations and so on.

On the other hand, jobs that are often considered to be the concern of the 'semantics routine' rather than the parser are delegated to ELI in SAM. For example, it is not sufficient for ELI to take 'John gave Mary a kiss' and produce something akin to 'GIVE<JOHN,MARY,KISS>'. The internal inference routines will be looking for a structure equivalent to 'KISS<JOHN, MARY>'. Since it requires knowledge about the English word 'give' to go from the first form to the second, it is ELI's responsibility to do so.

ELI embodies our claim (principle III) that separate syntactic processing cannot reasonably occur. Originally parsers were designed in such a fashion as to parse sentences without having any conception of the possible meanings of those sentences. This was due in part to the fact that many parsers knew little more about a word than its part of speech and its semantic markers. The meanings of the words themselves were not seen, much less exploited. But the amount of useful information contained in syntactic generalizations is very small compared to the amount of information a language understander needs. To say that 'write' and 'promise' are both verbs that take a subject, an object, and a recipient is to say very little that is useful for understanding the differences between 'John wrote Mary a letter' and 'John promised Mary a letter'.

With ELI we have not tried to get away with as little semantic knowledge as possible. If ELI has a word in its lexicon, then it knows, to some non-trivial extent, what that word means and how it is used. This knowledge is stored in the form of special routines that generate conceptual representations. These routines are attached directly to English words and their roots. When ELI reads a word, it often produces some fragment of the total conceptual interpretation immediately. At the least, reading a word will put the conceptualization-building routines attached to that word onto an active list, waiting for certain conditions to become true before executing them. Thus, during an analysis, ELI will have both conceptual knowledge of the form 'this text is about x, y, and z,' and processing knowledge of the form 'depending on conditions a, b, and c, this text may say d, e, or f.'

For example, when ELI interprets the sentence 'John was given a book by Mary', a routine attached to 'was' looks for a past participle. When this routine sees 'given', a CD form is partially built that says 'someone ATRANS something to a man called John'. Predictions are also set up looking for who is doing the ATRANSing and what is being ATRANSed. These predictions grab 'by Mary' and 'a book' respectively and the final interpretation produced is 'a woman called Mary ATRANS a physical object used for reading to a man called John'. (ATRANS is a Conceptual Dependency primitive action meaning 'transfer possession', see Schank, 1975). Let us consider this example in more detail:

Reading 'John' accesses and triggers a routine that builds the CD form 'a man called John'. A background routine saves this CD form in a special slot, which we will call TOPIC for the moment.

Reading 'was' accesses a number of routines attached to 'be'. One of them is looking for the past participle of a verb.

Reading 'given' triggers this 'be' routine which:

1. executes the routine attached to 'give' that builds the CD form 'someone ATRANS something to someone else';
2. puts the content of TOPIC—'a man called John'—into the recipient slot of the ATRANS;
3. sets up a routine looking for the word 'by'.

'Give' itself sets up another routine looking for a physical object. Thus, at this point in the interpretation, ELI has built the structure 'someone ATRANS something to a man called John', and has two routines pending—one looking for 'by' and the other looking for a physical object.

Reading 'a' accesses and triggers a routine that collects the adjectives and nouns that follow into a noun phrase. This routine finds 'book', makes the noun phrase 'a book', and builds the CD form 'a physical object used for reading'. This triggers the routine set up by 'give' looking for a physical object which puts the new form into the object slot of the ATRANS. Now ELI has 'someone ATRANS a physical object used for reading to a man called John'.

Reading 'by' triggers the routine that 'be' set up when it saw 'given'. This new routine says that the next noun phrase will be used to fill the actor slot of the ATRANS.

Reading 'Mary' accesses and triggers a routine that builds the CD form 'a woman called Mary'. The 'by' routine takes this and produces the final interpretation which is 'a woman called Mary ATRANS a physical object used for reading to a man called John'. This form can now be passed to SAM to find out exactly who these people are and what the action implies.

From this sketch we can see how ELI compares with an augmented transition network (ATN) approach like Woods' (Woods, 1970). First, ELI's routines are much more concerned with meaning than those found in ATNs. An ATN rule has a form similar to an ELI routine—i.e. 'if you see an X (reading from left to right) then build a Y'—but, in an ATN, these rules manipulate syntactic objects. For example, X might be 'noun' and Y might be 'noun phrase'. Most of ELI's routines are concerned with manipulating conceptual structures.

Second, ELI's flow of control is more dynamic than an ATN's. ATN rules are grouped statically into sets of alternatives and these alternatives can be attached to predefined points in the parse. The structure of an ATN is usually represented as a graph, where nodes represent distinguished points in the parse and arcs leading from these nodes represent the alternatives. This can be done in an ATN because only syntactic objects appear in the rules.

ELI, on the other hand, deals with conceptual structures. Rules about meaning do not come and go in an orderly fashion. They do not clump *a priori* into sets of alternatives. They do not map nicely onto any simple set of grammatical structures. Meaning rules must be dealt with in the same way that rules of inference are handled. ELI must search its long-term memory for potentially relevant rules. It must have reasons for activating the rules that it does and it must deactivate them when the reasons become invalid. It must know when rules are contradictory and when they are interdependent.

Third, part of the design philosophy behind ELI is that an understanding program should make the right decisions most of the time. This requires the availability of as much semantic information as possible. In contrast, the ATN approach is that syntactic decisions are fairly cheap and can be undone by unwinding the path taken through the transition net. An ATN analyser errs often and counts on back-up to lead it eventually to the right parse. We do not believe that people understand by trial and error. We feel that ELI is more intuitively natural in this regard than an ATN model.

At a more general level of comparison, ELI differs from most models of language understanding in several respects. First, ELI's knowledge about English is in the form of knowledge about specific words. Its dictionary contains a large number of specialized interpretation routines. Executing the routines for the words in a text produces the interpretation for that text. These explicit routines are consistent with principle VI which said that parsing was a memory process. One thing that has become clear in our study of story understanding by scripts is that everyday inferencing does not involve the application of abstract general rules. Instead, common inferencing involves the application of large amounts of very specific, often episodic, information.

Second, ELI's knowledge of a word's use stresses contextual dependencies. The routines attached to a word test for various conditions that previous words have set up, before building any conceptualizations. Further, one word may set up routines for interpreting other words explicitly. For example, one routine under 'write' tells ELI that 'write' means 'MTRANS information by physically making marks on paper'. It also says that the word 'down' may follow, but that the main action will still be MTRANSing.

Naturally, the inclusion of so much information can make a word's definition quite complex. For example, the definition for 'leave' is very complex because it has to deal with situations like 'leave a room', 'leave a tip', 'leave a table', 'leave a fortune', and just 'leave'.

The explicitness of ELI's definitions leads to a third distinguishing characteristic of ELI. Any word can manipulate conceptual structures, not just verbs and function words. Nouns may be as complex as verbs.

For example, the word 'of' can indicate very specific relationships when used in phrases like 'president of the company' and 'operator of the vehicle'. If we had to store all the possible uses of 'of' under the word 'of' the entry would be huge and unusable. In ELI however the rules for interpreting 'of' are part of the routines for the nouns 'president' and 'operator', just as 'write' defines a use of the word 'down'. The entry for 'of' contains only general routines for handling things like possessive and part relationships. When 'of' is used in some specific way, some previous word—noun or verb—has set up the appropriate routine for handling it. If no routine has been activated in advance, then the 'X of Y' will be interpreted using the general routines stored under 'of'.

A fourth distinctive aspect of the ELI model is that its knowledge of a word's meaning is oriented towards interpretation, not introspection. We believe that such processing knowledge is different from intuitive notions about what a word means on its own.

For example, if asked what the word 'give' means we say that it means 'to transfer possession of something to someone'. But clearly our interpretation procedure for 'give' is much more complex than this. It says that 'give' takes three cases syntactically. It says that with a physical object 'give' does indeed refer to transfer of possession, but that with noun phrases referring to actions—as in 'give a kiss'—'give' uses the conceptual structure of the action named.

The ELI model, with its contextually dependent routines, makes it very easy to see why people can understand immediately a word used in a sense that they cannot readily recall when presented with the word in isolation. To retrieve those senses requires generating enough of the right context to access and trigger the routine involved.

A fifth aspect of the ELI model is that it allows much more room for idiolectic variations in language understanding. This is because so much of ELI's knowledge is in the dictionary, rather than in the monitor routines that apply this knowledge. For example, the current dictionary for ELI has a definition of 'leave' that assumes that a PTRANS is occuring, as soon as the verb 'leave' is seen, but which rewrites this to be an ATRANS if a noun phrase is seen that does not refer to a place, as in 'leave a tip'. This definition will be given in detail later. However, ELI could instead handle 'leave' by assuming nothing when the word is seen, waiting until the end of the clause to make its decisions. This change would involve modifying only the dictionary entry for 'leave', not the monitor routines. The ELI model does not stand or fall by trivial differences in dialect.

ELI does make some predictions about processing behaviour though. One of them is that expected routines are always checked and used (if applicable) before general routines. For example, ELI as a model predicts that the sentence (example due to Mitch Marcus) 'John told the boy the dog bit Sue was coming' will require back-up. 'Tell' sets up a test action that says a clause describing the content of the message will follow the noun phrase describing the person told. When 'the dog' is read, the routine looking for the subclause takes 'the dog' and assumes that the boy is being told something about the dog. This turns out to be wrong, however. The actual use of 'the dog' is to introduce the relative subclause 'the dog bit' which describes the boy. There is a general routine that interprets noun phrase followed by noun phrase as 'the first noun phrase is being modified by the second'. But because there is a prediction from 'tell' waiting for a noun phrase, ELI (and apparently people) assumes the wrong interpretation of what role 'the dog' is playing in the sentence.

Sentences where predictions turn out to be misleading (as opposed to just unused) are not common. Normally predictions help in disambiguation and error recovery. We believe that prediction is a basic mechanism in understanding at all levels. People do not passively listen and connect everything new that they hear back to what has gone before. They listen actively, expecting to hear certain things, forcing what comes to fit what they have predicted.

Expectations are everywhere in ELI. Once they are set up by the routines attached to words, they control the interpretation of the words that are read next. The control flow between predictions, partially built interpretations, and not-yet-executed routines is the most sophisticated and complex part of ELI. To describe this flow correctly requires a number of special terms and numerous examples. Our description here will be fairly explicit, but we will try to remain close to intuitive concepts and examples.

First we must distinguish ELI's dictionary from its active memory (AM). The active memory contains the current state of the interpretation process. This includes routines that have been loaded from the dictionary but not yet run, predictions that are still unfulfilled, and partially built CD and syntactic structures.

These pieces are all interconnected. The partially built structures have holes in them, i.e. unfilled slots or gaps. (The terms 'slot' and 'gap' will be used interchangeably in this chapter to refer to holes in our frame-like structures.) To fill these slots certain predictions have to be satisfied. For example, some slots may be predicted to be human. This means that there is a prediction that that slot will be filled with some structure representing a human.

Each routine sitting in the AM is attached to some prediction. The routine is attached there because if the routine were executed it would build a structure satisfying the prediction. The structure built would then be put in the slot to which the prediction is attached.

For example, the AM might have a routine building the CD structure 'a man called John', attached to a prediction 'must be human', with this prediction in turn attached to the unfilled 'to' slot in the CD structure 'someone MTRANS information to someone'.

These three types of information—empty slots, predictions, and routines—are thus chained together in the AM. Slots have predictions and predictions have routines. We shall see shortly how routines in turn lead to more slots and predictions.

The information in the AM is built by loading information from the dictionary. The set of slots, predictions, and routines present in the AM is dynamically determined, based upon the static forms in the dictionary. We cannot write entries in the dictionary that specify exactly which prediction to attach each routine to and which prediction to put on each slot. A person's knowledge of how to use a word cannot specify every context in which the word will appear. Instead the entries must contain templates for routines and predictions. With these templates, ELI builds instances according to the needs of the AM.

For example, the word 'John' has a dictionary entry that says that it builds a 'man called John'. In analysing 'Mary gave John a book', this entry would be loaded into the AM as a routine that builds the 'man called John' CD structure and this routine would be attached to a prediction 'must be human', which would be attached to the conceptual recipient slot of the CD structure 'Mary ATRANS book to someone'. If the sentence had been 'A car struck John', then the entry would be loaded into the AM as a routine building the same CD structure, but it would be attached to a prediction 'must be physical object', which would be attached to the conceptual object slot of the CD structure 'car PROPEL something'. In both cases the structure built by the routine is the same, but the use to which it is put is different.

A dictionary entry therefore specifies a routine for building a structure. It does not specify a use for the structure, that is, it does not say to which prediction of which slot this structure should be assigned. This must be determined when the dictionary entry is loaded into the AM.

The simplest kind of routine used in the dictionary is one like 'build the structure "a man named John"'. This routine is direct and has no other effect. A slightly more complicated routine is one that places a condition on when (if ever) the routine can be executed. For example, one of the routines for the verb 'do' says 'if no noun phrase has been seen yet, mark this sentence as a question'. This routine has two parts—a test and an action. The test is 'no noun phrase has been seen yet' and the action is 'mark this sentence as a question'. The test is true in a sentence like 'Did John get to New York?' which means that the action is executed and the sentence is recognized to be (syntactically at least) a question. In the sentence 'John did get to New York' the test is not true and the action is not executed.

One problem in adding tests to routines is that tests naturally take the form 'slot X has property Y'. However, in the dictionary, which is where the test has to be written, the runtime status of the AM is not known. How then can we talk about 'slot X'?

In fact, a dictionary entry does not refer to slots explicitly. Instead, it makes references of the form 'the slot currently fulfilling the function of X'. That is, certain needs, i.e. slots, are almost always set up when a sentence is processed. For example, there is always a slot set up for the subject of the sentence. This slot may be left empty but it will have been prepared. There will be slots for the verb, for the final conceptual interpretation, for the conceptual time and for the syntactic tense. Most importantly there are slots where new input is placed. These are the slots referred to by tests like 'if a noun phrase follows'. Thus a dictionary entry can refer to 'the slot that is serving as the subject slot for this sentence'. The test for 'do' given about makes this kind of reference. This reference is made concrete when the test is loaded into the AM.

There is a special case of this functional reference to slots. When a dictionary entry builds some CD or syntactic structure, then that entry can refer to the slots that will be set up within that structure. For example, if an entry has an action that builds an ATRANS structure, then the entry can refer to the ACTOR slot, the OBJECT slot, and so on, of that ATRANS structure. We shall see examples of tests using generated slots shortly.

Having said this, we can now describe how a routine from a dictionary entry is loaded into the AM. First, for a routine to be in the AM it must be attached to some predictions already present in the AM. To do this, the structure that the action of the routine builds must be compared against each of the AM predictions. If a prediction is found that is satisfied by the structure, then the routine can be attached to that prediction. The prediction itself is attached to some empty slot. This is the slot that the routine will fill when it is executed.

Next, the test of the routine must be checked. If the routine has no test it is executable immediately. Also if the routine's test happens to be true already, it is executed. If its test is not true yet but might come true later, then the test must be added to the AM.

A test has the form 'the slot Y has the property X'. In the AM this becomes the prediction 'has the property X' attached to 'the slot Y'. That is, ELI takes the form 'execute ACTION only if TEST' and says 'since ACTION fits my expectations, expect TEST to be satisfied'. In this way, adding a routine to an expectation yields new expectations.

For example, the verb 'take' has a number of test-action routines attached to it, one for each way 'take' can be used. There are ones that handle 'take a book', 'take a bus', 'take aspirin' and so on. The routine for the first use mentioned says 'if a noun phrase referring to a physical object follows, then build an ATRANS structure'. The routine for the third use mentioned says 'if a noun phrase referring to medicine follows, then build an INGEST structure'.

Suppose we had the sentence fragment 'John had a headache so he took . . .'. Using SAM's inference routines on 'John had a headache' leads to the prediction that John will INGEST some medicine for his headache. When the routines for 'take' are checked, the one that says 'build an INGEST structure' is the one that satisfies a prediction in the AM. This routine is added to the AM but it is not executed since its test has not yet come true. The test portion of the routine is also added to the AM. This means that the AM now contains a prediction that a noun phrase referring to medicine will be seen. Notice that the conceptual prediction from SAM did not say anything of the form 'the object of the verb will refer to medicine'. This linguistic prediction was the result of a merger of ELI's knowledge about 'take' with SAM's knowledge about headaches.

When a routine is attached to a prediction, that prediction is the reason for that routine's presence in the AM. If the prediction is removed then so is the routine. This is the control mechanism that ELI uses to activate and deactivate routines. Only those routines that are linked to an existing need are kept in the AM.

A prediction disappears when the gap to which it is attached is filled. A gap may have zero or more different predictions attached to it. Each of these predictions may have zero or more routines. When any one of these routines is executed, the gap is filled. This means that all of the predictions on that gap are removed from the AM. This means that all of the routines attached to these predictions are removed. There is no longer any point in keeping them around.

For example, the verb 'be' has a number of different routines for filling in the main conceptualization of a sentence. One routine tests for a noun phrase following and produces a role membership form, as in a sentence like 'John is a doctor'. Another routine tests for an adjective following and produces a property prediction form, as in 'John is sick'. Yet another routine tests for the past participle of a verb. If one is found the structure that this verb normally builds is used but the slots are filled in differently. This is how passive constructions are done in ELI. It is one of the routines for 'be', not a high-level rule. There is another routine under 'be' that tests for the progressive form of a verb. In this case, the main contribution of the 'be' routine is the tense.

All of these routines attached to 'be' build a whole conceptualization—i.e. an event or state description as opposed to a simple object. None of these routines specifies a concrete structure itself. Instead they use the structure provided by the word following 'be'. If we have a sentence with a form of the word 'be' used, and there is an empty slot for a conceptualization, then all of these routines are potentially usable. Therefore they are all attached to the prediction testing for a conceptualization. This prediction in turn is attached to some empty slot. When any one of the routines goes off, e.g. when ELI reads an adjective or a past participle, the gap is filled with whatever structure the triggered routine built. Because the gap is filled, all of its predictions are removed. Because all of the predictions are removed, all of the routines set up by 'be' are removed.

Thus ELI dynamically sets up packets of routines that can be removed as a block. It takes those routines that are attached to a common empty slot and makes them alternatives. When the slot is filled the attached packet of predictions and routines is removed from the AM. These prediction/routine packets are not determined in advance by a dictionary or grammar as in an ATN. They are determined by the needs—i.e. the unfilled slots—set up by the active interpretation of the text.

To summarize, ELI is a conceptual predictive interpreter. When it reads words it gains access to routines that are responsible for the bulk of the understanding process. These routines build conceptual structures. Holes are often present in these structures and filling these holes drives the rest of the interpretation. ELI makes predictions about what will fill these holes and looks in the input stream for things to match these predictions. These predictions disambiguate the input by choosing those senses of words that match and rejecting those that do not.

With its conceptual structures and its predictions, ELI knows what it has and what it wants at every point in the analysis of text. It is this capability of ELI that makes it valuable as a general model of cognitive processing.

CONCEPTUAL ANALYSIS IN DETAIL

Having looked at ELI from the outside, comparing it with other models of natural language analysis, we shall now look at it from the inside. Our concern from this point on will be how ELI works: how its processing information is represented, stored, and applied. In talking about ELI's procedures, we shall be using the term *request* to refer to small test-action routines. Another name for such a routine is a *production*. Many arguments have been made in recent years for models using such routines, called production systems (Newell, 1973). With productions procedural information can be represented in small, easily manipulated chunks, and the flow of control becomes much more sensitive to the context. The term *request* will continue to be used here but the reader should understand that requests and productions are sisters under the skin.

ELI however is more than just another production system. In particular it has a highly developed control structure. This control structure, and the organization of productions that is implied, is one of the points of this chapter.

The basic idea in ELI's control structure is that of expectation. ELI builds large conceptual and syntactic forms. From these forms ELI makes predictions. A prediction says 'something with the feature X will be seen, because a form has been built with a hole that needs such a thing'. With such predictions, ELI can manipulate the requests that it has, preferring those that build structure matching the predictions over those that do not.

Controlling the flow of action with expectations is a top-down approach to analysis. As soon as ELI forms a larger overseeing conceptual or syntactic structure, it takes on a bias, looking in the input text for more things to fit the larger structure. Naturally when the input does not fit any of the expectations, Eli has to become bottom-up again, until it can build another larger frame to guide the processing.

To take a non-linguistic example derived from Minsky (1975), when we walk into a room, we activate a room-frame that contains empty slots for things like doors, windows, walls, ceiling, and floor. These slots contain constraints describing what a window looks like, what a door looks like, and so on. These constraints are applied to the perception routines. These routines are responsible for moving attention about the room, 'parsing' what is seen into edges and planes and so on. Thus, knowing that a room is being viewed biases the perception routines into looking for the edges and places and so forth that are proper to windows and doors and so on.

In our view, the major function of the frame approach is to provide a mechanism for organizing the expectations that we want to use to control the requests that process our perceptions. Large structures with their associated constraint/expectations form an expectation system. At any point in time, the contents of the expectation system represent what is assumed and/or expected. The contents of the request system represent the processing knowledge that is intended to fulfil those expectations.

The structure of a great many memory processes can be described with an expectation system combined with a request system. Since we view natural language understanding as a memory process, we have designed ELI to work as a memory process that uses these two mechanisms.

In ELI, the perception routine is one that reads text from left to right, one word at a time. For each word read, the routine looks in the dictionary for the packets of requests stored under that word. This is one place where the expectations become important. They bias the dictionary look-up, immediately disambiguating many words. Only those requests in the packet that produce a structure fitting an expectation are loaded. Those that are loaded are attached to the expectations that they fit.

For example, here is part of the dictionary entry for the word 'buck':

```
TEST: T
ACTION: # ANIMAL
SPECIAL ACTIONS: ADD PALIST (TYPE DEER)

TEST: T
ACTION: # MONEY
SPECIAL ACTIONS: ADD PALIST (TYPE DOLLAR)
```

There are two requests here. This first builds a base form representing an animal. Onto this form is added the predication that the animal is a deer. This added predication will be merged during analysis with any other explicit predications that were made in the text—e.g. that the deer is young in 'a young buck'.

The second request builds a base form representing money. Like 'waiter', 'money' refers to a role in a script. In particular, it refers to a script about buying and selling. One of the roles in this script is the thing that is ATRANSed to get the object being bought. The filler of this role is the base concept # MONEY, to which predictions, describing the kind of money (dollars, pesos, etc.) and the amount, can be added. In the example definition, there is the added prediction that 'buck' refers to dollars.

During analysis, if the word 'buck' occurs in a text, there will usually be some kind of frame set up into which one of the meanings of 'buck' is to be put. For example, in 'John spent a buck' there will be an ATRANS frame whose object slot is looking for something that is money. In this case, the animal sense of buck will not be loaded, but the money sense will. Conversely in a text like 'John fed the buck', only the animal sense will be loaded.

A request that is loaded is executed only if the test predicate of that request ever becomes true. If this happens, then the request builds a structure and this structure is put in the slot that had the expectation that the request would fit.

In terms of flow of information, there are three data stores in ELI which are linked by two central processes. One store is the *Input Text*. Words are taken from this store and their definitions are looked up in the second data store, the *Dictionary*. The dictionary entry in turn is taken by the routine INCORP and placed into the third data store, the *Active Memory*, where the processing structures are kept. This is where the expectations and active requests are kept. As processing occurs, the processing structures change, under the control of a routine called CONSIDER. A flow diagram of ELI is presented in Figure 8.1, where the boxes bordered by stars are processes. INCORP is the process which converts dictionary entries into requests suitable for processing the input text in the current context. CONSIDER is the process which manipulates the requests, executing them when their tests are satisfied, and removing those requests that are no longer needed.

The AM contains the expectation system and the request system merged into one data structure. In the AM there are three different kinds of nodes, *gap nodes* (GNs), *prediction nodes* (PNs), and *request nodes* (RNs).

A gap node represents a hole in some structure. When ELI builds large conceptual structures, they are frequently incomplete. They have holes which must be filled in, using information taken from the rest of the text.

For example, the meaning ELI produces for the sentence 'John gave Mary the book', is that John transferred a book from himself to Mary. In CD this is a conceptualization with the main act ATRANS. ELI waits until it sees a noun phrase referring to a physical object before making ATRANS the main act, because 'give' is also used in sentences like 'John gave Mary a kiss'. But when 'the book' is read, ELI can safely build the following ATRANS structure:

```
(ACTOR GN1 <=> ATRANS OBJECT GN2 to GN3 FROM GN1)
```

Here the gap nodes are GN1, GN2, and GN3. Each one is an unfilled slot in the ATRANS structure. Each one needs to be (and presumably will be) filled eventually, either by the text, or by some inference procedure.

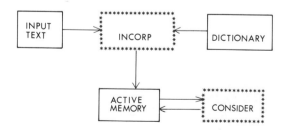

Figure 8.1. Flow diagram of ELI

The second kind of node in the AM is the prediction node. A prediction node is a predicate attached to some gap node. The prediction node describes one possible kind of filler for that gap. The gap to which the prediction applies is called the FOCUS of the prediction. The predicate to be applied is called the BODY of the prediction.

When ELI built the ATRANS form above, it also set up a prediction that the gap node GN1 would be filled with a human. This is a piece of conceptual knowledge about the act ATRANS, that is only done by humans. The prediction node for this looks thus:

```
FOCUS: GN1
BODY: (FEATURE HUMAN)
```

A gap node can have more than one prediction node if several different kinds of things can fill that gap. In script-dominated texts, there are times when the filler of some slot is expected to be something chosen from a finite list of possibilities.

For example, in a restaurant, you are served either by a waiter or a waitress. The sentence 'John was served a hamburger' is interpreted to mean 'someone ATRANSed a hamburger to John'. The 'someone' in this case is a gap node with two predictions on it, one for a waiter and one for a waitress.

For this reason, each gap node in ELI has the property PREDLIST. Under this property is a list of the predictions made for that gap.

For example, when ELI built the ATRANS structure for 'John gave Mary the book' above, it also had predictions for each of the gaps produced. The ACTOR gap was predicted to be a human, the OBJECT gap to be a physical object, and the TO gap to be an animate being. The gap node GN1 with its prediction node attached looks like this:

```
GN1:
PREDLIST: (PN1)

PN1:
FOCUS: GN1
BODY: (FEATURE HUMAN)
```

The third kind of node in the AM is the request node, which is the most complicated of the three. A request node is a test-action routine that builds some structure if its test becomes true. Each request node is attached to a prediction node. The job of the routine INCORP is to take a request entry (usually from the dictionary), find a prediction node that is satisfied by the structure it builds, and instantiate the entry as a request node attached to that prediction node. No request node is ever added into the processing structures unless it can be attached to some prediction node in this way.

A request-node routine may also specify special actions that modify other nodes in the AM, and it may contain pointers to dictionary entries. These parts of the request node are evaluated only if the request node is executed.

Thus, a request node has the following parts:

1. a prediction node which it satisfies;
2. a list of conditions specifying when the request node should be executed;
3. a function which builds some structure;
4. a special action function (perhaps vacuous);
5. a list (perhaps empty) of potentially new requests.

For example, in the ATRANS example that we have been following, when the word 'John' is read, INCORP looks it up and finds the following definition:

```
TEST: T
ACTION: (# PERSON FIRSTNAME JOHN)
```

The structure built by the ACTION satisfies the prediction node PN1, which is looking for a human. PN1 is the prediction node attached to the gap node GN1 (the actor of the ATRANS).

INCORP builds a new node RN1 with the following properties:

1. it attaches to the prediction PN1;
2. it has no conditions which must become true before it can be used;
3. it builds the structure for 'a person named John'.

Such a request node looks like this:

```
RN1:
SOURCE: PN1
ACTION: (# PERSON FIRSTNAME JOHN)
CONDITION: NIL
```

A prediction node can have zero or more request nodes under it, any one of which might eventually be the one to satisfy prediction. For example, in understanding the sentence 'The book was . . .' the verb 'was' provides a number of equally likely requests for filling in the main conceptualization of the sentence. These requests include:

1. one that tests for adjectives; this handles 'the book was red';
2. one that tests for past participles; this handles 'the book was read';
3. one that tests for noun phrases; this handles 'the book was a best seller';
4. one that tests for infinitives; this handles 'the book was falling'.

Each of these requests becomes attached to the prediction that ELI sets up looking for the main conceptualization. Hence, in ELI, each prediction node has a property SUGGLIST, which is a list of the request nodes which focus on the prediction.

Returning to the ATRANS example, in doing 'John gave Mary a book', ELI will build the following sequence of nodes to fill in the ACTOR of the ATRANS:

```
(ACTOR GN1 <=> ATRANS OBJECT GN2 to GN3 FROM GN1)

GN1:
PREDLIST: (PN1)

PN1:
FOCUS: GN1
BODY: (FEATURE HUMAN)
SUGGLIST: (RN1)

RN1:
SOURCE: PN1
ACTION: (# PERSON FIRSTNAME JOHN)
CONDITION: NIL
```

When a request node is added to the AM, its condition (if it has one) is represented as a prediction node. For example, there is a gap node where each word that is read is placed. This gap is given the reserved name GNWORD. Suppose INCORP had just added to the AM some request node—call it RN2—which satisfied some prediction node—call it PN2—by building the CD form for 'the inside of a place'. Suppose further that RN2 triggered off if the word 'to' was read. Then RN2 would look like this:

```
RN2:
SOURCE: PN2
ACTION: (INSIDE PART GN5)
CONDITION: PN3

PN3:
SOURCE: RN2
FOCUS: GNWORD
BODY: (EQUAL 'TO')
```

Note that the prediction node PN3 has a property SOURCE which specifies the request node that generated this prediction.

A chain of links from gap node to prediction node to request node to prediction node (with its implicit gap node) forms what we call a *processing tree*. With this structure ELI ties what it needs (the gaps and their predictions) to what it thinks will satisfy those needs (the requests), and at the same time it ties each request kept active to a reason (the gap and prediction) for keeping that request around. Such a processing tree is graphically exemplified in Figure 8.2.

When ELI interprets texts, it manipulates a number of these trees. Each gap node that ELI builds is capable of being the root of a processing tree whose function is to fill that gap.

For example, at the start of a sentence, ELI sets up four gap nodes which become the roots of processing trees:

1. one for the main conceptualization, called GNCONCEPT; under it is a prediction node looking for a CD form representing an event;
2. one for the main syntactic clause, called GNCLAUSE; under it is a prediction node looking for a syntactic form headed by a verb;
3. one for the first noun phrase, called GNSYNTOP; under it is a prediction node looking for a syntactic form headed by a noun;
4. one for the conceptual meaning of the first noun phrase, called GNCONTOP; under it is a prediction node looking for a simple concept.

Each of these prediction nodes has a request node under it. The four request nodes have the same basic structure. Each looks at the input stream for anything that will satisfy the prediction node to which it is attached.

The 'input stream' in ELI means three special gap nodes that are always kept around. They are:

1. GNWORD: this is where new words are put when read;
2. GNSYN: this is where new syntactic structures are placed when built;
3. GNCON: this is where new conceptual structures are placed when built.

Thus when a word is read, GNWORD contains the word itself, GNSYN contains its syntactic assignment, and GNCON contains its conceptual interpretation. These three gap nodes all have the following special properties:

1. they are the bottom-most gap nodes in processing trees;
2. they are not filled by requests, but by special routines in the main program of ELI itself; GNWORD is filled by the read routine, and GNSYN and GNCON are filled by the dictionary look-up routine;
3. their values are not fixed; i.e. once most gaps are filled, they stay unchanged from that point on; but these special gaps go through a cycle of being filled, emptied, and refilled;
4. all the prediction nodes on these gaps are inherited from the request nodes in the processing trees that terminate in these gaps;
5. a prediction node applied to them is always potentially true, because their values change; that is, when a normal gap is filled, any unsatisfied predictions on that gap are removed; this is not done for these special gaps with changing values.

Thus the monitor program in ELI fills GNWORD, GNCON, and GNSYN with values derived from the input text. Then the processing trees take these values and use them to fill the gaps in conceptual and syntactic frames.

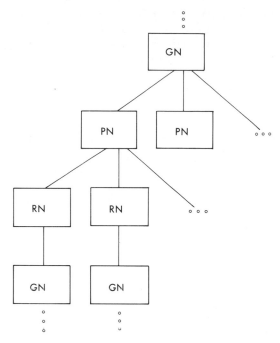

Figure 8.2. Processing tree showing links from gap
mode to prediction mode to gap mode

ELI deals with multiple processing trees. In this way syntactic knowledge is
merged with conceptual processing without forcing ELI into having a separate
syntactic phase to the analysis. A processing tree that builds and fleshes out a
syntactic description of a text can operate parallel to the more important trees
that provide a conceptual interpretation for that text. At the same time,
conceptual trees can be made with syntactic subtrees, when syntactic information is necessary to make conceptual decisions.

For example, ELI provides only a very sketchy syntactic description of
clauses while building very complex conceptual interpretations. For our next
example, we show how the syntactic description of 'John thanked Mary' is
arrived at. We chose this example because it is very simple. It is simple because
ELI needs little syntactic information to do this sentence.

In fact, at the clause level, ELI uses only two syntactic features: word order
and expected number of noun phrases. Word order of course plays an obvious
role. 'John thanked Mary' is different from 'Mary thanked John'. An expected
number of noun phrases is needed to help determine, when a noun phrase is
read, whether it is starting a new clause or is filling out a verb's case frame.

For example, when reading 'John gave Mary a book', it is clear that 'a book' is
filling out an expected noun phrase slot for 'give'. When reading 'John

thanked Mary a book', it is clear that there is no expected slot in which to put 'a book', and hence a new clause has to be started.

With this caveat given, we shall now show how a syntactic processing tree is applied to the text 'John thanked Mary'. Please keep in mind that when ELI interprets this sentence, the tree shown is only one of a number of trees being used. We shall see examples of conceptual trees in the more detailed examples given later.

First, at the start of the sentence, ELI sets up an empty slot called GNSYNTOP. This is intended to hold the first noun phrase of the sentence. To do this, a little processing tree is built with GNSYNTOP as its root:

```
GNSYNTOP:
PREDLIST: (PN1)

PN1:
FOCUS: GNSYNTOP
BODY: (FEATURE NP)
SUGGLIST: (RN1)

RN1:
SOURCE: PN1
ACTION: GNSYN
CONDITION: PN2

PN2:
SOURCE: RN1
FOCUS: GNSYN
BODY: (FEATURE NP)
```

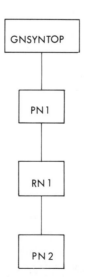

Figure 8.3. Processing tree to fill the gap GNSYNTOP in processing a text sentence

Note that the request node RN1 simply returns the contents of GNSYN if it matches the condition predicate.

Thus, the above tree will fill the gap GNSYNTOP with a noun phrase (PN1) provided by the request RN1 when a noun phrase is seen in the input (PN2). The tree is represented in Figure 8.3.

ELI also sets up another empty slot called GNCLAUSE. This is intended to hold the main clause of the sentence. To do this, a second processing tree is built with GNCLAUSE as its root:

```
GNCLAUSE:
PREDLIST: (PN3)

PN3:
FOCUS: GNCLAUSE
BODY: (FEATURE CLAUSE)
SUGGLIST: (RN2)

RN2:
SOURCE: PN3
ACTION: GNSYN
CONDITION: PN4

PN4:
SOURCE: RN2
FOCUS: GNSYN
BODY: (FEATURE CLAUSE)
```

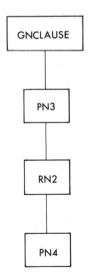

Figure 8.4. Processing tree to fill the gap GNCLAUSE

The above tree will fill the gap GNCLAUSE with a verb phrase (PN3) provided by the request RN2 when a tensed verb is seen in the input (PN4). This tree is graphically represented in Figure 8.4.

With these two trees set up, ELI is ready to do the syntactic side of 'John thanked Mary'. Several other processing trees have also been set up to do the conceptual side of the sentence in parallel.

ELI reads the first word 'John'. The dictionary entry for 'John' is matched against the prediction nodes attached to GNSYN, and the following request node is placed under PN2:

```
RN3:
SOURCE: PN2
ACTION: (JOHN)
CONDITION: NIL
```

Because there is no condition, RN3 is executed immediately, filling the gap GNSYN with the proper noun phrase 'John'. This triggers off RN1 which is looking at GNSYN for a noun phrase, and RN1 puts 'John' in GNSYNTOP.

Now ELI reads the word 'thank'. The dictionary entry for 'thank' is matched against the prediction nodes attached to GNSYN, and the following request node is placed under PN4:

```
RN4:
SOURCE: PN4
ACTION: (VERB THANK SUBJ GN1 OBJ GN2)
CONDITION: NIL
```

Because there is no condition, RN4 is executed immediately, filling the gap GNSYN with the verb clause for 'thank'. This triggers off RN2 which is looking at GNSYN for a clause, and RN2 puts the clause in GNCLAUSE.

Adding this clause frame to the AM also adds the two gaps, GN1 and GN2, that are holes in the frame, with a processing tree hanging off each:

```
GN1:
PREDLIST: PN5

PN5:
FOCUS: GN1
BODY: (FEATURE NP)
SUGGLIST: (RN5)

RN5:
SOURCE: PN5
ACTION: GNSYNTOP
CONDITION: PN7

PN7:
SOURCE: RN5
FOCUS: GNSYNTOP
BODY: (FEATURE NP)
```

```
GN2:
PREDLIST: PN6

PN6:
FOCUS: GN2
BODY: (FEATURE NP)
SUGGLIST: (RN6)

RN6:
SOURCE: PN6
ACTION: GNSYN
CONDITION: PN8

PN8:
SOURCE: RN6
FOCUS: GNSYN
BODY: (FEATURE NP)
```

The above processing tree is represented in Figure 8.5.

GNSYNTOP already has a value, 'John'. This satisfies PN7, triggering off RN5, which fills GN1 with 'John'. Thus the first noun phrase, which was saved in GNSYNTOP, is now placed in the subject slot of the clause frame for 'thank'.

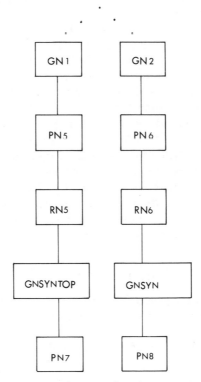

Figure 8.5. Processing tree for the two gap modes GN 1 and GN 2

Now ELI reads 'Mary'. The dictionary entry for 'Mary' is matched against the predictions on GNSYN. INCORP produces the following request node which is placed under PN8:

```
RN7:
SOURCE: PN8
ACTION: (MARY)
CONDITION: NIL
```

Because RN7 has no conditions on execution, it is executed as soon as it is added to the tree. This puts the proper noun phrase 'Mary' in GNSYN, which triggers off RN6, which fills GN2, the object slot of the 'thank' frame. This yields the final syntactic form:

```
(VERB THANK SUBJ (JOHN) OBJ (MARY))
```

Next the period is read which ends the processing of the sentence. When the next sentence is started, the processing trees will be reinitialized. Thus unfulfilled predictions disappear.

This covers only the syntactic processing that happened during the interpretation of 'John thanked Mary'. There was one syntactic prediction that was set up and never used. This prediction said that the word 'for' might appear, introducing the reason for John thanking Mary. In ELI this means that a prediction node was attached to the gap GNWORD waiting for GNWORD to be set to the word 'for'. This prediction node is the test of a request responsible for extending the conceptual representation of 'John thanked Mary'. Initially the representation says that John MTRANSed to Mary that she did something which pleased him. When 'for' is seen, the request node triggered adds more requests to fill in what it was that Mary did. In English this might be expressed with a verb phrase, as in 'John thanked Mary for driving him home', or with a noun phrase, as in 'John thanked Mary for the book'. In the second case, there is an implied ATRANS of the book from Mary to John. Therefore, there is one request which starts a subclause, with 'Mary' set up as the subject. And there is another request which takes a noun phrase referring to a physical object and builds the necessary ATRANS form.

THE DICTIONARY

We have described how the processing trees in the AM are used to interpret text in ELI. Now we will focus on what the dictionary entries, from which ELI builds these trees, look like.

ELI's dictionary contains blueprints for building GN, PN, and RN nodes. These blueprints are given to the function INCORP which converts them into explicit nodes in the processing trees.

The dictionary entry under a word is a list of request clusters, each of which looks like this:

```
request cluster:
LOADTEST: predicate
REQUESTS: REQUEST1
          REQUEST2
          . . .
```

A cluster of requests is accessed by reading the word in the text. It is loaded if its loadtest is true. The loadtests for most clusters are always true, but there are a few exceptions. For example, 'do' has two request clusters. One of them has an always-true loadtest, and this is the one that handles tenses. The other has a loadtest that is true only if no noun phrase has yet been seen in the sentence, and this is the one that handles the extra details needed for 'did' questions.

A request has the form:

```
request:
TEST: CONSTRAINT
ACTION: structure building function
SPECIAL ACTIONS: arbitrarily complex functions
SUGGESTIONS: SUGGESTION1
             SUGGESTION2
             . . .
```

CONSTRAINTs and SUGGESTIONs will be described shortly.

During analysis, the function INCORP is given an entry with the format above, and a list of prediction nodes. These prediction nodes are the ones that were attached to GNCON and GNSYN. That is, those processing trees which have GNCON or GNSYN as their terminal nodes are the ones that INCORP knows about when it loads the dictionary entries, and hence the ones that affect how those entries are processed.

INCORP looks through the list of prediction nodes for the first node that accepts the entry. An entry is accepted by a prediction node if the structure built by its action satisfies the BODY of the prediction.

When an entry is accepted by INCORP, an RN node is built. The ACTION, SPECIAL ACTIONs and SUGGESTIONs fields of the entry are copied over into the RN nodes. The CONSTRAINT becomes a PN node. The RN node then waits in the processing tree to be executed if its test ever comes true. If it is executed, then the SUGGESTIONs are given to INCORP, which produces a new set of RN nodes from them.

A suggestion has the form:

```
FOCUS: path description
REQUESTS: REQUEST1
          REQUEST2
          . . .
```

A path description is a list of role names. Conceptual and syntactic structures in ELI are built using a 'role-name filler role-name filler . . .' format. The filler for a role can itself be a structure of alternating role names and fillers. Using path descriptions, we can refer to any subpart of a conceptual or syntactic structure.

For example, in the conceptual structure representing the meaning of 'The book is red', which is:

```
(ACTOR BOOK IS (COLOUR VAL RED))
```

the following path descriptions are valid:

1. (ACTOR)—this leads to BOOK;
2. (IS)—this leads to (COLOUR VAL RED);
3. (IS VAL)—this leads to RED.

Dictionary entries refer to gap nodes in the processing tree by using path descriptions. For example, when an entry's action builds a structure, it is not known what names will be given to the gap nodes generated. However, the dictionary entry can refer to those nodes indirectly by means of path descriptions. If the action of a dictionary entry builds an ATRANS form, then other parts of the entry can refer to the ACTOR of that ATRANS, the OBJECT, the donor, and so on.

In particular, the suggestions attached to a request entry offer requests to be attached to the gap nodes generated by the action of that entry. When a request node built by INCORP from a request entry is executed it generates gap nodes. INCORP then turns the suggestions of the original entry into request nodes attached to these gap nodes.

There are also several special role names used in the path descriptions of dictionary entries to refer to the special gap nodes that ELI sets up. These role names are:

1. WORD—which refers to GNWORD;
2. CONINFO—which refers to GNCON;
3. SYNINFO—which refers to GNSYN;
4. CONTOPIC—which refers to GNCONTOP;
5. SYNTOPIC—which refers to GNSYNTOP;
6. CONCEPT—which refers to GNCONCEPT;
7. CLAUSE—which refers to GNCLAUSE.

Path descriptions are used in suggestions to say what gap node the suggestion is trying to help fill. The path description appears in the FOCUS field of the suggestion. This path description leads to some gap node in the processing trees and this gap node has a list of prediction nodes under it. The suggestion also includes a list of request entries. Each request entry is given to the function INCORP along with the list of predictions attached to the gap node.

For example, a request entry in a suggestion whose FOCUS referred to some gap node—call it GN5—would be INCORPorated using the prediction nodes attached to GN5. If GN5 had no predictions, or if none of them were satisfied by the structure built by the request, then the request would not be added to the processing structures.

The other field given in a request entry is its TEST field, which is filled with a constraint. A constraint is either a simple T, which means that the constraint is always satisfied, or a test predicate paired with a slot to which it should be applied. The latter have the form:

```
FOCUS: path description
BODY: predicate
```

The path descriptions look the same as those used in suggestions and have the same function.

When a request entry is made into a request node of a processing tree, its constraint is made into a prediction node. To do this, the path description is applied to find out which gap node is involved. Then a prediction node is made with this gap node as its FOCUS and with the BODY of the constraint as its BODY.

We now give examples of these entries as they appear in ELI's dictionary. In these examples, we will show simplified versions of the requests as they appear in the dictionary entries for various words. The simplifications involve deleting references to the LISP function QUOTE, adding labels to identify the functions of various elements in lists, showing only the important arguments passed to some functions, and omitting parentheses around single element lists. Also time and modality ('can', 'not', etc.) markers have been left out except where they are germane to the example.

Simple requests

A simple request for ELI is one with an always-true test and one structure building action. For example, under the word 'someone' is the following request:

```
TEST: T
ACTION: (# PERSON)
```

Because of the true test, whenever this request is accepted into the AM, it is executed immediately, causing the construction of the CD form representing some unknown person. Many of the nouns in ELI's dictionary have this simple form, varying only in the structure built by the ACTION field.

A simple request does not imply that the structure produced is simple. For example, under the word 'hospital' is the following request:

```
TEST: T
ACTION: (# ORGANIZATION ORGOCC ($HOSPITAL)
                        CONCEPTPOINTER (*HOSPITAL*)
                        ORGNAME (NIL))
```

This form has the base form # ORGANIZATION. SAM knows that organizations are groups of people, that they can be actors in conceptualizations, that organizations can be associated with scripts and particular physical objects, and that they often have special names attached to them. Thus the above entry refers to the hospital script ($HOSPITAL), which is the sequence of events that normally goes on at a hospital, the hospital building (*HOSPITAL*), and the name of the hospital (empty here, but in a noun phrase like 'the Veteran's hospital' it would of course be filled in).

Requests that add requests

A slightly more complicated request is usually attached to verbs. This request has a true test, a structure-building action, and some suggestions on how to fill out the holes in the structure built. For example, this is a request that appears under 'leave':

```
TEST: T
ACTION: (ACTOR NIL <=> PTRANS OBJECT NIL FROM NIL TO NIL)
        EQUAL (ACTOR OBJECT)
        ACTOR (FEATURE HUMAN)
        TO (FEATURE PLACE)
        FROM (FEATURE PLACE)
SUGGESTIONS:
        SUGGESTION FOCUS: ACTOR
                  REQUESTS: CONTOPREQ
        SUGGESTION FOCUS: FROM
                  REQUESTS: CONREQ

CONTOPREQ has the form:
TEST FOCUS: CONTOPIC
     BODY: T
ACTION: CONTOPIC

CONREQ has the form:
TEST FOCUS: CONINFO
     BODY: T
ACTION: CONINFO
```

and there is a second top-level request:

```
TEST: T
ACTION: (VERB LEAVE SUBJ NIL OBJ NIL RECIP NIL)
```

```
SUGGESTIONS:
        SUGGESTION FOCUS: SUBJ
                  REQUESTS: SYNTOPREQ
        SUGGESTION FOCUS: OBJ
                  REQUESTS: REQ1

REQ1 has the form:
TEST FOCUS: SYNINFO
     BODY: T
ACTION: SYNINFO
SPECIAL ACTIONS: (REDOLEAVE)

SYNTOPREQ has the form:
TEST FOCUS: SYNTOPIC
     BODY: T
ACTION: SYNTOPIC

SYNREQ has the form:
TEST FOCUS: SYNINFO
     BODY: T
ACTION: SYNINFO
```

In the first top-level request, there is a chaining of requests very typical in ELI. A top-level request builds a CD structure and offers several suggestions—i.e. new test-action pairs—that can be used to fill out the structure built.

In this case, the main structure is a PTRANS frame. Because the verb is 'leave', the structure needs to have an identity between the actor and the object of the PTRANS—i.e. the actor is moving himself. This identity is communicated by the line starting with the word EQUAL. Also, because the verb is 'leave' we have some information about the nature of the objects that can fill in the empty ACTOR, TO and FROM slots. In this case the information is no more than the minimum restrictions placed on any PTRANS.

When the action of this request is executed, a PTRANS frame is built. The constraints placed on the empty slots become predictions that have—so far—no attached requests specifying how they might be fulfilled.

The suggestions that follow in the main request body provide some of the needed requests. The line after SUGGESTIONS beginning with ACTOR offers the name of a request that might be used to fill the ACTOR slot. This is the request CONTOPREQ. It has a test that looks at the slot CONTOPIC, which is the slot filled by the first noun phrase. The test form is T, but this is conjoined with the constraint prediction on the ACTOR slot to produce the instantiated test (FEATURE HUMAN). The action of this request is to return the content of CONTOPIC, assuming it meets the test. This is how 'John left' is interpreted.

For the FROM slot a similar suggestion is offered, only this one—CONREQ—looks at CONINFO which is filled by each succeeding noun phrase. The test in CONREQ is conjoined with the constraint on the FROM slot to produce a test that checks later input for a reference to a place. If this test succeeds, that place is returned and hence will fill the FROM slot. This is how 'leave the city' is interpreted.

The second top-level request, the one dealing with the syntactic clause for 'leave', shows a set of requests for filling the clause frame similar to that for 'thank'. However, there is an important difference in the suggestion made for filling in the syntactic OBJ slot, which takes the first noun phrase after the verb. This suggestion has a call to the function REDOLEAVE in its special action slot.

This special action will be taken if, during the interpretation of a sentence with 'leave', the following sequence of events occurs:

1. the top-level request, which builds a clause frame, is successfully incorporated into the AM; this normally occurs because there is an empty slot set up at the start of the interpretation of a sentence looking for a clause;
2. the suggestion for filling the object of the clause frame is successfully incorporated into the AM; this normally occurs because the object slot is empty and the suggestion says no more than return the first thing in SYNINFO that fits the constraint of the object slot (i.e. that it is a noun phrase);
3. some later request builds a noun phrase and puts it into SYNINFO.

Thus, REDOLEAVE will normally be called whenever a noun phrase follows the verb 'leave'. It will be called in interpreting 'John left the restaurant', 'John left a tip', and 'John left the waitress a tip', but will not be called in 'John left' or 'John left quickly'. In these last two cases, the PTRANS frame built will stand as the main conceptualization of the sentence.

When a noun phrase does follow 'leave', however, it is necessary to check the conceptual interpretation of that phrase to see if it is a place. If it is, then the PTRANS can stay. If it is not, as in 'John left a tip', then the main conceptualization has to be redone, because the conceptual act should be an ATRANS.

The routine REDOLEAVE checks CONINFO when a noun phrase is built to see what should be done. REDOLEAVE is not a request, but a LISP program that looks like this:

```
REDOLEAVE:
    (COND ((FEATURE CONINFO PLACE) (RETURN NIL)))
    (SET CONCEPT
        (BUILD (ACTOR NIL <=> ATRANS OBJECT NIL FROM NIL TO NIL)
               (EQUAL ACTOR FROM)))
    (INCORP CONTOPREQ (GET ACTOR PREDLIST))
    (INCORP CONREQ (GET OBJECT PREDLIST))
    (INCORP CONREQ (GET TO PREDLIST))
    (INCORP SYNREQ (GET RECIP PREDLIST))
```

The first line of this function checks to see if the object is a place (note: FEATURE is used here with two arguments, which is how it is actually used; for simplicity, we omitted the first argument in our other examples because it was obvious from the context). If it is, then nothing has to be done and REDOLEAVE quits.

The next line resets CONCEPT, the gap node where the main conceptualization of the sentence is stored, to be an ATRANS frame where the actor and donor are equal.

The next three lines set up the processing trees that will fill in the ACTOR, OBJECT, and TO slots in the new conceptualization. The function INCORP is called explicitly with the names of requests and prediction lists. If the request satisfies one of the predictions then a request node is created for the gap node that provided the prediction list.

The last line sets up a request node to fill in the RECIP slot of the syntactic clause frame for 'leave'. This request will pick up 'a tip' in 'John left the waiter a tip'. The RECIP request is not in the suggestion list that builds the original clause frame, thus there is no competition between the RECIP slot and the OBJ slot for the first noun phrase after the verb. One thing that was discovered in working on the original MARGIE analyser was that there is no need to assign semantic significance to OBJ and RECIP. For our purposes, OBJ means 'the first noun phrase after the verb', and RECIP means 'the second noun phrase after the verb'. This ordering is induced by having the request for RECIP incorporated only when (if ever) the OBJ request is triggered off.

REDOLEAVE then rewrites the PTRANS structure initially generated by 'John left' into an ATRANS structure if a noun phrase not referring to a place is read. The two top-level requests given thus will handle the examples of uses of 'leave' that we gave. These requests are essentially what ELI has at the moment. A moment's thought, however, will show that REDOLEAVE actually has to be a bit more complicated. What we have given will handle 'John left the waitress a tip' but not 'John left the waitress'.

To handle both these sentences, REDOLEAVE needs to test the following cases:

1. is the object of a physical object or place? If so, quit;
2. is the object money? If so, build the ATRANS frame as above;
3. is the object a human? If so, set up a request to fill in the RECIP slot which will build an ATRANS structure as a side-effect if triggered.

The last test builds a request which will leave the PTRANS frame in the case of 'John left the waitress' but will replace it with the ATRANS frame in the case of 'John left the waitress a dollar'.

Passives

Passives are handled by a request in the dictionary entry for 'be'. This request looks for the past participle of a verb. If it finds one it modifies the requests attached to that verb so that the subject becomes the object and so on.

For example, when a phrase like 'was given' is read, the passive request attached to 'be' affects the INCORPoration of the entry for 'give'. Normally 'give' builds (in the simplest case) an ATRANS frame of the form:

```
(ACTOR (1) <=> ATRANS OBJECT (2) TO (3) FROM (1))
```

The numbers have been put in for convenience of references in the next paragraph.

'Give' attaches to slot 1 a request that fills 1 with the content of the CONTOPIC slot if it is human. 'Give' attaches to slot 2 a request that fills 2 with the first thing found in the input stream that is a physical object. 'Give' attaches to slot 3 a request that fills 3 with the first thing found in the input stream that is a human. These suggestions are written:

```
for slot 1 –– active version:
TEST FOCUS: CONTOPIC
     BODY: (FEATURE HUMAN)
ACTION: CONTOPIC

for slot 2 –– active version:
TEST FOCUS: CONINFO
     BODY: (FEATURE POBJ)
ACTION: CONINFO

for slot 3 –– active version:
TEST FOCUS: CONINFO
     BODY: (FEATURE HUMAN)
ACTION: CONINFO
```

Thus slot 1 is filled by looking backwards and slots 2 and 3 are filled in by looking forwards.

The 'be' passive request has to change this assignment of suggestions. To fill slot 1 we do not want a request that uses the content of CONTOPIC. Instead we want one that looks for a 'by' phrase, as in 'was given by Mary'. If a 'by' phrase is found then slot 1 can be filled if a human follows. To fill slots 2 and 3 we want, in addition to the requests already present, ones that look at the content of CONTOPIC. For example, in 'John was given a book', slot 3 is the one that gets the CONTOPIC, but in 'The book was given to John', it is slot 2 that is so filled. These suggestions look like this:

```
for slot 1 –– passive version:
TEST FOCUS: WORD
     BODY: (EQUAL BY)
```

```
ACTION: PREP-PHRASE DUMMY
SUGGESTIONS:
        SUGGESTION FOCUS: ACTOR
                    REQUESTS: REQ2
```

REQ2 has the form:
```
TEST FOCUS: CONINFO
     BODY: (FEATURE HUMAN)
ACTION: CONINFO
```

for slot 2 –– passive version:
```
TEST FOCUS: CONINFO
     BODY: (FEATURE POBJ)
ACTION: CONINFO
```

```
TEST FOCUS: CONTOPIC
     BODY: (FEATURE POBJ)
ACTION: CONINFO
```

for slot 3 –– passive version:
```
TEST FOCUS: CONINFO
     BODY: (FEATURE HUMAN)
ACTION: CONINFO
```

```
TEST FOCUS: CONTOPIC
     BODY: (FEATURE HUMAN)
ACTION: CONTOPIC
```

To generate the passive versions from the active, the request attached to 'be' must tell the function INCORP to modify its normal incorporation procedure to fit the passive situation. The request does this by setting the global flag PASSFLAG. Thus the passive request under 'be' is:

```
Passive request for 'be'
TEST FOCUS: WORD
     BODY: (FEATURE PASTPART)
ACTION: CLAUSE-DUMMY
SPECIAL ACTIONS: (SETFLAG PASSFLAG)
```

When INCORP sees that PASSFLAG is on, it starts monitoring the suggestions it is processing for the past participle. INCORP modifies which gap nodes the suggestions look at to get their information. When INCORP sees a suggestion with TEST FOCUS equal to CONINFO, it loads it, along with another suggestion whose TEST FOCUS is CONTOPIC and whose TEST BODY is the same TEST BODY as in the original suggestion. When it sees a suggestion with TEST FOCUS equal to CONTOPIC, it does not load it, but instead loads a suggestion whose TEST FOCUS is WORD and whose TEST BODY is '(EQUAL BY)'. This suggestion, if triggered off, asks INCORP to add another suggestion that will put the next structure in CONINFO into the gap that the original suggestion would have filled.

Thus, in effect, the 'be' request causes a transformation of other requests. This is a limited form of automatic programming and is one of ELI's special features. The set of requests in the dictionary, written to handle the active use of the verb 'give', were used to generate a set of request nodes in the processing trees that handle the passive use of the verb. This modification depended on the fact that the request entries:

1. had separate test focus and test-body fields; to create the passive versions, it was necessary to recognize and refocus any request whose test focus was CONINFO or CONTOPIC, while preserving the test body;
2. were limited in what they did; the more that a request does, the greater the possibility that refocusing would have unexpected side-effects.

In other words, the passive routine is an example how requests, i.e. productions, can be treated as data.

WHAT ELI CAN DO

The SAM project for understanding script-based stories and the PAM project for understanding plan-based stories have generated a number of paragraph-length texts for ELI to interpret. These are written on text files using normal punctuation. A routine to read upper and lower case was added recently by Rick Granger, and the ability to use this information when available for recognizing names was added by Anatole Gershman.

The examples that follow are taken from transcripts of various ELI runs made over the last year using such text files. Role names and their fillers (when the filler is NIL) have been deleted from the output CD structures. However, nothing has been added except the comments. For this reason, some of the examples are only upper case and some are mixed upper and lower. Also our beliefs about how certain things should be represented have changed somewhat in the past year. Thus the representations given are not totally consistent with each other or with other examples in this paper. However the differences are mostly cosmetic and hopefully will not confuse the reader.

Ex. 1: DID JOHN GO TO A TABLE?

```
((ACTOR (*JOHN*)
  <=> (*PTRANS*)
  OBJECT (*JOHN*)
  TO (*PROX* PART (*TABLE*)))
MODE (MOD2))

MOD2: (*?*)
```

This is easy for ELI; 'do' has a request that says 'if SYNTOPIC is empty (i.e. no initial noun phrase), then set the MODE to *?*; the 'go' requests build the PTRANS.

Ex. 2: Friday evening a car swerved off Route 69.

```
((ACTOR (# PHYSOBJ
        TYPE (*CAR*))
  <=> (*PTRANS*)
  OBJECT (# PHYSOBJ
        TYPE (*CAR*))
  FROM (*TOPOF*
        PART (# LINK
                SUPERSET (# ROAD
                          ROADNUMBER (69)
                          ROADTYPE (HIGHWAY))))))

TIME (TIM1))

TIM1:  ((BEFORE *NOW* X)
        (DAYPART EVENING)
        (WEEKPART FRIDAY))
```

'Friday evening' is done by a trap; these are requests kept in a library to be checked when input fails all expectations; here, a test for a time specifier is met, and Friday evening is put on the time.

Ex. 3: David Hall, 27, was pronounced dead at the scene by Dr. Dana Blauchard, medical examiner.

```
((ACTOR GNØ
  <=> (*MTRANS*)
  FROM (*CP* PART GNØ)
  INST ((ACTOR GNØ
          <=> (*SPEAK*)))
  MOBJECT ((ACTOR (# PERSON
                    FIRSTNAME (DAVID)
                    LASTNAME (HALL)
                    AGE (27)
                IS (*HEALTH* VAL (-10))))))
```

'27' is also handled by a trap; this one tests for a number and an immediately preceding named person; it makes the number the age of the person.

```
GNØ:
(# PERSON
  OCCUPATION (*DOCTOR*)
  FIRSTNAME (DANA)
  LASTNAME (BLAUCHARD)
  FUNCTION (*MEDEXAMINER*))
```

'Dr. Dana Blauchard' in the same sentence shows that the noun phrase routine (written by Anatole Gershman) handles titles, full names, and appositives.

Ex. 4: The passenger was extricated from the vehicle by the Branford Fire Department.

```
((ACTOR (# ORGANIZATION
          ORGOCC (FIRE/DEPARTMENT)
          CONCEPTPOINTER (*FIREDEPARTMENT*)
          RESIDENCE (# LOCALE
                      MUNIC (BRANFORD)))
  <=> (*PTRANS*)
  OBJECT (# PERSON
          FUNCTION (*PASSENGER*))
  FROM (*INSIDE*
          PART (# PHYSOBJ
                  FUNCTION (*VEHICLE*)))))
```

This shows the passive in action; the 'by' phrase request makes 'the Branford Fire Department' the actor of the PTRANS; this meaning of 'by' was set up by a 'be' request when it saw the past participle.

Ex. 5: JOHN LOVED MARY BUT SHE DIDN'T WANT TO MARRY HIM.

```
((ACTOR (*JOHN*)
  IS ($FONDNESS
      VAL (1Ø)
      OBJECT (*MARY*))))
```

This sentence produces two conceptualizations; ELI also sets a flag to note the presence of the 'but' link; the first clause is interpreted as a fondness theme relationship.

```
((CON
  ((CON
    ((ACTOR (*HUMAN*
             GENDER (*FEM*))
      <=> ($MARRY
           PARTNER (*HUMAN*
                    GENDER (*MASC*))
           PARTNER (*HUMAN*
                    GENDER (*FEM*)))))
     CANCAUSE
     ((ACTOR (*HUMAN*
              GENDER (*FEM*))
       TOWARD (*JOY*))
      INC (*PLUS*))))
   IS (*MLOC*
       VAL (*LTM*
            PART (*HUMAN*
                  GENDER (*FEM*)))))
MODE (MODØ)

MODØ: (*NEG*)
```

The second clause produces a form representing 'the idea, that if she married him, then she would be happier, is not in her long-term memory'—i.e. 'she did not believe marrying him would please her'; 'didn't' in this case sets the time (not shown) to past and the MODE (MOD0) to *NEG*.

Ex. 6: WHY DID MARY TELL JOHN SHE WOULD MARRY HIM?

```
((CON (*?*)
  LEADTO
  ((ACTOR (*MARY*)
    <=> (*MTRANS*)
    MOBJECT ((ACTOR (*HUMAN*
                     GENDER (*FEM*))
              <=> ($MARRY
                   PARTNER (*HUMAN*
                            GENDER (*MASC*))
                   PARTNER (*HUMAN*
                            GENDER (*FEM*)))))
    TO (*CP* PART (*JOHN*))
    FROM (*CP* PART (*MARY*))
    INST ((ACTOR (*MARY*)
           <=> (*SPEAK*)))))))
```

'Why did', along with 'what did' and 'how did', are handled by requests under 'do' looking at what is in SYNTOPIC; if 'why' is there, a frame for 'what lead to ...' is put around the form built by the rest of the sentence; note that the subclause is not introduced by a 'that'; 'tell' set up a request that said 'if a NP is seen and the TO slot is already filled, start a subclause for the MOBJECT'.

Ex. 7: WHEN THE CHECK CAME, JOHN PAID AND LEFT A TIP.

```
((ACTOR (*JOHN*)
  <=> (*ATRANS*)
  OBJECT (# MONEY)
  TO (*MANAGEMENT*)
  FROM (*JOHN*))
TIME (TIM2))

TIM2: ((BEFORE *NOW* X) (WHEN GN1))

GN1:
((ACTOR (NIL)
  <=> (*ATRANS*)
  OBJECT (*CHECK*)
  FROM (NIL)))



((ACTOR (*JOHN*)
  <=> (*ATRANS*)
  OBJECT (# MONEY)
  FROM (*JOHN*)))
```

This sentence produces two main concepts and one subconcept; the first main concept is 'John gave money to the management'; the time atom says that this happened at the same time as the subconcept GN1;

the subconcept says that someone gave the check to someone else; SAM, the script applier, makes the waiter (or waitress) the actor and John the recipient; it also determines that the check must have come BEFORE John paid it;

the other main concept is that John gave out some more money; although these simple forms don't show it, ELI's output does indicate that the text referred to only one John but two different amounts of money; SAM determines that this money was for the waiter (or waitress).

Ex. 8: ON THE BUS JOHN TALKED TO AN OLD LADY.

```
((ACTOR GN1
  <=> (*MTRANS*)
  MOBJECT (*CONCEPTS*)
  TO (*CP* PART GN1)
  FROM (*CP* PART GN1)
  INST ((ACTOR GN1
         <=> (*SPEAK*))))
  TIME (TIM1))



GN1:
  (# GROUP MEMBER
    (*LADY* REF (INDEF)
    REL
    ((ACTOR (PREVIOUS)
       IS (*AGE* VAL (6.)))))
    MEMBER (*JOHN*))
```

In this sentence, 'on' sees the name of a transport script and generates a conceptualization which is put on the time atom for the main concept; the main concept says that there was a conversation; a conversation is represented as MTRANSes by a group to and from the same group;

in this case, the group consists of John and an old lady (AGE is a relative scale from 1 to 10);

```
TIM1: ((DURING GN14) (BEFORE *NOW* X))
```

```
GN14:
((ACTOR (NIL)
  IS (*LOC*
    VAL (*INSIDE*
        PART (*BUS*)))))
```

the conceptualization put on the time atom says that someone was inside the bus when the conversation occurred.

Ex. 9: US NAVY TASK FORCE WHICH ABANDONED DA NANG TO THE NORTH VIETNAMESE LEFT THE TONKIN GULF.

This text is part of a new project that involves parsing headline-like news summaries; it demonstrates sub-clause parsing, and also how the noun-group function can handle a sequence of nouns (four in this case);

```
((ACTOR GN36
  <=> (*PTRANS*)
  OBJECT GN36
  FROM (*TONKIN-GULF*)))
```

the main conceptualization is that the NAVY moved from the Tonkin Gulf.

```
GN36:
(# GR-ORG
 PARTOF (# ORGANIZATION
         BRANCH (NAVY)
         PARTOF (*USA*))
 REL
 ((CON
   ((ACTOR GN36
     <=> (*DO*)))
   LEADTO
   ((CON
     ((ACTOR (# GR-ORG
              PARTOF (*NORTH-VIETNAM*))
      ISTOWARD (PCONT
              OBJECT (*DA-NANG*)
              INC (3))))
    AND
    ((ACTOR GN36
      IS (PCONT
        OBJECT (*DA-NANG*)
        VAL (∅)))))))))
```

The Navy is represented as a group organization belonging to the US.

The 'which' clause becomes a concept attached to the Navy; this concept says that GN36 (the Navy) did something which lead to North Vietnam getting more control of Da Nang and the Navy having no control there.

CONCLUSION

We might ask at this point if all we have said about ELI should in any way be taken to indicate that this is a theory of how humans process sentences. Although our initial loyalties in this work are to getting our programs to understand English, we feel that we also have here a viable theory of how humans process natural language. Of course, we have no experiments to back up our theories, therefore it may be possible straightaway to dismiss what we have said as mere conjecture with regard to people's processes. However, we have produced a working program. It has taken some three years to build and is still evolving. Nonetheless, it does constitute a form of test of our theories of natural language processing. (Test of our theories is an odd phrase here though; the program is not a test of our theory; the program is the theory itself.)

There is some question as to whether there could, in principle, be any other kind of test. Much of the psycholinguistic literature is devoted to testing isolated phenomena that occur in the processing of sentences out of context. Just as asking subjects to memorize a list of independent sentences seems a poor method for finding out how memory functions, so too does testing for how ambiguity is handled in the parsing of unrealistic context-independent sentences. If, as we have argued, the process of parsing is indistinguishable from other memory processes, it may well be impossible to design experiments that can tell us much about parsing *per se*.

Our parser does make some possibly testable psychological claims however, and we shall state them here, leaving them to those who choose to test them, either by controlled experiments or by larger and more comprehensive programs.

(1) Parsing is knowledge-based. Understanding a sentence involves accessing and using an entire set of knowledge related to the concepts being used. The more knowledge there is available to an understander, the faster he will be able to process what he hears. This is due to the effect of more knowledge creating more explicit predictions. Thus, in general, processing of sentences and coherent paragraphs should speed up towards the end.

(2) When information that was not expected appears in an input text, it is handled by trap routines that generate secondary expectations that are based on what has just been received. Thus, the '27' in 'Frank Miller, 27' is not predicted by the interpretation of 'Frank Miller'; when '27' is read, the frame for a human, which Miller is recognized as being, has a gap where the age of a person can be given. The trap routine generates a request looking for a number to put in the age slot, and this request picks up '27'. ELI predicts that the parsing of 'Frank Miller, 27' will be slower than a phrase like 'president of the company' because this 'age' request is not set up by a dictionary entry, but has to be generated dynamically.

(3) New input is always given first to the expectations. If they use the input, then the generation of expectations by trap routines never occurs. Thus, expectations hide secondary expectations from an understander. This causes people to miss ambiguities by making use of current context in processing. It can also cause errors to occur. As was described in the body of this chapter, the ELI model predicts the initial misparsing most people make when they read the sentence 'John told the boy the dog bit Sue was coming'. The expectation made

by 'tell' for a subclause tries to handle 'the dog bit Sue' and fails, causing back-up. (As Marcus notes, back-up is definitely not an unconscious automatic operation in this case.) The correct parse requires the generation of a secondary expectation—not unlike the one for 'Frank Miller, 27'—that says that a clause after a NP can be a modifier of that noun phrase.

(4) Parsing is a continuous left-to-right process. Information gleaned from the beginning of a sentence is available for use in the middle of a sentence. There is little or no back-up in the parsing process as most possibilities are eliminated by the conjunction of expectations obtained from what has already been processed. When the meaning is available for use, it is exploited.

(5) The ELI model claims that word definitions are not lists of possible meanings, but are routines that know when and how to generate such meanings. This means that ELI cannot generate the meanings for many words in isolation, because it lacks the context which the routines for these words interrogate. For example, ELI has routines for the word 'but' that know how to merge two conceptualizations, but it has no conceptual structure associated with the word 'but' itself. And in fact most people, who have no trouble using and under-standing the word 'but' in sentences, are incapable of giving a definition of the word. The kind of definition that is usually given for a word, such as 'give means to transfer possession', is not information that can be used to process that word, because it is too static, too insensitive to context. Such definitions are an interesting part of a person's knowledge of words, but they are not part of his parsing knowledge.

REFERENCES

Cullingford, R. E. An approach to the representation of mundane world knowledge: The generation and management of situational scripts. *American Journal of Computational Linguistics*. 1975, Microfiche # 44.

Hemphill, L. A conceptual approach to automated language understanding and belief structures: With disambiguation of the word 'for'. Ph. Dissertation, Department of Linguistics, Stanford University. (Published as AI-Memo 273, Computer Science Department, Stanford University.) Stanford, California, 1975.

Katz, J. J. and Fodor, J. A. The structure of a semantic theory. *Language*, 1963, **39**, 170–210.

Kuno, S. and Oettinger, A. Multiple path syntactic analyzer. In *Information processing 1962*. Amsterdam: North-Holland, 1963.

Minsky, M. A framework for representing knowledge. In P. H. Winston (Ed.), *The psychology of computer vision*. New York: McGraw-Hill, 1975.

Newell, A. Production systems: Models of control structures. In W. C. Chase (Ed.), *Visual information processing*. New York: Academic Press, 1973.

Riesbeck, C. Conceptual analysis. In R. C. Schank (Ed.), *Conceptual information processing*. Amsterdam: North-Holland, 1975.

Schank, R. C. Conceptual dependency: A theory of natural language understanding. *Cognitive Psychology*, 1972, **3**, 552–631.

Schank, R. C. Identification of conceptualizations underlying natural language. In R. C. Schank and K. M. Colby (Eds.), *Computer models of thought and language*. San Francisco: W. H. Freeman, 1973.

Schank, R. C. *Conceptual information processing*. Amsterdam: North-Holland, 1975.

Schank, R. C. and Abelson, R. P. Scripts, plans and knowledge. *Proceedings of the Fourth International Joint Conference of Artificial Intelligence*. Tbilisi, USSR, 1975.

Schank, R. C. and Abelson, R. P. *Scripts, plans, goals, and understanding*. Hillsdale, N. J.: Lawrence Erlbaum Associates, 1977.

Schank, R. C., Goldman, N., Rieger, C., and Riesbeck, C. Inference and paraphrase by computer. *Journal of the A.C.M.* 1975, **22**, 309–328.

Wilensky, R. Machine understanding of human intentionality. *Proceedings of the A.C.M. Annual Conference*. Houston, Texas, 1976.

Wilks, Y. An artificial intelligence approach to machine translation. In R. C. Schank and K. M. Colby (Eds.), *Computer models of thought and language*. San Francisco: Freeman, 1973.

Winograd, T. *Understanding natural language*. New York: Academic Press, 1972.

Woods, W. A. Transition network grammars for natural language analysis. *Communications of the A.C.M.*, 1970, **13**, 591–606.

Chapter 9

Inferring What is Meant

Herbert H. Clark

How do people comprehend what others say? The answer to this question depends on what one conceives 'comprehension' to be. Many investigators (see Fodor, 1975; Tanenhaus, Carroll, and Bever, 1976) seem to view it as the process by which listeners arrive at the literal or direct meaning of a sentence (as described by generative linguists). This I will call the *independence view,* for it is concerned with only those processes that apply to a sentence independent of its context. On the face of it the independence view seems overly narrow. It excludes much of what 'comprehension' is ordinarily thought to include— for example, the identification of referents. In an everyday conversation, if David said *He's crazy* and Nancy did not identify who 'he' was, she would ordinarily be said not to have understood David completely. Other investigators (see Bransford and Johnson, 1973; Bransford and McCarrell, 1974) view comprehension as the process by which listeners, relying on real world knowledge, build elaborate mental edifices for the situation a sentence describes. This I will call the *constructivist view.* Yet in critical ways this view seems too inclusive. On hearing *He's crazy,* Nancy might adventitiously be reminded of her mad Uncle Harry, which in the constructivist view would become part of her understanding of the utterance. But in the ordinary sense of 'comprehension', she wouldn't be said *not* to have understood David if she had not had this tangential thought.

In this chapter I will argue instead for an *intentional view* of comprehension, one that lies between the independence and constructivist views. In it comprehension is conceived to be the process by which people arrive at the interpretation the speaker *intended* them to grasp for that utterance in that context (see Grice, 1957; Schiffer, 1972; Bennett, 1976). Unlike the independence view, this view requires listeners to draw inferences that go well beyond the literal or direct meaning of a sentence. It insists that Nancy should identify who David is referring to in *He's crazy.* But unlike the constructivist view, it limits the inferences to those that listeners judge the speaker intended them to draw. It excludes stray thoughts about mad uncles. In this view the speaker's intentions are critical, but they can ever only be inferred. My aim in this chapter, then, is (a) to illustrate when and how people infer what is meant and (b) from there suggest some general ways for formulating a more satisfactory theory of comprehension.

INTENDED INTERPRETATIONS

In the intentional view of comprehension there is a distinction between the literal, or direct, meaning of a sentence and the intended interpretation of that sentence as uttered in a particular context. But what is the distinction? This question is not easy—indeed answering it is a major goal of philosophers interested in this view. Yet the essential distinction should become clear with some examples.

Take *He's crazy*. Considered in isolation, it presupposes that there is a male entity referred to by the definite noun phrase *he*, and it asserts that this entity is insane. This is roughly its literal or direct meaning. But when Nancy hears David say *He's crazy* in an ordinary conversation, she does not want to know merely that there *exists* a male entity to which *he* refers. She wants to know which of many conceivable entities it actually *does* refer to. For Nancy this poses a problem. There is nothing in the sentence *He's crazy* to tie *he* to the actual person it refers to. Nancy must go beyond the literal meaning and infer the connection, and that will not always be easy.

Or take *In Italy Margaret fell down and broke her arm*. In this sentence, *and* conjoins two clauses—*Margaret fell down* and *Margaret broke her arm*—with the result that both events are asserted to be true. Yet in most circumstances people would also take it that Margaret's fall was being said to be the *cause* of the break. People not drawing this inference would normally be thought not to have understood the utterance completely. Note that the causal interpretation is not a necessary one. The sentence could have meant merely that Margaret fell down at one time and broke her arm at another, in analogy with *In Italy Margaret visited Milan and met people in Rome*. So for this utterance people have to go beyond the literal meaning and infer the causal interpretation that they think is intended.

Or take *San Francisco always votes Democratic*. Its literal interpretation does not make sense. A city is an inanimate physical location that cannot go to its local polling place and cast votes. One way around this anomaly is to assume that *San Francisco*, in its literal meaning, is elliptical for *one or more persons connected with San Francisco*. But in ordinary conversations even this meaning will not do. In the right context *San Francisco* will be taken to mean 'a majority of people who actually vote in the election of interest', which is far more specific than the literal meaning. In other circumstances it will be taken to mean 'the mayor of San Francisco', as in *On the Council of Mayors San Francisco always votes Democratic*, 'a majority of the people on the city council', as in *Of the three city councils San Francisco always votes Democratic*, and so on. People are not satisfied with the literal meaning of *San Francisco*. In each context they try to find the specific category it is meant to pick out, and that requires inferences.

Or take this short conversation:

Alex: Are Levelt and d'Arcais psychologists?
Barbara: Is the Pope Catholic?

In answer to Alex, Barbara asked a question, but she did not mean it to be taken as merely a question. She was using it to say 'Emphatically yes' to Alex's question. He was meant to go beyond the literal meaning ('I request you to tell me whether or not the Pope is Catholic') to infer the interpretation actually intended. If he had failed to do this, he would ordinarily be said to have misunderstood what Barbara said.

In the everyday sense of 'comprehension' or 'understanding', then, people try to get at what they were meant to understand, and this ordinarily forces them to draw inferences that go beyond literal meaning. But what are these inferences? And how are they drawn? These questions are best approached, I will argue, with comprehension treated as a form of problem-solving. In the next section I will outline such a treatment, and in the following three sections, I will take up its consequences in three domains I have been especially interested in—indirect requests, definite noun phrases, and shorthand expressions.

COMPREHENSION AS PROBLEM-SOLVING

In getting at the intended interpretation of an utterance, listeners have a problem to solve: What did the speaker mean by what he said? The sentence uttered provides only some clues to the solution. Other clues must be sought in the physical and linguistic context of the utterance, the speaker's assumed beliefs, and all kinds of general knowledge. These other clues change from moment to moment, with some relevant one instant and others relevant the next. There is no algorithmic method by which listeners could anticipate all possible combinations of clues. They can only collect and weigh the evidence available and, by manoeuvres common to other types of problem-solving, infer what the speaker must have meant.

One view of this process is outlined in Table 9.1. First, there is the goal: find the intended interpretation. Next, there is the information, or 'data base', that is relevant to achieving the goal. This includes the sentence uttered, the time, place, and other circumstances of the utterance, the speaker's assumed beliefs, and general background knowledge about objects, states, and events that do or can exist in the real world. Third, there are the special assumptions that people make about the act of communication. These are set apart here as boundary conditions. As I will note later, these assumptions take the form of tacit

Table 9.1   Solving for the intended interpretation

Goal: What is the intended interpretation?

Data base: The sentence uttered; the time, place and circumstances of the utterance; the speaker's beliefs about the listener; general knowledge.

Boundary conditions: Various tacit agreements between speaker and listener about how language is to be used.

Mental operations:
  1. Build a candidate interpretation.
  2. Test the candidate interpretation against the boundary conditions.
  3. If it passes all the tests, accept it as the intended meaning. Otherwise begin at 1 again.

---

agreements speakers and listeners have with each other about how language is used. Finally, there are the three general mental operations people call on in solving problems. The first builds candidate interpretations; the second weighs the evidence for and against them; and the third registers one of them, if it passes muster, as the intended interpretation, the solution to the problem. I should stress that I have no special commitment to this particular way of characterizing the problem-solving, but it allows me to make a start on how the process might work.

Treating comprehension as problem-solving does not mean that the process is conscious. Most strategies listeners have available for building, testing, and registering interpretations are quick and efficient and carried out without awareness. Much of the process can probably never be introspected about. This is no different from problem-solving in arithmetic, algebra, geometry, and other domains, where most mental operations, especially on simple problems, are done without awareness.

Tacit agreements

Central to this characterization of problem-solving are the tacit agreements, the boundary conditions through which listeners weigh, accept, and reject possible interpretations. The notion of tacit agreement comes from Grice (1975), who proposed that in order to communicate successfully, people tacitly agree to cooperate with each other, to adhere to what he called the cooperative principle. In particular, it is agreed that speakers will ordinarily try to follow four 'maxims': (a) be informative, (b) be truthful, (c) be relevant, and (d) be clear. Thus, in composing utterances speakers will try to conform to these maxims, and in interpreting those utterances listeners will assume that speakers are trying to conform to them.

The cooperative principle and its four maxims, Grice has demonstrated, are critical in deciding what speakers mean. Consider the maxim 'Be truthful'. If people did not believe the things they asserted were true—if they did not have sufficient evidence for them—communication would be chaotic. Listeners would have no way of distinguishing what speakers believed from what they did not believe, and factual information could not be communicated. The maxim seems fundamental to communication. But it can also be used for conveying information indirectly. Imagine that after seeing an appalling production of Hamlet, Cleo says to Tony *Wasn't that an exquisite production!* He realizes she knows that he thinks it was a bad production and that he knows she thinks it was a bad production. Yet she appears to have said just the opposite, a blatant untruth. Even though she is flouting the maxim 'Be truthful', however, Tony has no reason to think she is not trying to be cooperative, so she must not mean what she said to be taken literally. She must be *implicating* that she is being sarcastic, that she means 'What a terrible production!' Thus, by reference to these tacit agreements, Tony has gone beyond the literal meaning of what Cleo said to infer what she meant. *Implicatures* like this, Grice has shown, can arise on the basis of the other three maxims as well.

In discussing the cooperative principle, however, Grice was rather sketchy. He did not elaborate on how it would apply to anything but a few well-chosen examples. So far it forms only the skeleton of a theory of communication, and it needs to be filled out before it can do the work it was meant to do. For each area I will take up, therefore, I will try to be more specific about what tacit agreements might be operating and how they would apply.

In summary, comprehension will be treated as a form of problem-solving. Listeners are faced with the problem of discovering what the speaker intended in uttering what he did. To achieve a solution, they sift and weigh all the evidence at their disposal—sentence, context, general knowledge, and judgments about the speaker's beliefs. They inspect the evidence particularly closely in the light of certain tacit agreements they share with the speaker about how language is to be used. These agreements lead them to apply specialized strategies that are particularly quick and efficient—that lead to the solution with the least amount of time and effort. Nevertheless, solving for the intended interpretation is not always easy.It takes measurable time and effort and leads to other behavioural consequences. In the next three sections I will consider some of these consequences for three types of expressions— indirect requests, definite noun phrases, and shorthand expressions. I have chosen these because they range in size from complete utterances (indirect requests) to single words (shorthand expressions) and I want to show how inferential strategies are required no matter what size of expression is considered.

INDIRECT REQUESTS

Requests are a type of interpersonal negotiation in which one person tries to get another to do something, like pass the salt. English has a construction especially designed for this purpose, the imperative. It is used for making direct requests, as in *Please pass the salt*. But requests can be made in other ways too, depending on the context, as in *Can you pass the salt?*, *Can you reach the salt?*, *I want the salt*, *If you don't pass the salt this minute, I'll scream*, and *This soup needs salt*. Since all of these use constructions other than the imperative, they are often called indirect requests. But how do people come to regard such utterances as requests? How do they arrive at their intended interpretations?

According to Austin (1962) and Searle (1969, 1975), people have tacit agreements about what constitutes a proper, genuine, or felicitous request. To be proper it must satisfy four 'felicity' conditions:

1. *Preparatory condition.* The speaker believes the listener *is able to* carry out the requested act.
2. *Sincerity condition.* The speaker *wants* the listener to carry out the requested act.
3. *Propositional content.* The speaker predicates a *future act* (the one being requested) of the listener.
4. *Essential condition.* The speaker counts his utterance as an attempt to get the listener to carry out the requested act.

People tacitly agree to make requests only when these four conditions are fulfilled. So when any one condition is not satisfied, requests go wrong. For example, Julia could not felicitously ask Ned to fly to the moon, because that is not something she believes he is able to do. The preparatory condition would not be satisfied. Requests go wrong in other ways when other conditions are not satisfied. Thus, like all other interpersonal negotiations, requests are made against a background of tacit agreements.

All this holds for indirect requests too, but they are identified as requests via the felicity conditions themselves. According to Searle (1975; see also Gordon and Lakoff, 1971) indirect requests fall into four major classes. First, speakers can ask whether, or state that, the preparatory condition holds—that the listener is able to do the requested act. In the right context one can say *Is it possible for you to pass the salt?* or *You could pass the salt* and it will be taken as a request. Second, speakers can state that the sincerity condition is satisfied—that they want the requested act carried out. This leads to such indirect requests as *I want you to pass the salt* and *I would appreciate your passing the salt*. Third, speakers can ask whether, or state that, the propositional content condition is satisfied—that the listener will do the requested act in the future. This class includes such indirect requests as *Won't you pass the salt?* and *You will pass the salt right this minute*. And finally, speakers can ask whether, or state that, there are compelling reasons for the requested act being done, as in *Why don't you pass the salt?* and *This soup needs salt*. These really belong to the second class, those having to do with the sincerity condition, since speakers should not request something unless they have good reasons for wanting it done and think there are no compelling reasons for it not being done. In short, speakers can *imply* they are requesting something merely by suggesting that one of the felicity conditions for that request is fulfilled. This is a powerful and useful method.

Central to this method is the notion that speakers can use one interpretation to imply another. Imagine that Helen tells Margaret *This soup needs salt.* Helen means her utterance to be taken literally—she is asserting that the soup really does need salt—but she is using this interpretation to do something further—request Margaret to pass the salt. That is, she means to convey both the assertion and the request, with the assertion being only a means to the request. So it is not that the construction *This soup needs salt* is being used as a request, but rather that the assertion that the soup needs salt—the interpretation of that construction—is being used to make a request. Listeners are meant to register both interpretations.

Chains of interpretations like this can become very long indeed. Imagine that George says to his son Ken, *Haven't you forgotten to clean up your room?* In the right context, this utterance will form a chain of interpretations something like this:

1. *Yes/no question.* Is it or is it not the case that you have forgotten to clean up your room?
2. *Assertion.* You have forgotten to clean up your room.
3. *Reprimand.* You haven't cleaned up your room, as you were supposed to.
4. *Assertion.* I want you to clean up your room.
5. *Request.* Clean up your room.

The direct interpretation, a question, is used to make an assertion, the assertion to make a reprimand, the reprimand to make a second assertion, and the second assertion, via the sincerity condition on felicitous requests, to make a request. Ken is meant to register all of these interpretations at once, but in relation to each other as the chain specifies. For example, if he says *No, I've already done it,* he has answered the first question in such a way as to nullify the force of the remaining four interpretations. Or if he says *But I wasn't supposed to,* he denies the reprimand, nullifying the prior assertion and question, and questioning the basis for the following assertion and request. In short, an utterance like this has an initial interpretation, zero or more intermediate interpretations, and a final interpretation. While the ultimate reason it is uttered may be to convey the final interpretation, it uses the prior interpretations in a particular sequence to do this.

Empirical Consequences

How do listeners arrive at the intended interpretation of indirect requests? The facts just considered suggest an approximate first answer, which I will present as a process model:

Step 1. Compute the direct interpretation of the utterance.

Step 2. Decide if the interpretations computed so far are what were intended. Are there sufficient and plausible reasons for the speaker to have intended these interpretations alone in this context?

Step 3a. If yes, proceed to Step 4.

Step 3b. If no, use the immediately preceding interpretation to compute an additional interpretation by way of the tacit agreements on speech acts. Then return to Step 2.

Step 4. Utilize the utterance on the basis of its collection of interpretations and assume that the final interpretation is the ultimate reason for the utterance.

This is one form of the problem-solving process presented earlier, for it builds candidate interpretations, tests them against the boundary conditions, and accepts them when they fit. But in its more specific form it has several testable implications. I will consider only four of them.

The first implication concerns the equivalence-of-interpretations assumption: indirect interpretations should have the same properties as the equivalent direct interpretations. The request interpretation of *Won't you go home?*, for example, should exhibit the same properties as that of *Please go home*, despite the fact that *Won't you go home?* conveys the interpretation only indirectly. This consequence has been tested in an experiment I carried out with Lucy (Clark and Lucy, 1975). In it people were shown a series of requests each accompanied by a picture. For each request they were to decide as quickly as possible whether or not the act being requested had been carried out in what was depicted in the picture. Several of the requests we used were direct, like *Please open the door*, while the rest were indirect, like *I would love to see the door opened*. We looked at whether the indirect requests showed the same pattern of verification times as the direct requests.

Requests like these can have either a positive or a negative force. The direct requests *Please open the door* and *Please don't open the door*, for example, are related as positive to negative, and so are the indirect requests *Can you open the door?* and *Must you open the door?*, *Why not open the door?* and *Why open the door?*, *I would love to see the door opened* and *I would hate to see the door opened*, and other such pairs. This contrast allowed us to make several crucial comparisons, for much was already known about verification times for positive and negative assertions. In a study by Clark and Chase (1972), for example, the time it took people to judge affirmative and negative assertions true or false of accompanying pictures were as follows:

True Affirmative. Star is above plus.	1810 msec
False Affirmative. Plus is above star.	1997 msec
True Negative. Plus is not above star.	2682 msec
False Negative. Star is not above plus.	2495 msec

These findings are typical (see Clark, 1976). Affirmative sentences are judged faster than negative sentences—here by 685 msec. And for affirmatives, true judgments are made faster than false ones, while for negatives, false ones are made faster than true ones. We thought that if the request interpretations of, for example, *Can you open the door?* and *Must you open the door?* are positive and negative in the same way, they should yield a similar pattern of latencies.

Indeed, they did. The following latencies are for only two of the ten pairs of requests we used, but they exhibit the main findings:

Direct requests

True. Please open the door.	1213 msec
False. Please open the door.	1610 msec
True. Please do not open the door.	1799 msec
False. Please do not open the door.	1644 msec

Indirect requests

True. Can you open the door?	1473 msec
False. Can you open the door?	1990 msec
True. Must you open the door?	2082 msec
False. Must you open the door?	1810 msec

First, the indirect requests exhibited virtually the same pattern of latencies as the direct requests. Second, both exhibited the main features common to studies of affirmative and negative assertions. Affirmatives were faster than negatives, and for affirmatives, true was faster than false, and for negatives, false was faster than true. Thus, these findings constitute evidence for one major consequence of the model outlined earlier: a request interpretation has certain properties no matter whether it is conveyed directly or indirectly.

A second implication of the model comes from what might be called the order-of-interpretation assumption: most indirect interpretations are computed on the basis of logically prior direct interpretations. For Helen's *This soup needs salt*, for example, Margaret computes the direct interpretation—Helen is asserting that the soup needs salt—and uses it to compute the indirect interpretation—that Helen is requesting Margaret to pass the salt. What this implies is that the longer it takes to compute the initial interpretation, the longer it should take to arrive at the final interpretation.

This implication was also tested in our study, at least for certain types of sentences. Two of our pairs of indirect requests were of this type:

(1) I'll be very happy if you open the door. (Positive)
   I'll be very sad if you open the door. (Negative)
(2) I'll be very sad unless you open the door. (Positive)
   I'll be very happy unless you open the door. (Negative)

In each pair the first request is positive and the second negative, but the way in which people should arrive at these interpretations for the two pairs is different. In (1) they should first compute a direct interpretation, making use of *if*, and use that to compute the indirect interpretation. In (2), the process should be the same except that the computation of the direct interpretation depends on *unless*. But *unless* is inherently negative—it means something like 'only if not'—and ought to take longer to make use of than *if*. Thus, if the model is right and people compute indirect interpretations on the basis of direct interpretations, they should take longer on (2) than on (1). They did. Pair (2) took about one second longer in our task than did Pair (1).

One caution here. In these two pairs it seems obvious that listeners must compute the direct before the indirect interpretations. How could they know whether the request was positive or negative unless they determined how the speaker's happiness was contingent on the door's position? In other instances, the point is not so clear. Some indirect requests, like *Can you open the door?* and *Why not open the door?*, may be idioms analogous to the 'die' interpretation of *kick the bucket* (Sadock, 1972, 1974). That is, the request interpretation of *Can you open the door?* is one of its two direct interpretations and is *not* dependent on its other direct interpretation—'I ask you whether or not you are able to open the door'. If so, the request interpretations of *Can you open the door?* and *Please open the door* would be dealt with alike in the model presented earlier, for both would be treated as direct interpretations. But the issue is even more complex. Indirect requests, like other constructions, probably lie on a continuum of idiomaticity (see Bolinger, 1975, pp. 99–107). Some may be dealt with directly, others indirectly, and still others directly or indirectly depending on the circumstances. At present very little is known about idiomaticity in comprehension, although the issue seems to be crucial.

A third implication of the model follows from the assumption that listeners register the whole chain of interpretations for an utterance—from its direct to its ultimate interpretation. If they register all these interpretations during comprehension, later, when asked to remember what had been said, they should be able to recognize not just the direct or the ultimate indirect interpretation, but the whole chain. Consider these three sentences, whose ultimate interpretations in context are on the right:

(3) The food is on the table. (Invitation)
(4) The food is on the table (Assertion)
(5) Please take the food on the table. (Invitation)

In their direct interpretations (3) is the same as (4), while in their ultimate indirect interpretations (3) is the same as (5). If listeners originally heard (3), they should therefore be able to distinguish it from both (4) and (5), since neither one contains the whole chain of interpretations of (3).

This point was tested in an experiment by Jarvella and Collas (1974). In it people were asked to take the part of an actor reading a script aloud. Later, in reading a second script aloud they were stopped at various points and asked whether or not the sentence just read was the same as one in the first script. One sentence in the first script, for example, was (3), and on the second script different people were asked about (3), (4), or (5). Averaged over many analogous examples, the findings were clear. People readily recognized (3) in the second script as being the same as (3) on the first. But they were reliably less willing to say that (4) or (5) on the second script was the same as (3). The percentages of 'same' judgments for (3), (4), and (5) on the second script were 89%, 77%, and 69%, respectively. Yet people recognized the content of (4) and (5) much better than chance. Faced with the invitation *The food is on the chair* in the second script, people were willing to say 'same' only 7% of the time. In short, people appear to retain the chain of interpretations behind indirect requests like (3), implying they compute and register the whole chain.

The fourth implication follows from the same assumption as the third—listeners register the chain of interpretations, not just the ultimate one—and it too concerns memory. Consider (6) and (7) (from Keenan, MacWhinney, and Mayhew, 1977):

(6) I think there are two fundamental tasks in this study.
(7) I think you've made a fundamental error in this study.

In their direct interpretations (6) and (7) are both assertions, but in the right context (7) would be interpreted indirectly as a reprimand. That is, (6) has a single interpretation in its chain, while (7) has at least two. If people comprehend and register the whole chain, they will have essentially one memory code for (6) but two for (7). With the two codes for (7), they have a better chance of recognizing it. They even have a better chance of distinguishing it from close paraphrases of its direct meaning, for many of these paraphrases will not lead to the right indirect interpretations.

These two predictions were tested indirectly in a study by Keenan and her colleagues. In it people who had attended a midday discussion were unexpectedly asked one or two days later to judge whether or not certain sentences had been uttered during that discussion. This recognition test included sentences that had actually occurred, paraphrases of sentences that had actually occurred, and plausible sentences that had not occurred. Of the sentences in the first two categories, half had what Keenan *et al.* called 'high interactional content'. Like (7) they contained 'information about the speaker's intentions, beliefs, and his relations with the listener'. The other half, like (6), had 'low interactional content'. From the examples Keenan *et al.* presented, it appears that the high interactional content sentences always had both a direct and an indirect interpretation, while the low interactional content sentences normally had only a direct interpretation. So this study provides a rough test of the fourth implication.

Keenan *et al.*'s findings were clear. The sentences with high interactional content—those with a chain of interpretations—were recognized far more readily than those with low interactional content—those with only a single interpretation. Indeed, the high interactional sentences were also more accurately distinguished from their paraphrases. As a control Keenan *et al.* asked people not at the lunchtime discussion to study the same high and low interactional sentences as lists of sentences and then take the same recognition test. Because the sentences were not heard in context, they were all probably interpreted more or less literally, hence were all essentially 'low interactional content' sentences. As expected, the two types of sentences were recognized about equally often. So it appears that the high interactional sentences were recognized better in context because they took on additional interpretations that made them easier to tie into the original conversation and easier to distinguish from literal paraphrases.

Indirect requests—and indirect interpretations in general—suggest that intentions are central to the comprehension process. On encountering an utterance, people ordinarily ask, 'Why did the speaker say that here and now?' and are not satisfied until they find a plausible reason. This often means computing the direct interpretation, asking whether or not it is sufficient in this context, and computing further indirect interpretations when it is not. The evidence cited here seems not only to fit these ideas, but to require them. Nevertheless, the details of this process are still far from clear.

DEFINITE REFERENCE

When listeners are confronted with a referring expression like *the woman* or *the knife*, they assume not only that such a woman or knife exists in some possible world, but also that the speaker expected them to identify the one he had in mind. Consider the following sequences:

(8) I met a man and a woman yesterday. The woman was a doctor.
(9) I went to a wedding yesterday. The woman was a doctor.
(10) A man fell to the floor murdered. The knife was dropped nearby.

In all three, listeners have to decide what is being referred to by the definite noun phrases. In (8), *the woman* almost certainly refers to the woman mentioned in the first sentence, but even that requires an inference. In the right context it could refer to another woman identifiable by another means. In (9), where there is no woman explicitly mentioned in the first sentence, listeners have a more difficult problem to solve. They must see that since the first sentence mentions a wedding, and since every wedding has a bride, *the woman* probably refers to the bride. In (10), the inference is also rather complicated. Listeners must assume that *the knife* refers to something about the event just mentioned, the man's murder. Since murders usually require weapons, and since knives are possible weapons, *the knife* probably refers to the weapon used in the murder. Definite reference, then, is an example *par excellence* of having to infer what is meant.

Like other expressions, however, definite noun phrases are used within the confines of a tacit agreement. This one, which happens to be part of an agreement Haviland and I have called the *given-new contract* (Clark, 1977; Clark and Haviland, 1974, 1977; Haviland and Clark, 1974), goes something like this:

> The speaker agrees to use a definite noun phrase only when he has a specific referent in mind and is confident that the listener can identify it uniquely from its description in the noun phrase.

For example, if Nancy were to say (10) to Jeffrey, she would have to have a specific knife in mind and fully expect Jeffrey to be able to identify it from what she believed he already knew. From Jeffrey's point of view, it is pertinent that Nancy had described the object as a knife, that she had just mentioned a murder, that knives are common murder weapons, and even that she assumed he could identify the knife uniquely from the little information she provided. Indeed, the last piece of knowledge—derived from the tactic agreement itself—is far more critical than one might suppose.

How do listeners solve for the intended referent? One hypothesis is that the problem-solving process in Table 9.1 takes on a specific form something like this:

Step 1. Compute the description of the intended referent.
Step 2. Search memory for an entity that fits this description and satisfies the criterion that the speaker could expect you to select it uniquely on the basis of this description. If successful, go to Step 4.
Step 3. Add the simplest assumption to memory that posits the existence of an entity that fits this description and satisfies the criterion that the speaker could expect you to select it uniquely on the basis of this description. If successful, go to Step 4.
Step 4. Identify this entity as the intended referent.

To see how this works, consider *the woman* in (11) and (12):

(11) I met a man and a woman yesterday. The woman was a doctor.
(12) I met two people yesterday. The woman was a doctor.

At Step 1, listeners would compute the description of the intended referent, namely that it is a woman. At Step 2, they would search their memories for such an entity. In (11), they would find the woman just mentioned. That entity satisfies the criterion that it could be selected uniquely on the basis of this description, so listeners could proceed to Step 4 and identify her as the intended referent of *the woman*. In (12), however, no woman has been mentioned, so listeners would have to proceed to Step 3. There they would add a bridging assumption, the simplest one possible, that posits the existence of a woman and still satisfies the criterion of unique selectivity. Without other information they would most likely add this assumption:

(12)a. One of the two people mentioned is a woman and the other is not.

The woman posited here fits the wanted description and could then be selected uniquely. But note that to get uniqueness, (12a) had to specify not just that one of the two people was a woman, but that the other one was not. With (12a) added, listeners would proceed to Step 4 and identify that woman as the intended referent of *the woman*.

The process just described is anything but complete. It doesn't say how listeners search their memories at Step 2. For example, do they try entities just mentioned first? Do they search the memory in a systematic order? Nor does it say when listeners give up searching (Step 2) and begin building bridging assumptions (Step 3). Steps 2 and 3 may work in parallel, with priority given to entities identified in Step 2. Nor does it say what the 'simplest' bridging assumption is, or how listeners go about building such an assumption. The model is incomplete in other ways too. If it has value, then, it is in providing a first examination on which one can build.

Empirical Implications

Yet the proposed model has several empirical implications. First, if listeners ordinarily compute referents in comprehending definite noun phrases, they should realize when they have failed to find what they believe to be the intended referent. Second, if they need to add bridging assumptions in order to compute an intended referent, they should show evidence that they have added them. And third, all of this process takes time. In earlier papers, Haviland and I (Clark and Haviland, 1974, 1977) discussed these and other implications in some detail. Here I will review only some of the pertinent evidence.

The first implication is almost too obvious. Listeners should object to speakers who violate their tacit agreement about definite reference. This agreement can be broken in several ways. For example, imagine that George, on meeting Margaret one day, says *He broke a ski*. Margaret's first reaction would be to say, 'I don't understand. Who is *he*?'. George has violated the part of the agreement covering computability—Margaret does not have enough information to find a plausible referent for *he*. Or imagine George telling her *Ken and Bob went skiing yesterday and he broke a ski*. This time Margaret would object, 'But which one broke the ski—Ken or Bob?'. George has violated that part of the agreement covering uniqueness. Although Margaret can compute a plausible referent for *he*, she cannot do so uniquely. At the same time listeners should realize when they should not be able to compute the intended referent. For example, when Jane overhears George tell Margaret *He broke a ski*, she should not be surprised if she cannot guess who 'he' is. George designed his definite reference for Margaret, and not necessarily for anyone else. With her current information Jane may or may not be able to identify the intended referent.

The second implication is that when bridging assumptions are necessary, listeners should show evidence of having added them. The major evidence for this is introspective. For definite reference in the appropriate circumstances, listeners readily agree that they have made certain bridging assumptions. The point can be made most vividly by considering several examples from a brief taxonomy of definite reference (Clark, 1977). Each example requires a bridging assumption, and merely reading them shows how readily and irresistably we build the right ones. The examples fall into three major types—direct reference, indirect reference to parts, and indirect reference to roles.

With direct reference the bridging assumptions are relatively simple, as illustrated in these four examples:

(13) I saw a play last night. The play I saw last night was by Tom Stoppard.
(14) I saw a play last night. It was by Tom Stoppard.
(15) I saw a play last night. The damn thing was by Thomas Dekker.
(16) I saw two plays last night. The brilliant one was by Stoppard.

In reading (13) and (14) we do not add any significant bridging assumptions. In (13) the referring expression *the play I saw last night* contains all the information we know about the play mentioned in the first sentence, so it is simple to infer what it refers to. In (14), although *it* contains only a scrap of that information, the inference is almost as easy to make. In (15), however, we are forced to add a significant assumption. Although the epithet *the damn thing* has the same function as *it* in (14)—it refers to the previously mentioned play—it forces us to add this bridging assumption:

(15)a. The speaker didn't like the play he saw last night.

In (16), *the brilliant one* picks the referent from a class previously mentioned, but we all add an assumption something like this:

(16)a. The play referred to by *the brilliant one* was brilliant, and the other one wasn't.

We seem to form this assumption effortlessly.

For indirect reference to parts, the bridging assumptions are more complicated—more obviously inferred—as in these three examples:

(17) Robert found an old car. The steering wheel had broken off.
(18) Robert found an old car. The radio was still in good shape.
(19) Robert found an old car. The letters F-O-R-D were still clearly visible.

We readily infer in (17) that the car had a steering wheel, in (18) that it had a radio, and in (19) that it had the letters F-O-R-D printed on it. We also infer that these are the objects being referred to by *the steering wheel, the radio,* and *the letters F-O-R-D*. But we did not add these bridging assumptions unthinkingly. While every old car has a steering wheel, few have radios, and even fewer have F-O-R-D printed on them. In (18) and (19), then, it was the referring expressions *the radio* and *the letters F-O-R-D* that led us to add the appropriate assumptions. We would never have made such strong assumptions without these goads.

With indirect reference to roles, the bridging assumptions get even more complicated. Consider (20) and (21).

(20) Yesterday there was a killing in Saloon Number Ten. The victim was Wild Bill Hickok.
(21) Yesterday there was a killing on Broadway. The getaway bicycle was later found in Central Park.

In (20) we readily assume that the victim referred to is the person killed in the killing mentioned in the first sentence. Killings necessarily have victims, so this bridging assumption is easy to make. But in (21) we just as readily assume that the killer made a getaway on a bicycle, and that that bicycle is the one being referred to. Yet it is not necessary or even usual for bicycles to play such roles in killings, even on Broadway. Thus, even though the bridging assumption for (21) is worked out from intricate pieces of world knowledge, it is one we make automatically. We are surprised, on reflection, that it is so complex and so indirectly inferred.

Bridging assumptions added in this process show up particularly clearly in experiments on memory. Keenan and Kintsch (see Kintsch, 1974) asked people to read one of these two sequences (and others like them):

(22) A carelessly discarded burning cigarette started a fire. The fire destroyed many acres of virgin forest.
(23) A burning cigarette was carelessly discarded. The fire destroyed many acres of virgin forest.

Later both groups were asked to judge whether *The discarded cigarette caused the fire* was true or false of what they had read. In (22), of course, this information is stated directly, so it is no wonder people almost always said 'true'. In (23), however, it is not stated outright. Rather, it is a bridging assumption people need only to identify the referent of *the fire*. But people in this group almost always said 'true' to the test sentence also, as they should have if they had added the assumption while reading the sequence. Yet for (23) one could argue that it was the test sentence, and not the earlier noun phrase *the fire*, that led them to infer that the cigarette had caused the fire. In fact, when people were tested immediately after reading (22) or (23), they were slightly faster at judging the test sentence for (22) than for (23). But if this alternative explanation were correct, they should also have been faster on (22) than on (23) when the test sentence was presented 15 minutes later, and they were not. Apparently, people judged the implicit information in (23) more slowly immediately afterwards, not because the information was not there, but because it was less available for conscious judgments. Thus, as many other memory experiments also show (see Clark and Clark, 1977, Chapter 4), people identify referents, adding the necessary bridging assumptions as they go along.

The third consequence to be considered is that it takes people time to search their memories and decide on the intended referent. This was demonstrated in a study I carried out with C. J. Sengul. We were interested in how long it took people to identify a referent depending on how recently it had been mentioned in the preceding discourse. So we composed a number of sequences, like (24), (25), and (26), which consisted of three 'context' sentences and a 'target' sentence with a definite reference (the definite noun phrase and its previous mention are in italics):

(24) *Referent mentioned in Sentence 1*: In one corner of the room was *an upholstered chair*. A broadloom rug in rose and purple colours covered the floor. Dim light from a small brass lamp cast shadows on the walls. *The chair* appeared to be an antique.
(25) *Referent mentioned in Sentence 2:* A broadloom rug in rose and purple colours covered the floor. In one corner of the room was *an upholstered chair*. Dim light from a small brass lamp cast shadows on the walls. *The chair* appeared to be an antique.

(26) *Referent mentioned in Sentence 3.* A broadloom rug in rose and purple colours covered the floor. Dim light from a small brass lamp cast shadows on the walls. In one corner of the room was *an upholstered chair. The chair* appeared to be an antique.

The target sentence in all three is *The chair appeared to be an antique,* but the referent of *the chair* is mentioned in the first context sentence in (24), the second in (25), and the third in (26). If people have to identify the referent of *the chair* before they are willing to say they understand the target sentence, they should take longer the less accessible that referent is in memory—roughly the farther back that referent was mentioned.

This prediction was confirmed. People were presented with typed versions of three context sentences like (24), (25), or (26). When they felt they understood them, they pressed a button that replaced the context sentences with the target sentence. When they felt they understood that, they pressed the button again and that ended the trial. The average times people spent comprehending the target sentence in sequences like (24), (25), and (26) are shown in Table 9.2. Also listed are the times people took on similar target sentences in which the definite noun phrase was *he, she, it,* or *them.* As these times show, people were reliably faster on the target sentence—about 300 msec faster—when the referent had been mentioned one sentence back than when it had been mentioned two or three sentences back. It was as if people searched through the entities in short-term memory—those in the last sentence or clause—earlier or more efficiently than they searched through entities not in short-term memory—those in earlier sentences or clauses. In less homogeneous sequences than ours, thematically prominent entities from earlier sentences would probably be in short-term memory too (Chafe, 1974). In any case, the more remotely in memory people had to search for the intended referent, the longer they took to comprehend the sentence, and this is consistent with the proposed model.

Identifying referents should take especially long when listeners have to add bridging assumptions. This prediction was tested in a series of experiments by

Table 9.2 Mean comprehension latencies (milliseconds) for target sentences in one of three contexts. (Referent mentioned in sentence 1, 2, or 3)

Type of noun phrase	Context sentence mentioning referent		
	1	2	3
Nouns	2174	2166	1802
Pronouns	2280	2133	1847
Means	2227	2150	1825

Haviland and myself (Haviland and Clark, 1974). In one study we composed sequences of context and target sentences like the following:

(27) Esther got some beer out of the car. The beer was warm.
(28) Esther got some picnic supplies out of the car. The beer was warm.

In (27), the referent for *the beer* is directly mentioned in the context sentence, but in (28), it is not. In (28), listeners have to add the bridging assumption in (28a):

(28)a. The picnic supplies mentioned include some beer.

If it takes listeners time to form this bridging assumption, they should take longer to comprehend *The beer was warm* in (28) than in (27).

Indeed, they do. In a procedure like the one described earlier, people were timed as they read and comprehended the context sentence and then read and comprehended the target sentence. They took about 200 msec longer, on the average, to comprehend the target sentence in sequences like (28) than they took in sequences like (27). Adding bridging assumptions, then, appears to take time and effort despite the speed and ease with which it seems to be accomplished.

Identifying referents for definite noun phrases, therefore, is a highly inferential activity. Listeners try to infer what is being referred to, and to do that they assume that the speaker has a specific referent in mind that he is confident they will be able to identify uniquely. Only on this assumption can they search their memories for referents they can test for specificity, intendedness, and uniqueness, or can they add bridging assumptions containing a referent that will pass these tests. In this brief section I have examined only some consequences of this view. My main purpose has been to demonstrate that this process is truly inferential, that it depends on tacit agreements, and that it has consequences for theories of comprehension.

SHORTHAND EXPRESSIONS

It is the common view that nouns correspond directly to categories perceived in the world—*neighbourhood* and *Picasso* correspond directly to what people think of as neighbourhoods and Picasso—and when these nouns appear in sentences they are meant to pick out the corresponding world categories and nothing more. In reality, nouns rarely if ever work this way—nor do other more complicated nominal expressions. Instead, they generally refer only obliquely, or indirectly, to the world categories they were meant to pick out. This point can be illustrated with a type of nominal I will call the shorthand expression.

Shorthand expressions are expressions that are rather obviously shortened versions of longer 'parent' expressions, as shown in these examples:

Parent Expression	*Shorthand Expression*
three works of art by Picasso	three Picassos
some Ajax soap	some Ajax
a Ponderosa pine tree	a Ponderosa
six cashmere sweaters	six cashmeres
two shorthand expressions	two shorthands

Many of these shorthands are so transparent in meaning that they are hardly thought of as shorthands at all. Yet they clearly are. *Picasso*, for example, is a proper noun, and proper nouns cannot themselves take plurals. When *Picasso* does take such an ending, it is short for a parent expression like *people named Picasso, people with the characteristics of Picasso*, or *works of art by Picasso*. Similar arguments hold for the other shorthands.

Every shorthand has a multitude of conceivable parent expressions. How, then, do listeners work out which one is intended? Faced with *three Picassos*, how do they decide that it means 'three works of art by Picasso', and not 'three people named Picasso', 'three works of art with the characteristics of one by Picasso', or any of the other conceivable interpretations? There is nothing in the shorthands themselves to say. Once again, listeners have a problem to solve: find the world category the speaker intended his shorthand to pick out. In most instances the problem is solved quickly and easily. Nevertheless, the solution typically requires intricate reasoning.

The interpretation of shorthands rests on a tacit agreement that goes something like this:

> *The shorthand agreement:* The speaker agrees to use a shorthand expression to denote a category (1) that is somehow connected with the explicit content of that expression, (2) that is specific, (3) that is coherent, and (4) that the speaker is confident his listeners can figure out uniquely on the basis of this information.

In illustration, consider the shorthand *William Blake*, as in *I just found a William Blake*. First, the category it denotes must have something to do with William Blake. For example, it might be his paintings, his books of poetry, his poems, quotations by him, books about him, or people with his name. Second, the category must be specific. *One William Blake* cannot mean 'either one painting by William Blake or one book of poetry by William Blake, whichever you happen to think of'. It can mean only one of these at a time. Third, the category must be coherent. *Three William Blakes* cannot pick out two paintings and one book of poetry by William Blake. Such a category lacks coherence. Unfortunately, I cannot yet characterize coherence any more precisely, but examples like this show that such a property must exist. And fourth, the category has to be one the speaker is confident his listeners can compute—and compute uniquely. If the speaker thinks his listeners do not know that Blake painted pictures, he cannot expect them to interpret *William Blake* as 'painting by William Blake' without other hints, as in *I just found a William Blake for my collection of nineteenth-century paintings.* But if he thinks they *do* know Blake painted pictures, he cannot expect them to interpret *William Blake* uniquely as a 'book of poetry by William Blake' without hints that eliminate the painting interpretation, as in *I just found a William Blake for my poetry collection.*

Indeed, it is this fourth criterion that demands the subtlest inferences. Consider our implicit reasoning for *I just saw three William Blakes at the art gallery.* First, as objects of *saw*, the entities denoted must be concrete, and that rules out non-concrete objects. Second, as entities seen in an art gallery, we can plausibly rule out all but 'paintings by William Blake', 'portraits of William Blake', and the like. If the speaker had meant something else, he would have been more specific, since with art galleries we naturally think of art works and the speaker knows that. Third, of the art works connected with Blake, the speaker must have meant Blake's own paintings. Blake is famous for these, and there are no other well-known art works connected with his name. More to the point, we are confident that the speaker believes we know that, and we are confident that he expects us to use this fact in our reasoning. It is this last assessment that enables us finally to rule out all choices but one.

Two cautions. First, although three *Picassos* may be thought of linguistically as a shorthand for *three works of art by Picasso,* it would be a mistake to assume that listeners reconstruct the parent expression in comprehending it. The model I have proposed assumes instead that listeners search directly for the conceptual category it was meant to pick out. Although this category is described by the parent expression—at least roughly—listeners do not need the parent expression to get at it. Second, listeners do not look for the intended world category itself; they search for its mental representation, however that is specified. Nevertheless, I will continue to speak loosely as if they searched for the world category itself. This is only a figure of speech.

Empirical implications

Although listeners probably never reason as explicitly as these examples suggest, they still cannot arrive at the right interpretations without collecting and weighing evidence as if they did. Somehow they must consult general knowledge and check candidate interpretations against the criteria of specificity, coherence, and unique computability. This view of shorthand comprehension, though formulated less precisely than the views for indirect requests and definite reference, has important empirical implications. I will take up four of them.

The first is that a shorthand will be rejected as unacceptable when it does not satisfy the shorthand agreement. For example, *I just bought five Abraham Lincolns*, without further information, makes no sense, and people reject it, saying, 'You can't say that'. According to the present view they reject it because they cannot find a specific coherent category connected with Lincoln that the speaker could have expected them to identify uniquely. The sentence has so many conceivable interpretations that they are at sea. However, when it is finished out with *for my collection of photographic portraits*, it suddenly becomes acceptable. Now people are able to find a specific coherent category they could have been expected to pick out uniquely.

The trees always vote Republican, without auxiliary information, would be rejected even more swiftly and adamantly than the last example. Unlike *three Abraham Lincolns, the trees* contains nothing to signal it to be a shorthand—it is a perfectly good plural—and trees do not vote. Even if it were taken as a shorthand, it is hard to think of sensible things it could pick out. And even if one could do that, it would be impossible to decide on the intended one uniquely. The sentence seems plainly unacceptable. Yet imagine a town divided into voting blocks by area, one in the river bottom, one on the bank, one up in the trees, and one in the meadowland beyond. With that it makes sense to say *The river bottom, the meadow, and the bank generally vote Democratic, but the trees always vote Republican. The trees* would be interpreted as 'a majority of the people voting in past elections from the area in the trees'.

Shorthands, therefore, are neither acceptable nor unacceptable in isolation. They are interpreted in relation to certain background information and are acceptable or unacceptable only in relation to that process. The lesson here may be general. To account for the semantic acceptability of a linguistic expression one may always have to refer to the process by which it is interpreted.

This lesson leads directly to the second implication: the interpretation of a shorthand changes with the background information as listeners assess what the speaker knows and why he said what he said. Consider *three William Blakes*, which, as we have seen, has a wealth of conceivable interpretations. There are four broad types of background, or contextual, information that listeners might consult in interpreting it:

1. *Local syntactic constraints.* Compare *I bought* versus *I met three William Blakes. Bought* and *met* require the three William Blakes, whatever they are, to be buyable and meetable, respectively.

2. *Global sentential constraints.* Compare *I bought three William Blakes at the art gallery* versus *at the rare book dealer's*. The entities buyable at art galleries and rare book dealers are quite different.

3. *Discourse constraints.* Compare the interpretation of *I bought three William Blakes* in a conversation about paintings versus poetry.

4. *Conversational participant constraints.* Compare *I bought three William*

Blakes spoken by a known collector of poets' letters versus a known collector of first editions.

It is because speakers can usually count on listeners making subtle judgments like these—especially types 3 and 4—that they can use shorthands in a potentially endless number of ways. But it follows that listeners must make just as subtle judgments in interpreting them. Unfortunately, too little is known about how listeners use these constraints.

The third implication is that for a shorthand to pick out the intended category of entities uniquely, it must retain the discriminating parts of its parent expression. Take *some Ajax soap*. In most contexts *Ajax* would be more discriminating than *soap*, and so it would be shortened to *some Ajax*, not *some soap*. Given *some Ajax*, listeners can uniquely pick out soap—Ajax is known for making soap—but given *some soap* they cannot uniquely pick out Ajax—there are many types of soap other than Ajax. Similarly, for the parent expressions given earlier, one would usually say *three Picassos*, not *three works of art*; *a Ponderosa*, not *a pine* or *a tree*; *six cashmeres*, not *six sweaters*; and *two shorthands*, not *two expressions*.

But the part of the parent expression that discriminates best in one context may not do so in another. Consider *three bottles of Coors beer*. In an opera house bar that sold many kinds of beer all by the bottle, one would order *three Coors*. If the only beer sold was Coors, one would order *three beers*. At a beer stand monopolized by Coors but selling it both by the bottle and by the glass, one would order *three bottles*. But if it sold the beer only in bottles, one would say simply *Three, please*. In the right circumstances all the other parent expressions given earlier can also be shortened in alternative ways.

The part of the parent expression that remains after shortening need not be a noun, as the examples so far might suggest. Indeed, it is hard to find a type of linguistic unit that cannot serve this function, as long as it is pronounceable. Here are examples of several other types of units, each set so that its interpretation is transparent:

(29) *Adjectives*. A team wearing *yellow* trunks played a team wearing *blue* ones. The yellows beat the blues.

(30) *Prepositions*. There were so many people driving *to* the supermarket trying to get by those driving *from* it that the to's got entangled with the from's.

(31) *Conjunctions*. There are people who drink spirits either before *or* after eating, and others who do so both before *and* after. The or's are more sensible than the and's.

(32) *Prefixes*. Some mothers in the study were interviewed *pre*natally and others *post*natally. The pre's gave much the same answers as the post's.

(33) *Auxiliaries*. Twenty people indicated they *would* go to the party, while another ten indicated they *might*. In the end, the might's outnumbered the would's.

In English many shorthands that fall into these categories have already become conventionalized and frozen. For example, *whites* and *blacks* are used for racial groups, *ins* and *outs* for political groups, *ifs* for conditions placed on actions, *pros* and *cons* for people for and against an idea, *haves* and *have nots* for rich and poor people, and *whys* and *hows* for explanations and means. Yet in all these shorthands—the fresh as well as the frozen—the part of the parent expression that is retained is the most discriminating part—typically the unit that forms a contrast with a related expression.

When what remains is a solitary noun, we are faced with an interesting question. Such a noun, in a particular context, can logically be considered one of two things: a full expression, or a shorthand for a fuller expression. In *Robert irritated his brother*, for example, *Robert* may be either a noun phrase complete in itself or a shorthand for *what Robert did*. But can these two cases be distinguished? My present conjecture is that they cannot. Virtually all nouns are intended to pick out categories that are more specific than the categories they literally denote. And if there are nouns that pick out exactly what they say, they are not distinguishable from the rest by any structural characteristics. My assumption is that a noun is rarely what it appears to be, so one must always look for the category it was meant to pick out in that context.

The final implication is concerned with memory: people should give evidence of having picked out a specific world category for each shorthand. Such evidence is available in a study by Barclay, Bransford, Franks, McCarrell, and Nitsch (1974) on memory for sentences like (34) and (35):

(34) The man tuned the piano.
(35) The man lifted the piano.

People listened to a list of such sentences and later, with phrases like *something with a nice sound* or *something heavy* as prompts for *the piano*, tried to recall each sentence. Any one person received only one sentence from each of 10 matched pairs of sentences like (34) and (35) and each person was given only one of the two possible prompts for that pair.

What prompts should work best? In (34), *the piano* is short for 'the musical apparatus within the piano', so *something with a nice sound* should be more effective as a prompt than *something heavy*. But in (35), *the piano* is short for 'the physical case of the piano', so in this case *something heavy* should be more effective. This is precisely the pattern that emerged. Prompts were more effective when they cued the specific coherent category the shorthand was intended to pick out. What people remember of a shorthand, therefore, includes its intended interpretation—the real world category it was intended to lead the listener to.

The study of shorthands is still in its infancy—there are far more questions than there are answers. How are world categories, as I have called them, represented in the mind? How do listeners search for the one that is intended? How do they bring the relevant evidence to bear in their decisions? My aim here has been to show how shorthands challenge traditional views of comprehension. Shorthands cannot be accounted for by assuming that listeners look up word meanings in a mental lexicon and mechanically select the corresponding world categories. Shorthands are indirect, and they require indirect means in their comprehension.

CONCLUSIONS

Intentions, therefore, are central to comprehension. Listeners strive to determine what speakers mean by what they say. This is not easy, since speakers rarely mean what they say. The direct meaning of their utterances is only a clue to what they mean, and listeners have to combine such clues with other information and infer the intended interpretations. So a speaker might assert *This soup needs salt* and expect listeners in that context to infer that it also means 'Please pass the salt'. Or a speaker might use *the victim*—describing something as a 'victim'—and expect listeners in that context to pick out the intended referent on that basis. Or a speaker might use *three William Blakes* and expect listeners in that context to see it was meant to pick out three paintings by William Blake. Since inferring what is meant is required for these three expressions, which range from complete utterances to single words, there is little reason to believe it is not also required for most, if not all, other types of expressions.

In this chapter I have focused on how listeners infer what is meant. I have stressed two points. First, comprehension is essentially problem-solving. Second, the problem-solving is accomplished within the confines of certain tacit agreements about language use.

When listeners comprehend an utterance, they in effect solve an intricate problem: What did the speaker mean by what he said? In solving it they use a variety of pieces of information. Why did the speaker say something here now? Why did he select this expression over another? What general knowledge does he expect his listeners to have—from broad facts about common objects and events to specific facts such as what William Blake is noted for? And what does he think they know about this particular context? These and other pieces of information must be gathered and weighed in coming to the right solution. But as in solving other types of problems, listeners sometimes make mistakes, missing a piece of evidence here and weighing a piece of evidence too heavily there. They do not always arrive at the interpretation they were supposed to arrive at.

This solution process relies heavily on tacit agreements people have with each other about the use of language for communication. The basic agreement is Grice's cooperative principle, but it divides into specific agreements. For indirect requests, there is an agreement about the felicitous performance of the speech act of requesting. For direct reference, there is an agreement about the use of definite noun phrases to enable listeners to compute intended referents uniquely. And for shorthands, there is an agreement about the use of nominals to pick out specific coherent categories uniquely. These agreements are litmus tests any candidate interpretation must pass to be accepted as the intended interpretation. Yet much remains to be learned about these agreements. How precisely are they incorporated into the comprehension process? How do they fit together in a system of agreements about communication? What role do they play in children's acquisition of language?

As the studies I have cited seem to demonstrate, inferring what is meant takes time and effort. Yet it takes so little time and effort that whatever problem-solving goes on must be quick and efficient. Indeed, listeners appear to use heuristic strategies for solving problems they encounter over and over again. The strategies conform to the tacit agreements, but avoid the cumbersome step-by-step reasoning they seem to require. Elsewhere Haviland and I have discussed a strategy listeners appear to use in identifying referents (see Clark, 1977; Clark and Haviland, 1974, 1977; Haviland and Clark, 1974), but little is known about other strategies. For example, given a shorthand expression, listeners seem able to find the right category quickly and without tedious reasoning. But what heuristics do they use in this search? Strategies of this kind, however, cannot be the complete answer, for they sometimes fail. When this happens, listeners seem able to fall back on first principles and use the tacit agreements to reason through what was meant. The strategies are tricks that work most of the time to make problem-solving simpler. Nevertheless, they are still a type of problem-solving.

Comprehension, in short, calls on people's general capacity to think—to use information and solve problems. Although people develop specialized strategies for comprehension, these are still built on their general ability to solve problems—to set up goals, search in the memory for pertinent information, and decide when the goals have been reached. Indeed, in inferring what is meant, people consider non-linguistic factors that are far removed from the utterance itself, and their skill at solving this problem is sometimes taxed to the limit. Comprehension is a form of thinking that should not be set off from the rest.

ACKNOWLEDGEMENTS

The preparation of this chapter was supported in part by Grant MH-20021 from the National Institutes of Health. I am indebted to Eve V. Clark for her comments.

REFERENCES

Austin, J. L. *How to do things with words.* Oxford: Oxford University Press, 1962.

Barclay, J. R., Bransford, J. D., Franks, J. J., McCarrell, N. S., and Nitsch, K. Comprehension and semantic flexibility. *Journal of Verbal Learning and Verbal Behavior,* 1974, **13**, 471–481.

Bennett, J. *Linguistic behaviour.* Cambridge University Press, 1976.

Bolinger, D. L. *Aspects of language* (2nd ed.). New York: Harcourt, Brace, Jovanovich, 1975.

Bransford, J. D. and Johnson, M. K. Considerations of some problems of comprehension. In W. G. Chase (Ed.), *Visual information processing.* New York: Academic Press, 1973.

Bransford, J. D. and McCarrell, N. S. A sketch of a cognitive approach to comprehension: Some thoughts about understanding what it means to comprehend. In W. B. Weimer and D. S. Palermo (Eds.), *Cognition and the symbolic processes.* Hillsdale, N.J.: Lawrence Erlbaum Associates, 1974.

Chafe, W. L. Language and consciousness. *Language,* 1974, **50**, 111–133.

Clark, H. H. *Semantics and comprehension.* The Hague: Mouton, 1976.

Clark, H. H. Inferences in comprehension. In D. LaBerge and S. J. Samuels (Eds.), *Basic processes in reading: Perception and comprehension.* Hillsdale, N. J.: Lawrence Erlbaum Associates, 1977.

Clark, H. H. and Chase, W. G. On the process of comparing sentences against pictures. *Cognitive Psychology,* 1972, **3**, 472–517.

Clark, H. H. and Clark, E. V. *Psychology and language: An introduction to psycholinguistics.* New York: Harcourt, Brace, Jovanovich, 1977.

Clark, H. H. and Haviland, S. E. Psychological processes as linguistic explanation. In D. Cohen (Ed.), *Explaining linguistic phenomena.* Washington D.C.: Hemisphere Publishing Corp., 1974.

Clark, H. H. and Haviland, S. E. Comprehension and the given-new contract. In R. Freedle (Ed.), *Discourse comprehension and production.* Norwood, N.J.: Ablex Publishing, 1977.

Clark, H. H. and Lucy, P. Understanding what is meant from what is said: A study in conversationally conveyed requests. *Journal of Verbal Learning and Verbal Behavior,* 1975, **14**, 56–72.

Fodor, J. A. *The language of thought.* New York: T. Y. Crowell, 1975.

Gordon, D. and Lakoff, G. Conversational postulates. In *Papers from the Seventh Regional Meeting, Chicago Linguistic Society,* 1971.

Grice, H. P. Meaning. *Philosophical Review,* 1957, **64**, 377–388.

Grice, H. P. William James Lectures, Harvard University, 1967. Published in part as 'Logic and conversation'. In P. Cole and J. L. Morgan (Eds.), *Syntax and semantics.* Vol. 3: *Speech acts.* New York: Seminar Press, 1975.

Haviland, S. E. and Clark, H. H. What's new? Acquiring new information as a process in comprehension. *Journal of Verbal Learning and Verbal Behavior,* 1974, **13**, 512–521.

Jarvella, R. J. and Collas, J. G. Memory for the intentions of sentences. *Memory & Cognition,* 1974, **2**, 185–188.

Keenan, J. M., MacWhinney, B., and Mayhew, D. Pragmatics in memory: A study of natural conversation. *Journal of Verbal Learning and Verbal Behavior,* 1977, **16**, 549–560.

Kintsch, W. *The representation of meaning in memory.* Hillsdale, N.J.: Lawrence Erlbaum Associates, 1974.

Sadock, J. M. Speech act idioms. In *Papers from the Eighth Regional Meeting.* Chicago: Chicago Linguistic Society, 1972.

Sadock, K. M. *Towards a linguistic theory of speech acts.* New York: Academic Press, 1974.

Schiffer, S. R. *Meaning.* Oxford: Clarendon Press, 1972.

Searle, J. R. *Speech acts.* Cambridge: Cambridge University Press, 1969.

Searle, J. R. Indirect speech acts. In P. Cole and J. L. Morgan (Eds.), *Syntax and semantics.* Vol. 3: *Speech acts.* New York: Seminar Press, 1975.

Tanenhaus, M. K., Carroll, J. M., and Bever, T. G. Sentence-picture verification models as theories of sentence comprehension: A critique of Carpenter and Just. *Psychological Review,* 1976, **83**, 310–317.

Author Index

Subject Index